RECOGNIZING THE PSYCHOLOGICAL AND CULTURAL STRENGTHS OF BLACK AMERICANS

This book examines the cultural beliefs and practices of Black folks in relation to psychological strength.

Divided into four parts, the book begins with a discussion on the history of African civilizations, including an analysis of faiths, architecture, and cultural diversity of the continent, followed by a meaningful dialogue on the history of slavery and plantations in North America. The later sections are a study on the contribution of the African American community toward America's prosperity. The book explores cultural values as a source of power, and uses historical, social, and psychological research to construct a framework of Black cultural values and psychological resolve. The author offers practical applications and interventions to demonstrate how this framework can be applied to training and policy matters on both individual and systemic levels.

Recognizing the Psychological and Cultural Strengths of Black Americans is essential reading for students and academics in the fields of Psychology, Sociology, Critical Race Theory, Political Science, and other related disciplines. It will also be a useful resource for professionals including policy makers, psychologist, counsellors, educators, and social workers.

Robert T. Carter is Emeritus Professor of Psychology and Education at the Department of Counseling and Clinical Psychology at Teachers College, Columbia University. He has devoted his career to issues of race and culture as they impact primarily people of color. He is known internationally for his work on racism, race-based traumatic stress, and racial identity ego statuses. He has authored more than 130 articles and nine books. More recently he writes about the traumatic stress effects of racial discrimination and Black culture.

RECOGNIZING THE PSYCHOLOGICAL AND CULTURAL STRENGTHS OF BLACK AMERICANS

Historical, Social, and Psychological Perspectives

Robert T. Carter

Routledge
Taylor & Francis Group
LONDON AND NEW YORK

Designed cover image: GettyImages via Smartboy10

First published 2025
by Routledge
4 Park Square, Milton Park, Abingdon, Oxon OX14 4RN

and by Routledge
605 Third Avenue, New York, NY 10158

Routledge is an imprint of the Taylor & Francis Group, an informa business

British Library Cataloguing in Publication Data
A catalogue record for this book is available from the British Library

Library of Congress Cataloging-in-Publication Data
A catalog record has been requested for this book

ISBN: 9780367629489 (hbk)
ISBN: 9780367629472 (pbk)
ISBN: 9781003111542 (ebk)

DOI: 10.4324/9781003111542

Typeset in Galliard
by Taylor & Francis Books

CONTENTS

TABLES

INTRODUCTION

My Journey to Discover Black People's Cultural Roots

The focus of this book is to document and trace the psychological processes Africans and Black Americans used to transmit their cultural patterns and practices to their descendants.[1] Their cultural values had to be passed on from generation to generation to allow Black African people to survive and flourish despite centuries of racial oppression. I contend that psychological resolve (i.e., determination, a flexible world view) and related cultural practices aided Africans and their descendants in holding on to and transmitting their core cultural values into unassailable hope and optimism. But it is, and was, also their psychological beliefs that provided what was needed to live and teach others their values and to build Black communities (Bennett, 1988).

Racial issues in the United States came to the forefront of social and political discourse during 2019–2021. Among other things were the actions of law enforcement personnel, with unarmed Black people killed with little accountability from law enforcement leaders or the legal community (Schwartz, 2020). Most officers who used what appeared to be excessive force against unarmed Black citizens were either not charged with violations of the law or, if they were charged, they were often cleared of any legal violations. When George Floyd, a Black man, was killed in May 2020 by police officers in Minneapolis, one officer held his knee on Floyd's neck, for over nine minutes, causing his death. The other officers did nothing to stop him. Protests erupted in some two thousand cities and towns across the country and in more than sixty countries around the world calling for an end to law enforcement's acts of racial injustice and systemic racism that seemed to be accepted and permitted, as well as in support of the Black Lives Matter movement (McGonigle, 2020). Some estimate that between 15 and 26 million people participated in these protests. The issues that people were

DOI: 10.4324/9781003111542-1

reacting to have been long-standing and date back many decades, even centuries. Eventually, unlike other officers across the country who committed similar acts, the Minneapolis officers were charged and later convicted of violating the law.

What stands out in the protests following Floyd's murder is that they occurred in the midst of a worldwide pandemic due to COVID-19, which itself revealed glaring racial disparities and inequities in health, health care, and economic opportunity (Trent et al., 2019). It has been widely reported that Black and Brown people have borne the brunt of the effects of the COVID-19 virus; they have been infected by the virus, hospitalized, suffered long-terms effects, lost jobs and homes, and died in greater proportion to whites (Gould & Wilson, 2020; Louis-Jean et al., 2020; Smith, 2020).

The confluence of the global pandemic, and the health and economic damage it caused to Blacks, and videos and events of police officers killing Black people have combined to put a bright spotlight on racial injustice in many sectors of American society. The damage has been so stark that people from many racial groups and generations have come out to protest, yet substantive socioeconomic changes remain elusive. There is an uptick in the coverage of the still crippling racial inequities that Black people confront today. As has been true historically, when Black people or their allies or advocates call for change and greater socioeconomic equality or simply for increased racial awareness, there is also greater and more strident white resentment and pushback to the calls for racial justice or awareness, so the issues are repeated and ongoing. This follows a similar pattern and, for the most part, has similar outcomes. When advocates share what they argue is and was happening to Black people, their contentions are grounded in the presence of racial bias and racism that account for the racial inequities in American society, yet what also is needed is an understanding of what is positive and affirming about Black people and their culture.

My Journey of Discovery: Learning Unique Aspects of Black Culture through Life Experiences

The goals and subject of this book began to matter to me at an early age in ways that were not obvious to me at the time. My brother and I were often taken out of our classes in kindergarten to be reprimanded, which seemed odd to me. I also noticed that we were often the subjects of ridicule by our teachers, which felt unjust. Later, as I grew older, I observed differences in interactional patterns that at the time I could neither reconcile nor comprehend. In my youth these differences became more apparent, especially when we moved from Manhattan to Queens, from a Black community to a mostly white one.

From my early years to the present, I have been interested in Black American culture, which operates in Black people's minds, emotions, and behavior. Many aspects of Black life and experiences have stood out for me, all of which contribute to my desire to document how Africans and their American descendants survived such harsh and degrading treatment for so many generations. While only several hundred thousand Africans came to the North American mainland, today there are millions of Black Americans, a fact that says in no uncertain terms that Black people endured and prospered despite the myriad obstacles that were put before them—and, as current events reveal, many obstacles still exist.

It is my view that the more we know about the strengths of Black people, the better off Blacks and other Americans will be. There are life-enhancing aspects of Black ways of living that should be more widely disseminated and used to address the problems that plague American society, especially race relations. Over my life I have noticed some positive and negative messages communicated in our society regarding Black people and their ways of being. I relay a few of these experiences to share how it was that I came to study Blacks' emotional and psychological strengths.

As I reflect on my life, I wondered if it was unique that, from a young age and throughout my life, I experienced many instances where I was singled out and received messages from whites and adults around me that my behavior was unacceptable, a communication that I received from various people and in varied situations—schools, family members, authorities, and so forth. I first assumed the problem was me, that I was lacking in some unseen way, but later I realized maybe it was not me, that I was not at fault. Perhaps the issues that marked my young life experiences reflected something larger than me: could it be that the messages were about the people to whom I belonged, meaning Black Americans? Was it possible that being a Black person triggered messages about being unacceptable? Yet even this possibility escaped my awareness since I thought that my race was not a significant part of who I was. I proudly proclaimed that I happened to be Black; it was my humanness that really mattered, so I thought.

Perhaps the best way to tell you about the connection between my life and this book is to tell this story in broad strokes since the book is not about me but about Black people as a racial and cultural group, descended from Africans and Africa. Yet the truth remains that during the course of my life I seemed to gravitate to the topic of this book. First came the realization that Black people were treated differently from whites and other racial groups in the United States. Second was the awareness that much of what was communicated and taught about Black people was extremely negative and demeaning. I also realized, third, that Blacks were encouraged to deny they were part of the group; by denigrating Black people as a group, as inferior and not worthy of social consideration or regard, portraying them as less than; therefore, the path to social acceptance for any Black person was to create distance from the group. Fourth, Black people did things that members of other racial groups did not do or as well. For instance, their ability with music and song has been recognized as unique and unlike members of other racial groups. Finally, fifth, I thought the experiences I had in my life were due to my actions and only my actions, but in time I saw there were forces beyond my control that contributed to my life outcomes. My life's direction did not result solely from my actions and decisions.

As I grew up, my awareness of race, Black people, and my own life was limited to the negative and stereotypical images and accounts presented in movies, media, and popular sources. The schools I attended taught little about Black people, and my school experience was that I was set apart from the other students for reasons that were not clear to me. It became obvious that educators were less interested in teaching me and more interested in controlling my behavior. While my world was predominately Black and I had only fleeting interactions with whites, the messages and ideas I was exposed to taught me Blacks were different from whites—they came from this dark and mysterious continent where the Africans lived in jungles, supposedly ate people, and lived among dangerous animals. Books and movies told me their protector was a white man called Tarzan, whom the people needed for guidance and protection. And it seemed that Blacks needed a lot of help for reasons that were not clear to a child, teenager, or young adult.

As I grew older and my family moved from an apartment in Manhattan to a house in a mostly white suburb of Queens, things changed. My family was one of only two Black families on our block, and I was confronted more directly with race and racism. I learned how unwelcome my family was and learned that I could not move freely in this area without being subjected to physical harm. One day the only other Black person around my age and I went to a local park to play basketball, and we were chased away by white teens wielding bats and other clubs. They destroyed my bike and came close to harming us both. The message was clear: Black people were not wanted or welcomed. Again I wondered why we were supposedly that different from whites—aren't we all American? As time passed the racial numbers changed and larger numbers of Blacks came into the area. Something I did not expect happened: people who did not know one another acted in concert to ward off the actions of whites, and a community formed. This was contrary to how Black people were popularly portrayed.

Perhaps the community had to act in concert to counter the reception Blacks received from whites, who in time left the area. But the messages I received in schools about my ability to learn were consistent, louder, and more pronounced by the time I attended middle and high schools, and the message was from all corners: "stay still and do what I say." In essence, I was asked to not learn, just do what I was told. The message and expectation created a problem for me since I wanted to learn, but it seemed that there was little or no teaching taking place. After trying several options to stay in school, the result was the same, so I dropped out.

I remember an incident in one class when the teacher was telling stories about his life, so I turned around to interact with a classmate. The teacher told me I had to listen to him, and I responded that I would as soon as he returned to the lesson. I was sent to the dean for misbehaving. My issue was that I wanted to learn, but it seemed there was little interest in teaching me. It seemed clear I was not worth the effort, yet I thought the problem was mine. So I left school and returned later to a school where I thought the educators wanted to teach me. It was at a community program and later college. The community college was Malcolm-King in Harlem (the section of Manhattan in which Blacks resided), which I was able to attend once I secured my high school general education diploma by passing the required exam. By then I was working full time and living on my own, so I took classes in the evening. The community college was established for people like me and was dedicated to help us advance and improve our lives. The school's president and administrator was a Black woman, another fact refuting what has been suggested to be true about Black people. Here was an instance of community support and collaboration. For me, the school's existence altered the course of my life.

By this time, I had enough experiences that I could see some of the differences between whites and Blacks. I did not hold what I knew in conscious form, but I came to grasp the reality of the same old prevailing messages about Blacks: they need help and assistance and have little to offer society unless it is music, sports, or physical labor. In part, the negative narratives of Blacks are based on the fact that they are descended from slaves, low-caste, and poor citizens in the society. This is a stigma that each Black person has had to overcome since people seem to think that we are forever scarred by that history and—more importantly, the story line goes—we are unable to care for ourselves and need whites' help to live. The poverty and damage from being slaves defined Blacks and created a sociopsychological world of disorder and chaos in which all Blacks lived. So we—and everyone in American society—were taught throughout our lives to believe whites' version of the story. Yet, as I learned more and observed more, I came to consider other possibilities, such as, Blacks had to have strengths and constructive values to survive generations of cruelty and oppression, and these strengths and values had to have been shared among the group and passed on to new generations.

The path of education that I began at the community college continued when I applied and was accepted to a four-year college, and then went on to pursue a masters' degree, and then a doctorate. Several things are important about this journey. While my efforts were supported and encouraged by many whites I encountered, I also experienced some whites saying to me, sometimes directly and other times indirectly, that I did not belong and should follow a different path. For instance, as an undergraduate at an Ivy League school, I had to find my own funding, which I did; I thought in reflection that it was an obstacle. I am not sure what happened with other students, maybe whites did the same thing; I am not sure. I doubt it, but I could be mistaken. The other factor that stands out for me is that along the way I encountered other Black people, some who became life-long friends; others cheered me on or helped me in specific situations along the way. It was the guidance of Black people who showed me the way forward and stood by me in times of crisis, struggles, and challenges that revealed a cultural connection between us that transcended the personal; I attribute it to their cultural investment in members of the larger Black group. Since many of these people were strangers to me when we met (see Carter, 2016), what we shared was our race, our identity, and mostly common experiences as Black people.

My educational journey during my graduate years provided me an opportunity to learn about race and people who were disadvantaged (typically then the term meant Black people). I recall a class, "Counseling the Disadvantaged," taught by white male and female professors who lectured about how disadvantaged people benefited from their commercially developed program designed to teach life skills to the disadvantaged. Throughout the course, I kept thinking: how did they know about the people they described, and had they overlooked something important about disadvantaged people? I had no answer, but I did consider the matter and later wrote a paper for another class I took, taught by a new Black professor, in which I proposed a mental health services center that would be based on knowledge of Black people and their preferred ways to receive mental health services in the community.

Some of the ideas I included in my paper were based on my direct experiences working as a community-based mental health counselor in a single-room occupancy (SRO) hotel where people who had been in such institutions as prisons and mental hospitals lived. I was charged with reconnecting discharged mental health patients to community-based mental health services that I would provide as their case manager. My task was to get the former patient to sign a document that allowed me access to their medical records and gave me permission to act as their case manager.

In this setting I was stationed in the social service office of the SRO hotel, where SRO residents would come for coffee, inexpensive meals, and assistance with city or state services. When residents visited the social services office, it was apparent who still had mental health issues, but there was no authority I could use besides persuasion to convince them to sign to allow me access to their records and be their case manager.

I worked in this position for a few years, and I learned a great deal about the mentally ill. What I had been taught about them in my college and graduate studies I found was not completely accurate. To make a long story short, I followed, at first, what I was taught in my masters' program in psychology classes about how to interact with people who were mentally ill and fell flat on my face. I failed to get anyone to sign the papers for me to be their case manager. Then I drew on a relational approach and did not use what I was taught such as the notion that mentally ill people could not form relationships due to their delusions and other symptoms; instead, I began to relate to them as I would any other member of the Black community (most of them were Black), and things changed. I developed a large case load. Once again, it seemed that something larger was at work here, that there was more to these people than was captured by their psychiatric diagnoses or what was said about what they could or could not do. My effort to have a relationship with them seemed to allow each of them to trust me, and many gave me access to their records and agreed that I could be their case manager. I had been taught this would not be possible, but I suspected, yet again, that there was something scholars and researchers were missing about Black people, about what was important to them and what they shared with most other Blacks.

This point is vital to emphasize. Blacks are almost always presented as if they are a single or monolithic racial group with few desirable or constructive traits or qualities. They are portrayed as a single community with one voice and little variation. In fact, Black people—even those with mental illness—are and have been quite diverse or heterogeneous, even though many have common or similar experiences and value some things that seem to be unique to them.

In the years while I obtained my masters training and encountered the newly hired Black male professor, I learned several important things; one had to do with what was emerging at the time in psychology, which was that researchers and scholars were advocating for understanding racial differences rather than the popular and widely held belief that Blacks were inferior or disadvantaged. The emerging line of scholarship at the time became known as the cultural difference perspective in psychology, which turned into what people in psychology call today multicultural or diversity. What mattered to me at the time was that proponents of the cultural difference perspective or cross-cultural psychology presented evidence and arguments that they claimed indicated how and in what ways Blacks and other racial minorities were culturally different from whites (Carter, 2005b, 2016). This scholarship confirmed for me the reservations I harbored about Black people being different; now I had language and theories to support my nagging suspicions.

The Black professor I met while in my masters' program introduced me to a possibility I did not know existed. He suggested I consider applying for entrance to doctoral programs in psychology, to earn a PhD. He had to show me the way, and he did. The white professors in the program expressed doubt and wonder at such an effort on my part, but a couple agreed to write letters for me. They—and I—were shocked and surprised when I was accepted to all the programs I had applied to, mostly due to the guidance provided by the professor who became a good and life-long friend and colleague (Carter, 2016). I moved away to study for a doctorate in 1981 and had no idea of what was before me. My good fortune continued, however; in my first year a Black woman joined the faculty, and she became my adviser, mentor, and valued friend (Carter, 2016).

I carried to this educational experience my focus on Black culture, which I had spent time studying, consuming all I could about what scholars said about Black culture being distinct and unique. The 1970s and 1980s was an era in which more attention was given to Blacks' experiences as more Black studies programs were established in many colleges and universities around the country due to protests by both Black and white people who thought this was an area of academic study that had been neglected. Prior to the 1970s and 1980s, the societal belief was that Black people were biologically and genetically inferior to whites, a view that seemed to be supported by scientific and social scientific research.

By the 1980s the cultural difference movement in psychology and other disciplines was well under way. Initially, the cultural difference emphasis did not include a large number of groups. Rather, its emphasis was on race as the primary source of the presumed cultural differences, thus contending that "race was also culture," an emphasis that led most articles and books in these decades to focus on the specific needs of members of certain racial groups. Over time "cross-cultural" became "multicultural," and by the 1990s scholars and researchers had developed psychological models based on the notion of cultural difference, where helping relationships that were cross-cultural began to be defined in terms of multiple sources of social difference such as gender, ethnicity, social class, and race (Sue et al., 1998).

So, back to my journey. I learned about Black culture and its unique aspects from scholarship and related sources that added to my personal observations and experiences, yet it struck me that empirical validation was lacking for many of the claims. While the descriptions and accounts of how Black people were different in terms of language, kinship, family roles and structures, beliefs about community connections, and spiritual and religious faith seemed accurate and plausible, I was hard pressed to find much empirical research evidence to support the claims about particular aspects of Black culture.

By this time I had begun my doctoral training, and during the first few years students needed to establish research competence by proposing, executing, and defending an independent empirical study. I proposed to study Black cultural values, employing a model of cultural orientations presented by Kluckhohn and Strodtbeck (1961) that used existential propositions to compare distinct groups' cultural preferences. This was done by way of an interview procedure in which a group's members would select one of three alternatives for each proposition or value orientation, including their view of human nature (evil/good/mixed), the groups' relationship to nature (harmony/master/subjection), its temporal focus (past/future/present), the preferred form of social relationships (lineal or follow elders/ collateral or group-based/individual), and the groups' preferred form of self-expression (emotional/being contemplative or being-in-becoming/action-oriented or doing) (Carter, 1991; Carter & Helms, 1987).

Empirical investigations employed instruments that captured the studies' constructs and psychological processes. To that end, I found a survey measure that used the Kluckhohn and Strodtbeck (1961) model, the Intercultural Values Inventory (ICV). I used the ICV to compare cultural values and racial identity attitude (one's psychological orientation to their racial group membership) instruments to capture within-racial-group variation.

I also used Black and white racial identity scales that operationalized the idea that all people, regardless of their race, assign different psychological meanings to their race (Carter & Johnson, 2019; Helms, 1990). It is the psychological meaning attributed to one's race that determines how an individual makes sense of the world and themselves as racial beings. The racial identity models and measures were relatively new at the time, and there were only a few published articles about Black racial identity attitudes and none for whites. My adviser was a coauthor on those papers. Theoretically, psychologically based racial identity resolutions were believed to influence, in different ways, a person's thoughts (cognitions), feelings and emotions, and behaviors and were considered by some to be an aspect of personality and racial socialization. In that sense, these resolutions would have particular relevance for understanding how individuals from specific racial groups might endorse cultural values. This is why racial identity attitudes were an important construct that I used to study within-group cultural value preferences since racial identity in this sense went beyond one's skin color or "race identity."

I believed that, with racial identity attitudes, I could study Blacks without comparing them to whites, which was the way research had always been conducted at the time. But my research committee (two other professors and my adviser) insisted that a white comparison group be included. Now this was a gigantic problem since I proposed to study Black racial identity status attitudes and related cultural value preferences. That is, would different Black racial identity attitudes be related to distinct and different value preferences? I suspected that, yes, they would. Including a comparison meant that I would have to have a racial identity instrument for whites, which at the time did not exist.

As it turned out, my research competence project and first empirical study involved the development of two instruments, the ICV, and the white racial identity scale (Helms & Carter 1990). Remember, I had just begun the doctoral program and, more importantly, had no research training. But if I wanted to complete my proposed project, I had to learn. So my adviser led the way. We constructed the white racial identity instrument based on my preliminary work and validated the ICV so it could be used (Carter, 1995; Carter & Helms, 1990; Helms, 1984).

In general, I found that whites and Blacks had different cultural value preferences when compared to one another and that racial identity attitudes for both racial groups were associated with distinctly different cultural value preferences. Yet, as expected, the within-group analyses using racial identity would reveal a different set of relationships when the racial groups were compared.

The investigation revealed several important things about cultural values and racial differences and similarities. Both whites and Blacks shared cultural values that were related to being American when compared to one another or when within-group psychological variation was not considered. However, when racial identity psychological resolutions were taken into account, differences emerged that related to their sociocultural and racial contexts. So my effort to establish empirical evidence for distinct Black cultural values was successful but more complex than I realized. My goal, then, was to learn more and strengthen my research skills.

As my studies and research training progressed, I took other opportunities, as I could, to delve more into Black psychology and cultural ways. I spent more time on racial identity and less on cultural values. However, I did hold on to the interest and learned more and more about race and racism through my work with white and Black racial identity.

The research and scholarship on racial identity development (Helms, 1990) has helped shape and influence how the discipline of psychology conceptualized, investigated, and treated the impact of racial group membership on people's lives and has helped build a better understanding of cultural preferences among Blacks. In that, the varied racial identity psychological resolutions reflected different cultural values. For instance, pre-encounter attitudes were associated with investment in dominant white American culture while the more mature and developed racial identity status attitudes were associated with preferences for ones' own race and culture. My shift to a focus on racial identity did not exclude consideration of cultural influences or practices. It instead gave my learning about Black culture a richer and more layered perspective since Blacks are a heterogeneous people and have always been so, contrary to popular beliefs.

Culture, Identity, and Human Development

I completed my doctoral degree, and while an assistant professor, my first book, *The Influence of Race and Racial Identity in Psychotherapy* (Carter, 1995), presented findings from my dissertation. The book was an opportunity to put forward the ideas that race and culture were integral aspects of personality and human development. In the book I discuss how race and racial identity are conceptualized and understood in mental health theory and practice, and I demonstrated how racial identity—how a person understood herself or himself as a racial-cultural being—influences therapy interactions and outcomes. I also described how race and culture are aspects of human development and, thus, individual identity and racial-cultural group formation. The human development and socialization process is integral to how people evolve self-concepts, and each person's sense of self is embedded in a cultural worldview, which is shared by the group of which the person is a part.

All people, regardless of race or culture, help their offspring learn to live and prosper; they must teach the young how to be in the world in which they reside. Children are taught the lessons and activities that are needed for healthy growth and change. Thus, children must learn to care for themselves and others and to participate in their respective families and communities. When people are members of groups that in some societies are held at the margins or in low-caste groups, additional instruction is needed; the lessons these groups are taught are influenced by the environment in which they live. The members of such groups also have to teach their children to cope and adapt to the rigors of their social position. Black Americans have had to live and raise their offspring in a society and teach them how to navigate a world that has held them in low esteem but relied on their labor.

In whatever situation a person is born, they must evolve an identity, a self-concept that contains information about who they are and how they matter in the world in which they live. In the mental health literature, there are many perspectives and theories about identity and development. Carter (1995) observes that developmental theorists lack any emphasis on culture and race and how they operate in the process of development and the formation of personality or personal-social identity. Human development theorists use the term "culture" to account for individual variation in humans. But culture usually refers to a variety of factors like geography, language, and customs. When cultural differences within the United States are considered, it is mostly done in terms of the special needs of deprived racial and social groups. One of the more influential theorists, Erik Erickson (1963), argues that healthy identity development means that one's sense of self is in line with one's social system. Yet this principle ignores cultural and racial stratification and hostility that erects barriers to social participation for Black Americans. While Erikson and other theorists acknowledge the role and functions of culture, less attention has been given to race. It has been suggested that developmental theorists have left out vital information and written as if sociohistorical facts and events have no role in the human developmental process.

Carter (1995) notes that

> because the effects of social history and customs on personality and identity development have been absent in the psychological literature, one might infer that race [and culture], as a central feature of social and historical life in the United States [and the world], has also been ignored or minimized, or thought about from the perspective of … racial/ethnic group inferiority or cultural deprivation.
>
> *(p. 75)*

Carter observes that the lack of attention to race in personality and human developmental models is curious in the face of information, mostly in the United States, that shows that children come to grasp the meaning of race and their social status by the age of three or four (Carter & Pieterse, 2020).

Human development begins with the fertilization of a woman's egg by a man's semen, and the binding of genetic material determines the gender, skin color, and other characteristics and attributes of the child. There is also some contribution to emotional and psychological predispositions that result from the pairing of genetic material. In the United States and in the colonies of years past, the markers for racial status have been skin color and physical features, both of which are derived from the genetic material from the parents of the child. At the same time, skin color and physical features matter a great deal in a society stratified by race and based on skin color, physical appearance, and language. Carter (1995) states regarding the physical and biological markers for race,

> They have considerable import in a racially segregated society that maintains social taboos about interracial unions and injects racial concerns at the point of human conception. A child's skin color, eye color, hair texture, and physical features will also be determined by genetic factors.
>
> *(p. 77)*

Thus, for Carter and other scholars, while racism and racial oppression are not biologically based, there are biological factors that have been used to establish racial categories and that have been enforced and reinforced with the power of laws and customs from the colonial period until the present (Carter & Scheuermann, 2020).

Individuals are conceived by parents and raised in a family and community of people usually including their guardians, relatives, and members of the larger community. As children mature, they learn about the expectations and rules/roles that govern the people and social groups to which they belong. What the theories of human development reveal are the mechanisms and interactions that are employed by people and groups to teach the ways of one's family and culture. In this way we each, as a part of a group, come to understand ourselves and our unique personality and place in the kinship network, community, and society (Bronfenbrenner, 1979; Lewin, 1935).

Bronfenbrenner's "ecological network" of human development (1979) states that multiple systems influence an individual's development. Bronfenbrenner's ecological systems theory suggests that people are influenced by five interrelated systems—the micro, meso, exo, macro, and chrono—each connected to the other. Children, at various times and in various aspects of their lives, receive different messages about who they are and, subsequently, all the messages contribute to who each of us become.

The microsystem is the immediate and direct environment, which includes parents, relatives, the community, and the physical environment. How the group or individuals interact with the child will affect how and what the child learns. Similarly, how the child responds to people in the microsystem will also determine how they treat the child in return. Supportive environments protect and promote the well-being of the child without enclosing the child, in contrast to an environment that lacks support, possibly leaving the child with doubts and fears (Bronfenbrenner, 1979).

The mesosystem is composed of the relationships among the parties in the microsystem, how parents and teachers interact, for instance. To focus on one system at a time and on its effects on a certain phenomenon is to simplify a reality in which various components in fact enhance or minimize each other's influence. In studying, for example, the relative influence that parents and peers have on a child, it is not valid to concentrate only on one aspect or set of influences. Rather, one should examine the ways in which supportive parents and nonsupportive peers both influence a child's behavior. All possible combinations of interaction need to be considered.

The exosystem refers to social systems that the individual is not necessarily a direct part of but that affect the person's life regardless. For example, children's lives are affected by what their parents do for a living, their parents' social networks, or by decisions made by parents and family at the social or community level. The social and physical environment of their parents, extended family, and community groups that are external but are part of where and how the family lives are all exosystems. It is not difficult to see that decisions made in these places can either support or stress families, social systems, and communities.

The macrosystem is the largest and most distant collection of people and places, and it has significant influence on the child in terms of social and cultural values. This level is the basis for the child's cultural teachings and what they learn about life's patterns and values (as in the cultural value orientations I studied); specifically, the child's dominant beliefs and ideas, as well as political and economic systems are contained in the macrosystem of people and places. Consider what values and lessons a child learns if the environment is one of hostility, war, and conflict compared to a setting characterized by support, cooperation, and peace.

The chronosystem adds the dimension of time, which demonstrates the influence of both change and constancy in the child's environment. The chronosystem captures changes in family structure, location, and parents' social and economic status, in addition to immense society changes such as economic cycles of prosperity, decline, and disruptions and climate as well as the physical realities of life.

The models of human development proposed by Bronfenbrenner (1979), Erickson (1963), and others show that, regardless of when and where a person is born and lives, there are various forces and factors that shape them.

Combined with the person's own decisions and choices, the forces interact and result in a unique person. Thus, each person also has a culture and learns the convictions, principles, and practices of the people in the community. Africans and their Black American descendants repeated the cycle of life and taught their offspring the rules and expectations during their time period, as well as the cultural practices and beliefs of their people for many millennia, instilling in their children the beliefs and values they learned and held dear. So the study of racial identity and race interjected the role and function of culture as it pertains to the development of individuals and the role of family, community, and the group's respective cultural orientations.

Culture, Race, and Community

I continued to write about racial identity status attitudes and their application to mental health interventions as well as how they could be used to capture the ways people's cultural orientations shifted depending upon how they viewed themselves as racial-cultural beings (Thompson & Carter, 1997). I extended the application of culture to a consideration of how it operated in organizations (Carter, 2000), and then I edited the two-volume *Handbook Racial-Cultural Counseling and Psychology* (Carter, 2005c), in which I was tasked with bringing together the leading scholars who were involved in promoting knowledge and research about racial, ethnic, and cultural groups and issues as well as people who developed and used racial-cultural perspectives of the various groups for mental health interventions and training methods. In volume 1 of the handbook, I addressed how I elected to use the term "racial-cultural," as opposed to "diversity" or "multicultural." I pointed out that it was difficult to know what people meant by the wide range of terms employed to refer to racial, ethnic, social, or cultural differences. I attempted to clarify the use of the varied terms in an article that first appeared in 1995.

I found it confusing and difficult to grasp what people meant by the terms "multicultural" and "diversity." Carter and Qureshi (1995) present a model to clarify what might be meant by such terms, the basis of which highlights the assumptions about cultural difference that seemed to be unstated and hidden in how issues of difference were being understood and presented. The problem is, mental health and professionals in other disciplines employ a wide number of terms, and what they refer to with the terms is unclear, like "diversity-sensitive," "ethno-cultural," "cross-cultural," "intercultural" or "working across cultures," "special populations," "culture-specific psychotherapy," "the culturally different," "the culturally diverse," "trans-cultural psychiatry," "multicultural," "cultural diversity," or "diversity." More often than not, the terms seem to be used to define cultural difference broadly, including a variety of socially defined group memberships (i.e., ethnicity, gender, social class, socioeconomic status, race, sexual orientation, sexual identity, age, or disability). Our model highlights unstated underlying assumptions of difference.

A brief review of the Carter and Qureshi model here might be of value. I use the term "racial-cultural" to identify my perspective and conceptual framework. I use the same framework in this book about Blacks and racial oppression. The assumptive types presented here are adopted from our early work (e.g., Carter, 1995; Carter & Qureshi, 1995), in which we presented what we believe are five unstated assumptions regarding what scholars mean by "cultural difference"; these assumptions are universal, ubiquitous, traditional, race-based, and pan-national. The tacit assumptions can be derived from the content and emphasis taken by the scholar or author in question. The description of the types of unstated assumptions about cultural differences are intended to highlight basic beliefs that remain unidentified when people use the language or terms such as "diversity" or "multicultural" or some variant.

Universal: The universal assumption equates cultural difference with individual differences. The essential idea is that humans are alike, and they vary primarily as unique individuals. Therefore, only secondarily do experiences and identity formation derive from group memberships (e.g., ethnicity, race, gender). Culture is noted and understood as characteristics of an individual (e.g., age, gender). Psychological and mental health theory and practice is guided by the universal assumption of cultural difference. The universal approach, in effect, takes a colorblind view of race and culture wherein racial group differences are of little or no relevance.

Ubiquitous: The ubiquitous assumption holds that all differences associated with group membership(s) are salient. All forms of social or group membership are essentially cultural. Cultural difference can be a driven by geography, income, gender, age, race, religion, ethnicity, disability, and sexual orientation, to name a few. Those who operate on the assumptions of the ubiquitous perspective would contend that there is a fundamental difference in culture between a gay white male and a straight white male. This assumption underlies many of the definitions of diversity and multiculturalism. The view of difference as common experience or group identity presumes that one's shared group membership cuts across dominant or nondominant American social and racial-cultural group patterns. Thus, white, Asian, and Black American men and women share gender cultures and are considered culturally different due to their gender group membership. Yet, some would also contend that race is a source of cultural difference.

Traditional: The traditional assumption is grounded in anthropology, which defines culture in terms of one's country of origin, with a common language, values, beliefs, rituals, and so forth. One is a member of a cultural group by birth and national influence. Central to beliefs about differences due to culture based on this assumption is that culture is defined as common experience and as a function of socialization and environment from one's country or nation.

Race-Based: This assumption holds that race is the primary form of culture in North America in that cultural groups are identified and classified based on skin color, language, and physical features. Race-based theorists hold that the definitive aspects of culture—for example, cultural values (see Carter, 1991)—ultimately vary according to psychologically (e.g., racial identity) and socially based racial categories. The race-based approach assumes that the experience of belonging to a racial group supersedes all other experiences in the United States because race is the most visible of all "differences" and because of the history of racial segregation and racism that exists in the United States. Race has been and continues to be the ultimate measure of social exclusion and inclusion.

Pan-National: The pan-national position views race in the global context as definitive of culture. The focus of this assumption about cultural difference is in the role of oppression and violence rendered by the legacy and practice of colonialism and imperialism primarily directed at people of color throughout the world. Whites in the United States and Europe, for example, developed their society and social structures based on racial-cultural violence and exploitation.

The assumptive typology is intended to help clarify what one might assume when they use the words "multicultural" or "diversity." Clearly, for much of American history through today, the basis of differences between social groups has been due to race and, through race, culture since it has been proclaimed that Black people are culturally and racially distinct. Yet this view has changed over time and shifted from considering Blacks as less than human or as uncivilized savages to considering Blacks people who need guidance and who need to be taught the ways of white European Americans.

Teaching about Race, Racism, and Culture

My career path led to academic positions in universities where I taught undergraduate and graduate classes designed to help students become racially and culturally competent. In the process of designing and improving the classes, I found that a cultural-historical perspective was an effective way to promote self-awareness with respect to issues of race and culture (see Carter, 2005a). Objectives of my racism course were for students to learn how racism affected both the oppressor and the oppressed and to increase their ability to understand racial issues in terms of knowledge, with less emphasis on personal opinions, which tends to characterize such discussions.

The course provided a historical overview that focused on Native, Asian, Latin, and African contributions to humankind as well as documented events in American history. The historical perspective demonstrated that disenfranchised Americans lived in complex and elaborate civilizations long before the rise of European powers. The material I used and shared in this course instilled in me an appreciation for the importance of looking at culture, race, and racism from a historical perspective (Feagin, 2014). I began to wonder how Africans and their descendants survived the centuries of racial oppression and whether there are things they still do to exist as a people in the North American mainland today.

Culture and Psychology in the Context of Development

Jones (2003) argues that people are motivated to grow or improve to protect themselves from threats to their being or person. Actions to protect or grow are both undertaken by individuals and as members of a targeted group such as Black Americans.

Some scholars believe that minority group members, because of their low social status, develop negative attitudes and beliefs about themselves and their racial group. They hold denigrating views of themselves and the people to whom they are presumed to belong. Clearly, some actually do hold such negative beliefs about self and groups members. Jones (2003) argues that this may not be so for all, contending that oppressed people can have positive regard for themselves and their group. And he presents an African-based cultural worldview associated with positive psychological well-being for Black Americans, which he contends was true for some Black people. According to Jones, worldviews are both cultural (that is, they have existential propositions that are guides to behavior and attitudes) and psyche (that is, the existential propositions are expressed through patterns of thinking, emotions, and actions that are represented through symbols, ideas, and values, and these also guide actions). Jones states that present-day Black Americans' culture is connected to their African origins. The way Black culture evolved is best described by two processes, one reactionary and the other evolutionary. As members of African cultural groups, Black people had to cope and adapt (react) to their circumstances as oppressed captives and had to evolve new ways to act over time. They had to learn how to handle the loss of their freedom and how to deal with being dehumanized. This was the evolutionary mechanism that held the core African cultural ethos. That is, these aspects enabled "the recovering [of] certain forms of physical and psychological freedom" (Jones, 2003, p. 223) and set the basis for regaining humanity in a hostile setting. Black Africans found ways to hold on to and pass on their culture, but the situations they encountered also meant they had to devise new ways to do so and adopt new beliefs. My inquiry is, how was this accomplished? What did Africans and their descendants do to survive psychologically, emotionally, socially, and as a community?

The book charts the course over time of African beliefs, practices, and behaviors and psychological perspectives and follows the people from Africa to the North American mainland, later the United States. It examines how, or if, people who were subjected to such horrible racial oppression came through with their minds and culture intact. More importantly, it identifies their strengths that were central to their culture and mental well-being.

Conclusion

I came to the topic of psychological and cultural strengths of Black people through personal and academic research activities and social experiences. I discovered there were many unanswered questions about how Africans and their descendants survived the centuries of hostile racial oppression. I looked for evidence to show that, through determination and trusting their beliefs to guide them, Africans brought with them a range of beliefs and values, some of which they managed to retain and pass on to succeeding generations. Some contend that not all Blacks did this since they were an ethnically diverse people. At the same time, historians and scholars also point out that Africans exhibited common themes and experiences that pulled them together, and these commonalities could have triggered the processes that contributed to their being able to get through the worst of their treatment.

But what was true of Black Africans in the 1600s, 1700s, 1800s, 1900s, and 2000s is not the same; it is important to consider that many events and actions occurred, and things changed and varied by location. Nevertheless, as Johnson and Carter (2020) found in their study of Black cultural strengths, there are psychological, social, and cultural beliefs and values that can be discerned, and these could have helped Blacks to adapt and push forward or survive. By using secondary and a few primary sources, I document what was known about Africa and its varied people. I trace their efforts to build and establish communities and social structures, and I explore the range of beliefs and practices that existed prior to contact with Europeans, primarily along the West Coast of the continent. I follow Africans to the New World and describe their experiences and reactions to unearth possible evidence of their psychological and emotional reactions, and I examine how they settled on particular practices that came to define them as a people, in part, including some practices that were influenced by and taken from white European-American race and cultural practices and beliefs.

Plan of the Book

The text is organized into four parts and 14 chapters. Part 1, "Africans at Home," consists of two chapters: chapter 1, "African Civilizations and Culture," reaches into the ancient past and traces the history of civilization on the African continent, including the development of social structures. Chapter 2, "African Life and Ways Expressed in Cultural Patterns," examines the cultural ways, practices, and psychological perspectives of African people from ancient times through the Middle Ages and first contact with Europeans, and it describes how Blacks were traded away from West Africa.

Part 2, "Africans in the New World," has four chapters, starting with chapter 3, "Building a Life in the New World from the Foundations of the Old," which covers the transatlantic slave trade and how Blacks from Africa, the Caribbean, and South America survived life in the colonies. Chapters 4 and 5 examine Black lives by region. Chapter 4, "The First Generation of Slaves and Servants," discusses life in American colonies for the Charter generation. Chapter 5 "The Rise of the Plantation in the Colonies," explores the effect of plantations on Blacks and colonial life. Chapter 6, "The Revolutionary Era and Beyond," covers the colonies' struggle for independence, including actions toward ending the slave trade.

Part 3, "Africans' Conversion to American Life and Their Contributions to Its Prosperity," begins with chapter 7, "The Expanded Union and Blacks as the Engine for Progress," which discusses the expansion of slavery as the new country grew, the new government's failure to give Blacks rights under the Constitution, and slavery as the engine of the industrial economy; chapter 8, "Black Freedom Blocked: The Churches, Land, and Schools," and chapter 9, "Jim Crow Reality," picks up the narrative during Reconstruction, a time that could have brought equality for Blacks but instead brought a new form of subversion with sharecropping and Jim Crow laws; Blacks responded by establishing churches, schools, and other organizations to strengthen their community. In chapter 10, "A Century of Black Activism, 1920s–2020s," covers Black activism beginning after World War I and looks at how white supremacy was maintained over the 20th century.

In part 4, "Integrating Black Cultural Strengths into Psychological Practice," racial identity theory is examined in chapter 11, "Elements of Black Culture" shows the progression of Black cultural values and beliefs over time; chapter 12, "Critical Differences among Blacks and Others Regarding Race and Cultural Value Preferences," focuses on the ways Blacks vary psychologically and culturally, since the group is heterogenous; the application of cultural strengths to teaching and practice in mental health is discussed in chapter 13, "Applications for Black Cultural Strengths in Training and Practice", and chapter 14, "Applications to Programming and Policy."

Note

1 I use the term Black American, instead of African American, because any person regardless of race, white or Asian, who is native to Africa, and comes to the U.S. to live, can be considered an African American, including white South African leaders or citizens. Black was a term chosen by the collective of Americans of African descent.

References

Bennett, L. (1988). *Before the Mayflower: A history of Black America.* Johnson Publishing.

Bronfenbrenner, U. (1979). *The ecology of human development.* Harvard University Press.

Carter, R. T. (1991). Cultural values: A review of empirical research and implications for counseling. *Journal of Counseling and Development*, 70, 164–173.

Carter, R. T. (1995). *The influence of race and racial identity in psychotherapy: Toward a racially inclusive model.* Wiley.
Carter, R. T. (Ed.). (2000). *Addressing cultural issues in organizations: Beyond the corporate context.* Sage.
Carter, R. T. (2005a). A cultural-historical model for understanding racial-cultural competence and confronting dynamic cultural conflicts: An introduction. In R. T. Carter (Ed.). *Handbook of racial-cultural psychology and counseling*, Vol. 2, *Training and practice* (pp. ix–xxvi). Wiley.
Carter, R. T. (2005b). Teaching racial-cultural counseling competence: A racially inclusive model. In R. T. Carter (Ed.). *Handbook of racial-cultural psychology and counseling*, Vol. 2, *Training and practice* (pp. 36–56). Wiley.
Carter, R. T. (Ed.). (2005c). *Handbook of racial-cultural psychology and counseling: Training and practice.* 2 Vols. Wiley.
Carter, R. T. (2016). The road less traveled: Research on race. In J. M. Casas, L. A. Suzuki, C. M. Alexandria, & M. A. Jackson (Eds.). *The handbook of multicultural counseling* (4th ed., pp. 71–80). Sage.
Carter, R. T., & Helms, J. E. (1987). The relationship of Black value-orientations to racial identity attitudes. *Measurement and Evaluation in Counseling and Development*, 19, 185–195.
Carter, R. T., & Helms, J. E. (1990). White racial identity attitudes and cultural values. In J. E. Helms (Ed.). *Black and white racial identity attitudes: Theory, research, and practice* (pp. 105–118). Greenwood Press.
Carter, R. T., & Johnson, V. (2019). Racial identity statuses: Applications to practice. *Practice Innovations*, 4(1), 42–58.
Carter, R. T., & Pieterse, A. (2020). *Measuring the effects of racism: Guidelines for the assessment and treatment of race-based traumatic stress injury.* Columbia University Press.
Carter, R. T., & Qureshi, A. (1995). A typology of philosophical assumptions in multicultural counseling and training. In J. Ponterotto, M. Casas, L. Alexandria, & L. Suzuki (Eds.). *The handbook of multicultural counseling* (pp. 239–262). Sage.
Carter, R. T., & Scheuermann, T. D. (2020). *Confronting racism: Integrating mental health strategies with legal reform.* Routledge.
Erickson, E. H. (1963). *Childhood and society* (rev. ed.). Norton.
Feagin, J. R. (2014). *Racist America: Roots, current realities, and future reparations.* Routledge.
Gould, E., & Wilson, V. (2020, June 1). Black workers face two of the most lethal preexisting conditions for coronavirus-racism and economic inequality. *Economic Policy Institute.* https://files.epi.org/pdf/193246.pdf.
Helms, J. E. (1984). Toward an explanation of the influence of race in the counseling process: A Black-white model. *The Counseling Psychologist*, 12, 153–165.
Helms, J. E. (Ed.). (1990). *Black and white racial identity: Theory, research, and practice.* Greenwood Press.
Helms, J. E., & Carter, R. T. (1990). The development of the white racial identity inventory. In J. E. Helms (Ed.). *Black and white racial identity: Theory, research, and practice* (pp. 67–80). Greenwood Press.
Johnson, V. E., & Carter, R. T. (2020). Black cultural patterns as sources of strength and psychological well-being: An empirical analysis. *Journal of Black Psychology*, 46 (1). doi:10.1177/0095798419889752.
Jones, J. M. (2003). TRIOS: A psychological theory of the African legacy in American culture. *Journal of Social Issues*, 39(1), 217–242.

Kluckhohn, F. R., & Strodtbeck, F. L. (1961). *Variations in value orientations*. Row, Peterson.
Lewin, K. (1935). *A dynamic theory of personality*. McGraw Hill.
Louis-Jean, J., Cenat, K., Nkjou, C., Angelo, J., & Sanon, D. (2020). Coronavirus (COVID-19) and racial disparities: A perspective analysis. *Journal of Racial and Ethnic Health Disparities*, 7(6), 1039–1045. doi:10.1007/s40615-020-00879-4.
McGonigle, L. B. (2020). Imperatives of the present: Black Lives Matter and the politics of memory and memorialization. *Netherlands Quarterly of Human Rights*, 38(4), 239–245.
Schwartz, S. A. (2020). Police brutality and racism in America. *Explore*, 16, 280–282.
Smith K. A. (2020, September 17). Covid and race: Households of color suffer most from pandemic's financial consequences despite trillions in aid. *Forbes*. https://www.forbes.com/advisor/personal-finance/covid-and-race-households-of-color-suffer-biggest-pandemic-consequences/.
Sue, D. W., Carter, R. T., Casas, M. J., Fouad, N. A., Ivey, A. E., LaFromboise, T., Manese, J. E., Ponterotto, J., & Vazquez-Natall, E. (1998). *Multicultural counseling competencies: Individual professional and organizational development*. Sage.
Thompson, C. E., & Carter, R. T. (Eds.). (1997). *Racial identity development theory: Applications to individual, group, and organizational interventions*. Erlbaum.
Trent, M., Dooley, D. G., Douge, J., AAP Section on Adolescent Health, AAP Council on Community Pediatrics, AAP Committee of Adolescents, Cavanaugh Jr., R. M., *et al.* (2019, August). The impact of racism on child and adolescent health. *Pediatrics*, 144(2), e20191765.

PART 1

Africans at Home

1

AFRICAN CIVILIZATIONS AND CULTURE

As with any good story, it is important to begin at the beginning (Silverstein, 2019). In the chapters to follow I chart the course of African history and cultural ways, from the emergence of humans to the period when Europeans began to take Africans as slaves from the West Coast of Africa to Europe, the Americas, and Caribbean islands. Then I follow the events that unfolded in the North American mainland, from colonial times through to the present, documenting and describing what Black people did to survive and the actions they took that aided in their survival.

Western Europeans (mostly Christians) became interested in the African slave trade in the 1400s, and they continued the practice for several centuries. Trading people as slaves was widespread both in Africa and the world. But what it meant to be a slave had different purposes and objectives in most of the world. Slaves in some societies had opportunities for educational and cultural advancement. It was also true, for instance, that among Africans who were Muslim, slavery "was not an institution utilized primarily for the production of goods from which wealth could be derived" (Franklin & Moss, 2000, p. 34). Instead, slaves were employed as servants, absent the strict and harsh treatment that came to characterize life for slaves in North America. It was also the case that slavery was not used in Africa to establish wealth; rather, it was a reflection of it. Yet in North America, slavery was the means to acquiring wealth.

Slavery has existed in many shapes and forms throughout world history and into the present. However, one version of slavery is set apart from the others. The enslavement of Africans in the New World and what became the United States was particularly harsh because of the status to which slaves in this system were relegated and because the slaves were a source of wealth, which came through their unpaid labor. While slaves in many other countries and times throughout history were treated harshly, abused, and stripped of some human

DOI: 10.4324/9781003111542-3

rights, slavery in the New World colonies and, later, the United States, regarded slaves as nonhuman property (Watkins, 2001). Yet Africans found ways to maintain their humanity in the face of being relegated to the status of property.

It is well established that Black people in the United States have been subjected to centuries of racial oppression of different forms. What is not established is what the people who were racially oppressed did to survive and what cultural values and psychological strengths they possessed to survive more than four hundred years of captivity (Johnson & Carter 2020; Stewart, 1999). To fully understand Blacks' cultural strengths and the psychological practices, we must visit the past with a focus on the psychological perspectives and cultural practices and patterns of Africans and their descendants. We must learn how Africans thought and behaved, and learn about the features of West Coast African societies before Africans were traded to Europeans. Historians (e.g., Dodson, 2002; Franklin & Moss, 2000; Horton & Horton, 2005) continue to debate the matter of the survival of what Herskovits (1990) calls Africanisms present in Black American culture; Herskovits (1990) cites several scholars who claim that Africanisms did not exist, while Mintz and Price (1972) say there is a blend of African and European ways that can be detected in Black life, and Asante (2019), Bennett (1988), Holloway (2005), and Franklin and Moss (2000) argue that African ways, patterns, and practices can be identified among African descendants.

Harms (2018) refers to Africa as the mother land, and Stampp (1956) describes it as the place where underdeveloped people resided. Historians, archaeologists, biologists, and scientists (e.g., Harms, 2018) have presented numerous perspectives on the people who were Africa's inhabitants. While Stampp (1956) argued that African people have contributed little of value to human history and knowledge, Holloway (2005) and other historians (e.g., Bennett, 1988) take the view that, in fact, African people contributed a great deal to humankind. Take for an example the contributions made by the Egyptians.

The existence of great ancient civilizations like the Egyptians before the birth of Christ is acknowledged, but many attribute that society to people of non-African origins, and others (Harms, 2018) contend that the building of the pyramids and Egyptian civilization itself was the work of Europeans. Nevertheless, there are scholars who document the opposite, claiming that those are the achievements of Africans (Harms, 2018). While many factors are at play regarding these debates, it seems that the enslavement of Africans and their relocation to the New World and Europe, along with the subsequent colonization, subjugation, and exploitation of much of the African continent, is a dark cloud that obscures our knowledge of Africa and its people. Indeed, it is difficult to attribute astonishing contributions to people who have been enslaved and dominated for so many centuries.

The irony is that science has various sources of information and evidence to show that, in fact, Africa is the mother land of humankind, that the people who occupy the world came out of Africa, and that some of the world's ancient civilizations originated there as well (Asante, 2019). In the evolution of humankind, the topography of the African continent is vital to understanding the climate and physical environment in which many Africans had to cope and live. Davidson (2005) notes that the settings and environments where many Africans lived were harsh and demanding, which affected their psychological perspectives. It also explains the view of the cosmos that many African people evolved to make sense of their lives and relationships. Historians mark the beginning of life for *Homo sapiens* as the point when beings walked upright and began using tools in Africa (Davidson, 2005).

Prehistoric Times

Humans, or *Homo sapiens*, evolved from a range of hominids or other human types who had existed on the planet for several million years. It is said, based on fossil evidence, that *Homo sapiens* lived with other human types (e.g., Australopithecus and Neanderthals) as well as ape-like primates dating back some 315,000 years. The notion that *Homo sapiens*, hominids, and primates are related is an accepted fact established by both anthropologists and biologists (Davidson, 2005).

It is believed that the human branch sprang from the African continent, yet the exact nature and details of the evolution remains controversial. What is clear, it seems, is that there was a group of human-like beings that existed over time, and some of these grew into what we call *Homo sapiens*. It is said that the first movement or significant development of steering of hominids took place some 23 to 5 million years ago in the Miocene period, which is distinct from the more recent Pleistocene period (3 million to 11,700 years ago) in which tools, symbols, and evidence of culture emerged some 10,000 years ago. Due to changes in the environment, there were also changes in hominids, one of which was being bipedal or walking upright, which was not unique to humans; however, walking in strides was a form of movement that was unique and became one of the more significant developments that made humans distinctive. Historians, archaeologists, biologists, and other scientists contend that adaption to the environments of Africa and other parts of the world contributed to the survival of the hominid subgroups, which led to *Homo sapiens* in three time periods known as the Stone (Paleolithic or Old Stone Age, 3.3 million–11,650, BP [calibrated before the Present]; Mesolithic or Middle Stone Age, 10,000–8,000, BP; and Neolithic or New Stone Age, 8,000–3,000, BP), Bronze, and Iron Ages, which are discussed here in order.

Stone Age

In this time, people mostly used stone tools, and it is suggested that the evolution of both the hands and brains progressed during the Pliocene and

Pleistocene around 5 million to 12,000 years ago years ago. The tools that were used became more diverse and complex. Ornaments for the body have been found, along with implements made from a variety of material, such as bone, stone, wood, ivory, and shells. It appears that these tools were used for a range of activities such as fishing, while spears, bows, and arrows were used for hunting. Some items were polished and ground, which indicated that beads, pendants, and related objects of art were created. There is also evidence that fire was used, although when is not clear.

Beings that existed in the Old Stone Age were cave dwellers or lived in huts and hunted and gathered for food. They learned to use fire and to cook their meals, which consisted of animals and included fruits and berries. They created cave art and crafted figures from stone, bones, and other material. It is said that this period was marked by climate changes and migration.

Bronze Age

The Stone Age was followed by the Bronze Age, which occurred from about 3000 to 1300 BCE (before the Common Era), which was characterized by the use of metals for weapons and tools with polished points made of bone and wood as well as bows and arrows. These advances set in motion the use of the plow and wheels, which helped advance many aspects of daily life such as in textiles and clothing as wells as the construction of homes. It also appears that the people moved around and established settlements near water, and they began planting foodstuffs. The new era witnessed agriculture as a means of food production, and some animals were domesticated. Tools for food production such as plows emerged. With the settlements came advances in farming, home construction, art, pottery, and sewing/weaving. It was possible to build stone houses with thatched roofs. With more stable villages came the advent of law, governments, and conflicts. It is during this time that the Egyptians built pyramids and introduced symbols and writing.

Iron Age

Many developments happened during the Iron Age, which took place from about 1300–900 BCE (some mark this period as extending into the first century of the Common Era). One of the more significant developments was the use of iron, which overtook the use of bronze. Ways to heat and make iron meant that weapons and tools could be mass produced, and homes could be built that were larger and had more rooms. In some cases stables were added for animals, defenses from outsiders in the form of forts were possible, and palaces and water systems were constructed. Developments in buildings, art, religion, and writing changed how people lived, as can be seen from the brief overview of Africa by Basil Davidson (2005):

> The regional variation of *homo sapiens* continued, one may note, through all these transformations: as between north and centre-south, no doubt, partly because the Saharan belt remained uninhabitable, much as it is today, throughout a great deal of the Middle Stone Age. But at some time after 10,000 BC, the climate of the Sahara grew cooler and less dry. Pastures appeared. Rivers flowed. Much land became fertile. This marked another turning point, and may be regarded as a highly progressive period in African prehistory.
>
> *(p. 10)*

The now-welcoming Sahara encouraged people to move into and around the area, and to interact with one another, resulting in the exchange of ideas, tools, methods, and techniques.

As Davidson (2005) notes, the changed climate and physical world made it possible for Africans in the Sahara to farm as well as to improve how they lived and worked. It also provided a foundation for the civilization in this region to advance other areas of the continent.

The growth of human civilization took place during the Neolithic period, saw the development of complex and elaborate social, economic, and cultural advances as evidenced by the emergence of the Pharaonic Egypt around 3500 BCE in the Nile valley. To fully understand the significance of the physical changes that took place and how those changes affected the African people who lived in many areas on the continent, we must understand how the land mass is configured.

The Lands of the Continent

Africa is the second-largest continent in the world after Asia, yet it is often discussed as if it were merely a country. Africa has a land mass of some 12 million square miles (or more than 30 million square kilometers). The distance from Tunisia, its northern-most point, to the southern tip at Cape Town is about 4,725 miles, and from east to west at its widest points spans some 4,600 miles. The land mass of Africa is larger than all of North America (9.4 million square miles), and three United States of Americas (3.8 million square miles) can fit on the African continent.

It is important that the reader grasp the vast size of the land mass and its varied spaces—some livable, others not. The people in this land had to survive these varied environments and find ways to thrive given the environmental challenges. The land contains lakes, rivers, mountains, forests, high grasses, and low-grass areas. Wild animals and naturally growing fruits and vegetables also are present. Its inhabitants had to manage, grow, and learn to use the land to their advantage.

Harms (2018) uses the travels of two people who go north and south and west and east to describe the various landscapes, terrains, and environments of Africa. Both begin their travels from the city of Mbandaka in the Democratic Republic of the Congo, which is at latitude 0. Here the day and night are equal length, all year long. And it should be noted that the four seasons (winter, summer, spring, and fall) that most people are familiar with do not describe the African climate; instead, it is best to refer to rainy and dry seasons. The travelers' starting point gets considerable rain given that Mbandaka is encircled by tropical rain forest. Looking down from the sky, the rain forest appears to have trees that are interconnected and cover the land tightly, with the tallest trees 100–150 feet high. Below the visible growth is called understory, which is collections of smaller trees with large leaves that absorb the sunlight that pierces the canopy of the taller trees. As a result of the two levels of trees, the floor of the forest is dark and neither warm nor hot. There are many birds (more than 400 types), amphibians, and plants (thousands of types) in the rain forest.

Our travelers start in the center city with traveler A going north for about 2,594 miles and traveler B, south for about 2,350 miles, both using routes in a straight line. If we follow traveler A north, she treks through the rain forest and encounters some clearings that have fields of naturally growing crops like yams, cassava, and oil palm trees as well as plantains and bananas. The climate about 300 miles north of where she started is in the dry season. Along the northward route, trees shorten and the overcover diminishes. At about 500 miles north, the rain forest gives way to woodland savanna that has an open, park-like appearance.

Here the dry season lasts for some six months, with about 24 inches of rain per year and temperatures in the 90s (Fahrenheit). The woodland savanna extends for some 400 miles and is covered with tall grass, trees in spots, and gallery forests near streams and rivers. As the traveler progresses and leaves the woodlands, she comes upon the grassland savanna with short grasses, which spans the next 200 miles. After the grassland savanna, she enters the Sahel region, which lasts for the next 300 miles, before entering the Sahara Desert. The desert region is dry for three-quarters of the year and is rainy only in July, August, and September. People who live in this region herd animals or engage in irrigated farming close to river floodplains. The area has considerable short grasses, spiny plants, and shrub-like acacia trees with small green leaves. The temperatures increase as the traveler gets closer to the desert. The Sahara is not an endless beach of sand but, rather, as Harms (2018) notes, is

> a variety of landforms such as regs, ergs, mountains, and oases. Seventy percent of the Sahara surface is covered by regs, which are plains of sands and gravel that are remains of prehistoric sea and riverbeds. Ergs, which are sand dunes up to 1,000 feet high, stretch for hundreds of miles and cover 20 percent of the desert's surface. There are three mountain ranges in the Sahara with peaks reaching as high as 11,000 feet. Oases form

> around underground water sources that reach the surface via springs and wells.... All the oases in the Sahara put together take up only 800 square miles, which is about 0.02 percent of the desert's total surface. Yet 75 percent of all the inhabitants of the Sahara live in those Oases, the rest are camel-herding nomads who move from place to place with their herds in search of water and pastures.
>
> *(p. 15)*

As traveler A leaves the Sahara, she is about 200 miles from her destination when she comes to fertile plains that receive about 20 inches of rain a year. To her left are the Atlas Mountains, which indicates that she is now in a Mediterranean climate zone with olive trees and vineyards, cereal crops, and fruit trees. The climate path along the coastal plains is cooler, averaging about 77 degrees Fahrenheit, as traveler A reaches Tunis, her destination.

Traveler B, who is moving south, will first journey through rain forest, like traveler A, for the first 300 miles, then through woodland savanna; however, in the southern direction the woodland savanna takes about 1,000 miles to traverse. Once that region is passed, traveler B comes to the grass savanna, and this exists for some 400 miles, upon which he comes to a semidesert area known as the Kalahari, which is similar to the Sahel region that traveler A encountered going north. Still heading south and 300 miles north of Cape Town, the traveler finds a climate that is like the one in the north, but here the rain that falls is about 20 inches per year, and there are vineyards but no olive trees. In Cape Town the weather is mild, with temps in the 70s. The terrain that each traveler found dictates how people lived on the land, given the vegetation that could grow in each area. It rains more nearer to the equator and less as one moves away from it. But the north–south pathways do not tell the full story of the land in Africa. We must now learn about the east and west landscapes.

Our travelers will now go east and west starting in Goma, another city in the Democratic Republic of Congo. It is 100 miles south of the equator, and the paths the travelers will take parallel the equator. Goma is located among mountains and lakes on the western side, and it is on the north shore of Lake Kivu, a mile above sea level, and has an average temperature of 78 degrees Fahrenheit with lows of 59 and with 47 inches of rain each year.

Traveler A will go 759 miles east to Malindi, Kenya, on the Indian Ocean coast, and traveler B will head west 1,416 miles to Port-Gentil, Gabon, on the Atlantic coast. As traveler B goes westward, he descends the Virunga Mountains through an alpine tundra to a bamboo and montane forest for 200 miles, leaving the mountains and coming to the rain forest, which extends for 1,200 miles to his destination in Gabon. Traveler A, heading east toward the Indian Ocean coast, also goes through mountains for about 200 miles. She comes to the shores of Lake Victoria, the largest lake in Africa and the source of the Nile, the worlds' longest river, at some 4,000 miles. Upon leaving the lake she comes to what is known as the Serengeti, a large plain. First there is a savanna with medium-high grasses and acacia tress, which changes to treeless grasslands with mostly short grasses. A variety of wild animals (e.g., wildebeest, zebras, gazelles) migrate here from January through March. Traveler A then comes to a semidesert grassland that is also home to wild animals, but they are different here, for example, lions, elephants, and giraffes. The trip is complete, and soon the traveler is at the destination of Malindi, Kenya, on the Indian coast.

The People of Africa

The continent has a center marked by the equator, and the climates and vegetation are for the most part similar north and south of the equatorial zone. The central area is characterized by green forests and frequent rainfall with monsoons. Changes in altitude affect this pattern in the eastern and southeastern regions.

> Africa is not the all-over forest-covered steaming jungle that popular belief often assumes it to be, and the zone of rain forest in now greatly restricted as a result of some two to three thousand years of cutting and burning by [humans]. Most of the continent is covered by a wooded savanna [i.e., mixed woodland and grass or lowland, or pasture] where deciduous trees predominate. The further removed from the equator, the longer the winter or dry season, lasting up to six months or more.
>
> *(Curtin, 1971, p. 20)*

Today Africa comprises some 54 countries, several territories, and independent states (some not recognized). Most of the countries are in the Northern Hemisphere (above the equator), and the remainder are in the Southern Hemisphere (below the equator). Africa has a population today of some 1.3 billion people. It is separated from Europe by the Mediterranean Sea (on its northern coast) and from most of Asia by the Red Sea (on its eastern coast). Africa and Asia are connected at a northern point known as the Isthmus of Suez. Africa has plateaus, plains, mountains, rivers, lakes, and a few islands.

The climate in Africa has several different zones. It is hot in the lower plains and deserts of North Africa as compared to the Congo basin (central regions) and Guinea coast (west region), and sometimes the temperatures can cool in the desert areas. In East Africa, the temperatures cool due to the elevations of the mountains and the proximity to the ocean. This also occurs more in the southern regions, which have less width than does the north. Apparently, the climate was ideal for the evolution of humans.

Scientists contend that Africa is where humans evolved. It is the oldest inhabited land on the earth, with fossil evidence showing that humans resided in various parts of the continent as far back as 7 million years ago. It is believed that *Homo sapiens* date to some 350,000 years ago on the African continent. At that time Africans were hunter-gatherers and lived in small nomadic groups, as previously discussed. It is suggested that the early humans left Africa and traveled to other continents and populated the world. Vansina (1995) observes that

> the great variety of cultures … flourished in Africa until recent times—hundreds of cultures in endless variations, like so many flowers in the same bed. Yet despite the differences, all have grown from humble and very similar origins, and underneath all the variation common themes can still be discerned, themes and patterns that stretch back into the hallowed past. The unity, then, derives from the roots, for these African cultures have grown up in the surroundings where they flourished for thousands and thousands of years ever since the first of our direct ancestors, homo sapiens … emerged … in Africa. Africa has been inhabited ever since, and ever since cultures have developed there.
>
> *(p. 1)*

While the past for Africa extends over many millennia, most historians mark the period when African people began to produce food, farm, raise and care for animals, and use iron tools as a point of departure to report on its history, since prior to that time there are few sources upon which to anchor definitive information about what occurred, partly because the hunter-gatherers were nomads and lived in small groups to sustain themselves. Their food production during the Neolithic Age (8000–3000 BCE) involved less effort and did not require stable settlements. So there was less material from which researchers could draw conclusions about how people lived. It is thought that, at that time, only people who lived in proximity to rivers were able to live in larger or stable settlements since they were able to fish and live on wild plants, grasses, or yams and palm trees, which were natural crops. Yet people still had to tend to the daily cycles of life and find ways to manage the requirements of living, and the unit to manage life was the family. The needs of survival were borne by each family unit, among those who were usually related.

Asante (2019) asks, when a child is born to a man and woman, what is required of this family group?

> They need food to eat. They need shelter, to protect themselves from the weather. They need something to cover their bodies in order to keep warm if the temperature gets too low. They need tools and weapons to defend their lives from predatory animals. At the fundamental level they will need these things; hence we say food, shelter, clothes, and tools. The infant will need to be cared for while the mother and father gather food.

> How will the child be tended during the time the mother is working? There are some options or choices. The child could be left alone, with one of the parents, or with friends, or carried to work. What we see in African history is that the mother carried the baby with her, most often wrapped tightly to her back.
>
> *(p. 16)*

There also is a need to know who is who, a way to distinguish one child from another, when there is more than one, both within and outside a family group. So naming was used to make these distinctions. If naming children was related to ancestors, the ancestors had to be named in some way, or maybe the seasons or events were used for naming. Regardless of what one was named, this aspect of life required language to express the cycles of life between birth and death as well as to name and express or share experiences. The people who dealt with these complex issues were Africans, and all these tasks had to be done as a process over time, and each had to be developed. They needed a way to mark time and the changes in time, from day to day and so on.

As communities and villages were established, gathering food gave way to the production of food, and the climate and environment were less dominant factors in the social and cultural lives of the people. In addition to the collection of food, how decisions were made also needed to be handled in a way that promoted unity, and that was not possible if one person in such small groups was the chief. It was more likely that groups of elders dealt with issues that arose among groups of people, which could be about 20–50 or 100 or more people, but seldom would the size exceed that number. It is also likely that the groups were kinship based. As was previously noted, while many Africans were foragers, there were also settled villages, usually near water, where fishing was possible; while rare, these villages nevertheless existed and were the precursors to the establishment of larger communities. Such settlements could number from 100 to 1,000 people and required a different social structure than was common among the hunter groups. There needed to be a different way of dealing with the essential tasks in a settled village, and households needed a different governing mechanism.

> Fishing probably required a greater division of labor by gender than hitherto existed. The equipment required for fishing led to the development of notions of property, both common and personal, and hence to the practice of inheritance, certainly for equipment, such as dugouts, that had been fashioned with great labor input and could be used for many years. Notions of property and inheritance provided a new focus for the household. Meanwhile communal activities continued, but may have involved smaller groups than a collective hunt for big game did. Fishing with nets required the cooperation of a few adults only. That, too,

affected the overall spirit of solidarity in the community. Under such circumstances, it is likely that public authority began to be formalized and that an ideology to justify leadership developed in such settlements. *(Vansina, 1995, p. 4).*

The various issues that arose in the settled communities meant that a balance was needed between the households and the larger settlement, and peaceful relations must be maintained between the different groups. Coupled with the idea and facts of property, the people needed social cohesion, and it had to be expressed in their beliefs and rituals. It is possible that the need for social cohesion brought about the use of sanctions such that people were taught to be afraid of sanctions if they did not cooperate with the wishes of the group; this could have been a force that helped maintain group solidarity. In modern times, witchcraft and sorcery have been used for these purposes. If it was the case that people in the community acted in ways that the people disapproved or they set themselves apart, then they might be branded a witch or sorcerer. To avoid being named a witch or becoming the target of a witch, people would comply with social expectations. These early settlements helped establish community leadership, build institutions, and set the foundation for many values, beliefs, and rituals that emerged over the generations that contributed to the transition to more stable settlements and communities. As stable villages grew, the primary means of communication among them turned out to be fishermen, who traveled up and down the water ways with items to trade and stories to share and ideas to communicate (Vansina, 1995).

Building Communities and Populating the Continent

A considerable amount of early history in Africa was not recorded or documented, and the evidence we do have from various sources is scant, so it is difficult to know all the things that occurred over time. Yet a few things are clear: that as hunters and gatherers shifted to living in more stable communities and became sedentary, they had to find ways to produce more food. The once fertile Sahara became less so, and the climate there turned drier—conditions that lasted for some 1,500 years. With less rain, vegetation could not survive, and the soils that once were fertile and food producing turned to dust in the desert.

Even so, some people moved and others adapted to the harsh life of the desert; some stayed in the northern and southern sections of the Sahara, and over time they moved further south to portions of northern Niger and northern Mali, where their descendants can be found today. Those who stayed in the desert had two options: farm near oases (the sources of water) or be nomads, herding sheep and goats (cattle could not survive the dry conditions). Later (100 BCE–5 CE) camels were introduced and were used by the desert dwellers.

The new harsh environment of the desert required a way to govern that worked equally well when the population was large and when people were in small groups, given the nomadic lifestyle that enabled habitation in various parts of the desert. "New social systems were invented to cope with this dual way of life. One of these, the *deep segmentary kinship* system, eventually became universal life in the Sahara" (Vansina, 1995, p. 13). The people who lived in large groups descended from one ancestor, usually from the male line. The groups are known as "tribes" or "clans," and these groups could have subgroups who were descended from lesser ancestors.

In many ways the issues of food production and farming led to the population of the continent. People had to cultivate large tracts of land to farm but could stay only a short time because the soil would be depleted of its nutrients and they would need new land on which to plant. Thus, they moved around and settled much of the continent:

> Once food-producing economies had taken root, populations came to be more firmly tied to territories and a foundation was laid for the growth of regionally distinct societies and cultures.... Once food was produced populations could grow more rapidly than before, even if the rates of growth remained highly irregular. Once communities were settled further technological processes in agriculture, husbandry, metallurgy, or other industries could be perfected. At the same time interactions between settled communities for mutual advantage (trade, intermarriage, medicine, mutual security) could from now on proceed in more predictable ways. Thus, the foundation for the various types of African societies and cultures of later times were laid in the centuries following the acquisition of food production.
>
> *(Vansina, 1995, pp. 26–27)*

In general, north of the equator, people were farmers and herders; south of the equator, there tended to be more hunter-gatherers living in rain forests. The migration of Bantu speakers that occurred over some 4,000 years aided in the population of the continent; many such speakers occupied much of the tropical rain forests, and as they traveled, their language did so as well. Knowledge of how to smelt iron aided progress for the growing populations, but overall, farmers and cattle herders dominated the land while the hunter-gatherers lived on the margins of the land.

Using Language to Track Expansion

Language is one method that linguists have used to track and trace how people have moved throughout the continent. According to Vansina (1995), in one example of linguists documenting how various groups have similar words—like the word the Kongo people on the Atlantic coast have for "people" and a similar word in Swahili, as in the case for the Duala of Cameroon—linguists noted how much alike the words were and concluded the various languages shared a group they called Bantu. Linguists surmised that the group of terms and languages had a common ancestral origin that was called Proto-Bantu, or the first language. Language groups typically belong to a single family with a common origin, yet languages change and evolve over time, particularly from one generation to the next as words change and meanings are altered. As population groups separated from one another, often their common language would diverge to some extent. Thus, as separations of groups of people grew, so did the language forms that emerged, similar to what might be captured in a family tree. Vansina (1995) describes five families of languages that have been documented by linguists; Bantu languages accounted for the spread of languages in most of southern Africa, west to east. More than six hundred versions of Bantu have been identified. The spread of these languages is attributed to migration and population movement. In some situations, one group, presumed to be larger, imposed its way of speaking on a smaller group; in other situations, a smaller group with more advanced technology or civilization dominated, and their language was adapted in the new area. Porto-Bantu is associated with ceramics and farming crops like cereals and roots as well as with the use of goats. Linguists contend that such migration occurred before 3000 BCE and accounts for the dispersion of people in Africa. Vansina (1995) describes three areas where Bantu speaking people settled and contributed to the growth of farming and the use of advanced techniques. These were North Bantu, which was an area that extended west to east just below the Sahara, and West Bantu southwestern sections of the continent, and East Bantu bordering the southwestern areas and extending to the Indian Ocean.

Distinctions between North Africa and Other Regions

The early history of Africa is marked by small and slow evolution and population growth. The people also interacted with non-Africans, given Africa's proximity to Europe to the north and Asia to the east, particularly in the northwestern area, which is nine miles from Europe, across the Mediterranean Sea, and in the northeastern corner, which is accessible to Asia via the Isthmus of Suez and the Red Sea; at the southern end of the Red Sea, it is 20 miles to the Arabian Peninsula.

By 800 CE there existed a thriving Iron Age that had spread throughout the continent. Farming evolved, as did metal-based technology. Communities had been established with well-developed religions, social and political organizations, and communities that ranged from small villages to powerful states like Ghana. People developed elaborate systems of democratic village governance, and this formed the foundations for recent societies.

> From this Early Iron Age until the colonial period of the nineteenth century, the course of continental Africa's development remains, with a few important exceptions, steady and continuous. Unbroken by any major outside intervention through ten centuries and more, highly various in form, repeatedly successful in its settlements and mastery of a difficult and sometimes harsh environment, this development offers a remarkably special but also remarkable unified chapter in the history of mankind.
>
> *(Davidson, 2005, pp. 23–24)*

It is important to point out that the Sahara Desert functioned as a field for communication and interaction, while during the Middle Stone Age, people who lived in North Africa tended to be seen as different from those who lived in the southern regions. While the Sahara served as an area that fostered intercommunication, in many ways the people of the north evolved differently than those south of the Sahara. "While the peoples of the North developed as part of the whole Nile-Near Eastern-Mediterranean complex of cultures, those in the south were left in isolation to problems and solutions of their own" (Davidson, 2005, p. 24).

The two regions, those north of the Sahara and those south, varied in terms of the climate and environment, and people had to adapt to the situations they found. What emerged were kingdoms north and south of the Sahara and along the Nile River. As we look back in time to, say, 7,000 years ago, farmers planted barley and wheat and other crops in the Nile River valley, yet the people moved away as the desert became dry, which meant people had to move closer to rivers and away from the desert. Archaeological data reveals that several hundred years later people built canals and dikes to direct the water, so the water could be stored and used later. It was also apparent that complex administrative systems and organizations were established to oversee these complex projects.

Egypt and the Origins of Its People

The foundation of the Egyptian state was first created from the far south, not in the north.

> The Egyptian state that King Narmer [from southern Egypt] created in 2950 BCE by uniting the Two Lands would last for over 2,600 years before it was conquered by Alexander the Great in 331 BCE. During that long stretch of time, more than 177 pharaohs, as the kings were called, ruled over the state. More of them were men, but women ruled as queens or regents on at least 10 occasions. Historians have grouped the rulers of Egypt into 30 successive royal **dynasties**. The longest-running dynasty (the Eighteenth) ruled Egypt for 247 years, while the shortest

> (the Twenty-Eighth) ruled for only 5 years. A typical reign was about 100 years long. Throughout the long history of ancient Egypt, periods of administrative unity alternated with periods of chaos and disorder. The periods of unity have been named the Old Kingdom, the Middle Kingdom, the New Kingdom, and the Late Period. The periods of disorder are known as the intermediate periods.
>
> *(Harms, 2018, p. 51)*

To the south of the Egyptian state were kingdoms and village-states located in what is known as Nubia, such as Kush and Meroe, up the Nile between the first and sixth cataracts (barriers created by water cascades or falls), and while different from the Egyptian state, these kingdoms nevertheless interacted and intermingled with one another. They also competed for control of the area as well as for trade routes.

Regarding the ancient civilization known as Egypt, many thought that its people were not African but actually came from outside of Africa. Many historians and scientist held that the Egyptian people were not Negros or Black African people, so its history was considered to be separate from that of Africa and its natural people. There is debate about which peoples populated this vast region; many say the races were mixed, while others contend that most of the people were African and Black (e.g., Asante, 2019; Bennett, 1988; Davidson, 2005; Harms, 2018; Vansina, 1995; Williams, 1987).

> The Egyptians of the Pharaonic Age were not Negroes, it was argued, and therefore they were not Africans; and so, their civilization, no matter how firmly and enduringly planted on the soil of Africa, should be left outside the African context. This view has little to be said for it. It now seems perfectly clear that the vast majority of pre-dynastic Egyptians were of continental African stock, and even of central-western Saharan origins, there is likewise serious dispute among the authorities even as to whether the hypothetical "dynastic race" associated with the foundation of Pharaonic Egypt has come from outside Africa. These early populations [without doubt] … included the descendants of incoming migrants from the Near East. But to argue from this that the vast majority of the inhabitants of old Egypt, not being "Negro" were therefore not African is as little tenable as to argue the same about the Berbers and the Ethiopians, whom nobody has yet proposed to erase from the list of African peoples.… Whatever their pigmentation or physical appearance the Egyptians of Pharaonic times were an intimate part of African history.
>
> *(Davidson, 2005, pp. 25–26)*

The strength and power of their civilization and achievements seems to be at odds with the perception of Black people as savage and uncivilized. But Harms (2018) places the debate in the context of the notion that humans are "pure races"; thus, some scientists have proclaimed that the ancient Egyptians were white and from Europe, while other scholars make the opposite claim, that they were Black people. Harms states that evidence from anthropology and biology has essentially dismissed the favored racial categories; he suggests looking instead for evidence of biological connections between neighboring peoples. For instance, studies of skulls from 4000 and 3100 BCE from southern Egypt, when compared to skulls from Nubia or Kush (neighbors of Egypt), show more similarities than to skulls from southern Europeans. Thus, it is clear that biological data shows that Egyptians were African.

The Egyptian people have a long list of remarkable achievements, among them the construction of the pyramids and numerous temples and cities. The kings or pharaohs who were worshiped as gods and divine leaders created many institutions and structures to oversee the land in which they ruled. The Egyptian people, led by their pharaohs, developed their own written language—hieroglyphs, a complex set of symbols, pictures, and phonetic symbols—that could form words and sentences. They then created a literate cadre of citizens who could use and read their language, and these people would administer the holdings of the Pharaoh. The writing was for record keeping but was also used for religious, historical, and poetic purposes. Architects, engineers, medical doctors, and astronomers were also supported by the pharaoh. In time, artists and craftsmen were employed, and they adorned the pharaoh's palaces, temples, and burial place. The elaborate states that served the pharaoh were expensive and required armies of people to work as scribes, intellectuals, priests, artists, and administrators. Thus, common people were used for these tasks. To ensure needed resources, the pharaoh collected taxes. There was no currency, so taxes were tributes in the form of grain that were carefully tracked and measured to gauge the taxes from each village. The pharaoh at first would travel to the villages, then appointed governors for newly created provinces in the Nile valley. Common people were for the most part poor, while the government officials lived comfortable and often luxurious lifestyles.

Other African Civilizations

Beyond Egypt were other civilizations in Africa, many of which were large and complex. One was called Nubia, located in the middle Nile region, and one of its well-known city centers was Meroe, northeast of Khartoum in Sudan. It dates to 2000 BCE and survived until the second millennium CE (Connah, 2016). The development of cities and states in this region was parallel to that of Egypt and was not brought on by Egypt's ascendance. The cities in Nubia evolved through the effort of its people. Similarly, the relatively isolated mountain highlands of Ethiopia and Eritrea had fertile soil. The state of Aksum had cities and urban centers in the last few BCE centuries; in addition to urban centers, Nubia had its distinct language and writing, coins, and evidence of unique buildings and monuments. There are also indications of extensive trading inside and outside of Africa. The society appears to have been highly structured and ruled by kings but perhaps not autocratic ones. Religion was central to this area. "From the fourth century AD onwards, for both the later Aksumites and subsequent Ethiopians, the principal religion has been Christianity of a distinctive Ethiopian type" (Connah, 2016, p. 143).

There was also life and settlement in the western savanna, in the region west of Lake Chad, set between the Sahara Desert in the north and the tropical rain forest to the south. Isolated by borders that were difficult to breach, this area nevertheless participated in trade, in part because of the introduction of the camel, which appeared in the early CE centuries, making trans-Sahara trade possible. The ecosystems and terrain were varied in this region, ranging from swamps, deserts, rain forests, woodlands, and savannas. Each had its resources and limitations; for instance, salt was in the desert but less so in the savanna, and the forest had few animals, but animals were plentiful in the savanna. These conditions sparked regional trade rather than external trade, which did occur. As Connah (2016) states,

> It would appear that the West African savanna by the beginning of the first millennium AD already had a sound agricultural base ... and already had a varied iron-based technology. Developing social complexity is already evident ... and it seems quite probable that during the first millennium AD, and prior to Arab contact [through external Sahara trade] stratified societies were emerging.
>
> *(p. 184)*

The tropical rain forest region along the west coast had many names—the "Gold Coast," "Ivory Coast," and so on—but was small in relative size. It extends from Cameroon to Ghana, and to the south its borders are the coastal swamps of the Atlantic Ocean. On the opposite coast, the eastern side near the center of the continent, were several towns and cities in what is now Tanzania and the coastal islands. Connah (2016) contends that the presence of large and complex settlements in this region is due in part to trade with Asia via the Indian Ocean; rather, what seems more plausible is that Africans developed a complex and stratified social system that was able to take advantage of the trade that came its way.

An area north of South Africa between the Zambezi and Limpopo Rivers and the Kalahari Desert and the Indian Ocean is an area that covers the modern nations of Zimbabwe (formerly Rhodesia), southern Mozambique, northeastern Botswana, and South Africa. Evidence from the Great Zimbabwe site reveals urban living and state formation in the second millennium CE. Scientists found stone wall structures that seemed to bound a series of huts that indicate urban life for elites in the area as well as smaller sections with similar structures. Connah (2016) states: "The stone structures that have dominated archaeological research housed a small ruling elite, who governed settlements varying in size from the capital city of Great Zimbabwe itself, with a population of perhaps 18,000 to smaller regional towns" (p. 297). Similar development occurred in Central Africa in the region where the Congo Republic, Democratic Congo, Angola, Zambia, Rwanda, Burundi, Uganda, and western Tanzania are today. Many cities and states were settled near the equator, but south of it.

The evidence of African people's development throughout the continent is well established. Egypt was not the only thriving civilization that emerged. The people farmed, grew crops, hunted, made weapons and utensils, built homes and villages, established complex systems of government, and had religious systems that served them well over time. They struggled with a range of environments and resources that varied from place to place, and they had conflicts with one another and with non-Africans. At the same time, they traded and gained information and commodities, crops, animals, and other objects of value. Much of this took place in the millennia shortly before and after the birth of Christ. I turn now to the rise of some significant city-states.

The Rise of City-States

For about 3,000 years before the Common Era, Egypt was ruled, grew, and maintained its status through many dynasties. There were periods of "confusion and decline" as well as times of renewed stability. The Egyptians employed centralized government with effective administration through intermediaries, and they accumulated wealth and established stability. Egyptians sent expeditions into the western and southern regions of the continent via the Red Sea. "After the end of the third millennium, however, Egypt began to exercise a direct military and political power over the southern and to the lesser extent her western neighbors" (Davidson, 2005, p. 31).

Black people fathered the civilization of Egypt, the Egyptian people depicted themselves in paintings using black-reddish-brown-yellow hues. Egyptians and Nubians (dark-skinned people) had intimate contact, with each conquering the other over 5,000 years. For centuries Ethiopian (Nubian) kings held the office of pharaoh. African kingdoms, those in Egypt and beyond, existed for more than 2,000 years before the birth of Christ and some endured well into the 15th century. Around 500 years CE, three large and powerful states in the western Sahel (located between the Sahara to the north and the forest of the Guinea coast to the south) successively emerged: Ghana (not the current country, and not where it is located today), Mali, and Songhay. These states reached the peak of their power during the Middle Ages, from the fifth to the 15th centuries.

Harms (2018) points out that the various settlements, villages, and towns in the region were numerous yet independently governed; to complicate matters further, they created distinct political organizations based on their unique languages. He uses English terms to identify the various West African political models. He states that the leader of a village was known as a chief. Groups of chiefdoms were considered kingdoms, and empires comprised both chiefdoms and kingdoms. When empires were established, kings became vassal kings, and their areas were considered vassal kingdoms or chiefdoms.

Empires form when a greater power or leader overtakes weaker leaders, kingdoms, or chiefdoms and the former rulers pay tribute to the more powerful leader of the empire and agree to their status as lesser or vassal states. In this instance, the former states remain intact with their vassal rulers and political structures. What changed in leadership was the addition of a new higher level of authority with an upper-level organizing structure. As empires weakened, vassal entities could break away and reestablish their former station and status as the ultimate ruler. Thus, there was always some form of political stability.

It is difficult to reconstruct the events that preceded the rise of these empires in Africa since not many records exist and, as Harms (2018) and Asante (2019) tell us, much of what is known is drawn from oral histories and traditions that have advantages and disadvantages. The oral traditions and the few written documents help to fill in details. Asante (2019), for instance, used the writings of several ancient scholars, for example, Ibn Battuta and Leo Africanus (see pp. 120–121), to gather information about this period in history.

Legend has it that Ghana was established by the Soninke people led by Diabe Cisse between 500 and 700 BCE. Cisse had cavalry troops from the wilderness's four corners of the central provinces of the kingdom. In the beginning, the chiefdoms and kingdoms were overtaken and incorporated into an empire. Some were tribute vassals and others were not, but all were ruled by the king of the empire.

Asante (2019)—drawing on three sources of information about this period: scholars' books, oral histories, and archaeological evidence—argues that the formation of a trading kingdom around 300 BCE was the foundation for the Ghanaian Empire. He contends that the name of the empire was in recognition of the paramount king, which was "Ghana" in the Soninke language; the people referred to the empire as Wagadu.

> Kings came from the descent lines of the first ancestors … usually female. Most African societies prior to Islam and Christianity were matrilineal.… A king of Wagadu could command an army of many thousands, use the services of many servants and messengers, and employ many traders and interpreters to deal with the Amazighs [Berbers], Wolof, Serer, and other peoples.
>
> *(Asante, 2019, p. 122)*

For any society to grow and thrive, it must have an economic foundation. For this new empire, the economy was grounded on trade and gold, and the city where trade and governance took place was called Kumbi Saleh, a cosmopolitan city of some 18,000 people, with a lively social and economic life. Traders came and went; some married local women, and some became local merchants. The wealth of the ancient Empire of Ghana came from taxes levied on gold and other items brought and sold, like salt, ivory, copper, spices, and ebony. It was a diverse city, with poor and middle-class residents as well as artists, thinkers, and merchants. Many of the city's citizens had become Muslim. The army that defended the empire was large and armed with weapons such as iron-tipped spears. No other power could match its might. Ghana dominated the Sudan for more than three centuries but declined in its power and influence by the 13th century (Harms, 2018, p. 133).

Mali, located between the Senegal and Niger Rivers 350 miles to the southeast of Ghana, is where the new empire was created. The area had access to well-watered grasslands with proximity to Bure gold mines. The people were Mande, and they used a social system divided by categories and groupings such as nobles, commoners, slaves, and work-based guilds (e.g., blacksmiths, wood carvers, bards). Membership in the categories and groups was based on birth and lineage, and intermarriage was forbidden among the various guilds and groups.

The Kingdom of Mali grew through conquest. Once conquered, the Mali rulers imposed obligations upon its new vassal states; some were left as autonomous chiefdoms with tributes to pay, and some states were independent vassals. It used the vassal system to impose its will, but their system gave local leaders considerable authority, provided they bowed to the king of the empire. What was sought in the conquest were the towns at the center of trade and commerce. A visitor to Mali in the 14th century observed how the Mande disliked injustices. The cities of the state were recognized far and wide. Some, like Timbuktu, were known as centers for culture and learning.

> Timbuktu, during Askia's reign, was a city of some one hundred thousand people, filled with gold and dazzling women. One of the most fabled and exotic cities in the medieval world, the Sudanese metropolis was celebrated for its luxury and gaiety…
>
> The towering minarets of two great mosques dominated the face of the city. From the Great Mosque, flat-roofed houses (of wood covered with plaster) radiated in all directions. The older Sankore Mosque, to which was attached the University of Sankore, was the center of intellectual life. Both buildings were cut of stone and lime.
>
> *(Bennett, 1988, pp. 18–19)*

Goods from North Africa and Europe could be purchased in the stores and shops in the city. In the streets, scholars mixed with the Black shopkeepers. Young people came to study law and medicine. The universities held sizable stores of manuscripts in many languages, and scholars came from faraway places "to check their Greek and Latin manuscripts" (Bennett, 1988, p. 19).

After Mali's rise as the center of power in the region, it declined in the 15th century and was replaced by Songhay. One leader, Sunni Ali, used his army and ships in the city of Gao to capture Timbuktu and Jenne as well as other lands so he could control the gold and salt trades. While Muslim, he was not devout and did not respect the Islamic scholars who resided in the city, so many of them left. Askia Muhammad took over as ruler in 1493, and his dynasty lasted until the decline of the Songhay Empire. Over time the empire was challenged by its vassal states, who in time broke away.

> In the sixteenth century, as the capital of the Songhay Empire, Gao had a population of between 38,000 and 76,000 not counting the nomads who camped around its edges. Feeding such a large population in a semiarid grassland was not easy. Vegetables and melons could be grown in the wetland left by the annual flood of the Niger, but grain had to be grown elsewhere and shipped in by large boats that could carry as much as 20 tons. To feed the royal court, Askias maintained plantations in the flooded rice lands farther up the Niger, which were worked by royal slaves and supervised by slave officials.
>
> *(Harms, 2018, p. 141)*

The empire relied on taxes of trade products, like salt and gold, for revenue and to generate wealth, but paying the taxes left many people unable to survive. There were also tributes from other vassals as well as the spoils of war, particularly captives who were sold as slaves. Other leaders of the empire created libraries and paid scribes to copy books. The books grew in number and subject matter to include math, geography, medicine, and other subjects, and scholarship excelled through the 1500s. The wealth and influence of the empire got the attention of other leaders, who also wanted to control the trade routes, such as the ruler of Morocco, Ahmad al-Mansur. In 1580 al-Mansur sent troops to take the salt mines, but this was not successful, so he set his sights on Timbuktu, Gao, and Jenne. The invaders, the Arma, took Timbuktu and settled there, becoming the new ruling class. Their influence waned over time as the Portuguese and Dutch became major traders in gold from the Atlantic coast.

Between the 8th and 10th centuries, Swahili-speaking merchants established trading outposts on the coastal islands off the east coast of Africa, making trade from the sea the lifeblood of the coast. The merchants used family lineage to assert their status but were content to rule their respective towns and trading areas by operating as middlemen between the traders who sailed there and the people of the interior. The elite in these trading towns were able to live well and were comfortable, but they had little interest in land acquisition. Unlike the people on the west coast, the cultural practices and influence of Islam led to different ways of being on the east coast, in part due to the influence of ideas and beliefs that came from trading with Arabia, India, and other countries. Gold was traded along both the east and west coasts, and this activity influenced trade in other items, including an active trade in slaves where some 4.8 million Africans were sold and taken to locations in Europe and the East, some captives taken to India as well (Harms, 2018).

The people on the west coast reveled in their good fortune with joyous activity and engaged in excessive merriment. These civilizations declined in the 17th century, "and the reign of the great West African States came to an end" (Bennett, 1988, p. 22). The decline is attributed to clashes between Islam and Christianity, while others contend the decline was because of the European slave trade (Bennett, 1988). Yet, the view of Africans held by Europeans was not one that depicted them as leaders of empires or states but as uncivilized people.

> The popular myth depicts the conquering white man carrying the blessing of civilization to the naked savages who sat under trees, filled their teeth and waited for fruit to drop into their hands. The truth is less flattering to the European ego. On the West Coast of Africa, from whence came most of the ancestors of American Negroes, there were complex socio-economic institutions. Political institutions ranged from extended family groupings of village states and territorial empires. Most of these units had all the appurtenances of the modern state—armies, courts, and internal revenue departments.
>
> *(Bennett, 1988, p. 22)*

The Trade in People

During the Middle Ages, around the 1100s, the European city-states of Venice and Genoa created sea-based empires. By controlling the sea-faring trade routes, they gained access and dominion of the spice markets of Asia. Over the next 300 years they expanded to secure coastal areas and traded for slaves, set up plantations on Mediterranean islands, and had conflicts with several adversaries. But these city-states dominated economic activity in this region. At first the slaves were white, usually Turks and Tartars, who were used as soldiers, laborers, and domestic servants. In time the supply of white slaves declined, and the merchants looked to North Africa for captives (Harms, 2018).

Following the lead of Genoa and Venice, Portugal and Spain sought to expand and locate the riches that marked the actions of its neighbors, yet efforts to take by force a major trading area in North Africa failed. Therefore, in 1415 Prince Henry of Portugal instructed his people to sail down the west coast of the continent to secure gold and other products. It took a while for the sailors and captains to figure out how to navigate the southward journey and return trips along the West African coast. By 1430 the navigation problems were solved, and by 1498 they were able to reach any part of the Old World (i.e., Europe, Africa, and Asia) by sea. They had traveled to India and returned. So it is not a surprise that by the 1500s, Spain and Portugal had evolved thriving economies that extended to many parts of the world; the expansion came about through wars where land and people were claimed.

The economic and war-related operations that were used around the world varied, yet several countries (e.g., Spain, France, Portugal, England) claimed large tracts of land in the Americas and established plantations to grow crops of sugar and tobacco, and they used cheap and slave labor to produce the needed products. In Asia, they created and chartered companies to administer their authority and will over the areas where they conducted business and formed colonies and other arrangements. In Africa, they engaged in trade and created posts on the coasts for those purposes. They did not take land or claim power or authority over the rulers of African city-states and kingdoms; however, the primary object of trade by that time was captured Africans.

Summary

Most Americans have been denied reliable and accurate information about the African past and, more important, Africans' achievements. This chapter acquaints the reader with the ancient and prehistoric events that took place on the African continent. To fully understand Black American culture, it is imperative to highlight and teach that culture's roots in Africa. We visited the past with a focus on how Africans lived and organized their lives and communities.

The vast size of the continent, with its varied environments and its settings and topography, has shaped the lives of its inhabitants, who for many centuries evolved highly complex and sophisticated societies—far from the images of unclad people with spears and bows who were often shown as cannibals and savages in cartoons and movies. Egypt is recognized as a civilization that has contributed a great deal to humankind, and many scholars now acknowledge Egypt as an African civilization; yet I suspect there are still some who deny that fact.

The empires and kingdoms located in other regions of the continent are not as well known, but they also reveal a lot about African people. Kinship played a central role in Africa's villages and larger governing units. This chapter also discusses Africa's social and economic systems prior to contact with Europeans.

Slavery was part of world societies, and many slaves were sold to various locations in the Old World. This is one point of commonality—in the face of considerable diversity of languages, places, climates, social organizations, and history—between Africa and other parts of the world.

Africans believed in life and death and valued their connection to the spirits and nature since they were surrounded by nature and its many wonders. While Africans are not one cultural group but many, it has been suggested that there are some overarching beliefs and practices that can be generalized to the numerous African cultures.

Scholars and historians have focused their attention on West African societies because it is from this region that most Africans brought to the New World colonies came. There are several aspects of African life that characterize many ethnic–cultural groups and peoples. In political life Africans established entities that were organized around the family; in some instances, these entities grew in size to reflect a state or village-state. In some instances, kingdoms and empires were organized around clans or family networks. Other entities were not kin-related but had leaders or small councils that provided the decision-making that the people required (Thornton, 2012).

Economic life was, for the most part, agricultural. Land was held by its first occupants and was considered, beyond the first occupants, to belong to the entire community, not individuals. Artisans also contributed to the economy, and iron tools and products were used and traded. According to Franklin and Moss (2000), Africa was "therefore never a series of isolated, self-sufficient communities, but an area that had far-flung interest based on agriculture, industry, and commerce" (p. 20). Their industry and commerce meant that they traveled and traded with others near and far. In some regions trade was a centuries-old endeavor.

African people who were captives, as well as their descendants, managed to hold on to various aspects of their original cultures. And due to their interactions with white Europeans, these cultural practices were transformed and altered so that Africans could adapt to their situations of bondage and racial oppression.

References

Asante, M. K. (2019). *The history of Africa: The quest for eternal harmony* (3rd ed.). Routledge.

Bennett, L. (1988). *Before the Mayflower: A history of Black America*. Johnson Publishing.

Connah, G. (2016). *African civilization: An archaeological perspective* (3rd ed.). Cambridge University Press.

Curtin, P. D. (1971). The emergence of African history. In A. Adu Boahen, A. M. Josephy Jr., & A. Josephy (Eds.). *The Horizon history of Africa* (pp. 6–15). McGraw-Hill.

Davidson, B. (2005). *Africa in history: Themes and outlines*. Simon & Schuster.

Dodson, H. (2002). *Jubilee: The emergence of African-American culture*. National Geographic.

Franklin, H. J., & Moss, A. A. (2000). *From slavery to freedom: A history of African Americans* (8th ed.). McGraw Hill.
Harms, R. (2018). *Africa in global history with sources.* Norton.
Herskovits, M. J. (1990). *The myth of the Negro past.* Beacon.
Holloway, J. E. (2005). *Africanisms in American culture* (2nd ed.). Indiana University Press.
Horton, J. O., & Horton, L. E. (2005). *Slavery and the making of America.* Oxford University Press.
Johnson, V., & Carter, R. T. (2020). Black cultural strengths and psychological well-being: An empirical analysis with Black American adults. *Journal of Black Psychology*, 46(1), 55–89.
Mintz, S. W., & Price, R. (1972). *The birth of African-American culture: An anthropological perspective.* Beacon.
Silverstein, J. (2019). The 1619 Project: Introduction. *New York Times Magazine*, 4.
Stampp, K. M. (1956). *The peculiar institution: Slavery in the ante-bellum South.* Vintage.
Stewart, C. F. (1999). *Black spirituality and Black conciousness: soul force, culture, and freedom in the African-American experience.* Africa World Press.
Thornton, J. K. (2012). *A cultural history of the Atlantic world, 1250–1820.* Cambridge University Press.
Vansina, J. (1995). The roots of African cultures. In P. Curtin, S. Feierman, L. Thompson, & J. Vansina, (Eds.). *African history: From earliest times to independence* (2nd ed., pp. 1–26). Longman.
Watkins, R. (2001). *Slavery bondage throughout history.* Houghton Mifflin.
Williams, C. (1987). *The destruction of Black civilization: Great issues of a race from 4500 BC to 2000 AD.* Third World Press.

2

AFRICAN LIFE AND WAYS EXPRESSED IN CULTURAL PATTERNS

African people for thousands of years, from 3000 BCE to the 15th century, populated and spread to various regions on the African continent. In this chapter I examine some of the cultural ways, practices, and psychological perspectives of African people from ancient times through the Middle Ages, up to the time of contact with Europeans on the west coast of the continent, which resulted in Africans being taken as captives to the New World beginning in the 1400s. While scholars and historians have shown that Africans developed significant, complex, powerful civilizations and societies (Davidson, 2004, 2005), we also know that Africans lived day by day in environments that were less than welcoming to humans. The history I have reviewed so far has not given any clear indications of the beliefs and behaviors that guided Africans' actions, including the nature of their cosmology or view of the world or universe and their cultural practices or worldviews (Bodley, 2017; Kluckhohn & Strodtbeck, 1961).

As is discussed in chapter 1, the African people managed to navigate their environments and to prosper and expand. They learned to go beyond gathering and hunting food to harvesting crops and expanding their food supply so they could trade with others in their areas and beyond. They evolved languages and crafts, made tools, and built communities. Their communities were often small, yet many grew to be cities, states, and empires of significant size and import. In particular, in the northwestern region of the continent, before the Christian era, several large empires evolved and dominated their regions. The best known was the Egyptian Empire.

For about thirty centuries before the Common Era, Egypt was ruled, grew, and maintained its status through many dynasties. While there were periods of "confusion and decline," these were short-lived. The Egyptians employed centralized government with effective administration through intermediaries, and

DOI: 10.4324/9781003111542-4

they were able to accumulate wealth and expand their territory. Even after the decline of Egypt and other powerful kingdoms, several West African empires reached the peak of their power between the 5th and 15th centuries during the Middle Ages. So how did the people of Africa live, work, and interact?

Africa's Demanding Environment and How It Influenced Core Beliefs

Africans had to cope with the demands of nature and find ways to live in settings that were difficult to harness. Significant parts of the continent's soil were not fertile, many of its trees offered little sustenance, and vast stretches of land were filled with brush. The appearance of natural wealth did not always conform to reality. Added to the soil issues were dangerous animals and insects, like the tsetse fly, and other parasites, like jiggers and locusts, that left both humans and animals sick with disease. Davidson (2004) observes that the soil was not fertile, so farmers had to limit the time they used it, working sections of their fields and allowing other sections to lie fallow. To maintain nutrient-rich fields, they would also move locations, usually in the same general vicinity. Once farmers changed to a new field, the abandoned area would return to its natural state.

> The crucial invention in improving this situation, in enabling longer periods of settlement and new processes of growth, seem to have lain in the metallurgy of iron: … How greatly its uses were appreciated by Stone Age farmers may be guessed from the mystical rites and beliefs, linking it to an immanent spiritual power, that continued in later times [350 BCE–500 CE and beyond] to surround the working of iron and other metals including copper, gold, and tin … a process exercised by specialists under divine protection that was both physical and spiritual, demonstrating man's command of nature as well as nature's command of man, in an idiom perfectly at one with African conceptions.
>
> *(Davidson, 2004, pp. 33–35)*

As tool making became more efficient and effective, it was possible to produce surplus foods and other items, so there could be excess food stores. This meant a larger number of people could be fed, thus freeing some people from the work of farming so they could concentrate on other skills and activities to enhance the lives of the community. This allowed industry to grow, as did the population; the division of labor allowed others to learn and use knowledge in different areas, expanding the knowledge and skills of the community, which also fueled change and growth. Consider the challenges that these early African people and isolated groups had to confront and overcome in the early years of the Common Era and beyond, yet they established even larger empires between the 5th and 15th centuries.

Africans established their cultural foundation from their knowledge, existential propositions, and experiences; they followed customs and conventions; honored their ancestors and the life forces that their God created; and they valued and honored nature as they worked to have harmony and balance with it. They valued family and the related rules that held the community above the needs and desires of individuals. It is suggested that during the Stone and Iron Ages African people were isolated from the rest of the world, and from one another, yet they seemed to have developed common notions about their respective worlds. Davidson (2004) illustrates this with examples of various groups around the continent who had similar ideas and beliefs about creation and their origins. The Dinka of southern Sudan held that God was once among the people. Then, due to human error, God left to reside in the heavens and made it so man would not have direct access to him, requiring that humans fend for themselves.

Some thousands of miles away in the rain forest of Ghana, the Akan people had the same notion. It is clear that this idea about creation replicated itself across the land for reasons that are not clear or hard to fathom but nevertheless occurred. While the details of the creation stories varied, the pattern was the same (Davidson, 2004, 2005; Sweet, 2003; Walker, 2011). The common beliefs held by many African people, such as the Mossi, Fon, and Dogon, as Davidson (2004) notes, is contained in the concept of movement between opposites—high and low, odd and even, right and left, male and female; these opposing forces reflect yet another important idea, which is that

> the universe … is based, on the one hand, on a principle of vibrations of matter and, on the other, on a general movement of the universe as a whole. The pairs of opposites support each other in an equilibrium which the individual being conserves within itself.
>
> *(Davidson, 2004, p. 39)*

Such propositions were used to establish life principles and behavioral guides. For many Africans, in life there must be balance and equilibrium between opposite forces (Falola, 2000; Horton, 1967). According to this view, Africans came to see the world in similar ways and invoked common perspectives about the universe and themselves.

Religion/Spirituality

Early Africans believed that all things have forces that are vital and that come from God, the supreme being, yet not in the Judeo-Christian sense. In Judeo-Christian theology, there is a single God who does not change. Africans believed in God, yet God was often not singular, as Sweet (2003) notes regarding African cosmology, which was distinct from that of Europeans. This was often not understood by Europeans, whose perceptions and interpretations of Africans were often racially biased. Europeans thought Africans were uncivilized heathens, despite the fact that Africans followed Christian, Islamic, and traditional religions in conjunction with Africans' unique perspectives and applications. According to Sweet (2003),

> In most [traditional] African societies, the supreme being was not conceived as a universal creator, but rather as the creator of a particular people. This "original ancestor" was concerned only with the well-being of his descendants; not with all of humanity. Many Africans also believed that the creator could be transformed in accordance with political, economic and social change.... Religious beliefs and everyday secular activities were intimately connected. Thus, change in the secular world often impacted religious beliefs and practices, including humans' relationship with the supreme being.... A variety of separate and distinct ancestral spirits and deities were the spiritual arbiters of the temporal world.
>
> *(p. 107)*

From this perspective, Africans considered most things of importance to be local and specific to a group of people; moreover, the gods guided and influenced daily and local life. Sweet (2003) observes further that the spirits that mattered were often the spirits of those who recently passed and had the most say in the lives of those still living. Deities were known to the African people usually by name, location, personal attributes, and, more importantly, the harm they could cause. Africans did not conceive of a place like heaven, which implied that life on Earth was less than what could be experienced in heaven; rather, for many Africans the soul of the departed joined the legions of ancestors and, as such, could still influence the lives of their kin and others. Africans used religion as a mechanism for managing and solving day-to-day issues. Their religion aided in their ability to explain, predict, and control life events, and their rituals and beliefs were important for dealing with the everyday world, with its misfortunes, diseases, droughts, and so on (Aderajew, 2019; Horton, 1967). Embedded in their spiritual practices was their worldview, which was centered on the activities of the living. For Africans, science and religion were intertwined; both explained their world, day-to-day events, and odd happenings, and both represented their connection to their gods. Effective natural remedies had spiritual relevance and meaning.

From their spiritual/religious bases, Africans preferred temporal foci on the present and past. Their African spiritual orientation comprised communalism beliefs, meaning that Africans valued the group (e.g., family, village) and that the needs of the group mattered over the wishes, wants, and needs of individuals or over personal obligations. A guiding principle was that the people must follow in the ways of the ancestors; it was said that people should do as their fathers had done (Davidson, 2004). When it was necessary, Africans also knew when to try different things; they understood when to change and adapt—and did so while honoring their customs and traditions.

Davidson tells of the Lou-speaking people who lived in the hot grasslands of the southern Nile region. They raised and cared for cattle and farmed millet in lands that had contrasting seasons. The formidable climate meant that they had to follow long-established rules regarding social relations and how they tended the land. Yet, as Davidson (2004) points out, the Lou-speaking people also

> became a people of wanderers who experimented with a copious range of new ideas. They adopted variant forms of religion, helped to found prestigious dynasties of kings, lived repeatedly on the ideological as well as physical frontiers of "somewhere else" and "something different."
>
> *(p. 31)*

In the African system of meaning, history was passed along in stories, such that it was the ancestors who started life and located the people in their respective lands, and when the ancestors passed, they left their legacy to their people (Aderajew, 2019).

As was noted before, people had to relocate often. The reasons for leaving or dispersal were many, such as failed succession or lack of authority, which occurred as populations grew in size and complexity. Some may have been disappointed by their new situation and status in their original homeland and elected to move to new lands. So they set out with others to find and establish new villages where they would have more say and influence (Curtin, 1971). Some of the seekers settled communities through conquest or found unoccupied areas in which to settle (Josephy, 1971). Scholars ask us to consider Africans' situations and the dynamics of change and growth (Falola, 2000). The breakaway groups were usually small in number and had few women and children (Walker, 2011). Each group that settled a new land left their original community weaker than before, and they also left their ancestral links and connections, creating some degree of anxiety and fear for the breakaway group.

So the breakaway group would adapt to their new settings. The most important task for the migrant group was to establish a new identity to lessen anxiety and risk. To do so, they needed rules and customs (Williams, 1987). These issues required an ancestral line with which to anchor its identity. The people would select the ancestors who were connected to lines of succession from their past, and this gave power to living humans and provided a way to protect the here and now, thus making the future possible and "generally assuaging the doubts and worries of pioneering groups in the wilderness where they wandered and settled" (Davidson, 2004, p. 49). In the new village, the people had to reinvent themselves after receiving the blessing from their ancestors. But as communities grew both in size and complexity, how would they organize themselves?

Social organization was grounded in religious beliefs and practices. Upon settling in a new area, people would erect a shrine with which to connect to their founding ancestors as well as with the locally recognized ancestors who were important as well. The shrines would aid in the valued connection to the ancestors. This was imperative since the ancestors blessed the land and guided them to prosperity in their newly established village. The people took great care in making legitimate the blending of the newcomers and those who existed in the land, which was done by linking the spirits of the land with the honored and important ancestors, since only the Spirit of the Earth could grant proper title to the land.

> They could do this only through a process of spiritual reconciliation sanctioned by appropriate rites. Otherwise the Spirit of the Earth would not recognize their legitimate existence in the land. Failing this act of connexion, even the appointed ancestors of the incomers would lose their spiritual power, for they would be cut off from its divine source.
>
> *(Davidson, 2004, p. 52)*

African's beliefs were expressed in art objects, which were concrete illustrations that could be used in religious ceremonies. The art was visible manifestation of their beliefs and principles, and in time the objects were present in shrines, rites, and rituals. By doing so, the people could govern and form stable and organized communities. For Africans, what mattered most were the ancestral links that provide legitimate spiritual connection to the life force since it was this life force that was the foundation of daily life. For Africans, God and the life force were not separate (Horton, 1967). As noted previously, the culture of African people was focused on the life of those in the present, in the context of family, and those who lived before and the life forces the ancestors provided the living.

Some people followed tradition and sought new ideas and ways to function since the physical environment which they inhabited required adjustments and adaptations. Yet as the groups grew, so did the range of issues that needed to be attended to and the lineage system did not handle these issues well. To address the aspects of society and community that pertained to economic, political, and military issues, a different form of governance had to be established. There also needed to be additional guides for proper personal behavior and agreement about the accepted uses of social influence.

Ghana, Mali, and Songhay, as discussed in the previous chapter, were large and powerful empires characterized by the large cities and towns that were the core of trade and government. Walker (2011) suggests that one of these cities might have been Jenne, whose population by AD 500 had grown to some 20,000. Evidence of the existence of other cities and towns has been found dating into the BC era, as far back as 1000–800 BC. Also found is evidence of trade and related activity as well as walls around the cities for protection (Walker, 2011; Williams, 1987).

Robert Harms (2018) points out that, for the most part, Africans lived in small villages and towns that were mostly independently governed using distinct political systems. Larger states such as empires came about when a powerful leader overtook weaker kingdoms or chiefdoms, making the former kings vassal rulers who paid tribute to the leader of the empire. In this instance, the former political and leadership structure of the state remained intact.

As Africans spread throughout the continent, they adopted various notions about themselves and the world around them as ways to comprehend their lives and environments. They came to tell and pass on stories and tales that told of how they came to be and how they should live.

The ideas about what was acceptable behavior also applied to principles of right and wrong. In particular, in the context of how to manage community affairs, the issues of descent lines became more complex as village and group populations grew. This also brought about more conflict between groups, so they needed to find a way to settle disputes to maintain order and peace among the people. One solution was to elect a chief to manage the affairs of the villages.

> A great many "small societies" seem to have found themselves in this growing contradiction between lineage loyalty and the welfare of the community. Many of them began appointing chiefs, with increasing powers, [for] at least ten centuries and sometimes more.
>
> *(Davidson, 2004, p. 69)*

Even for those groups that found another solution for population growth and the increased competition for land and trade, the primary principle that undergirded actions was that of the collective. The moral code that dictated behavior was also based on choosing the best options for the group.

Community Formation

How people governed themselves in precolonial African life is subject of some debate, mostly about how best to describe the political systems. According to Nwaubani (2000), scholars have proposed several ways to classify political systems. Some scholars contend that there were two types of political systems, centralized and decentralized, and that all political systems had some degree of segmentary or hierarchical elements. Others have identified systems characterized as segmentary kingdoms, in which key functions were centralized, such as the delegation of authority and control of the military, but there were also weak links between the central authority and its vassal states.

Four distinct models of government have been described, including one in which ultimate authority in a community rested with the kinship group(s); another in which vested authority was held by both the kinship groups and associations or guilds; a third that extended the second to include centralized authority, the king or state leader, who shared authority with the kinship groups and associations; and a fourth in which all authority in the state resided with the leader of the central government.

Nwaubani (2000) points out that many of the descriptions of states rested on an assumption that may not apply to precolonial Africa—that a state refers to a set area in which government resides. Yet in many areas and regions of Africa, the people moved about, and "many of these empires and kingdoms also lacked the slightest 'probability of permanence' since it was in their nature to give way to stronger state-formations" (Nwaubani, 2000, p. 276). Nwaubani suggests instead that African societies should be thought of as acephalous or stateless, meaning they had no governing head or chief; he proposed three types of government: (1) societies governed by segmentary lineages (i.e., divided); (2) those structured on age groups or classes; and (3) those governed by associations or councils, with limited formal membership.

The most common state system of government was segmentary kinship. Such political arrangements needed to manage how lineages operated as corporate entities, so that the social influence of parties from various lineages were handled effectively. The area geographically had to be understood as well, and there needed to be organizational mechanisms designed to handle interlineage disputes. It also needed to be clear how far these arrangements went. Who was able to hold high and consequential offices needed to be sorted out as well, in that the social power needed to be balanced within and between lineage and kinship groups. As an example, the Tallensi people of Ghana were organized by the kinship system in such a way as to effectively embed kinship into its social organization. Regarding the Tellensi, Davidson (2004) notes that they were a people who had no central authority; instead, they used several layers of arrangements to guide their community. The lineages and kinship groups were tied to one another to guide knowledge of their respective obligations. Beyond this, their notion of moral codes and mutual obligations kept the peace and ensured their social order and balance. Another system that was used involved organizing the contributions to the community along age groups so villagers' obligations would be dictated by age-specific tasks and roles.

Regardless of the society or clan, whether ruled by a king or no ruler at all, the role of kinship existed. While its form and patterns would change and shift to afford many variations, its presence was always necessary and a vital aspect of the social structure. Some societies ruled themselves and other groups established central rulers, usually governed by kings and other leaders and assisted by administrators and armies. The age-group approach, as with most things on the African continent, varied (Nwaubani, 2000).

Nwaubani (2000) reports that age groups were used by some people to create alliances and to set the bounds of moral order. The groups are described as members who are taught at the same time and brought into the group's rules and obligations together and thus are subject to the authority of elders. Davidson (2004) tells of the Tirki, who reside in western Kenya and used as their legal unity seven age groups. Around the age of 10, a young boy or girl had limited obligations and duties; then they are initiated, which was designed to mark the transition to manhood or womanhood, which involves enacting and learning the ritual tests and activities that need to be completed. Everything, all learning, is done in and by the group upon the orders of the group leaders. The youths live together and eat, dance, bathe, and learn all tasks as a group.

Rituals and ceremonies accompany the training and learning, some of which involve lectures and teaching from the elders about the importance of following the rules and of age-based membership and responsibilities. The youths are taught to respect elders, honor one's sisters and brothers, and defend or care for the people. Upon completion of the training, the youth becomes a young adult and is able to participate in community affairs. The next age group is that of warrior, which takes more than a decade to reach. By the age of 40, adults, usually men, may become elder warriors who govern community matters; in time, they are able to sit as judges when they reach the next age set. As adults age, they are eligible to tend to the shrines of the villages, where laws are modified and adjusted as needed. After the age of 80, adults become honored elders, retired from active social life.

Not all societies used as many age groups—the numbers range from a few to many. People who lived nearby, the Karimojong of Uganda, used just two groups, leaders and followers. Nwaubani (2000, p. 278) observes that "examples of acephalous political systems based on age grades were found mainly in East Africa.... Since membership was universal, age-grades cut across the boundaries of kin group." In this system, status changes were group-based and occurred for the set of people in the age grade; the changes were automatic and mandatory. The age groups provided structure and guidance for how to act and behave when not with the larger group.

The age groups provided guidelines for how to behave in myriad situations so when people of the group gathered, all would know what was needed in a given situation and they could act in common. Similar age-group arrangements used the assumption that those who violated the moral codes or defied the elders' wishes had been bewitched or were under the influence of evil.

Nwaubani (2000) also discusses associations as acephalous political systems, which have groups-based membership usually based upon a criterion other than birth date or kinship. The group could be formed using ritual practices, or they could be secular organizations with their own rules, and some could be arranged by using combinations of both. What matters here is that the group was able to use social and political power to direct the actions of nonmembers. Some associations were also called secret societies as a means to maintain order. But the secret societies as a political mechanism had limits and, in many instances, had little effect on maintaining individual behavior and compliance with social expectations.

People still had issues and conflicts with one another, and in some situations the social structures were not able to resolve these matters; moreover, the social codes could not address personal distress or impairment. So a way to define and address personal distress or impairment was needed. The social objective was balance with the spirits, nature, and the ancestors. There needed to be a way to communicate with these forces and a way was needed to heal the ill as well as the distressed, from both physical and mental illnesses. At the same time, there needed to be systems to assign responsibility for misfortune and failure.

In a world where balance was needed, where good and evil existed, and where malevolent forces were expressed through adverse events, this upset the balance between people and nature. Only those who knew the techniques of the divine that cause missteps—witches and sorcerers—could act on behalf of the people to address and deal with evil, failures, and misdeeds and could divine the path forward or heal the ills in people's bodies and minds.

It was a strong, enduring belief and conviction among Europeans, laypeople, scholars, and missionaries that Africans had no culture of note, no ideals, no generational messages, no inventions, no thoughts of merit (Davidson, 2004; Herskovits, 1990). The European colonial officials also held that Africans had little in culture or knew few things of values, beliefs that were held for many centuries. Yet, when some colonial Europeans listened, they learned of the history of African ancestors and kings of past times, and while the stories that were told had spiritual meaning for the storytellers, the stories had political and social meaning as well.

Life Centered on the Family Unit

Much of the African social structure was built on economic maintenance of the family unit. Even as new communities were established and grew, this governed the daily life and actions of African people. Before and up until the 5th century, the family unit typically resided in an area that was small and consisted of usually three generations—parents, children, and sometimes grandparents. Beyond the 5th century, larger villages and communities emerged, but many were still family centric.

It is presumed that the family unit supported itself and consumed what it produced. Recall that people occupied the land, but the Spirit of the Earth was its owner, and that the people sought to live in balance with the spirts and their ancestors. As the family groups grew, they tended to occupy areas near the central family unit or compound; thus, it is likely that larger villages emerged as families expanded and multiplied. The family units in such a community were linked and provided both security and identity to its members.

> It came about that all property and productive relations had to be conceived in terms of kinship relations, since it was the sum of the family groups, combined in a jural [recognized rights and obligations or legal] community, that was seen as having devised the saving balance with nature. This means that political action was necessarily kinship action. But this in turn required that every individual must play an expected social role. To the ecological balance, there corresponded another in the field of human relations—an ideal balance of kinship rights and obligation, occasionally quite simple, often very complex, and nearly always structured in terms of countervailing pressures between different … lineages and groups of lineages.
>
> *(Davidson, 2004, pp. 56–57)*

The group could survive only if the balance with nature was kept and individuals abided by the proper behavior and conduct. Sweet (2003) and Davidson (2004) describe the situation this way: individuals could exercise their rights provided the rights were exercised within the context and for the benefit of the community. In this sense, what was legal was determined by the obligations of the person to the community. This is contrary to the statement of the individual's rights, which is the hallmark of European and American cultures.

An issue with the extended family line was that one could not mate within the family. Its members had to mate and marry people outside the family, someone not in their lineage. Because of this, lineal groups became interdependent. For example, when a woman from village 2 married a man from village 1 and the union produced a child, all the men from village 2 (the woman's village) were obligated to protect the child, who is considered their "sister's son"—and they are the "mother's brothers"—and they are expected to act on behalf of the mother and child, who are now part of a different descent line but are still connected to the kinship group of village 2.

In terms of psychological perspectives, the Africans believed that it was important to abide by the principle of "enough is enough"—to maintain the proper balance in the community, each individual was not to strive for more than was needed; achievement beyond what was required was considered an act of injustice to the people. Davidson (2004) describes the principle this way:

> For the ideal balance always supposed enough but not much more: enough for a given community in a given place, taking for granted that whenever the community grew too large for local sustenance, for the achieved balance, some of its members would find new land elsewhere.
>
> *(p. 66)*

In the 1580s the ruler of Morocco, Al-Mansur, challenged Songhay, the last of the West African empires. The African empires during this era did not impose a singular political culture, nor did they centralize their administration; rather, they left local chiefs and kings alone and ruled through them. The empires operated based on personal relationships and economic motivations. They did not impose or create laws to bolster their rule. Instead, they relied on divine blessings, as was true of African traditional beliefs. In different ways, each ruler followed the ways of the people and the religious practices accepted by most people.

The Europeans

In Africa, European ships engaged in trade and created posts on the coasts for that purpose, but they did not take land or claim power or authority over the African people or of the rulers of African city-states and kingdoms. However, the primary object of trade by that time was captured Africans. Before the 1400s, travel and trade with the outside world in Africa was through the Sahara Desert or via the Indian Ocean. The Atlantic side of the continent had not been breached. Once it was, Africans and Europeans began to interact from the Atlantic coast and from some of the islands on the west side of the African continent, interactions and encounters that took several forms.

There is considerable debate about the transatlantic African slave trade. As was noted previously, it was common to buy and sell slaves in various regions of the Old World, including inside and outside of Africa. The transportation of captives to the New World was different from the practices that had taken place for more than a millennium. The debate centers on the role and manner of participation Africans themselves may have played in the transatlantic slave trade. There are many viewpoints about this, with some contending that Europeans duped Africans or manipulated them into selling their people, which was not in their best interest and in fact deprived them of needed populations. Another perspective is that Africans did not view slavery the same way that Europeans did, and they did not know how the slaves they traded to Europeans would be treated or regarded (Harms, 2018; Thornton, 1998).

The notion of slaves as property or the notion of individual or personal property, as it was understood and defined by Europeans, was not consistent with Africans beliefs. Thornton (1998, p.74) notes that "slavery was rooted in deep-seated legal and institutional structures of African societies, and it functioned quite differently from the way it functioned in European societies."

In most societies there needs to be a way to produce wealth and economic activity so there are resources with which to expand and grow. In Europe's legal model, ownership of land afforded private citizens a means of revenue; in this sense, land could be used to generate revenue, for instance, through agriculture, provided there was a pool of labor to work the fields. In this way the landlord-tenant relationship was a version of serf or peasant labor provided to nobles who benefited from the revenues, and this type of relationship was widespread. In Africa the economic situation was different; "slaves were the only form of private, revenue-producing property recognized in African law" (Thornton, 1998, p. 74). Land was owned by the community, not by private or individual owners.

In the case where land was legally personal property, the said owner had the right to use the land and whatever was produced from it. Since the land itself was just dirt and grass, it could be rented or used or taxed to generate revenue. In Africa, land was community property, so wealth was reflected in the number of slaves one had, not in their labor. Thornton (1998) shares the parallel between African concepts of economic production and that of Europeans, when he states

> just as ownership of land as a factor of production establishes a right to the product of that factor, so, too, ownership or control of labor (people or slaves) can provide the same right. African law established claims on product through taxation and slavery rather than through the fiction of landownership.
>
> *(p. 76)*

Trading in slaves was an economic activity that African elites used to grow their wealth and influence; the more slaves sold or used, the greater the elites' economic well-being. Thus, the practice of selling slaves was widespread on the continent and was done in the Old World for hundreds of years.

Having control of labor was a source of wealth and enterprise, and it allowed one to grow economic resources. Furthermore, the notion of being a slave was not the same in Europe and Africa. Slaves held subordinate status in the family in which they labored and were treated, as some might say, like a dependent child. However, the contributions that slaves made differed in Europe and Africa. In Europe, it was possible to secure land and use that land to produce income, either by renting it out or having workers toil (often serfs or the poor) on the land for productive gain. In Africa, slaves were "treated no differently from peasant cultivators, as indeed they were the functional equivalent of free tenants and hired workers in Europe" (Thornton, 1998, p. 87). For some observers, slaves were deemed so in name only. They were given freedoms, and many served in a range of roles in African societies. They could be soldiers, royal advisers, or administrators as well as miners or farm workers. In essence, Europeans and Americans legal and economic systems regarding slavery diverged considerably. Thornton (1998) observes that

> African slaves were typically used in two different ways. First of all, slaves became the preeminent form of private investment and manifestation of

> private wealth—a secure form of reproducing wealth equivalent to land-owning in Europe. Second, slaves were used by state officials as a dependent and loyal group, both for production of revenue and for performing administrative and military service in the struggle between kings and executives who wished to centralize their states and other elite parties who sought to control royal absolutism.
>
> *(p. 89)*

From this perspective slaves were the markers of wealth in Africa. While there were other forms of wealth, having slaves was one of the most common. They were also a centerpiece of social and economic systems in many African societies, but not the basis of wealth.

At the same time, observers have argued about whether Europeans drove the slave trade through direct or indirect means, using economic, political, or technological (suppling weapons) forms of enticement to Africans to wage war and to increase the number of captives available for trade. It is true that the relatively smaller sizes of African states contributed to conflicts and acts of aggression; it is also the case that Africans seemed to act for their own reasons and purposes. In an analyses of these issues Thornton (1998) concludes that

> we must accept that African participation in the slave trade was voluntary and under the control of African decision makers. This was not just at the surface level of daily exchanges but even at deeper levels. Europeans possessed no means, either economic or military, to compel Africans leaders to sell slaves.
>
> The willingness of Africa's commercial and political elite to supply slaves should be sought in their own internal dynamics and history. Institutional factors predisposed African societies to hold slaves, and the development of Africa's domestic economy encouraged large-scale trading and possession of slaves long before Europeans visited African shores.
>
> *(p. 125)*

Conclusion

The focus of this chapter is on the cultural practices and beliefs that were unique to African people and how their world views and values shaped its people. The cultural practices and themes held by Africans across the continent were in many ways similar, although there was considerable variation, and there were several shared ideas and beliefs, such as the connection and reverence for God and the life force, both of which were reflected in nature and represented what was good and proper. They also believed in a Supreme God, along with lesser divine spirits, often ancestors, who guided and permitted people to live and prosper.

The core unit of social and moral life was the family with its kinship ties and its place as the foundation of community life wherein all acted for the good and benefit of the community and village. Centralized political systems were also tied to God, the ancestors, and kinship lines, but political models and people could often go astray. The people devised ways to recognize and address such behavior and thus maintained the needed balance in the affairs of the family and community. It was imperative that nature, God and the spirits, the life forces, and ancestors be recognized and respected in all things. At the same time, good lived side by side with evil, which was often understood through magic, sorcery, or witchcraft. The people engaged in activities, ceremonies, rituals, and rites of passage to affirm and honor the spirits, ancestors, nature, the community, and God.

The values expressed by traditions, customs, and ceremonies were contained in religious beliefs that were used to heal the ill and deal with social disruptions, but not in the way Westerners thought about religion.

Africans valued communalism as cultural practice and cultural spirituality as expressed in religion, and they practiced oral traditions in which Africa's history and customs were communicated and passed to succeeding generations. For Africans, the present included the past such that the cultural-temporal focus was a fusion of these two time frames. The oral traditions were supported and represented by Africans through artistic symbols, speech, and other expressions and activities (e.g., masks, shrines, pottery, clothing, and other art objects), the use of rhythmic music and dance was employed to honor and communicate their traditions and to recognize the power of nature, the spirits, life forces, and their gods.

The cultural patterns developed over millennia changed and evolved, yet some patterns held firm across place and location. The core beliefs and engrained cultural ways that defined Africans at home traveled with those who were taken and sold to Europeans.

The strong evidence of the long time span that characterizes prehistoric and ancient Africa, including during the Middle Ages, suggests that Africans were able to hold on to their deeply engrained worldviews and values, and these changed due to circumstances, expanding and evolving in the New World (Belgrave & Allison, 2019). In the next chapter we will see the forces that influenced these changes and will follow the manner of adjustments that Africans made to their worldview as well as how they passed their values down to their descendants.

References

Aderajew, A. (2019). African systems of thought: Whether they fit scientific knowledge. *Journal of Philosophy and Culture*, 7(2), 14–25.

Belgrave, F. Z., & Allison, K. W. (2019). *African American psychology: From Africa to America* (4th ed.). Sage.

Bodley, J. H. (2017). *Cultural anthropology: Tribes, states, and the global system* (6th ed.). Rowan & Littlefield.
Curtin, P. D. (1971). The emergence of African history. In A. M. Josephy (Ed.). *The Horizon history of Africa*. American Heritage Publishing.
Davidson, B. (2004). *The African genius*. James Curry, Ltd.
Davidson, B. (2005). *Africa in history*. Simon & Schuster.
Falola, T. (Ed.). (2000). *Africa*, Vol. 1, *African history before 1885*. Carolina Academic Press.
Harms, R. (2018). *Africa in global history: With sources*. Norton.
Herskovits, M. J. (1990). *The myth of the Negro past*. Beacon.
Horton, R. (1967). African traditional thought and western science: Part 1. *Africa*, 37(1), 155–187.
Josephy, A. M. (Ed.). (1971). *The Horizon history of Africa*. American Heritage Publishing.
Kluckhohn, F. R., & Strodtbeck, F. L. (1961). *Variations in value orientations*. Row, Peterson.
Nwaubani, E. (2000). Acephalous societies. In T. Falola (Ed.). *Africa*, Vol. 1, *African history before 1885*. Carolina Academic Press.
Sweet, J. H. (2003). *Recreating Africa: Culture, kinship and religion in the African-Portuguese world, 1441–1770*. University of North Carolina Press.
Thornton, J. K. (1998). *Africa and Africans in the making of the Atlantic world, 1400–1800* (2nd ed.). Cambridge University Press.
Walker, R. (2011). *When we ruled: The ancient and mediæval history of black civilisations*. Black Classics.
Williams, C. (1987). *The destruction of the Black civilization*. Third World Press.

PART 2

Africans in the New World

3

BUILDING A LIFE IN THE NEW WORLD FROM THE FOUNDATIONS OF THE OLD

In the first two chapters I discussed how African people, over the course of several thousand years, from 3000 BCE to the 17th century, populated and spread to various regions on the continent. Several beliefs and behaviors guided Africans' actions, and they constructed shelters, made tools and art objects, and created stories and tales to convey their ideas and beliefs.

Bodley (2017) notes that, for a culture to survive, it is imperative for its people to pass along to later generations the culture's principles, beliefs, practices, and so on. Given the limits of an individual, groups are required so that information can be shared and distributed. At the same time, the expanded group needs to organize the growing information the people collect. Conflict is also likely, especially in a challenging physical environment, so sociocultural systems are subject to flux and change. In these ways "culture" can be characterized as the collection of knowledge, art, laws, and beliefs that humans use in their social lives. Thus, what the people think, make, and do reveals their cultural ways as well as their psychological and behavioral tendencies (Bodley, 2017).

As discussed in chapter 2, Africans had a variety of beliefs, but some common patterns were identified, including their belief in the power of the life force and the existence of a supreme being who was particular to the people in question since their God was also their ancestor and was worshipped as such. The religious and secular were intertwined and reciprocal. The recently departed joined the ancestors in that they looked after the living and thus were always the objects of respect and reverence.

Africans' beliefs were used to foresee events and to settle conflicts and disputes, unlike the Europeans' and Americans' belief that science and religion were separate. In the African cosmology, their spiritual practices

DOI: 10.4324/9781003111542-6

represented their science and understanding of the universe (Sweet, 2003). Africans adjusted to their environments, and their numbers grew over time; as they learned, they also modified what they knew in accordance with the situation and changes in their circumstances. Often the climate and changes in their life circumstances would mean they had to change how things were done or understood.

Considering all this, African people held in high esteem the family, community, the life forces, and their ancestors; they valued the needs of the group over that of the individual. They respected and valued nature and its dangers and benefits. They sought harmony with their surroundings. Their economic and political organizations were usually built on the fundamental notions of family and community. The spirits held and owned the land, and the people simply worked it for sustenance. Parts of the African continent were isolated from the outside world, while some regions, in closer proximity to Europe and Asia, experienced less isolation and engaged in trade and commerce, exchanging and sharing goods and ideas across the seas and oceans. Contact with the outside, and Europeans in particular, increased with the Europeans' ability to travel along the west coast of the continent in the 1400s (Berlin, 2003).

The End of African Isolation

The world known to many Africans, especially those on the west coast, changed in the 15th century in ways unforeseen by many. The Atlantic islands of Sao Tome, Principe, and Cape Verde off the west coast of Africa were uninhabited until around 1450, when the islands were settled by the Portuguese. Prior to this time the Atlantic was impossible to navigate both north and south. As Thornton (1998) states,

> No sailor could ignore the patterns of prevailing winds and currents on the ocean. This was crucial for the development of Atlantic navigation, for the winds and currents created barriers to traffic for thousands of years. They limited contact between the Mediterranean and Africa for a very long time.
>
> *(p. 15)*

In the later years of the 1400s (1440–1470), when Europeans began to raid and explore the west coast areas of the continent, they found it difficult to prevail in attacks on African people.

> The Europeans had little success in their seaborne attacks on the mainland. As a result, the Europeans had to abandon the time-honored tradition of trading and raiding and substitute a relationship based more or less completely on peaceful regulated trade....

> African naval power made raiding difficult, it also allowed Africans to conduct trade with Europeans on their own terms, collecting customs and other duties as they liked.
>
> *(Thornton, 1998, pp. 38–39)*

In time, Africans and Europeans began trade and exchanges of goods. Some Europeans established themselves on coastal islands, and others lobbied to locate trade centers or forts on African soil. Goods and related commodities were sold, including people, usually war captives or criminals. Africans were partners in the trade of people because slavery was an integral part of African society; it was embedded into their social, economic, political structures and institutions, and was even codified in Africans laws and legal customs. Yet it is important to be clear that slavery in Europe and in the British and European colonies in the Americas was distinctly different, both in legal and economic terms. Thornton (1998) describes the distinction this way:

> Different legal structures led Africans and Europeans to develop the institution of slavery in substantially different ways. Consequently, the conventional wisdom concerning slavery developed from the study of European or colonial American societies with landed private property simply cannot apply to Africa.
>
> *(p. 89)*

In Africa, slaves were treated as human beings, not as property, for Africans slaves or servants provided valuable services and were considered part of the family or community, and some were able to acquire wealth in their own right.

In the North America mainland, African slaves were regarded as nonhuman or inferior heathens, and they were treated as such. It is vital that these differences between Africans, Europeans, and Americans be clear. Regarding cultural views and beliefs, it is not always possible to know the worldview of others; it is more common to think that people have the same view as you do even when there is no way to know that their worldview or belief system may vary from yours. Inner mental processes are not visible or knowable unless there is more intimate contact with the parties involved. So Africans participated in the slave trade, and Europeans benefited from the labor provided by the people who were sold to them.

There is considerable debate about whether captives in Africa who became slaves upon arrival in the New World were able to retain their cultural ways. I have suggested in the introduction and chapter 1, based on scholarship and research evidence about the lives and ways of Black American adults, that they did indeed retain their cultural ways. Yet many scholars and historians (e.g., Herskovits, 1990; Mintz & Price, 1976; Sweet, 2003; Thornton,

1998) have argued that they could not retain their worldview or cultures, and others have put forth the notion that they could and did.

African Cultural Strengths Pre-Contact with Europeans

As Herskovits observes, people who lived in the heart of the slave-trading regions were the Akan-Ashanti of the Gold Coast, the Dahomean, Yoruba, and the Bini of western Nigeria. He described the economic, social, and political lives of these peoples as a way to convey some aspects of Black American survivals from African culture. The African economy was able to support the leaders and nobles as well as the commoners of the social system. The social system was organized by levels, and the distribution of labor was based upon kinship lines. In trade and agriculture, women had important roles since they were often the sellers at markets. African laws recognized kinship lineage in varying ways. For the Yoruba, maternal inheritance determined one's social position, while one's spiritual connections came from the father. The extended kinship system helped build and maintain stability in African social systems.

Africans believed that life did not end at the point of death; rather, those who passed on were an important part of life, with nobles having greater power as ancestors than commoner ancestors. Burial rituals reflected these notions about the value of the dead since many Africans believed that ancestors were in close communication with the gods. Herskovits (1990) observes:

> In … [the west coast], in fact, the funeral is the true climax of life, and no belief drives deeper into traditions of West African thought. For the problem of New World survivals this is of paramount importance, for whatever else has been lost of … customs, the attitudes toward the dead as manifested in meticulous rituals cast in the mold of West African patterns have survived.
>
> *(p. 63)*

Africans lived in family compounds consisting of groups of physical structures or huts that were separated, usually by a wall or barrier, from other family compounds, thereby unifying the family unit psychologically in the village. In family compounds, wives had their own huts that they shared with their children. In this way children were closer to their mothers. Wives (if there was more than one) rotated visits to the husband's hut.

Political organizations had many versions but all shared one essential feature: they were usually independent. There was always loyalty to the local leaders. Even when the political units grew, each operated with efficiency, and the administration of justice worked well, as did the actions needed to defend the village or the state. It was expected that the people would serve in the armies when needed. The states and related political entities were maintained through the imposition of taxes. These were levied through the structure of leadership in which the family leader was responsible to the village chief, and he to the district chief and so on, to the next level up. Leaders would consult a council of elders, and these groups handled disputes and other issues that arose.

Another aspect of African life that was as important as politics was religion or cultural spirituality. Many observers believed that Africans were "Fetish" worshippers, which seems to refer to magical practices or the use of charms and other devices for various reasons. This characterization applied even to those who were Christian or Muslim. The Ashanti, Dahomeans, and Yoruba's religious principles and practices involved notions that a great God created all things and left men to handle what was created for them. God was believed to have been part of several family groups, which reflected the forces of nature and operated to ensure that people lived good lives.

Africans formed cult groups to worship the various deities. These were what some called lesser gods or forces, such as Fate, among the Dahomey, and Yoruba, specially trained diviners often spent decades learning how to understand the divining system. The principles associated with the practices of divining were centered around an important set of beliefs. One was that each person's life was predetermined but, at the same time, it was possible to avoid one's fate if you could invoke the good will of the gods. For Herskovits (1990), this fact of African belief, where one can alter fate and change a negative predetermined course to a positive one, was central to understanding how Africans may have held on to their cultures in the context of oppressive racial exploitation. He notes that Africans were predisposed to not allow fate to determine their life courses. Their deeply held spiritual orientation offered another view and course of action. To hope and preserve that view was necessary.

Another important factor of Africans' religion was that they had no desire to promote their views or beliefs and get others to follow them; in fact, Africans were willing to accept new deities that others followed, usually from outside their clan or tribe. If one set of people was conquered by another, then the people accepted the gods of the group in power. This way political change also carried with it religious change. Gods were for the protection of the people.

Another element in the African religious practices involved the use of charms and what many called magic. Charms and magic were part of each person's daily activities. At the same time, there was fear and concern about the various forces in the world. Herskovits (1990) reminds us that, for Africans, this perspective was normal. He says of the objects people used,

> For if these are dangerous, they are also helpful.... So, with the West African's gods, and so with magic. What can potentially harm, if not handled properly, can also be of great aid; ... in West Africa priests and

> diviners and dealers in magic charms are … on hand to exercise the proper controls.
>
> (*p. 74*)

Africans used stories and tales to communicate about various aspects of life, and they had a range of aesthetic expressions such as wood carvings and other ornaments. They employed music, folk songs, drums, and other musical instruments in their rituals and ceremonies in which they danced and sang.

The Transatlantic Slave Trade

Harms (2018, p. 170) draws upon information from the Trans-Atlantic Slave Trade database, which reports that there were about 35,000 slave ships that traveled across the Atlantic between 1400 and 1866. The scholars who estimated the numbers in the database used statistical analyses to project the approximate totals, and they filled in gaps in the data to show that some 12.4 million captives were transported out of Africa during that period. Close to 2 million Africans did not survive the journey, and some 11 million arrived in the New World, most of whom went to South America and the Caribbean islands, with around 400,000 arriving on the North American mainland. Dodson (2002) contends that about 10 million Africans were transported, and 450,000 arrived in North American ports, mostly in the north. More than five centuries later, the estimated number of Black people in the United States is about 46.8 million (Tamir, 2021), although there is no way to know how many are descended from enslaved Africans.

Africans came with their cultural ways, but they were not allowed to express these ways in their lives as servants and slaves. Regardless of where Africans came from, their ways were suppressed in North America (less so in the Caribbean and South America, where Africans outnumbered whites). Historians contend that if one were looking for particular patterns of behavior among Africans brought to the New World, then where they came from might shed some light on this matter.

Herskovits states that most African captives transported to the New World were from the west coast region of the continent, such as Gambia, Senegal, Goree Island, Guinea (the Gold Coast, Winward Coast), Angola, Congo, Sierra Leone, Liberia, the Ivory Coast, East Africa, Togo, Dahomey, and the Niger Delta (Herskovits, 1990, pp. 48–49). Thornton (1998) identifies three main regions from which captives were transported. The western coast (from the Senegal River to Sierra Leone), the Gulf of Guinea, and the west-central region (from Cameroon to the Cape of Good Hope). Harms (2018) believes there were multiple regions involved in the slave trade over the course of the 250 years in which it took place; his list, from north to south names Senegambia, Sierra Leone, Gold Coast, Blight of Benin, Niger Delta, Kongo, and

Angola. Harms notes further that captives typically were taken no farther than 250 miles from the coast and that by 1700 the framework and structures for slave trading were well established.

Mintz and Price (1976) believe that Africans did not bring their cultures with them. They state that this was not possible because the captives were more different than they were similar; they contend that neither Africans nor Europeans who came to the New World were able to transfer much of their ways of living from one place to the other. They suggest, however, that it was possible that African ways might have survived on deeper psychological and behavioral levels. This could be seen in the behavior and beliefs of West and Central region Africans and their descendants, many of whom were taken to the Caribbean and South America where they encountered fewer constraints in practicing and establishing their traditional customs and re-creating their native institutions. Many of the Africans' cultural habits and ways found in the New World, they argued, were linked to particular African societies, "Suriname or Jamaica to the Ashanti, Haiti to the Dahomeans and so forth" (Mintz & Price, 1976, p. 15). While my focus is the North American mainland, it is important to recognize that Africans were transported to South America and Caribbean islands in the New World in larger numbers and for a longer period of time. Some, perhaps many, of these Africans, over time, were brought to the North American mainland.

Mintz and Price (1976) argue that the store of knowledge and information held by Africans from their respective ethnic-cultural groups were enacted and used in their new situations to deal with matters that were in front of them, which required that they build connections in whatever way was possible. They suggest that this bonding occurred from the outset—upon capture, while being held in factories waiting for transport to the New World, and during the Middle Passage. The bonds were made often between members of the same sex since men and women were separated during these early phases of their captivity. The Africans were not passive victims in this situation; they acted to assert their values, and many fought back and died. Some killed themselves when possible, and some took over the ships and tried to return to Africa. Many of these acts took cooperation, but those who could not communicate effectively had limited options to act. For Mintz and Price (1976), it is the adaptations and bonds formed in varied situations before entering the New World that set the foundation for what they called new African-based cultural patterns and social systems. For example, symbols and designs shaved into their hair that were visible when they were forced to dance on the ship's deck were used to communicate with other Africans, even those whose language differed. The meaning and application of the shipmate bond, they argue, was akin to family ties, and shipmates were regarded as brothers and sisters. Thus, Africans found ways to express aspects of their core cultural ways.

Mintz and Price (1976) also believe that West African people shared an openness to cultural difference and that this tendency was shared among the varied African ethnic groups. Africans experienced assaults on their personal identity, which was combined with the constant threat of death and physical violence; these elements gave Africans an appreciation and a deep value for personal, unique attributes and characteristics, which found expression in improvisation and rhythm. So, to express themselves and their unique identities, many found simple means of self-expression such as their style of walk or form of dress, like the slant of a hat. Africans understood that these personal qualities and forms of individual expression could not be taken away. The combination of personal qualities and the tendency to be open to cultural differences meant that Africans placed an importance on fueling creativity and innovation, which infused dynamic change in the cultural practices of enslaved Africans who lived in Jamaica, Haiti, Suriname, and the North American mainland.

Africans who landed in South America and the Caribbean demonstrated some survival of traditional African customs and beliefs, as presented and demonstrated by several scholars and historians (e.g., Blassingame, 1972; Herskovits 1990; Mintz & Price, 1976; Sweet 2003). For Sweet (2003) and Mintz and Price (1976), Africans created a culture of their own. Mintz and Price (1976) state that the

> deep-level cultural principles, assumptions, and understandings which were shared by the Africans … would have been a limited though crucial resource … [that] could have served as a catalyst … by which individuals from diverse societies forged new institutions, and could have provided certain frameworks within which new forms could have developed.… The Africans in any New World colony … became a *community* and began to share a *culture* only insofar as, and as fast as, they themselves created them.
>
> *(p. 14)*

According to Sweet (2003), family, gender, sex roles, kinship ties, and religion were elements of culture that were also transported to the Americas irrespective of the differences among the various African ethnic groups, and these elements were retained and survived in the New World slave communities. He traces the movement of Africans to Brazil from the middle of the 1400s to the 1770s. Sweet contends that shared cultural notions were brought from Africa and passed on to their descendants.

Many aspects of African cultures were demonized and debased by Europeans, who had the power to suppress a lot of slaves' behavior. Nevertheless, many elements of European morals and conduct were rejected by the slaves, and their concepts of morality and family prevailed in spite of the European Christians' efforts to impose their ideas of marriage and family. For instance, Sweet observed that in many Central African societies, sexual life was a way to honor and celebrate the process of reproduction, and it was encouraged and taught to youth without stigma assigned to sexual activity, unlike the notions of Westerners, who proclaimed only married partners should have sex, and the unmarried should abstain from any sexual activity. Moreover, Europeans believed in monogamous marriages and Africans did not. Sweet (2003) states:

> The code of Christian morality that the Portuguese applied to their own sexual relationships was absent in many African societies, where there was a distinction drawn between the communal obligations of marriage and individual carnal desires. For those who were sent to the Americas as slaves, … many of the same attitudes and African type arrangements would persist.
>
> *(p. 35)*

The situation with relationships and marriage is, for Sweet, an example of how Africans applied their common cultural understandings to re-create through language, religion, and child-rearing a common or familiar cultural foundation that they passed on to their children. He points out that slave households during the 1730s were not simply composed of male, female, and their offspring.

> The willingness of households to adopt non-kin "outsiders" was a prominent feature of some African societies and allowed for the development of a mixed web of kinship on certain large Brazilian properties.
>
> *(Sweet, 2003, p. 49)*

Regarding religion, Sweet argues that practices in Central Africa and those in the Americas reveal that Africans' core assumptions and beliefs that undergirded their religious life were not destroyed and that Western Christian practices and beliefs did not take over or replace the practices and beliefs of Africans. Yet, since far fewer Africans arrived on the North American mainland, and since they came later in time, fewer of these cultural patterns might be visible in North America.

Europeans and Africans in the North American Mainland

In the early years of the North American mainland colonies, people who provided labor were indentured servants, and people of all skin colors and religious backgrounds held the status of servant (Fredrickson, 1988). Historians tell different stories of what happened (Bennett, 1988; Berlin, 1998, 2003; Dodson, 2002; Fredrickson, 1988; Thornton, 1998, 2012). Yet, between 1619 and 1640, a small number of Africans were introduced into the Virginia colony as servants. "Some, and perhaps most, of these early arrivals were freed after a limited term of service," (Fredrickson, 1988, p. 193), as was the case with most indentured servants irrespective of race.

Some of the 20 or so people who landed in the Virginia colony in 1619 were Creole, or mixed race, part African and part European. Many Creoles were the offspring of marriages or unions between European men and Africans women in the towns that had sprung up around the forts or factories that were established to make trade possible and efficient on Africa's west coast (Berlin, 1998).

The debate continues over whether the Africans in the North American mainland colonies were slaves from the outset. People also have different views about what factors contributed to Africans eventual low social status. Some contend that international law meant that Africans were slaves regardless of where they were taken; others argue that race prejudice combined with physical differences were determining factors that sealed Africans' fate to be chattel slaves (Bennett, 1988; Berlin, 1998; Dodson, 2002). In the course of 20 years, by 1640, while the colonists' ideas about race and race relations were still in flux, it was nevertheless clear that white and African servants were treated differently; thus, they were seen as different (Dodson, 2002). This is best illustrated by the treatment of three servants who ran away together in 1640, a precursor to further efforts to set Blacks/Africans apart from whites. Two white and one Black indentured servant ran away seeking to be free, and they were captured and punished. At this point the differences between them emerges: the two white indentured servants had years added to their contracts of service, while the Black servant was sentenced to remain in service for his entire life. Racial distinctions like the one revealed in the punishment of the indentured servants and in other aspects of colonial life were followed by laws that established racial restrictions, and these legal limits and distinctions made racial slavery part of the fabric of the North American mainland colonies.

Colonies passed laws that, in most instances, were guided by English common law. But Virginia's 1662 colonial provision (contradicting English law, which held that children were linked to their fathers' status) mandated that the status of Black children be determined by their mothers' status or position. Therefore, any child born to a Black slave woman (even if the father was white) would be a slave. This change in the law achieved two goals: it helped to increase the supply of slaves, and it codified the racial distinctions between slave and free.

Other American mainland colonies followed Virginia's 1662 colonial provision with statutes of their own, such as ones that outlawed interracial marriages and relationships. For instance, a 1664 Maryland law said that if a free white woman married a Black male slave, she could become a slave. In South Carolina in 1691 an explicit slave code was established designating Negros and Native Americans as slaves. In 1705 Massachusetts laws were passed that banned interracial relationships. By the 1700s other colonies followed this action. In time, the slave's status as property was written into colonial law throughout the various colonies, yet it appears that, by 1640, racial distinctions were clear and unambiguous. Racial customs and practices were established (Wright, 2017).

In spite of the colonial laws and customs, Africans and their Black and mixed-race descendants' lives in the first century of the North American mainland colonies shifted between servant and slave, and they intermarried and mixed socially with whites and Native Americans. Berlin (1998) presents the early years in the North America mainland in terms of different colonial regions and distinct generations. He called the first generation the Charter generation. It was during this period that the first Africans arrived in the colonies. They, like those after them, survived the Middle Passage and had to manage the psychological trauma of capture, transport, and being thrust into a strange and brutal world. During this era Africans were seldom brought directly from Africa; instead, most came to the mainland by way of the Caribbean islands or South America, and they were considered seasoned. Included among them were many mixed-race Atlantic Creoles.

The North American mainland colonies, as described by Berlin (2003), consisted of four regions: the North; the Chesapeake; the coastal Low Country of South Carolina, Georgia, and Florida; and the Lower Mississippi Valley. Each region had its own unique and distinct terrain, economy, and social structure. Berlin (1998) argues that these regions of colonial America shifted between societies with slaves and slave societies. Societies with slaves had a social structure in which the lines and boundaries between slaves and other laborers were fluid and the population of slaves was small; while in slave societies, where the economy was based on slave labor, the boundaries were firm and rigid. Labor was a pressing issue in slave societies because they often produced crops like rice, tobacco, and similar commodities, which were labor intensive and in high demand in the international trade markets. In the regions, the size and makeup of the Black/African labor pool varied along several dimensions. For instance, in some regions (identified in the forthcoming sections), some of the slaves came from European countries, had European names, practiced Christian religions, and spoke European languages. Many were Atlantic Creoles. Bennett (1988) states:

> The "good servants" came from different backgrounds with different experiences. Quite a few, as we have noted, came from England, where Blacks had lived since the middle of the sixteenth century. Many came from Spain, Portugal and the West Indies. Significantly, many were Christians, baptized either in Spain or Portugal or on the high seas. In 1624 Johns Phillip testified in a Jamestown court and his testimony against a White man was admitted because he had been "christened in England twelve years since."
>
> *(p. 37)*

Atlantic Creoles were part of the Charter generation and were among the first groups of slaves in the colonies during the founding years. They were skilled at trade and agriculture, knew the European languages or spoke lingua franca used by traders and merchants, and they knew European laws that were used in colonies and trading centers in the Americas, Europe, and Africa.

To grasp the unique place of Atlantic Creoles requires that we step back a bit in time and place to before the 15th century in Africa. It is here that Atlantic Creoles began—they were part African and European. Europeans arrived on the west coast of Africa around the early 1400s, first on the west coast islands near the continent. By the middle to late 1400s Europeans had established trading posts or forts near the coast on the African continent, and towns grew around these numerous settlements.

One of the first such trading centers was Elmina, built by the Portuguese in 1492 (and later taken over by the Dutch in 1637). The trading posts were meeting places for African and European traders. Berlin (2003) states that

> the people of the enclaves [towns around the trading forts and factories]—long-term residents and wayfarers alike—soon joined together geographically and genetically. European men took wives and mistresses among African women and before long the children born of these unions helped people the enclaves. Elmina sprouted a substantial cadre of Euro-Africans ... men and women of African birth but shared African and European parentage, whose swarthy skin, European dress and deportment, acquaintance with local norms, and multilingualism gave them an insider's knowledge of both African and European ways but denied them full acceptance in either culture. By the eighteenth century, they numbered several hundred in Elmina. Along the Angolan coast they may have been even more numerous.
>
> *(p. 25)*

What was important about these Africans of mixed race was their use of a lingua franca, or Guinea speech or Negro speak, which became the language used in the Atlantic world, in Europe, Africa, and the Americas.

Atlantic Creoles lived in a world that was neither African nor European but between the two. Many resided in the towns that came about around the trading forts and factories, and from this position they learned to speak to both Africans and Europeans. They were instrumental in the growth and use of a pidgin language used to communicate in the trading centers of the African coast and in many trading locations in the New World and Europe. Because Africans did not fully accept Atlantic Creoles as Africans but were considered African or Black by Europeans, they constructed a place between the two worlds, and in this place they pressed to their advantage some degree of recognition as trade brokers. When members of this group were transported to the New World as slaves, they were able to forge some favorable spaces for themselves and their families in the New World's North American colonies, to varying degrees of success.

The Atlantic Creoles were a segment of the newly arriving slaves, and while the lines between slave and servant were fluid at first, life was less constrained for Blacks, slave or free. Creoles could take advantage of what they knew to secure a better place in colonial society. Both groups, African slaves and Creoles, pressed for more rights and recognition in the courts and used the laws of the colonies to improve their status. They formed small communities, they worshiped in the churches in their respective regions, and they established families as best they could, which was difficult since most slaves were male. They learned the language spoken in their colonial region. Many used their skills and knowledge as traders and merchants to operate in the colonies and to assume essential roles as interpreters and middlemen between the local people, traders, and the slave populations.

Bennett notes that by the time of the American Revolution, white indentured servants outnumbered slaves in most of the colonies. While the numbers of Blacks compared to whites were small, their presence was still obvious, and it raises the question—who were the Blacks in the first generations of the colonies? Bennett (1988) proclaims that they were Africans, regardless of the routes they traveled to North America; some came from Europe and others from other colonies in the New World. He continues:

> Africans brought their mind and ethos to America with them. The important point here is that the first generation of African-Americans were carriers of an African world view. They had ideas about social organizations and the nature of forces that controlled the universe. They also had technical skills ... in the area of agriculture, which was well developed in Africa.
>
> *(p. 42)*

The nature of slave life changed from the broad and more independent model that was used during the years of the Charter generation to the more restricted and confined life of what Berlin (1998) called the Plantation generation. The model of plantations that was used in other parts of the New World was brought to North America and employed to produce crops such as sugar, rice, and tobacco and to maximize profits on large, confined estates and set in motion a new social order and ruling class, the white planter elite. Life for Africans and Creoles changed dramatically under the new circumstances of plantation life, which we examine in chapter 4.

Conclusion

Regardless of the origins of Africans, and irrespective of their being seasoned prior to arrival in the North American mainland, the process of being taken and oppressed had its effects on individuals, families, groups, and social relationships. That Blacks were seen as different and set apart from whites was clear, even though many whites shared a similar status and were friends and allies with Black people. The connections among the varied racial groups of servants began to change rather quickly. While some members of the Charter generation were accepted and assimilated into colonial society, there were others still impacted by being held as slaves; as time went on, their rights and opportunities were further restricted. Thus, Blacks' status came with a psychological and emotional cost. Africans' cultural and spiritual beliefs provided a means to cope with the rigors of their new circumstances.

The Charter generation's members brought with them some elements of their homeland's cultural ways that were expressed more fully in the other colonies of South America and the Caribbean, but some Africans did infuse these African customs and practices into Black people's lives in North America. Not long after their arrival, Blacks were seen as inferior because of their race. Despite being set apart during the first few decades of colonial life, some Blacks in some colonies acquired and accumulated land, participated in elections, gave testimony in courts, and interacted with whites as their equals.

Blacks in the New World lived in ways that demonstrated elements of the cultural ways of their African ancestors as they established extended families, had flexible gender roles, had religious faith, and employed their farming skills. In essence, they adapted.

References

Bennett, L. (1988). *Before the Mayflower: A history of Black America*. Johnson Publishing.

Berlin, I. (1998). *Many thousands gone: The first two centuries of slavery in North America*. Belknap Press of Harvard University Press.

Berlin, I. (2003). *Generations of captivity: A history of African-American slaves*. Harvard University Press.

Blassingame, J. W. (1972). *The slave community*. Oxford University Press.

Bodley, J. H. (2017). *Cultural anthropology: Tribes, states, and the global system* (6th ed.). Rowan & Littlefield.

Dodson, H. (2002). *Jubilee: The emergence of African-American culture*. National Geographic.

Fredrickson, G. M. (1998). *The arrogance of race. Historical perspectives on slavery, racism and social inequity*. Wesleyan University Press.

Harms, R. (2018). *Africa in global history with sources*. W.W. Norton.

Herskovits, M. J. (1990). *The myth of the Negro past*. Beacon Press.

Mintz, S. W., & Price, R. (1976). *The birth of African-American culture: An anthropological perspective*. Beacon Press.

Sweet, J. H. (2003). *Recreating Africa: Culture, kinship and religion in the African–Portuguese world, 1441–1770*. University of North Carolina Press.

Tamir, C. (2021). *The growing diversity of Black America*. Pew Research Center.

Thornton, J. K. (1998). *Africa and Africans in the making of the Atlantic world, 1400–1800* (2nd ed.). Cambridge University Press.
Thornton, J. K. (2012). *A cultural history of the Atlantic world, 1250–1820*. Cambridge University Press.
Wright, D. R. (2017). *African Americans in the colonial era: From African origins through the American revolution* (4th ed). Wiley Blackwell.

4

THE FIRST GENERATION OF SLAVES AND SERVANTS

The life and manner of living for Africans and Blacks in North America shifted and changed depending upon time and place. There are several ways to mark the shifts and changes; one way is to look at the regions of the North American mainland in which they resided, and the other, to examine Black lives by time period. Berlin (1998) used generations to describe the phases of Black life in the colonial era, a span of more than 200 years. I focus in this chapter on the span from the founding of colonies beginning in 1619 to the 1740s, some 120 years.

I begin with the early colonial settlements, what Berlin has named the Black Charter generation, or the first African arrivals, their children, and grandchildren. I touched on some of what happened with and to the initial arrivals in chapter 3. I concentrate more on their children and grandchildren in this chapter.

Colonial America and the Charter Generation

According to Berlin (1998), there were four regions during the colonial era: The *North*, which included the colonies known as New York (New Netherlands) and Pennsylvania; the *Chesapeake*, which included the colonies of Maryland and Virginia; the *Low Country*, which consisted of the Carolina colony (what is now North and South Carolina and Georgia) and parts of Florida; and the *Lower Mississippi Valley*, which included the colonies located in what is now Louisiana, western Florida, and Mississippi (these colonies were not part of the British domain).

Wright (2017) identifies colonial regions in a similar but slightly different way. The *Chesapeake* includes the Virginia and Maryland colonies; *The Low Country*, the Carolina colony and part of northern Florida; the *Lower*

DOI: 10.4324/9781003111542-7

Mississippi Valley, western Florida and colonies in Mississippi and Louisiana; and *New England and the Middle Colonies*, farming settlements in what is now Connecticut, Long Island, the lower Hudson Valley, and industrial areas of what is now southern Pennsylvania, New York, Rhode Island, and Massachusetts. The lives of colonist and their captives varied by region, so each of the four regions will be described in a little more detail.

In the early years of the North American colonies the British settlers were struggling to compete in the international Atlantic trade markets, where other Europeans had been successful. All New World settlement employed the forced labor of Native people and Africans, with many Africans transported in the 1500s. For the most part, colonies in South America and the Caribbean islands exported goods like sugar to their respective European colonizer countries. The need to establish a profitable crop was pressing, and the British settlers in North America started with tobacco (which Native Americans had taught them to grow), which required considerable labor to produce.

When the first Africans arrived, the colonist used indentured whites from Europe as their labor as well as the forced labor of Native Americans. European leaders and governments placed enormous pressure on the colonists to succeed in the newly established colonies as well as pressure to operate and succeed in the larger Atlantic economic system of North and South America, various Caribbean islands nations, Africa, and various European countries, including Spain, the Netherlands, England, and France, to name a few. The stakes were high, and the settlers had to find and establish viable crops to export. "Spanish success at staple-producing agriculture in American colonies gave English speculators the idea that they could support similar ventures, and the crown was all for such schemes" (Wright, 2017, p. 65). Yet the regions varied in terms of climate and topography as well as in the people who came as settlers. There was variation in the nature and type of contact colonists had with Native people and in how the colonists chose to administer their settlements. Some colonies were more religious than others, and different crops were possible in the varied regions as well.

The Chesapeake Region

The Chesapeake region consisted of colonies in Virginia and Maryland. Even before African captives entered the North American mainland colonies, Africans were guides and trackers for European expeditions to the New World in the 16th century. So, in fact, those who arrived in the early 1600s were not the first Africans to set foot on North American soil.

The colony in Virginia was settled in 1607, more than 100 years after slavery was operating in South America and on Caribbean islands. The colonists started out as traders and found that planting or farming would be more beneficial; by 1617 they had settled on tobacco as their main crop for export while other staples were grown for subsistence. The issue, however, was that to grow tobacco they required labor. It was a demanding crop, but they thought the supply of landless Englishmen would be adequate to meet their labor needs (Berlin, 2003; Wright, 2017). They also had access to Indigenous people to supplement the labor of English servants.

In 1619, 20 Africans disembarked at Jamestown, Virginia, and were engaged as servants, like their European counterparts, thus adding to the labor force. Historians go back and forth about these developments in the colonies. Many contend that at least in the Chesapeake between 1620 and 1670, there was less of a color line in that, among servants and slaves, there were few differences. They labored alongside one another, and the fact that African people composed a very small portion—between 2% and 5%—of the colonial population made it somewhat easier to include them into colonial life (e.g., Bennett, 1988; Berlin, 1998; Dodson, 2002; Horton & Horton, 2005). The status of slaves had not been fully defined or articulated, which allowed many African people to live out their terms of service and contribute to the colonial society (as noted in chapter 3). The story of Antione the Negro illustrates the point that slaves often were freed and became productive members of the social structure.

Antione, listed as a Negro in documents from the era, was sold into service in 1621. He worked on the Bennetts' plantation in Virginia. He was respected by the landowners, who also became his patrons. While a slave, he was able to farm independently, marry, and have four children baptized. By 1650, he and his family were freed from their service and moved to the shore area of Virginia, and by 1651, he had acquired cattle and a land grant of some 250 acres. He is known to have changed his name to Anthony Johnson and functioned as a full member of the colony. For instance, in 1655, he used the courts in a successful legal challenge to reclaim one of his servants after a white man took the servant from him. The Johnson family continued to prosper in the region, with John Johnson, the son to Anthony, awarded 550 acres of land and the headrights that allowed him to import eleven whites as servants. Another son also was granted land for the same reasons. So some of the early African settlers fared well.

In fact, between 1664 and 1677 in one Virginia county, 2% of the households were Black landowners who raised livestock, traded, resolved disagreements in courts, and had large social networks. Overall, however, the number of Blacks remained relatively small in the Chesapeake; for instance, of the 13,000 residents, some 300 were Black, or about 2% (Berlin, 1998; Wright, 2017).

The life of an indentured servant, regardless of race, was difficult and unpleasant. Planters expected the workers to toll for long hours to generate as much profit as possible to accomplish the planters' economic goals. But the rights of workers were determined by English law and customs, as colonial servants enjoyed the same laborers' rights as those in England. In 1650 people were not allowed by law to work all day Saturday or on Sunday during the summer, most were permitted to work fewer hours in winter and have long lunch breaks, and many enjoyed holidays off.

More important, planters in the early years of the colony provided servants, food, shelter, and clothing. How servants were disciplined was limited and had to be presented to the courts to be implemented, a circumstance that applied equally to whites and Blacks. During these years slaves were accorded the same rights as servants. At the same time, landowners were far away from royal rules and common-law enforcement in England, and many ignored the customs and laws in order to squeeze as much work as they could from both servants and slaves. They had more say over the labors of slaves than servants, and some landowners employed harsh measures while others chose to use incentives. For instance, some planters, in exchange for servants and slaves having independent time, agreed to allow them to clothe and feed themselves for a share of their independent efforts. This practice was well established in Europe and in the Caribbean islands dating back to the 14th century.

> But in the colonial Chesapeake during the seventeenth century, the kaleidoscopic movement of tobacco prices, particularly their dramatic decline in the 1630s, encouraged planters to allow slaves to work independently in periods of economic depression.
>
> *(Berlin, 1998, pp. 33–34)*

The details of the independent labor system were in flux and were fluid, with both parties pushing for concessions. Slaves lobbied for more time off, such as Saturdays, and for late and early days; planters countered by requesting that slaves assume more responsibility for their own care. The outcome was the existence of two economic systems. The nature of the slave economic system was fairly extensive. They had to have land to grow corn and vegetables to feed themselves and their families, and they also grew tobacco for export as well. They raised hogs and cattle, and some slaves produced large amounts of tobacco. Some made handicrafts and shoes, while some engaged in carpentry to add to their farming income, and they sometimes sold their time for pay (Reiss, 1997; Wright, 2017).

The slave economy meant that to sell their goods and buy supplies, the slaves needed loans and people to invest with them. Usually, these moneys were provided by landowners and neighbors. These economic transactions required that slaves be free to move around the area; so they learned about the physical layout and terrain of the Chesapeake. They traded with planters and merchants and acquired debts and rented land; some also willed property to relatives. The planters grew uneasy with this secondary slave economy. As their discomfort grew in Maryland and Virginia, local officials joined with their own disapproval, and they began to prohibit slaves from engaging in trading activities. The planters issued pronouncements to abolish it, but it was not enforced. The planters went to the courts, but the practice continued after the courts added its prohibition.

The slave economic arrangement meant more working hours for slaves, but the benefits provided some modicum of control as well as economic and social opportunity and, for some, a chance to buy their freedom. The arrangements brought to the Chesapeake a new economic system that overlapped with the planters' system of staple production for international export. The free time allowed slaves the opportunity to establish their own gardens, raise livestock, hunt, fish, and make items for sale in the markets. In the face of these developments, planters used harsh methods of discipline to squeeze more from their slaves and servants, and they began to view the workers as commodities.

The agreement with indentured servants was they would work until the end of their terms of service and then would be able to secure land and livestock to start their own farms. Several factors disrupted this arrangement. One was a high mortality rate for Europeans in the new land (many died due to illnesses against which they had little immunity), coupled with the reality that much of the viable land was taken by the time their terms of service ended, and tobacco prices fell by 1640. This situation meant that not many indentured servants were able to turn their status into landowners.

The situation meant that the freed servants became landless and unemployed, yet many of them were also armed (for protection in the colonies), and they began to rebel against their circumstances. Many planters tried several options to remedy the matter and ease the displeasure of landless servants. For instance, in 1676 Nathaniel Bacon, an English merchant, led an armed revolt known as Bacon's Rebellion, which included Black and white men who were former or current indentured servants, small farmers, and slaves, all of whom felt deeply dissatisfied with their lot in the colony. The rebels succeeded in capturing and destroying Jamestown, colonial Virginia's capital. Their uprising was directed at the colonial governor, and it marked the first of this type of insurrection in the British colonies. Bacon's Rebellion was followed by similar unrest in Maryland a year later. Landowners were deeply disturbed and sought to prevent similar unrest.

> Landowners tried several methods of preventing the growth of these poorer classes, including lengthening terms of servitude and seeing to passage of laws preventing those without property from voting. Still, the problem remained. Servitude had provided a labor force, but it had brought with it a disruptive class of young men. The circumstance might have been different had the landowners in Virginia and Maryland been able to own these men as chattel slaves for the duration of their lives and the lives of their offspring.
>
> *(Wright, 2017, p. 72)*

Complicating the situation further for the colonists and planters prior to the rebellion by Bacon and other armed groups, there was tension between the Native Americans and colonists; it seemed to be more difficult to maintain friendly relationships. Given that the colonists had come into the Natives' home, Native people were displeased with how matters developed. By 1622 there was open conflict between them, and the colonists' efforts to enslave Native Americans only added to the increased hostile relations. Among the Indigenous people who were enslaved, many were not suited to the rigors of the labor required to grow tobacco, and they died or ran away.

Planters were not willing to enslave other Europeans or their "own" people—people from their own race. But it was clear, at least in their minds, that they needed a labor force that could be controlled. Various factors combined to decrease the supply of white servants for the Chesapeake planters, such as competition from other colonies for English servants, wars involving England and its people, and declining English birth rates—all of these factors contributed to the decrease in numbers of white servants. By 1680, while planters still imported whites (mainly Irish criminals) as servants, they also sought to change course for their labor needs. Wright (2017) observes that several factors converged to change the labor force. He notes that

> the decline of sufficient numbers of servants, coupled with the hint of the availability of larger numbers of Africans, the result of English and Dutch shippers participating in the carrying trade from Africa to Barbados and Dutch colonies, helped bring Virginia and Maryland tobacco growers to make the same decision to switch to African slaves that their counterparts on sugar plantations in the Caribbean had made almost half a century earlier.
>
> *(p. 74)*

By 1665 the population of the Chesapeake had grown to about 1,700, of which 300 were Blacks, and a small Black community had grown on the Eastern Shore of Virginia and Maryland with some 40 adults and children. In the late 1600s planters in the Chesapeake began replacing indentured servants with captured Africans. But instead of being brought from the West Indies, slave traders began direct importation from Africa to North American mainland ports. For instance, by 1695 there was more activity in adding slaves to the colony. By 1700 Chesapeake landowners imported some 3,000 Africans, which equaled the total had they imported in the previous twenty years. Consider the change this way, in 1660 the population of Blacks in the Chesapeake did not exceed 1,700, and by 1680 that number was around 4,500 African captives. By the end of the 1600s the African population had grown to some 13,000 (Wright, 2017).

During the early years of the slave economy, Blacks gained experience of the colonial world; they had respite from the fields and farms and were able to meet and get to know colonists from various social stations; and they established social networks with their clients and customers. They were able to use these relationships when disputes or questions about their character were raised. This would also help them when questions were raised about their activities. These relationships could also be sources for investment and loans, and they could leverage these connections and income to secure their freedom.

Nevertheless, the views and opinions of many colonial citizens toward Blacks, free and slave, was clouded by their general status as slaves. They were seen as unworthy and debased, views that were dominant prior to any legal proclamations about their condition as slaves. Yet they were servants, like all others who labored in the colony.

> But the free Blacks' presence in growing numbers subverted the logic of racial slavery in the eyes of white and black alike. As long as the boundary between slavery and freedom remained permeable, and as long as white and black labored in the fields together, racial slavery remained only one labor system among many. If the stigma of color condemned some black people to lifetime servitude, so the stigma of poverty, criminality, immorality, uncertain lineages, and alien religion condemned others—men and women of European pedigree prominent among them—to terms of servitude in which they labored and lived no better than slaves. That black people could, and on rare occasions did, hold slaves and servants themselves suggested that race—like lineages and religion—was just one of many markers in the social order [of the Chesapeake] that Atlantic creoles understood well.
>
> *(Berlin, 1998, p. 38)*

In 1688 the laws in all the Chesapeake region colonies changed to restrict and remove the gains made by many of the Charter generation Africans including Atlantic Creoles; the laws declared that all free Negros were to be slaves.

The Low Country

In the Low Country of the Carolinas and part of Florida, transformations regarding slavery were similar to that in the Chesapeake; the difference was that the exported crops in the Low Country were rice and indigo, which became sources of wealth for planters. The Low Country British colonial settlements emerged in an uneven fashion, with very distinct and varied circumstances for each. The Carolina colony was settled first, followed by Florida, which had been settled by the Spanish. The economic activity of each colony was fragile and tentative at the beginning of this era. Settled in 1670, the Carolina colony was founded by families of successful planters from

South America. The planters had farms, swamps, and marshes converted to plantations in the first decade of the 18th century.

The colonial settlers in Carolina were English, Dutch, French, Scottish, Irish, and Blacks who came from other Atlantic colonies where they spoke English, Spanish, and Creole and most were Christian (Protestant or Catholic). Slaves came along with their owners and knew the language and religious beliefs and practices of Europeans. The colony began during the end of the 17th century and had an economy based on farming and raising livestock; the crops and animals were raised to be sent to the sugar plantations on Caribbean islands, on Barbados, and in South America. The labor pool included white servants, Native Americans, and Black slaves who arrived in small groups. At first the success of the colony required that all groups—whites, Blacks, and Natives—worked together, owners, indentured servants, and slaves.

Like in the other colonies, labor demands in the Carolina colony created uneven equality among the working class. There were also dual threats—one from Spanish Florida to the south and one from Native Americans to the west. These threats meant that it was necessary for slaves to defend the area and be armed. In fact, in 1710 Blacks were part of the colonial militia, and they fought in a few of the armed conflicts of the period.

This combination of external threats and the needs of the economy gave Black slaves an advantage. Furthermore, slaves who objected to harsh treatment could flee into the lowland swamp or into the back country, and some slaves established small and hard to maintain maroon communities. The options that Black slaves had made the colonists see the benefits of less harsh treatment and the value of giving slaves some degree of independence.

Colonists could not monitor slaves' activities on their farms in the early years because the farms were small and needed all-hands-on-deck to maintain them. The situation also called for slaves to take on a range of duties, to be jacks of all trades. They were cattle chasers and field hands, and they assumed other roles as well. This meant slaves were able to set the pace of work, determine standards, and decide on the division of labor. Given the nature of the economy, the colonial settlers agreed that slaves would provide for their own subsistence. As happened in other colonial regions, this generated a slave economy since the slaves often had surpluses of what they made or grew.

Altogether, slaves had considerable freedom and flexibility to move about, trade, earn income, and socialize. These developments unnerved the colonial leaders so much that by 1683 they outlawed some of the slaves' activities. They forbade slaves and servants from engaging in trade, and in 1682 they outlawed use of the owners' land for profit. Other laws were enacted to forbid whites from trading with slaves. Laws passed in 1691 prohibited slaves from being free on Saturdays, and in 1714 slaves lost the right to own hogs, cattle, and horses. However, the laws did not stop the practices as many were hidden from view and went on nonetheless. As the new century came, slave economic activity was deeply rooted in the colony of the Low Country. The range of slaves' activities was broad, including farming, hunting, and fishing. In 1712 lawmakers decreed that slaves must give their income to their owners. The population of Blacks doubled by 1720 and by 1760 comprised 60% of the population of the region. During this time laws were enacted in the Low Country to strip slaves of all rights. Berlin (1998) observes that

> slaveholders and other settlers complained bitterly and frequently about slaves traveling unsupervised through the countryside, congregating in the woods, and visiting Charles Town to carouse, conspire, or worse. But knowledge of the countryside and a willingness to hunt down cattle or stand up to Spaniards were precisely the qualities that slaveholders valued in their slaves. They complained but they accepted it. Indeed, to resolve internal disputes within their own community, European settlers sometimes promoted black participation in the affairs of the colony far beyond the bounds later permitted slaves or even black free men.
>
> *(pp. 69–70)*

The area of the Low Country region known as Florida was settled by the Spanish in 1565 as an outpost built by slaves and guarded by a slave militia from 1672 to 1683. In Florida the situation for slaves was somewhat different under Spanish rule in that the colonial officials sought allies to help then hold back the expansion of the English in the Carolinas. Spanish colonialists reached out to slaves in the Carolina colony to flee and settle in Florida. The English and Spanish conflicts began in earnest in 1686 when the Spanish raided an island off of the Carolina coast and captured a dozen slaves and refused to return them. Instead, they paid them wages, instructed them in Catholicism, and allowed them to marry, all in an effort to build up their colony and to assist the Spanish Crown. In 1693 Spain offered freedom to runaway slaves to the colony. The promises made to runaway slaves were attractive yet hollow. Most escaped slaves who found their way to Spanish territory were enlisted in its militia and sent to raid the lands of their former owners. These forays into each other's colonies went on for some years, erupting into war in which Blacks served to defend both colonies.

North of St. Augustine, the main settlement in the Florida colony, the governor of Florida established a Black settlement, Fort Mose, to house the growing number of Black runaways. In this fort Blacks were able to farm and subsist. The existence of the Spanish settlement served as an irritant to the English planters until 1763, when Florida was taken over by the English.

The Northern Colonies

In the Northern colonies, as in the Chesapeake colonies, the number of Black people was small, and most came from the Caribbean and South America.

Landowners in the north preferred seasoned slaves, with twelve or more years of experience, but by 1708 there was a shift in where slaves to the Northern colonies were imported from. Prior to this shift, Africans came to the north in small lots of two or three, or no more than 12, from the Caribbean; many had been in Barbados for three or four years. Thus, many were familiar with the Atlantic world and their slave status. During the Charter generation a few had established families and their numbers grew through natural increases. The following illustrates the source of slaves in one Northern colony:

> In New York, with the largest slave population in the North, Caribbean imports continued to outnumber African arrivals well into the eighteenth century. Between 1715 and 1730 the count was more than three to one in favor of West Indian slaves; and during the first three decades of the eighteenth century, fully 70 percent of the slaves arriving in New York originated elsewhere in the Americas.
>
> *(Berlin, 1998, p. 49)*

Like in the Chesapeake, Atlantic Creoles stood out in this colonial region because they were able to integrate into colonial society by building relationships with institutions and people with power and influence, and they used the courts to expand their rights or petition for freedom. In New Netherlands, Black labor was essential since there were limits on immigrants and indentured servants. Many of the immigrants preferred trade over farming, leaving a void that the Dutch West India company had to fill. In 1638 there were 100 Blacks in New Amsterdam, which equaled 30% of the population, the largest Black population of any colonial settlement; by 1664 Blacks were 20% of the city's population but only 5% of the entire colony, as was true in the Chesapeake. Also as in the Chesapeake, newly arrived Blacks lived in barracks, and some were able to work on their own. They learned the language and joined the Dutch church; they took marriage vows and baptized their children in the local church. Some adopted children who had lost their parents, which formed kinship ties. In 1635, ten years after the arrival of Blacks to the colony, some Blacks asked the Dutch West India company's leaders in Amsterdam to give them wages but were denied. Blacks worked alongside the white settlers, and they were involved in all phases of colonial life, as was true of Blacks in the Chesapeake. Some were granted freedom, and some of the free did well as members of colonial society. Some Blacks built small communities on the outskirts of Manhattan. In 1664 the English took control of the colony from the Dutch, where a few Blacks were free, had property, and engaged in independent economic activity.

> During the first century of settlement in the North, black people composed a small fraction of the population of New England and the Middle colonies. Only in Rhode Island did they approach the proportion of the

> population achieved in New York, and that did not occur until after midcentury. In most Northern colonies, the proportion was considerably smaller. At its height, the black population totaled only 8 percent of the population of New Jersey and was less than 4 percent in Massachusetts and Connecticut. No visitor could confuse New England or the Middle Colonies with the plantation regimes of the sugar islands where the slaves constituted upward of 80 percent of the population.
>
> *(Berlin, 1998, p. 54)*

Even with their small numbers, they still made up a good portion of the population in the northern region and constituted over half of the workforce. They worked in industrial settings forging iron and in factories, and they worked on farms in New England, the Hudson Valley, and northern New Jersey. In the Northern region, unlike on large plantations, many slaves worked in small groups with their owners and other whites, and their tasks were varied—working the fields, operating a boat, or driving a wagon.

Many planters made no provisions for slaves to live; many slaves were packed in cellars or they lived in garrets, back rooms, closets, and outbuildings. So, with their owners' consent, slaves engaged in economic activities to provide for self-subsistence. They took on trade and, as a result, moved about the region, traveling from the country to the cities for trade and socializing. In the cities they would socialize with servants and the poor citizens of the colony.

> The intermingling of these impoverished, often disaffected, men and women was made easier—particularly in the Middle Colonies—by the fact that many white men and women were also servants, the legal property of a master who could sell, trade, and discipline them at will. Bemoaning disorders caused by "servants apprentice boys, and numbers of Negros," authorities generally lumped white servants and black slaves together. The respectable class in the northern colonies widely shared the perception that the social cleavage ran between free and unfree—not white and black.
>
> *(Berlin, 1998, pp. 59–60)*

Some mixing occurred among Blacks and Native Americans wherein they were able to create a world for themselves. These associations were looked down upon by the members of the upper classes of colonial society in the region, and they tried to prevent the social mixing of races. Even with the objections of the white landowners and officials, when slaves had time to themselves, they sought out their own kind, preferring to be with people of similar status, origins, and circumstances. In the 1690s whites objected to Blacks gatherings on the weekends because they were seen "dancing in the manner of their several nations in Africa, and speaking and singing in their native dialects" (Berlin, 1998, p. 61).

The gathering of Blacks, both free and slave, led colonial officials to outlaw such activities, with particular attention to Sunday, and they forbade the sale of liquor. The legal prohibition had little effect since the nature of urban life made it possible for Blacks to gather regardless of the objections and displeasure of the regional colonial leaders.

Furthermore, during the charter years in the Northern colonies, Black life involved activities like social gatherings, births attended to by Black midwives, consensual marriages, and African burials. Berlin (1998) says the burial ceremonies constituted the first Black created institution in the Northern colonies. For instance, in 1699, some 20 years after Blacks' arrival in Philadelphia, a section of a graveyard was designated for Blacks. Many of the planters avoided being involved in the burials of departed Blacks, so it was possible for Blacks, both free and slave, to accord the dead appropriate dignity and respect of their traditions. They dressed in their finest garments, sang and played music, and marched in groups to the burial grounds, often while being led by an important community member. Following what they recalled of African practices, they would often leave gifts for the departed, who might be dressed with beads, amulets, and other objects, and from time to time they would include food and drink so the spirit would be nourished. With the burial rites left to Blacks to perform, this was the only aspect of their lives free of interferences and control; all other activities were constrained by the planters and colonial officials.

The activities and accomplishments of northern Blacks reveal something about their thinking and feelings. For instance, when given the opportunity, they sought out one another so they could socialize, revealing emotional ties to what they knew of their past lives and ancestors. They showed deep emotional commitment to the burial rites, which were extremely important for Africans. With their ability to move around the colony came the opportunity to gather knowledge about the people and to learn about the sentiments of the ruling class. And their social activities with other servants as well as their proximity to whites that they worked for provided more data for them to assess other options and opening points with which to gain their liberty. Many of the slaves knew the basics of the system; they were often seasoned, having lived and worked in other Atlantic settlements prior to coming to the North American mainland. They often sought ways out of their slave status or, at the minimum, tried to lessen the burdens of their lives. Blacks sought each other out for socialization, and, when doing so, practiced what some could remember of their African traditions.

As in the other regions, the number of slaves in the Northern colonies increased, and there also was a rural/urban difference in slave life. In this region, slaves were actively discouraged from having families since many lived in small homes of whites, in closets, attics, and related spaces, so there was less room for families. Moreover, slaves were allowed to dress like their owners, unlike the slaves in the hotter southern colonies who lacked garments. Northern slaves were also allowed more freedom of movement, as some would be hired out to other people in town. Nevertheless, as slaves in the Northern colonies grew in numbers, the ruling class saw fit to "close the vice" on them, and new harsh restrictions were enacted.

The Lower Mississippi Valley

The French settlers in the region had ambitions of creating a colony that was like the Caribbean islands they knew, where slave labor was dominant. To meet their goals, the planters requested African slaves from the French Royal Charter company that oversaw the settlement in the Lower Mississippi Valley. The charter officials were content for the settlement to operate as a military outpost, so around 1715 Native Americans became the major labor source along with a handful of Africans. The few Africans who came to the French outposts were Atlantic Creoles who knew their rights and obligations and spoke French. For the most part, the colony was unable to focus on developing farms and viable crops for export. The white French immigrants, mostly servants, poor men, and former criminals, were not up to the task of clearing forests and swamps for planting. The colonists instead took on the ways of Native people, and many colonists intermarried with the Natives. In fact, Native Americans were essential for the survival of the colony. They provided food, clothing, medicine, and protection from rival tribes. The Native allies provided captives through their battles with other tribes in the region, such that in 1722 it was determined that some 200 Native Americans were held as slaves in French Louisiana.

By 1721 the colony grew with the arrival of some 7,000 white former servants who were castoffs from French or German countries; they showed little appetite for clearing the land for farming and, worse, few had knowledge of agriculture. So planters again requested of the Crown African slaves, saying they would leave the colony if they did not get them. Between 1721 and 1731 some 6,000 Africans slaves were brought directly from Africa to Louisiana (although many did not survive the journey), and the arrival of the survivors altered the labor pool in the colony. In time, the Africans assumed many skilled and unskilled tasks. Many Europeans servants fled the colony, while those who stayed lived in cities like New Orleans.

Africans who were brought to Louisiana directly from Africa had a rocky road since many died due to neglect and the rigors of the passage from Africa. For instance, the saga of one slave ship tells the story of some 450 Africans on board when the ship left Africa in 1729. Nearly 100 died along the way, with 363 making it to the Mississippi river port. But many of them were so ill upon arrival that two-thirds died soon after entering the port; in the end, fewer than 100 remined alive, and about 350 Africans had lost their lives in the journey.

The Africans slowly overcame the challenges of living in the new setting, and by 1731 the Black population had grown to approximately 4,000, which was 60% of the Lower Mississippi Valley colonial population. French Louisiana became a Black-majority colony, and the slaves had many roles and duties since they were the primary source of labor. This meant that the slaves interacted freely with all sorts of people and had a central hand in the economic life of the colony. More important, they were able to quickly learn the ways of the European colonists.

Colonists, with the aid of the African slaves, were able to build an agricultural base in tobacco and indigo, and more land was cleared for farming, making it possible to export crops in larger quantities. As conflicts with Native Americans increased, the French colonists enlisted African warriors in the defense of the colony. All of these developments opened a path for free Black people to exist and prosper.

In the Lower Mississippi Valley, the slave system changed to one in which slaves became part of society. In this region there were fewer restrictions, unlike in the plantation system, in part because there was less emphasis on international exports; instead, the economy was diverse, as was the work slaves undertook. They were able to develop a range of skills and were expected to tend to their own needs, which meant they had to feed and clothe themselves and furnish their homes. This environment encouraged family formation and sparked independent market activity on the part of slaves, who were able to devote part of their day to self-sustaining activities, mostly for profit. In addition, like in the 17th century, slaves worked alongside whites and Native Americans. The area also saw changes when its rulers changed from the French to the Spanish, who were open to slaves being released from slavery.

The Planters' Power

As some historians (Berlin, 1998; Harms, 2018; Reiss, 1997; Thornton, 1998; Wright, 2017) tell it, when the colonial leaders contemplated the matter of how to secure sufficient labor to meet the needs of the growing colonies, there were multiple options. They could bring in more white European servants, enslave larger numbers of Native Americans, or import more Africans. The white servants had the ability to run away and evade capture by blending into the population; the Native people knew the area and had allies among their fellow Native Americans and could run and mount considerable resistance to being held captive. Africans, on the other hand, were isolated, had no defenders, and could escape but not hide since their skin color gave them away. While they did run away and resist, their lack of allies and visibility made them ideal for exploitation, and they were less expensive to own since the white servants could only be held for the length of their contracts, but Africans could be held for life. Not to mention, there seemed to be an endless supply of Africans.

Across the regions, British colonists passed laws that were contrary to English common law, like the law of 1662 that determined the fate of Black children based on their mothers' statuses. The colonial laws achieved several goals: they increased the supply of slaves, and they maintained the racial distinctions between enslaved and free persons. As other colonies followed the legal processes to limit the lives of Africans and to further racial distinctions, such as specifically forbidding interracial marriages and relationships, the obstacles to Black freedom grew in number and were aimed at fundamental areas of life, family, and interpersonal relationships. By 1750 the slave's status as property was well established (Horton & Horton, 2005). Africans were set apart from white European colonists and servants. Gradually more and more rights were accorded to whites and denied to Blacks, and free Blacks became rare.

Planters' Views of Africans

Another factor in the treatment of Blacks was Europeans' views of them, including perceptions and views of Black men and women as childlike. Europeans are said to have had a negative perception of Africans based on early contact with them in the 15th century, and Europeans made negative assumptions about the meaning of differences in physical appearance and culture between them and Africans that led to their views. For instance, Blackness was equated with being evil and uncivilized in the language and customs of Europeans. Many Europeans and Americans of all stations believed that Africans and their descendants had no distinct culture of their own:

> In … North America, people of African descent have seen their homeland portrayed as a primitive society in an arrested state of development and themselves as a congenitally backward people.… The governor of South Carolina asserted what would become conventional wisdom for most white Americans.… The African negro is destined by Providence [Divine intervention] to occupy a condition of servile dependency.… It is marked on the face, stamped on the skin, and evinced by the intellectual inferiority and natural improvidence of the race.… They are in all respects—physical, moral, and political—inferior … [and] are doomed to this hopeless condition by the very qualities which unfit them for a better life.
>
> *(Berlin, 2010, p. 3)*

So Europeans had set in their minds the low status of Blacks, and Europeans' treatment of Africans communicated much of their sentiment about the captives. For some colonists, the Africans' appearance—with facial scars, filed teeth, languages the colonists could not understand, and strange customs—meant these people were brutish and savage. The presence of Africans made whites uncomfortable, and they saw a need to regulate their lives; for instance, in the 1640s and 1650s legal decisions defined how Blacks and whites would live on different terms. With many arriving Africans weak from the horrors and the psychological shock of captivity and the Middle Passage, colonists sought to weaken their spirits further by denying Africans their given names and labeling them with random first names to diminish their sense of identity and weaken their sense of heritage to remove Africans kinship lineages.

By 1640, 20 years after the initial arrival of Africans, a major obstacle for Africans was erected: life servitude was made legal. And while the ideas about race and race relations were still taking shape, it was nevertheless clear that white and African servants would be treated differently. The racial distinctions made in practice or in daily life were followed by statutes that set the foundation for many of the limits enacted by laws that made slavery part of the fabric of the country (Carter & Scheuermann, 2020).

The process of stripping Africans of their sense of self occurred, during the 17th and 18th centuries, after the importation of Africans increased. In their first few months in the colony, many would be taken to specialized areas, away from the main farms and fields, where they would be forced to perform menial repetitive tasks that required little knowledge and skill. This was to acclimate them to their role as laborers. During this time they were kept in barracks segregated by sex and given meager rations of food, clothes, and medicine. The colonists' goal was to create completely dependent people. In the latter decades of the 17th century, as more Africans arrived, attitudes toward them continued to harden.

Africans' Experiences and Reactions

While it seems customary to tell the story of Africans from their entry to the North Americans mainland in 1619, I want to capture not just the events of that time but Africans' experiences and psychological states, as best as can be done with limited available evidence, since this book is about what they did to survive the oppression, racism, and inhumane treatment visited upon them. What were the psychological, emotional, and cultural adjustments required for their survival and, indeed, prosperity? While it is important to know how they were treated, it is equally important to know how they reacted to that treatment. Complicating these questions is the fact that there are few records or documents from Africans from their points of view. I am left to infer or to imagine from what evidence does exist the potential reactions and internal processes they may have had.

In the previous chapter, I discussed the issues of whether Africans held onto their cultural ways, but I did not discuss their emotional and psychological experiences. How did they feel and think after being captured and taken through the door of "no return" (exits from forts or camps, where they were taken to ships as cargo)?

Historians and scholars (e.g., Harms, 2018) have done a good job of documenting the numbers of ships that carried slaves and the estimated number of slaves transported to the New World. While knowing the scale of the slave trade is vital, that scale also obscures the individual's experience. Less is known about the person's experience, and what is known is mostly from which regions of Africa many captives came from (see chapter 3). I also presented in that chapter some of the Africans' cultural beliefs, with glimpses into how individuals might have responded to their capture. We also learned about how Atlantic Creoles came into being and how they used their in-between status to prosper in the Atlantic world.

Yet it would help us to understand Africans experiences better if we follow them from the point of capture to their sale in North American mainland colonies. I acknowledge that, before the New World slave trade, some Africans were sold in the Old World long before slave markets emerged in North America, but the New World era is the focus of this volume.

Historians (e.g., Asante, 2019; Harms, 2018) say the Atlantic slave trade lasted for many centuries, and Wright (2017) states that it

> began shortly before 1450 with the export of enslaved Africans to continental Europe and sugar plantations on the Atlantic islands off Africa, and lasted until after the middle of the nineteenth century.
>
> *(pp. 23–24)*

In telling the story of Africans, historians and scholars (Bennett, 1988; Berlin, 1998, 2003; Harms, 2018; Reiss, 1997; Wright, 2017) have tended to focus more on the horrors of the Middle Passage and less on what happened upon capture and before being placed on slave ships for transport. Wright (2017) points out that "the hardships Africans encountered from the time of capture to the point of sale are frequently overlooked because of the absence of evidence" (p. 46). He posits that the voyages to the New World lasted for one to two months, while the time from being kidnapped or captured to boarding a slave vessel could last from six months to a year. Some have suggested that it was this part of the captives' experience that accounted for more death and illness than the Middle Passage (Wright, 2017).

A description of Africans who were marched to the coast from the interior reveals that their legs were tied together, two-by-two, in such a way that they could only walk slowly. They were kept in small groups and were fixed to one another by the neck. At night each captive's hands were bound as they slept, and food was in short supply (Equiano, 2003). The varied environments that African captives had to pass through would mean they could be struck with diseases not common to their home regions. People not accustomed to forest could develop sleeping sickness, while those who lived in dry or higher elevations and were taken through low wet areas could, and some did, develop malaria and yellow fever. Added to the shock of capture was the probability of becoming sick. To add to their burden and to aid their captors, they were made to carry trade goods, some weighing 30 to 50 pounds, as they marched to the coast. Once at the coast they often would have to wait in dungeons, camps, or forts for several months for ships to arrive. "It is clear, however, that the African man, woman or child presented for sale to a ship captain for conveyance to the New World was already a survivor" (Wright, 2017, p. 47).

While the history of slavery occurred over the course of 400 or more years, and several million Africans were captured and transported to the New World, each person might have been a father, mother, wife, husband, sister, brother, son, uncle, or daughter. Each was part of a family and community. Each person had their life interrupted, including the daily activities, and the place each had in their village or community. Each had strengths, personal qualities, and a personality. Each had wisdom, wishes, dreams, aspirations, and activities that they enjoyed or pain they endured. Each contributed to their family system, with its unique history, and each had talents, abilities, and phases of life to look forward to.

Consider what each endured moving through daily activities like you or I do—then, in a blink of an eye!—their lives changed in ways that none could have imagined. As discussed in previous chapters, slavery was common in Africa, but there slavery did not negate the person's humanity; a slave in African communities still mattered and was respected as a person. Not so in the New World Atlantic slavery system: the person's life as they knew it ended for the price of five and a half pounds in 1680 (before that, somewhat less), which rose to 20 pounds by 1780. That was not much, it could be argued, for a life that could not be lived on its original terms (Wright, 2017).

Olaudah Equiano's (2003) description of his kidnapping provides a glimpse into these events. He was born in 1745 and was tasked with keeping watch over the village where he lived (which suggests the villagers knew about the kidnappings) while other village residents cared for the community crops, which were a distance from the village. He describes how the villagers worked collectively to tend to the food crops and how they had to defend the village from attacks, which were common. Often these attacks would come while they were tending the fields. He tells how he witnessed a battle near him in which the village adults prevailed. On the days that adults would go to work in the fields, children would gather in one place where they would have protection from potential assailants or kidnappers. He tells it this way:

> One day, as I was watching at the top of a tree in our yard, I saw one of those people coming into the yard of our next neighbours but one, to kidnap, there being many stout young people in it. Immediately, on this, I gave the alarm of the rouge, and he was surrounded by the stoutest of them, whom entangled him with cords so that he could not escape till some of the grown people came and secured him. But, alas! ere long it was my fate to be thus attacked, and to be carried off, when none of the grown people were nigh. One day, with all of our people were gone out to their works as usual, and only I and my dear sister were left to mind

> the house, two men and a woman got over our walls, and in a moment seized us both; and, without giving us time to cry out, or make resistance, they stopped our mouths, tied our hands, and ran off with us into the nearest wood: and continued to carry us as far as they could, till night came on, when we reached a small house, where the robbers halted for refreshment, and spent the night.
>
> *(Equiano, 2003, p. 47)*

We can grasp how this 11-year-old and his sister were ripped from their lives, home, and family. The overwhelming reactions to being kidnapped was extreme distress and terror. One moment their lives were on a normal and expected course; the next moment it turned to an unknown course and a set of terrifying experiences. Wright states that once Africans encountered Europeans, usually upon arrival at the coastal forts or factories, they were subjected to new traumas. One was meeting foreign people who some Africans thought were spirits or had caught them for meals. Add to this shock the visual of the large ships in the waters, these images and sights brought on new horrors and fears. Many Africans were petrified that the whites were going to reduce them to foodstuffs or oils; in essence, they feared certain death. Wright (2017) states that "the psychological effect of the entire experience on the captive cannot be measured but some witnesses described a continued state of depression as the norm for Africans through much of the time following their enslavement" (p. 53).

Africans were weakened to the point that it was easier for them to contract European-borne illness, and some were so destroyed and distraught that they took their own lives (Reiss, 1997; Wright, 2017). Their trauma continued as they boarded the ships, where they were washed, shaved, some branded, and again put in chains. The Africans' experiences on these voyages were not extensively documented, but sometimes captains or surgeons wrote their observations and perspectives of the Middle Passage, writing to stop the trade or to justify slavery. Wright (2017) states:

> Recent studies focusing on the statistical evaluation of thousands of voyagers aid … in doing so [evaluating the human toll]. They show that efforts toward more or less humane treatment of the captives mattered little to the way uprooted Africans coped. Random influences, or at least factors largely beyond the control of even the most experienced captains, had greatest effect on slave health and mortality between Africa and the Americas.
>
> *(p. 54)*

Many of the captives were young men, who were preferred by planters, but women and children were also put to work alongside men at early years of the slave trade. The sex ratio favored men, and kidnappers avoided taking children and older people, but this was not always possible if captains wanted their cargo holds to be full. The horrors and traumas continued once the ships set sail. Africans were placed in small spaces lying chained in spooned positions. There was no provision for waste disposal. On occasion they would be brought to the deck to jump as a way to exercise, but they received limited food rations. Many died due to disease and dehydration, a common condition on board slave vessels. Yet some historians attribute African survival to their intimate connections to one another (Smallwood, 2007).

No studies are available to reveal the full extent of the psychological damage done to the people captured and transported, but it is possible to infer trauma reactions. Today a lot more is known about trauma and its attendant reactions and symptoms, but we can assume these would also apply to the people in the 15th and 16th centuries. When faced with traumatic experiences, people seek to fight, they run away, or they freeze. When freezing, the person becomes emotionally numb and cut off from their feelings; they dissociate, deny, and repress their emotions; and they are subject to a range of reactions and manifestations to these responses. They would attribute what was happening to them to the spirits, ancestors, or God's will. Others would think they were being punished for bad acts or thoughts they had. Perhaps they felt guilt and some responsibility for being caught and taken to who knows where.

If they survived the voyage—and many did not—they were met with new forms of brutal treatment. They continued to be treated as objects as they were prepared for sale, quarantined, and allowed time to regain strength. Some were brought to an island near the mainland of North America, while others arrived in northern ports, where Africans often encountered new illnesses. This transitional period could last weeks or months, and more would die. One estimate is that, between 1710 and 1718, 5% or more of those who arrived in North American ports died before being sold, and more died within the first year. Wright (2017) notes that about one-quarter of the new arrivals in the Chesapeake and more than one-third in the Low Country did not survive the first year.

The psychological and emotional harm was extreme, and the surviving captives were bewildered to be cast in the role of beast of burden, laboring from dawn to dusk under the constant threat of violence as well as actual assaults. Regardless of how Africans were characterized by Europeans and North American mainland colonists, they were individuals, and many functioned in a fog and state of psyche numbness. In this inexplicable circumstance some tried to connect with their fellow captives to regain their sense of self. It seems possible that in the minds and hearts of many who were transported to this new reality was a resolve and determination to hold onto as much of their humanity as possible and to find a path to survival and freedom. They did not come to this situation as empty shells; rather, they came with their personalities from families and communities with traditions, beliefs, knowledge, skills, and emotions.

Adjusting to life in the colonies was a difficult process for most Africans. For the Atlantic Creoles, it was a bit easier since they knew some of the languages, commercial practices, and cultural ways. They had lived in proximity to Europeans in South America and the Caribbean, and they were part European, which gave them an advantage in the colonies. Their African brethren had a more difficult adjustment as little of the North American life was familiar, not the environment or the social or cultural ways of the new, strange people.

Many of the African captives were also enraged and bewildered. Not only were they swept away from their families and kinship networks, but they were also removed from the connections they made with others during capture and transport. Wright (2017) contends that these early experiences were the most trying and difficult because the African was alone, having been suddenly removed from all that was normal and comforting. There were no social, economic, or psychological anchors for them. These were gone, and to survive they had to create new emotional and psychological anchors.

There is considerable debate about how Africans reacted to slavery and what they did to protect themselves emotionally. It seems fair to say that they reached inside and used what they knew to anchor themselves in their new reality. They also used what was available and what they could gather from one another to forge their lives in North America. The process was slow and hard, Wright (2017) explains:

> In trying to cope and build new lives, the uprooted Africans tended to cling to their own cultural traditions and ways of doing things. These included a sense of personal identity; a language; a worldview that usually involved a religion; ideas of time and space, family life, and work; social customs; historical traditions; and a good bit of general know-how.
>
> *(p. 120)*

Yet, there were also considerable regional variation among Africans since some identified with white colonists and sought to follow European ways; some were content to survive the best way they could in the close confines of colonial life; and others were happy to be immersed in Black communities. Many sought out other Africans to socialize and build connections. Despite the complex relationships between Blacks and whites, Blacks were able to enact their own traditional practices (Bennett, 1988; Berlin, 1998; Dodson, 2002; Reiss, 1997; Wright, 2017). What were the elements of Black culture that began to be expressed during the colonial era?

There is evidence that Africans exhibited a range of behaviors and expressed thoughts related to their traditional ways, some observed by colonists; these may have been more evident in the early years of the settlements in each of the regions. It is fair to argue that the people who lived during the charter years in mainland North America were heterogenous and reflected a variety of psychological, emotional, and behavioral reactions. The majority seemed to accept their fate and status and acted in ways that might inspire acceptance from the colonial leaders and citizens. Some sought to assimilate into European society; they spoke, dressed, acted, worshipped, and lived like Europeans, as much as that was possible, given how Europeans looked down on them as a group and as individuals. There had to be some who were not sure of what to do, so they did what was possible to survive. In could also be that the terror and trauma of the Middle Passage and years of enslavement numbed many to their situation, so they surrendered to the power of the colonial life and circumstance. Perhaps they were in denial of the situation, believing that what had happened was not so bad and that the ancestors and God would provide. There could be the process of splitting off oneself and living one's life in psychological compartments such that their true self could not be touched. Many may have lost touch with reality altogether and were lost in their own minds.

Some African may have taken solace in the knowledge that others, regardless of race, were dealt the same fate and lived under the same sorts of oppression and domination. Yet others likely refused to surrender and found ways to push back and reclaim their humanity through death or escape. While others plotted rebellion, a few acted out in small ways. But, when it was possible, Africans sought an outlet and built connections and kinship groups. They used these opportunities to speak their native tongue or pidgin languages and recreate their native music and dance. When possible, they held on to and practiced important rites and rituals learned in their homeland. They sought to earn their way to freedom and to free their family members; it seemed that this objective may have been at the forefront of their minds.

The road to freedom was wider for the members of the Charter generation since racial distinctions then were not as firmly established as they would become. Still, the Charter generation would have needed a patron to press their case for freedom, and colonial officials needed to be open to such requests. Such achievements likely took many years or decades to accomplish and may have required a confluence of factors for success.

There is the story of Francis Payne—"who began slave life in the Chesapeake in 1637 as 'Francisco a Negroe'.... When Payne's owner ... married a Maryland planter and left Virginia for her new husband's estate" (Berlin, 1998, p. 36)—whose mistress entered into an arrangement with him in which he would run the property; in exchange, he could earn his freedom and for his family. In 1656, after 20 years as a slave, Francis Payne was a free man, and he later extended that arrangement to secure the freedom of his family. He had made a seemingly impossible bargain based on a desperate desire for freedom and an extraordinary ability. When his obligations had been discharged, the Payne family took its place alongside the Anthony Johnson family, who we met at the beginning of this chapter, in the ranks of the Chesapeake's free families.

References

Asante, M. K. (2019). *The history of Africa: The quest for eternal harmony* (3rd ed.). Routledge.

Bennett, L. (1988). *Before the Mayflower: A history of Black America*. Johnson Publishing.

Berlin, I. (1998). *Many thousands gone: The first two centuries of slavery in North America London, England*. Belknap Press of Harvard University Press.

Berlin, I. (2003). *Generations of captivity: London, England*. Belknap Press of Harvard University Press.

Berlin, I. (2010). *The making of African America: The four great migrations*. Viking.

Carter, R. T., & Scheuermann, T. D. (2020). *Confronting racism: Integrating mental health strategies with legal reform*. Routledge.

Dodson, H. (2002). *Jubilee: The emergence of African-American culture*. National Geographic.

Equiano, O. (2003). *The interesting narrative and other writings*. Penguin Classics.

Harms, R. (2018). *Africa in global history with sources*. Norton.

Horton, J. O., & Horton, L. E. (2005). *Slavery and the making of America*. Oxford University Press.

Reiss, O. (1997). *Blacks in colonial America*. McFarland.

Smallwood, S. E. (2007). *Saltwater slavery: A middle passage from Africa to American diaspora*. Harvard University Press.

Thornton, J. K. (1998). *Africa and Africans in the making of the Atlantic world, 1400–1800*. (2nd ed.). Cambridge University Press.

Wright, D. R. (2017). *African Americans in the colonial era* (4th ed.). Wiley Blackwell.

5

THE RISE OF THE PLANTATION IN THE COLONIES

The previous chapter describes the experiences of Africans and Atlantic Creoles as they entered the mainland North American British colonies. The story of the Charter generation's participation in the various colonies was similar; slaves had some degree of independence and engaged in some economic activity. These opportunities afforded them the ability to have families and, in some instances, form communities. More importantly, some Africans and their descendants sought to be part of the social structure of their respective colonies by joining churches, being baptized, having their marriages registered, and availing themselves of the legal system—and some were even able to end their bondage and join the ranks of landowners (Reiss, 1997).

Yet, as the colonies matured and became more stable, there were shifts in the racial makeup of the labor pool and in the viability of the crops that were being produced. Some historians characterize the middle decades of the 17th century through the later decades of the 18th century as the Plantation generation for Blacks (e.g., Berlin, 1998). The changes in colonial life during this era were uneven; nevertheless, in most regions of the North American mainland, most colonies shifted from societies with slaves to slave societies. Each region produced crops and other commodities, and some established one or two staple crops that were responsible for the colony's economic growth. For instance, in the Chesapeake, the staple crop was tobacco; in the Low Country of South Carolina, the staples were rice and indigo; in the Lower Mississippi Valley, sugar and cotton were the crops that served as the basis of the economy; while the Northern colonies manufactured industrial supplies, provided educational and technological aid, and imported slaves to southern colonies (Franklin & Moss, 2000).

The focus of this chapter is on the developments of the Plantation generation in the North American mainland regions and the implications for white colonial

DOI: 10.4324/9781003111542-8

inhabitants and Africans. The chapter proceeds with a discussion of the regions and the actions of the planters, followed by a discussion of Africans' reactions to their lives in bondage and to the circumstances that they had to endure.

The Growing Colonies and the Plantation Generation

In some colonial regions, the means and methods of crop production differed on the small, owner-operated farms and the larger estates or plantations. With these changes in crop production, where more landowners invested in larger estates and began to grow crops in larger volume, the lives of Blacks also became more constrained as farms grew to large estates; in particular, how Blacks/Africans were characterized, perceived, and treated also changed. Slaves in society offered more liberty and the means to earn additional income and have expanded social relationships. But when farms became plantations, slave societies also emerged. The transformation from societies with slaves to slave societies occurred differently in the four regions: the Northern colonies, the Chesapeake, the Low Country, and the Lower Mississippi Valley. The regions grew somewhat different crops and had varied climates and different labor needs.

In some regions, slaves were part of the labor pool (societies with slaves) along with other workers, servants, and small farmers. When the former collaborative working arrangements became predominately Black/African workers, white servants eventually left the area since they could not compete for work with the planters' forced laborers. Moreover, slaveholders were able to dominate and dictate to the regions' legislative bodies and government officials, thus legislatively creating slave societies. The planters had slave codes enacted that bestowed upon them the right to control the lives of their slaves. During the years of the Charter generation, slaves and servants were for the most part equals as they traveled, gathered together at will, held property, and traded in markets; these were societies with slaves. Later these types of activities were curtailed in some regions.

> Slaveholders elaborated the logic of subordination, generally finding the sources of their dominance in some rule of nature or law of God.
>
> Since slavery became exclusively identified with people of African descent in the New World, the slaveholders' explanation of their own dominance generally took the form of racial ideologies.
>
> *(Berlin, 1998, p. 9)*

The Chesapeake Region

In the Chesapeake region, planters in the 1650s settled on tobacco as the crop for international markets. They reasoned that it would be viable and more profitable if more land and labor were dedicated to growing tobacco.

One of their actions that reshaped the labor pool was making slavery legal. The regional authorities declared in 1660 that the status of Africans and their descendants would be that of slaves for life. In this pronouncement the reliance on indentured servants was reduced as more Africans, who were less costly to acquire, began to replace white servants and Native Americans in the region (Fredrickson, 1998).

One of the events that took place after lifetime slave status was established and confirmed the planters' thoughts about their labor needs was the revolt on the region's capital, Jamestown, Virginia, led by Nathaniel Bacon in 1676. The restlessness and demands of the wayward former white servants and slaves sealed, for the landowners with large holdings, the decision to use slaves as their labor source and expand their production of crops for international export (Horton & Horton, 2005).

The number of Africans brought to the region increased; one estimate is that between 1675 and 1690, 3,000 Africans entered the region. The colony was still majority white, but that was changing as planters relied more on slaves and as the source of slaves shifted from the Caribbean to Africa. During the Charter generation, slaves were experienced and came in small groups from the Caribbean islands, and these slaves had knowledge of the Atlantic world, could speak the language, knew the cultural practices, and were able to participate in colonial society. However, the more recent arrivals came directly from the African continent.

> By the turn of the century—eighty years after the first black people arrived at Jamestown and some forty years after the legalization of slavery—newly arrived Africans composed nearly 90 percent of the slave population, and their dramatic influx into the Chesapeake profoundly transformed black life.
>
> *(Berlin, 1998, p. 110)*

The new African arrivals came weak and dispirited, as well as unaccustomed to what was expected of them, so planters devised methods to season and communicate with them. The new Blacks would spend their days laboring on farms and plantations. To accomplish their orientation, planters created training facilities used for acclimating the new workers. The newly arrived Africans lived in gender-specific barracks and spent their days doing repetitive, menial tasks, and they learned to respond to the European or random names assigned to them—another means to reduce their will and sense of self and to instill dependency.

The planters understood that while Africans had few connections, did not understand the language, and did not know where they were located, they still had to be controlled, usually with violence. So violence—sanctioned by legislative action—was used and grew in complexity and frequency to induce fear. In essence, Africans were subjected to acts of torture and physical assaults to get them to work and act in ways that planters and colonists found acceptable.

Force and violence were needed to maintain the planters' dominance, so the colonial authorities made legal and permissible the power to commit acts of violence against slaves using the rod, lash, and branding irons; in 1669 it was no longer a crime in Virginia to maim or kill a slave. "In the years to follow, Chesapeake lawmakers expanded the power of slaveholders and diminished the rights of slaves even further," and a slave code was enacted in Virginia in 1705 (Berlin, 2003, p. 61).

In the process of importing more and more Africans, little attention was given to their health and well-being. From capture to sale, many died along the way. For the planters, the high rate of mortality was solved by increasing the numbers brought to the mainland since Africans were inexpensive relative to financial gains.

Planters wanted to limit the movement and interactions of Africans in order to maintain strict control and reduce growing fears that the people being forced to work would object, perhaps with force. To assuage their fears, planters established more rules and so-called safeguards. Planters were mindful of the interracial relationships that had formed between free farmers, servants, Native people, and slaves in the earlier years of the colony, and they wanted to stamp out any possible new connections. So in 1705 new laws required slaves to have a pass granting travel outside of their home plantations. Slaves were also not permitted to gather in groups larger than four and could only gather for brief periods of time. To ensure compliance, planters levied fines on one another.

In response to the growing Black population, planters, landowners, and local authorities decided to unite the poor and working-class whites and the white elites, shutting off connections with Blacks by elevating whites and pushing down Blacks who previously had some freedom and opportunity. To accomplish the goal of elevating poor whites, it was necessary to make skin color a status symbol for whites and a mark of inferiority for Blacks, thus creating a new social order based on race. White servants were elevated to a higher status in the social order—irrespective of their circumstances—based on their skin color. Whites who were not landowners and not part of the political system were raised to where they could assume roles reflecting their new status. It made sense to enlist them as slave catchers, overseers, stewards, slave drivers, and other roles that supported the landed gentry. In these roles they were often required to hand out punishment to control the slaves who might run or resist the control of the landowners. For example, one planter, Robert "King" Carter, who had a large plantation, petitioned the court for permission to maim one of his new Africans for running away.

As the wealth of the planters grew, so did their influence and their ability to dictate legislation, create new laws, and determine the outcome of court decisions. "The grandees steadily expanded their holdings and tightened their grip on colonial legislatures and county courts" (Berlin, 1998, p. 117).

> The assumption of near absolute sovereignty reflected the rapid expansion of the planters' power during the first decades of the eighteenth century. Having enslaved back people and confined the remaining white servants to a subordinate place in Chesapeake society, the grandees knit themselves together through strategic marriages, carefully crafted business dealings, and elaborate rituals, creating a style of life which awed common folks and to which lesser planters dared not aspire. By mid-century, the great planters had forged an interlocking directorate, tied together by family loyalties, business partnerships, political allegiances, and grand displays at taverns, cotillions, and courthouses.
>
> *(Berlin, 1998, p. 117)*

In their minds, the planters thought of themselves as fathers or parents who wielded authority and required deference; at the same time that the planters' empires grew, so did the population of Africans. But more than that, enough time had passed for Blacks to reproduce and for the number of American-born slaves to increase.

Increases in the international demand for tobacco and the particulars of its cultivation required fresh soil on a regular basis (every three years), which stretched planters to look for other crops and new land; this led to diversified farming. New products were introduced, and planters began to grow grains and corn, and to raise livestock. Planters on the Eastern Shore of Virginia and Maryland settled on growing wheat as their main crop, and as the Atlantic market for it grew, others elected to grow rye and oats. In this way the Chesapeake region became more economically diverse.

The change in crop production also altered labor needs and the demands on slaves. Tobacco cultivation was a year-round endeavor, but not so for cereal crops. The slaves' activities changed since grains had to be stored, milled, marketed, and shipped. Wagons and other related tools needed to be maintained, and livestock were needed to pull wagons. This generated new activities and tasks for slaves to undertake. Many varied tasks came with the nonfarming world as tasks that were in the past the province of white servants shifted to Blacks, and many took on skilled craft occupations that whites—who were living on a new social level in the region—no longer held.

Alongside the commercial growth of the diversified economy came new cities, and trade centers sprung into being in cities such as Norfolk and Alexandria, Virginia, and Baltimore, Maryland. The urban centers increased the need for artisans and skilled manufacturing workers. Planters found a market for renting their slaves to fill the labor void. Being rented or hired for work outside the plantation opened a window into a once-closed slave economy. Alongside the new slave economy was the allowance system of the plantation where landowners would ration clothes and other provisions. Blacks were able to forge new levels of social engagement despite the planters' displeasure in the development of this new slave economic activity. Little was done to stop its development; yet, as the decades moved to the last quarter of the 18th century, rumblings of the discord with the British Crown and whispers of liberty slowly began to spread among planters in the region.

The newly arrived Africans could see how they or others were treated if they ran away or objected in any way to the planters' efforts to humiliate and dehumanize them. The colonists' actions were visible and could be understood as the new arrivals watched. They knew they were being forced to labor for long hours each day in the tobacco fields, and this activity dominated their days and hours. Their new lives were structured by following the routines needed to bring the crop to market. They could not know what existed beyond their immediate surroundings, but maybe they could surmise given the lack of voices that spoke about or acknowledged their plight. Maybe those who came before them were able to convey the full weight of their situation. Nevertheless, the newly arrived Africans had to figure out what was going on and the limits of what they could do to survive. Berlin (1998) states:

> Violence, isolation, exhaustion, and alienation often led African slaves to profound depression and occasionally to self-destruction. But slaves contested the new regime at every turn—protesting the organization, pace, and intensity of labor and challenging the planters' definition of property rights. Over time they perfected numerous techniques to foil their owners' demands and expand control over their own labor and lives.
>
> *(p. 119)*

The ways of being on the part of Blacks became more African as reflected in language, music, and spiritual beliefs; at the same time, their growing numbers were not equal; there were more men than women, which limited family formation. The direct importation of Africans also brought more death and illness.

There was a small free Black community in the Chesapeake, but the colonist saw all Black people as one group with few if any distinctions between free and slave. Berlin (1998) states:

> Chesapeake lawmakers systematically carved away at the privilege the free black members of the charter generations had enjoyed prior to the plantation revolution. To the extent that such liberties contradicted the logic of racial slavery, they would not be permitted.
>
> *(p. 123)*

Yet, by 1740, a new generation of native-born Blacks began to outnumber the recently arrived Africans, or "saltwater" slaves. No longer were slaves unable to communicate, as the native-born knew the language, landscape, and economy of the region. Slaves were now able to establish families. By midcentury they composed four-fifths of the slave population in the region. Yet while American Blacks did not embrace African ways in total, their birth and death rituals reflected their African heritage. Some Blacks, however, did warm to Christianity or European American ways.

The American-born Blacks understood enough about the planters' ways to find areas where they could use the planters' beliefs to their advantage, such as planters' beliefs about being fatherly to their slaves. For instance, slaves wanted to have stable families and pressed for permission to visit spouses on other plantations or to reside in the same households. Planters did not see much benefit in these arrangements, but some were swayed by the manner in which these requests were made and the fact that, if they denied men the ability to visit wives off the plantation, the men would go anyway, withdrawing their labor to do so.

Slaves' desires for family life took hold, and planters came to grant their requests so much so that by the 1750s it was believed to be a slave's right. Once secured, other related concessions were made; women wanted time to attend to newborns and be relieved of field work when expecting and caring for newborns. Blacks also asserted their right to name their children, which was once the province of the planters. They also began to leave inheritances to their offspring, and skilled slaves would pass those skills on to their young. As part of establishing families, they lobbied for cabins. Thus, slaves strove for recognition that they were entitled to privacy. Black family life was established to some extent, and its existence was contrary to the core tenets of slavery, which held that the slave was not human. But Blacks in their actions forced recognition of their humanity.

The tobacco planters in the Chesapeake had to move fields every few years, so the slaves had to move about as the plantations expanded and fields moved; this meant more interactions with other plantations, and relationships evolved beyond the home plantation. And because some plantations were populated with family members, many adults had to look beyond their home plantation for husbands and wives; thus, some established families on other plantations.

A struggle occurred during the 18th century about how slaves worked. Blacks sought to ease some of the burden they endured by complaining to the overseer or planter that the work was too much. They requested limited working hours. By 1750 they had regained some days off as planters shifted from reliance on tobacco to other, less labor-intensive crops like wheat; this opened opportunities for slaves to take on a wider range of activities, many beyond the confines of the plantation. The diversification of crops also led to the emergence of trade towns in the Chesapeake region, which also meant more opportunity for slaves to be hired for their skills and labor. These developments created yet again a small slave economy, but not to the extent to which it had grown in the 18th century; yet slaves were able to supplement their allowances and eat and dress better.

The Low Country

The colonies in the Low Country developed in a parallel fashion to that of the Chesapeake region; however, there were dramatic differences, the first difference being that the international export products were naval stores (residue from pine trees used for ships of the day), indigo (a dye), and rice. The region also had large plantations rather than farms. The colonial rulers imported more Africans for labor on the plantations, and Africans' lives were restricted in similar ways as was done in the Chesapeake.

Blacks, however, were divided between those who resided in urban areas and those who lived in the country. The urban Blacks took on the goals and aspirations of the former generation Atlantic Creoles, seeking to assimilate. Blacks isolated in the country gravitated toward their African roots and heritage.

The urban landscape of numerous towns, such as Charlestown, South Carolina; Savannah, Georgia; and Wilmington, North Carolina, became desirable destinations for the new colonial ruling class of the Low Country. The new white elite, the wealthiest in the mainland, began to knit together a family-based ruling class through marriage, alliances, and assuming leadership roles in the local and region governments, and planters oversaw their properties through chains of command. They hired overseers, stewards, and drivers (Blacks) who saw to it that the work was completed since rice and indigo required considerable attention to a range of details. The planters' wealth made it possible for them to build estates and to enlarge their plantations and homes on their lands and in the cities.

With the chains of command in place on the plantations, planters assumed roles that had more to do with handling disputes and seeking innovation to improve the production of their holdings. By 1750 "planters as fathers" became the lens through which all social relationships in the region were viewed. Planters allowed slaves Sundays off and permitted them to have gardens to grow their own provisions. In addition, they provided allowances for food, clothes, and medical attention. Some planters allowed slaves to have property, and these concessions allowed slaves to generate an economic system using their time off.

The growing of rice and indigo both required considerable infrastructure and additional processes to grow and ship the crops. The absence of white skilled laborers also meant that slaves had to fill the void and assume many of the skilled positions needed on the plantations. Berlin (1998) observes that slave

> hydraulic engineers built and controlled the canals that irrigated the rice fields. Slave coopers made barrels to house rice and vats to process the indigo; slave brickmakers and masons fashioned bricks and built the kilns to cure the indigo; slave blacksmiths cared for horses and mules, while slave carpenters kept the plantations in good repair. In addition, slave watermen connected the great estates with Charles Town and other lowland ports, bringing messages and supplies to the plantation and hauling staple produce away.
>
> *(p. 168)*

Planters became alarmed at the number of skilled slave workers and requested of government leaders in 1730 that they stop training slaves to be skilled workers, an effort that failed.

In the Low Country, slaves and planters lived in separate yet intersecting worlds in which much of the planters' demands were challenged by the slaves, but mostly those on the plantations and less so by urban Blacks, who sought to be like their white owners.

The Low Country colonies were based on slavery from the outset; its core crop took time to be identified, but it was the goal from the beginning that slaves would be the means of labor. In the Low Country, plantations with between 10 and 50 slaves were the norm. Many plantations were dedicated to rice cultivation, which was even more physically demanding than tobacco. Indigo was added to diversify production. Slaves in the Low Country, living on large plantations rather than the smaller farms of the Chesapeake, were isolated from whites more than was true in the Chesapeake.

Plantation life offered more opportunity for Blacks to acquire skills and have a wider array of social relations. These developments, along with such advances as roads, allowed more interaction between plantations for Blacks, which led to "black families with links going back through generations" (Wright, 2017, p. 129).

They also established relationships with the broader Black communities beyond their specific plantations, and by the time of the American Revolution, Black life had been established in such a way that they could express their own worldviews and beliefs. While individual Blacks still labored under the watchful gaze of whites both on and off the plantations or farms, many Blacks had by then established kinship ties and incorporated African ways into religious and spiritual beliefs and had created their own forms of music, dance, work, and play that reflected their distinct cultural practices.

The Africans and native-born Blacks resisted by holding onto their cultural practices and using what they knew to build their lives in the new colony. Resistance from slaves happened when landowners tried to change stewards or overseers or introduce new crops, tools, or techniques. Changing the slaves' routines was met with disfavor, and planters were reminded that the so-called savages or natural mudsills had human will and resolve, and if this was ignored, it would be costly to their enterprises. The struggles between planters and slaves grew, as did the complexity of the production undertaken on the plantations.

The planters of the Low Country retreated to towns in urban areas to enjoy their newfound wealth; with them came slaves who assumed a range of artisan, skilled, and domestic roles. They soon were hired out, and many set their own terms for the work they did outside of their primary duties. So urban and country slaves led distinctly different lives. Berlin (1998, p. 159) notes that "mobile, skilled, and cosmopolitan, urban slaves improved their material condition and expanded their social life even while the circumstances of the mass of rural slaves deteriorated in the wake of the rice revolution."

The foundation of family was recreated on rural plantations by the 1750s, and the role of the family was acknowledged by the planters. Europeans and American colonists regarded blood kin as family, which was usually limited to parents and children. Yet Africans' beliefs about family were broader and considerably more inclusive, and, given their situation, it is possible that these combined forces triggered a re-formation of family for Black people. For example, captives who survived the slave ships together thought of each other as family.

Overall, as was the case in Africa, the family and the kinship network were at the core of Black life and culture in the North American colonies; these ties were tenuous and fragile but were still formed and nurtured. Religion was also a core source of hope, humanity, and survival. It was where Black souls and spirits were fed and strengthened no matter the abuse to their bodies. Africans and their descendants held firmly to their spirits and the convictions of their beliefs in God, whom they worshipped. Their bodies could be beaten and bent, but their souls and spirits could not be suppressed. Housed in the subconscious were the memories and knowledge of their former lives among their former families and communities; these were reinforced and amplified by the continued presence of their African countrymen.

African kinship systems could not be recreated in North America because Africans had been torn from their family ties and bonds, which could not be restored. However, Blacks took what they knew from their former lives and redefined family to fit their new lives and their new reality. Kinship was simulated during the Middle Passage, as was noted earlier, and on plantations. Children were taught to respect elders and adults by employing terms of authority and respect like "aunt" and "uncle," when appropriate. Since parents and even grandparents could be separated from children, it was customary for members of the community to take up the responsibility of childcare for these unrelated children.

Another core aspect of Black culture was their spiritual beliefs and practices in the colonial era. The Black spiritual beliefs and practices were both personal and collective; it was where their souls could be free and where they could seek and affirm hope of returning home. Black spiritual practices were expressed in ideas about the role of spirits in daily life and in magic, taboos, and ornaments to ward off evil, which were part of their reality. Spirits inhabited objects around them, both living and not.

The Northern Colonies

In the Northern colonies slavery evolved unevenly and only in some parts of the region. The colonists in the middle colonies turned to slavery more frequently than in New England, and cities were ahead of the countryside in the use of slave labor. Yet involvement in Atlantic international trade was the impetus for the increased use of slaves.

During the middle years of the 18th century, the protracted wars in which England was engaged decreased the numbers of white indentured servants from coming to the colonies, which led to a growing reliance on slave labor in the Northern colonies; yet the number of Blacks fluctuated with the economy. During recessions the numbers of white servants decreased. In the 1740s, 15% of the working population in some Northern cities, like Philadelphia, were slaves.

While most people lived in the country, those who lived in such cities as Newport, Rhode Island; Boston, Massachusetts; or New York City relied on slave labor. The slaves worked as domestic servants and artisans and were the main source of labor at seaports and on small farms in Pennsylvania; Northern New Jersey; the Hudson Valley and Long Island, New York; and New England. The planters in the country also expanded their use of slaves as the decades of the 18th century progressed.

As was noted, Blacks' numbers in the region grew during this era, for instance in Rhode Island, between 1720 and 1750, the slave population increased from 500 to 3,000, which represented an increase in the proportion of Blacks in the overall population. Elsewhere, the growth of the population for whites and Blacks increased in equal proportion, with slaves keeping pace with that of whites. In New York and other colonies, the pattern was similar as colonists depended more on slave labor. Yet, the increase in the slave population did not alter their status among the working class in the colonies of the north; slaves still typically worked in small groups alongside servants and wage workers, both Black and white. The larger proportion of Blacks resided in cities in the north during the 18th century; for instance, in 1750, 40% of slaves in Pennsylvania lived in Philadelphia, which was similar to the percentage of slaves in large cities in other colonies. The activities that slaves undertook also increased, and they did more work as artisans and domestic hands. In part since many of the slaveholders were themselves tradesmen and artisans, they were involved in industries such as trade and maritime-related fields in which they and their slaves made boats, sails, and ropes.

In the 1730s slavery had become an essential component of the economy of the Northern region, and wage workers in the region complained that the widespread use of slave labor had made it difficult for them to earn a living. The residents in the country also followed the lead of their city neighbors, particularly as grain farmers turned to slaves as their labor source in the 18th century.

Corresponding to the increased numbers of slaves was their place of origin, which in the past had been the Caribbean, and they arrived in small lots. In the 18th century, however, Africans arrived in the northern region by the shiploads from Africa. In fact, by 1750 70% of the Africans arriving in northern ports were from Africa while just a few decades prior the opposite had been true, with 70% coming from the Caribbean.

Newly arrived Africans were infused into the slave population, yet they tended to be young men, which is what slaveholders desired. Unlike in the Low Country and Chesapeake regions,

> Northern slaveholders discouraged their slaves from marrying, by making it difficult for slave families to reside in the same abode. They routinely separated husbands from wives and parents from children, and only reluctantly extended visitation rights. Women with reputations of fecundity found few buyers, and some owners sold slave women at the first sign of pregnancy.
>
> *(Berlin, 1998, p. 185)*

Thus, the lack of family life was such that few Blacks in the north knew their grandparents. Black life in the northern region was in a state of disorder characterized by low birth rates and high mortality.

The Northern region was for all intents and purposes a slave society during the middle decades of the 18th century as the colonies revised and updated the slave laws and codes that made the slaveholders stronger and the slaves weaker by limiting considerably what slaves could do and tolerating fewer independent activities.

In should not come as a surprise that slaves resisted the regime in which they had to live. Their pushback took several forms. The African-born slaves rejected much of colonial life and ways. Efforts on the part of missionaries and religious people to convert the Africans were unsuccessful. Most slaves did not trust the religious principles being taught to them and held on to their traditional religious views and beliefs. They also used traditional African practices including in their personal relationships, embracing polygamy, which was in direct opposition to the Christian principles of the colonists. Berlin (1998) observes:

> The rejection of Christianity was just one manifestation of the reorientation of black culture stimulated by the importation of African slaves. Newly arrived Africans, although a minority of black society, had a powerful effect on the native black population, infusing it with

> knowledge of Africa and African ways. Sometimes it was just the presence of African men and women walking the streets of northern cities and the byways of the northern countryside, bearing ritual scars and speaking the language of a land most black northerners knew only from second- and third-hand accounts. At other times, newly arrived Africans reawaked black Americans to their African past by providing direct knowledge of the west African society.
>
> *(p. 190)*

In the late 1760s and 1770s, in the midst of the colonial claims for liberty from British authority, slaves in the region began to assert their rights to be free as well, with some petitioning the British Crown directly to set them free. But the slaveholders held firm in the face of arguments to abolish slavery. The region began to resemble a society with slaves as the end of the century approached, and slaves' calls for freedom and liberty from the colonists were more frequent. Berlin (1998) states that

> in some parts of the North, slaves initiated legal suits for their liberty. In other places, they bargained with their owners or simply fled. The unrest that surfaced in rumors of insurrection and in veiled threats that slaves would side with the British in any contest for empire suggest how the simultaneous maturation and politization of African-American culture cleared the way for the refashioning of black life and the transformation of the North from a society with slaves to a free society.
>
> *(p. 194)*

The Lower Mississippi Valley

The colonies in the Lower Mississippi Valley region were slow to find a viable export crop or make slave labor the center of the regions' economy. The French colonists wanted to establish a plantation system but fell short of their goals. The importation of Africans by the French slowed to a crawl after 1731 and did not pick up until the Spanish, after the Seven Years' War, seized the colony in 1763. Several developments frustrated Spanish aspirations to bring larger numbers of Africans to the region, and it was not until the region changed hands again, in 1780, this time to the British, that Africans were imported in much larger numbers.

The lack of slave labor in the desired numbers between 1730 and 1780 meant French planters had to reconsider their labor needs. Since they could not import slaves, the colonists turned their attention instead to encouraging family formation among Blacks to build loyalty and to increase their numbers. The colonial leaders provided better working conditions and used less harsh treatment with slaves to convince them of their more liberal intentions. Changes were made on plantations, such as replacing barracks with cabins and outbuildings, easing workloads for women, and facilitating male–female interactions. The planters registered marriages, baptized children, and some stood in as godparents. The number of native-born Blacks grew and by 1740 exceeded 4,500, which was more than the white population; and by 1763 it was estimated that their numbers in the region had grown to some 6,000 native-born Blacks.

But the economy stalled, and plantation expansion was hampered such that, instead of the population expanding into the countryside, more people lived closer to the port of New Orleans. It was estimated that the population around this central regional city was one-quarter Black and one-third white, and the remainder other races. Slaves in the region tended to live in households rather than on plantations.

The economy and slaveholding were, for the most part, based in cities. Yet planters still grew tobacco, indigo, and naval stores, and still cut lumber and raised cattle. So the economy remained diverse, which meant that slave laborers worked closely with other colonists, and Native Americans and whites alike assumed a wider range of roles and occupations in homes, wharfs, and factories. The diversified economy offered slaves opportunities in part because planters required them to take care of their own needs for food, clothing, and medical care. Slaves had Sundays and parts of other days to grow crops, tend to livestock, and make crafts for sale. Their activities grew into a large and lucrative economy, which allowed some slaves to buy their freedom. Planters became uncomfortable with the slaves' freedom of movement and economic activity, so they set out to outlaw much of slaves' economic activity, which by then had become an accepted and valued part of the region's economy and social life. Blacks had more interactions with whites and Native Americans, extending to interracial marriages, which increased the mixed-race population.

The plantation was a major development in many of the colonies in the North American mainland, yet it did not reach the Mississippi Valley region during this era. In this region the previous slave society became instead a society with slaves. The labor force became more varied, and the effort to establish plantations faltered. As in time past, slaves were able to establish their own economy in the region, and they were enlisted in the local militia. The Black slaves in the militia fought with whites against Native Americans and other combatants in support of the French and Spanish Crowns. These activities helped Blacks establish a foothold in white society, and some were able to free themselves as a result.

In the region, reactions by the French Crown to the Natchez rebellion and other unrest led it to end its control of the colony. The termination of the administrative companies' oversight resulted in a break in importing Africans to the colony in Louisiana. The Louisiana colony changed administrations in 1763 when the Spanish took control from the French at the end of the Seven Years' War. The Spanish resolved to return to importing slaves from Africa, but events in the years following their takeover slowed their progress, the American Revolution was one of several events that interrupted the Spanish plans to enlarge the slave population. Therefore, few ships from Africa arrived at the ports after 1731 until the Spanish began to bring some slaves to the colony in the 1770s, several years after taking over the colony. From the cessation in 1731 to the start of new arrivals, slaves arrived slowly through other colonies in the region. The result of these events meant that there were few new African workers, and those who were there would have little direct knowledge of Africa since most came from other slave societies to the region.

It was not until the 1780s, when the American interests took charge of the colony, that the slave trade from Africa resumed. In essence, the planters in the area were not able to increase the labor pool for some fifty years (1730–1780), so they had to manage with the existing labor pool. They relied on the natural increases of the slave population by easing restrictions and promoting families to grow and prosper. These policies and practices had the desired outcome, and the Black population increased and expanded beyond the whites in the colony.

Slaveholders saw few advantages to their slaves' economic activity but believed it to be too engrained to abolish. The market activity in the cities offered occasions for Blacks to gather, interact, and socialize without the watchful eyes of the slaveholders. It provided an outlet for Blacks to practice and celebrate their African heritage. The socializing crossed racial lines, and interracial bonding occurred. The ports and urban centers were prime for liaisons and forbidden partnerships. Thus, a mixed-race population grew and offered a higher status in the social order for some Black women who partnered with white men.

> By midcentury slaves in the lower Mississippi Valley—a largely creole group leavened by a sprinkling of African and Caribbean transplants—had begun to establish their own unique culture. That culture drew from Africa as well as Europe, the Caribbean, and Native America. It was most visible in the creole lingua franca that fused various African tongues with French and Native-American languages into a new language with an African grammatical structure and a French vocabulary.
>
> *(Berlin, 1998, pp. 208–209)*

However, Blacks behavior was meet with displeasure and was despised by the colonial officials and slaveholders who sought to prohibit their independence and relationships with white and Native American residents.

The struggles endured by the French colonists were transferred to the Spanish, who sought to reinvigorate the colony. The Spanish encouraged immigration and new settlers by offering land for reasonable costs and with subsides for staple crop production. But their efforts, which had modest success, were slowed by the American conflict with Britain and other external and internal issues, and they were unable to establish the international staple economy they strived to achieve.

Black Perspectives

In this section I address Blacks' perspectives and their response to being held as property. I also explore how they viewed their life circumstances as slaves.

By the 1770s, some 100 or more years after the first arrivals, many Africans and their Black descendants in the North America mainland colonies had established families, kinship networks, and informal communities that had developed unique cultural practices. Many aspects of Black life that evolved during the 17th and 18th centuries set the foundation upon which Black life would be built going forward. Blacks had survived in America for multiple generations, so by this time there were both African- and American-born Blacks.

Individual Africans working in proximity to whites and isolated from other Blacks might have had a hard time holding on to African ways and traditions. Even small groups in similar isolation might have struggled to recall past practices from what might have been a long-ago past; such was the case in the Chesapeake and some parts of the Northern colonies. Yet, the same might not be true for larger groups of Blacks who lived and worked some distance from whites, such as those who lived in the Low Country. Blacks in large groups could form families and communities; in doing so, they could recall the old ways, or the group as a collective could fashion practices from their distant recollections of home and family. More important, the presence of recently arrived Africans, or saltwater slaves, could also enhance their recall of the ways of the homeland. In families, even fragile and tentative ones, it would be possible to teach the young about their life situation and their heritage from the recent and distant past. As has been the case throughout the discussion to this point there were regional variations in how Africans responded to their situations and circumstances. However, there were common themes across the colonial world.

Africans' lives were dictated by their oppressors, the planters and colonists and especially the landowners; white colonists who had small landholdings or even no land also took part in oppressing Africans. Landowners had power over Black people's lives, and they regarded them as property. Nevertheless, Blacks were humans, and their labor could not have been of much value if they, as landowners portrayed them, were actually "beasts of burden," simple-minded children, or "Sambos." It is this reality of slavery that marked the struggle between landowners and slaves; the agency of Blacks could not be ignored or dismissed. Rather, this fact meant that many of the actions taken to control and dictate Black lives and labor had to be negotiated. While many rights enjoyed by white in the colonies were denied and limited for Blacks, they still had some say in how they lived and worked.

> Evidence of the degradation of slave life was everywhere. Violence, isolation, exhaustion, and alienation often led African slaves to profound depression and occasionally to self-destruction. However, most slaves refused to surrender to the dehumanization that accompanied the plantation revolution. Instead, they contested the new regime at every turn—protesting the organization, pace, and intensity of labor and challenging the planters' definition of property rights.
>
> *(Berlin, 2003, pp. 64–65)*

The colonial planters tried to make it seem that the slaves were content and accepting of their lot, but many knew this was far from the truth since slaves were resistant and rebellion—active or indirect opposition—was just below the surface. Wright (2017) and other historians (e.g., Bennett, 1988; Berlin, 1998, 2003) offer as evidence of the planters' knowledge the various laws that were enacted to prevent Africans from being able to free themselves. Wright (2017, p. 174) observes, "As slave populations grew, suspicion, distrust, and fear filled the minds of white colonists and became manifest in colonial statutes." The colonist in the 1700s enacted slave codes that forbade group meetings, prohibited access to or use of weapons, limited movement to farms or plantations, and made it illegal to be on the streets after dark. It was also deemed illegal for slaves to use musical instruments such as drums or horns. Slaves chanced capital punishment if they set fires, poisoned anyone, stole repeatedly, tried to incite insurrection, or would not submit to being questioned by authorities or landowners.

The laws alone were not enough to remove Black people's agency, so white groups were enlisted both in rural and urban settings to keep a watch over Blacks' movements and activities. Some justices, planters, and overseers added torture to the tactics employed to keep slaves in line, and many of the tactics were legal. Slaves were branded, flogged, burned, had limbs cut off, and many were executed, all to control their behavior. Compliant, docile people were desired, and considerable effort was expended to portray Blacks as just that, docile and childlike.

In the face of numerous assaults, Blacks adapted and held on to their vision of being free. Some accepted their status, and some sought to be like their oppressors, while others found indirect means to resist. They forgot, were clumsy or careless, stole, broke tools, became ill or pretended to be unwell, and struck back with hidden words in speech or songs (Levine, 2007; Stuckey, 2013).

Others ran off; some engaged in armed revolts. The final act of rebellion and the ultimate form of resistance: some elected not to live any longer and took their own lives. For the owner, there was no profit, no work; for the slave, there was no humiliation. They sent a message—their lifeless bodies—to others symbolizing their refusal and rejection of their captivity and bondage to strangers; their bodies were messages, shouting NO. However, some opted for life and survival, and there were multiple paths that an individual could follow in pursuit of maintaining their lives and that of their people and families (Bennett, 1988; Berlin, 1998, 2003; Harms, 2018; Levine, 2007; Stuckey, 2013).

Africans who arrived in the 17th and 18th centuries, saltwater slaves, often ran off after they arrived in the colonial settlements. The slaves who knew European ways also found intellectual responses to express their resistance to being enslaved. In the minds and hearts of many individuals was a rejection of the world of forced labor. They found indirect and subtle ways to resist as a way to affirm their humanity and at the same time live, while others sought more direct paths to assert their resolve not to give in to control of the planters.

In contrast to the former generation of Africans, who often worked side-by-side with whites or with their owners, the new arrivals of the Plantation generation were kept apart from whites. One effect of the Blacks' isolation and their growing numbers was a new social order in which whites of similar status were elevated above that of Black slaves; thus, a new racially based social order was created, a social order we would recognize today as systemic racism (Feagin, 2006), but then only its bare outlines were forming (Wright, 2017).

The lives of Blacks were dramatically altered in a way that afflicted many Blacks with psychosocial trauma as well as physical and emotional torture, followed by fear and isolation. The psychological and emotional impacts had to be staggering and, for some, crippling. My focus, while not exclusively, is on the new African arrivals to the colonies, the group that made up the Plantation generation. It is extremely difficult to know what it was like for these Africans. When they arrived, there were no reporters or film crews to document their experiences, and few people seemed interested in their stories at the time. The evidence that does exist from the 17th and 18th centuries is usually from landowners' records and diaries, official records of court proceedings, or colonists' letters. These sources do not capture the captives' perspectives; the few slave narratives that do exist are also limited as sources of objective evidence; nevertheless, this is what is available. I am left with having to infer psychological states and emotions from behavior and actions of Africans recorded in the few sources, much of which historians documented only in broad terms (see Wright, 2017).

After surviving passage and sale, Africans made a binary choice, live or die, with many electing to live while others selected death—some directly, others indirectly. Then there were those who fled, usually for short periods of time, since considerable effort was expended to return runaways to their owners. It is not clear how many slaves escaped and stayed away, but the record seems to suggest not many did so.

Africans had to overcome many challenges, the first of which was learning the new language, followed by making any type of meaningful connections with others. Narratives from former slaves indicate that connections were made during the Middle Passage (Mintz & Price, 1976; Sweet, 2003) and that these connections served the purpose of rebuilding kinship ties. Evidence of these efforts indicates that captive Africans were able to address their distress through establishing relationships with other captives, and while they were unable to recreate relationships as they existed in Africa, they created what was possible given their new situations. I suspect this effort worked to ease some of the distress of their capture and removal from their former lives. It would also serve to motivate Africans to cobble together a way to communicate, which went a long way to helping them reestablish connections and relationships with fellow Africans. This may have also served as a tool for healing the deep trauma they endured and still carried with them (Sweet, 2003).

However, another challenge was maintaining any connection in the face of unexpected disruptions among friends and families (Dodson, 2002; Wright, 2017) since, at the will or whim of the owners, slaves could be sent away for a range of reasons—to work for another person or be willed to a family member, and so on (Kulikoff, 1986). This meant family and friendship networks had to be rebuilt and recreated, time and again.

The timelines here are important and need to be restated and the events reviewed, and there was regional variation to consider. I use as an example the Chesapeake region to illustrate the issues and challenges. Kulikoff's description of life in the region highlights some of the critical events and issues. He contends that Africans were too diverse to form a single culture in America; rather, they drew on the shared aspects of their respective cultures such as kinship and lineages to recreate a new cultural world that reflected how they lived and interacted and how they coped with ordinary life tasks like working, eating, and loving. Kulikoff (1986, pp. 317–318) states: "The social institutions they developed were neither imposed by Europeans nor directly taken from African communities, but were a unique combination of elements" from both European and African worlds.

Three periods of Black life occurred in the various regions. In the first, from 1650 to 1690, Black peoples' presence increased, followed by greater and more harsh repression of Blacks as they became more numerous. The period from 1690 to 1740 was characterized by the significant increases with the arrival of saltwater Africans, which disrupted the lives of American-born Blacks who were enslaved and created conflicts between the two groups. Many Blacks worked on small plantations, making it difficult for them to establish communities, except in the Low Country, where Blacks on large plantations often outnumbered whites. During the last period, from 1740 to 1790, the number of Africans brought from their homeland declined and then stopped, the sizes of plantations grew in the Chesapeake, the overall Black population increased through reproduction, and internal conflicts among Blacks dissipated. The overall outcome was that Blacks, many of them American-born, established stable communities (Kulikoff, 1986).

Each Black person who came to the New World was a unique person with attributes, attitudes, emotions, intellect, aspirations, and dreams, and each longed for human affection and regard. Each looked to those around them during their formative years for guidance and protection. Individuals had access to their senses and were able to feel pain and joy. Historians tell us about events and occurrences that affected a broad segment of the Black people. This is valuable and important but at the same time does not help us know or see the range of responses that Black people had to their situations.

African people came from a land that was demanding and required considerable efforts to tame the hostile environments that surrounded them. Nevertheless, African people managed to prosper and multiply, and they developed complex religious, social, economic, and political systems and organizations. All of this knowledge, skill, and experience came with the captives. Individuals were multilingual as well, and had knowledge of farming, agriculture, herbs for medicines, and other skills.

Their psychological states varied, from shock and trauma reactions to despair, anxiety, and depression. The loss of connection from relationships and places in Africa may have been overwhelming, and they directed their remaining energy at escape in one form or the other. Choosing to escape could have been a way to honor their ancestors, a wish to be with them, or simply a rejection of a life path that would dishonor the family, past and present. I suspect there are many more possibilities.

The options for the living were numerous, and for those who knew the ways of the Europeans and shared their blood, the path to integration and acceptance seemed reasonable and psychologically consistent for people who lived on the edges of African and European worlds. This path, in an environment that was not hostile and restrictive, was the one taken by some between 1619 and 1690, before the colonist decided to rely on Africans as the primary source of labor.

Recall that Blacks had allies and relationships with others of similar station. Given these circumstances, the rewards and benefits to assimilation were far greater then than in later periods. Not to mention that some of the Blacks were Creoles, of mixed racial heritage and lineage, which helped them to be accepted. Psychologically, the path with the greatest reward was to adapt the ways of the dominant white colonists and strive to be like them in all ways possible. I suspect that even then, some did not embrace this path but elected to renew and honor their African ancestors and traditions. There were also those who, when interacting with other Blacks, followed Africans' practices out of the gaze of whites. Still others may have been unsure how to proceed or which path to follow, so they became stuck in place, moved by external forces, lacking little internal will. They may have been buffeted back and forth, not knowing which direction to go; perhaps they chose paths that had the least resistance and resolved to accept what came their way, to not create any disturbance.

Those who had more opportunity to observe whites and learn their ways might have used this information to figure out how and when they could safely express themselves. Then, in the presence of whites, they exhibited one side of themselves while, outside of whites' watchful eyes, they expressed another side of themselves. This path might have made it possible for Blacks to evade some of the harsh treatment they experienced and for some degree of intimacy and individual expression. Recall the story of Anthony Johnson from the last chapter, who arrived in the colony in 1621, worked independently on a plantation, married, and had four children baptized; three decades later, in 1651, he and his family were released from service. As free colonists, they acquired cattle and a land grant. Johnson left an inheritance to his sons, and his family maintained their estate. The paths and psychological perspectives I described could reflect the thinking and feeling of people in the Charter generation like Johnson and his family. But, as has been pointed out in previous chapters, the fortunes for Blacks changed.

Starting in the late 1660s increasing restrictions were imposed as time passed, until in the mid-18th century when the status of slaves was relegated to that of property. This is when their status as slaves was legalized, whereas from the beginning of the transatlantic slave trade it was merely custom and tradition to treat and regard Africans as cargo or property. This new status of legally enslaved had to alter the psychology of Blacks and introduce other emotional coping mechanisms and psychological defenses. During the period from 1690 to 1740, the colonial population grew wherein both Europeans' and Africans' numbers increased, and Africans were brought directly from their homeland. And with them came new and different challenges for Africans who were already in the colonies. The saltwater Africans did not wish to assimilate, as was the practice of some of the earlier Blacks, and their status and treatment was significantly more restrictive and less equal (Thornton, 1998). The saltwater slaves were directly tied to their native traditions and worlds, unlike Blacks from the Charter generation or those who were born in North America. And the new arrivals had to learn the language and grasp the meaning of their new lives as slaves, forced to work under the threat of harm and death. One of the first things owners did upon the purchase of a slave was to change their name from who they knew themselves to be, to select their new name. Kulikoff (1986) describes it this way:

> Not only were Africans forced to work for harsh masters in a strange land, but masters usually stripped them of their names, their last personal possession. Africans imbued names with great meaning, and naming often followed a ceremony at birth or coming of age.... Masters in the Chesapeake, without ceremony, forced Africans to adopt English names and required that they be used in daily exchanges between whites and blacks.
>
> *(p. 325)*

Many newly arrived Africans became ill soon after they came to plantations and thus were unable to work. It seems reasonable to suggest that all of the changes forced upon them led to their poor health, which was both physical and psychological.

References

Bennett, L. (1988). *Before the Mayflower: A history of Black America*. Johnson Publishing.

Berlin, I. (1998). *Many thousands gone: The first two centuries of slavery in North America*. Belknap Press, of Harvard University Press.

Berlin, I. (2003). *Generations of captivity: A history of African Americans slaves*. Belknap Press, of Harvard University Press.

Dodson, H. (2002) *Jubilee: The emergence of African-American culture*. National Geographic.

Feagin, J. R. (2006). *Systemic racism: A theory of oppression*. Routledge.

Franklin, H. J., & Moss, A. A. (2000). *From slavery to freedom: A history of African Americans* (8th ed.). McGraw Hill.

Fredrickson, G. M. (1998). *The arrogance of race: Historical perspectives on slavery, racism a social inequity*. Wesleyan University Press.

Harms, R. (2018). *Africa in global history with sources*. Norton.

Horton, J. O., & Horton, L. E. (2005). *Slavery and the making of America*. Oxford University Press.

Kulikoff, A. (1986). *Tobacco and slaves: The development of southern cultures in the Chesapeake, 1680–1800*. University of North Carolina Press.

Levine, L. W. (2007). *Black culture and consciousness; African American folk thought from slavery to freedom*. (30th anniversary edition). Oxford University Press.

Mintz, S. W., & Price, R. (1976). *The birth of African-American culture: An anthropological perspective*. Beacon.

Reiss, O. (1997). *Blacks in colonial America*. McFarland.

Stuckey, S. (2013). *Slave culture: Nationalist theory and the foundations of Black America* (25th anniversary edition). Oxford University Press.

Sweet, J. H. (2003). *Recreating Africa: Culture, kinship and religion in the African-Portuguese world, 1441–1770*. University of North Carolina Press.

Thornton, J. K. (1998). *Africa and Africans in the making of the Atlantic world, 1400–1800*. (2nd ed.). Cambridge University Press.

Wright, D. R. (2017). *African Americans in the colonial era: From the Africans origins through the Americans revolution*. (4th ed.). Wiley Blackwell.

6

THE REVOLUTIONARY ERA AND BEYOND

In this chapter the discussion moves into the later decades of the 18th century. I review where the population of the colonies stood regarding the census of white and Black residents as well as the varying distribution of residents from region to region and within each colony. After examining the colonial census, I turn to the events that occurred during the later decades of the century (1750–1810) since it was during this period that major changes occurred concerning the status of the colonies and the colonists' relationship with the British government. After the overview of the events of the century, I consider how Black people reacted to the myriad developments of this era.

The Colonial Census

Up to this point, I have discussed the events and developments in the colonies by regions, but now a focus on individual colonies is warranted to delineate where Blacks resided and how many were in each colony.

Virginia

I begin with the colony of Virginia, where 300 Blacks resided in 1650. As time passed, more arrived, and by the 18th century the Black population grew at a significant rate. By 1708 there were 12,000 Blacks and 18,000 whites, yet by 1756 the numbers rose to 120,156 Blacks and 173,316 whites, and in some counties Blacks were dominant.

The colonial leaders in Virginia created a comprehensive slave code, based on codes used in the Caribbean islands, that became a model for other colonies. It restricted slaves' movements to their plantations unless they had written permission to leave the confines. Slaves who killed someone or

DOI: 10.4324/9781003111542-9

engaged in sexual assaults were hung. If a slave robbed someone, they would receive 60 lashes. If they engaged in petty offenses, like being unresponsive, or if they interacted with free Blacks or whites, the punishment could be whipping, losing some part of their body, or being branded. Virginia slaves were generally complacent, which was attributed to the harsh punishments and surveillance by law officers, courts, and nonslaveholding colonists (Franklin & Moss, 2000).

Maryland

The Maryland colony introduced slaves early in its settlement (1634), but slavery was not legally recognized until 1663, when the colonists proclaimed all Blacks to be slaves, even those who had been free, and the status of a slave would pass to newborns based on the mother's status.

At first, the fact that Africans were not Christian slowed their entrance into Maryland, but by 1671 a law stated that converted Africans would be acceptable. By 1708 there were 800 Africans in the colony; by 1750 Blacks numbered 40,000 compared to 100,000 whites. Like in Virginia, laws were passed designed to control the slaves' behavior and to quiet colonist fears of Black revolts (Franklin & Moss, 2000).

The Carolinas

The Carolinas were established with an eye to building plantations much like those in the Caribbean and following the success of such estates in Virginia and Maryland. Blacks were brought to the Carolina colony while it was being settled. In fact, the Carolina colonial leaders in 1663 attracted settlers with land grants of up to 20 acres for each Black male slave owned and 10 acres for each Black female slave owned. This led to a population in 1715 of 10,500 Blacks and 6,250 whites; ten years later the Black population was three times that size, at 30,000 (Franklin & Moss, 2000). As was the colonial custom, laws were enacted to restrict Blacks lives by limiting their movement, forbidding them from having weapons without a permit, and prohibiting them from engaging in trade. Blacks could also be searched or punished by white patrols at any time and in any manner if they were judged to be in violation of peace and good order (whatever that meant) (Franklin & Moss, 2000).

Georgia

Georgia was established in 1733 by the English with the provisions that no land grants would be offered, nor would alcohol or slavery be permitted. Yet these ambitions were resisted and altered by Georgia settlers. The prohibition against slavery was rescinded in 1750, and by 1760 the colony had about

6,000 whites and 3,000 Blacks; by 1773 there were 18,000 whites and 15,000 Blacks. Slave codes were adapted from the South Carolina code (Franklin & Moss, 2000).

The Middle Colonies

The New Netherland colony was settled initially by the Dutch, who used slave labor to create plantations in the Hudson Valley beginning in 1638. The Dutch approach to slavery was humane regarding the personal rights of the enslaved and considerably milder compared to other colonies. The Dutch imported fewer slaves, so the issues of large populations of slaves did not exist. The English took over control of New Netherland in 1664 and by 1665 the ruling bodies recognized slavery; it was a legal institution by 1684 in the province now known as New York. By 1698 the New York colony's population was roughly 18,000 whites with 2,100 Blacks; by 1723 Blacks numbered 6,100; and by 1777 Blacks accounted for 20,000 of the 168,000 people in the New York colony. Like in other colonies, slave codes justifying and determining the status and behavior of slaves were enacted. Slaves could not bear witness for someone who was free and, if baptized, could not seek freedom. In New York City, Blacks were prohibited from being on the streets after dark.

South of New York was New Jersey, Pennsylvania, and Delaware. These colonies promoted slavery as well, and Blacks' numbers grew: by 1745 there were 4,500 Blacks among 61,000 people. Only in Pennsylvania did the slave population grow slowly, in part due to the Quakers' ideological opposition to slavery. In 1721 Blacks were estimated to be about 2,000 in total, yet by 1790 there were 10,000 Blacks, and about one-third were slaves. The Pennsylvania colony's treatment of Blacks was quite humane, and some people from the area became leaders in the movement advocating Black freedom. Blacks in Pennsylvania were able to attend churches and schools, marry, and establish families.

At an earlier time, Delaware was part of Pennsylvania and followed similar laws and colonial practices. Delaware separated in 1703 as its own colony. Its slave population grew because it tended to resemble colonies to its south. By 1750 Delaware had a population of about 27,000 with about 1,500 Blacks.

The New England Colonies

Slavery was an accepted institution in New England, but interest in slavery was a bit different. New England was focused more on the trading of slaves in the international market than ownership of them, but some slaves were used in Massachusetts and Connecticut in the construction industries to build homes and forts. The founding settlers of Rhode Island used slaves in the early years of their settlement, so slavery was an important commercial and economic engine for the region.

From 1713, New England was flush with traders in various products including humans, both going out of the area and coming in, through its ports in Boston, Salem, Providence, and New London. In 1700 the total population of the entire region was about 90,000, with only 1,000 Blacks. Massachusetts by 1776 had some 5,200 Blacks; Connecticut counted about 3,600 Blacks in 1756; and Rhode Island in 1774 had 3,700 Blacks. Very few Blacks lived in New Hampshire (Franklin & Moss, 2000).

The presence of Blacks in all the colonies was well established after more than a century and a quarter. While the overall number of Blacks in relationship to the general population was small, by 1775 there were about 935,000 whites in the 13 colonies and about 236,500 Blacks, about 20% of the population; Blacks' role in the colonial economy was integral and central. The laws and regulations putting Blacks at the margins of society were also clear and common across the colonial world. The regional variations were significant in that there were far more Blacks in the Chesapeake and Low Country regions than in the Northern region and, while not under English control, in the Lower Mississippi Valley region.

The Break with Britain

The colonies became unhappy with being governed by the British Crown and political leaders from Britain, with many reasons put forward for their displeasure, but primarily the colonists sought liberty and equality, and they rebelled against the government that had established their settlements. Lepore (2018) notes that the war for independence took many years, ideas, principles, positions, actions, actors, and advocates, all proclaiming rights to liberty, freedom, and equality (see also Goldfield et al., 2014). To set the scene and to briefly recount what took place, I begin in the 1750s when the British and French were engaged in conflicts over land in North America in the area known today as the Midwest. The French had settled into the western regions of the Ohio valley, Canada, and Louisiana, while the British claimed lands on the eastern coastline of the North American mainland. The first skirmishes between the French and British took place in 1754 when the colonial militia encountered the French in its territory and the colonial troops suffered a humiliating loss. The skirmish motivated delegates from colonies to gather in New York to consider how they would respond and defend their territory. At the meeting it was proposed that the colonies join as a defensive union. The idea was accepted by the delegates attending the meeting, but it was rejected by the respective colonial assemblies (Lepore, 2018).

Yet in spite of the initial defeat at the hands of the French in North America, the British engaged the French at other locales, with each engagement about something different: trade, fishing rights, shipping, and sugar production. England declared war in 1756. The French and Indian War, or Seven Years' War, brought the colonies together in part because the British sent troops to mainland North America because the Crown did not trust the colonists to defend themselves, as they had done in the past with American militias. Unexpectedly, British troops attacked and sacked colonial properties and people, so many colonists came to fear the British troops. The commander of the British military in the colonies reassured the colonial people that the war would be paid for by the Crown, as the British and Americans fought together against the French and Indians in North America.

In Canada the conflict was joined by the Iroquois Indians on the British side, turning the advantage to the British and American forces who prevailed, and by 1760 the North American conflict came to an end. Some three years later, in 1763, the arranged peace meant that France gave up any claim to Canada and to New France, which included all French-held lands east of the Mississippi. The land west of the Mississippi went to Spain, while the Spanish gave Britain Cuba and half of Florida.

Waging war of the magnitude undertaken by the British emptied its treasury and grew its debt. Native Americans remained a threat in North America, who had seized forts in the Ohio valley. So troops were needed to defend the expanded colonial area that the British had gained as a result of the war. In an effort to raise needed revenue, the English Parliament enacted the American Revenue Act, also known as the Sugar Act, to pay down debt and cover the costs for the defense of the North American mainland. Colonists objected to having taxes levied on them by a body in which they had no voice or representation. The reaction by colonists and colonial governments was to argue that such taxes without a voice were the equivalent of rendering them (the colonist) to the status of slaves (Lepore, 2018). The colonists reacted in a similar manner to the next law passed by Parliament, The Stamp Act, which required the issuance of a government stamp on all paper items for tax purposes throughout the British Empire. The theme that they were being treated as slaves was again raised by the colonists, who referred to themselves as the sons of liberty. Lepore (2018) states:

> The sovereignty of the people, the freedom of the press, the relationship between representation and taxation, debt as slavery: each of these ideas, with origins in England, found a place in the colonists' opposition to the Stamp Act. Still Parliament professed itself baffled.
>
> *(p. 83)*

The protests against British taxes led colonists to march in the streets with cries of liberty, which triggered again calls to end racial slavery. In 1766 the Stamp Act was repealed by the British Parliament, but at the same time it passed the Declaratory Act, which gave Parliament the authority to pass any law it deemed fit. This was followed by the Townshend Act, which placed taxes on lead, paper, paint, glass, and tea. Colonists reacted with protests, boycotts, and riots; Britain reacted by sending troops to enforce the law.

Horton and Horton (2005) note that during the pre-revolutionary conflict, there was considerable agitation between colonists and the British government. Blacks participated on both sides of these exchanges and protests, not knowing which side would prevail and having differing loyalties; Blacks especially sympathized with colonists' claim of their right to be free and not be oppressed. Adding to colonists' discontent was the presence of British troops in many colonial cities and towns.

Many historians point to 1770 and the actions attributed to Crispus Attucks, a fugitive slave, and other colonists who, while socializing in a Boston tavern with other sailors, encountered a British soldier. A conflict between civilians and soldiers ensued, continuing into the evening. Attucks is said to have led a group of 20 to 30 Irish, Black, mulatto, and other sailors, who confronted British guards at the Boston Common House. The group of Americans taunted the British soldiers, and the group eventually was fired upon, killing several and injuring others. Attucks was among the dead. Some consider this the first battle of the American Revolution.

The British Parliament in 1773 issued a new law focused on taxes, the Tea Act, which lowered the taxes on tea but reinstated Parliament's right to impose colonial taxes. The result was an uproar over the importing and sale of tea. Several ships with tea on board docked in Boston harbor and were boarded by colonist who dumped the tea into the harbor. Parliament reacted to these events by passing the Coercive Act of 1774, which effectively closed Boston harbor and rescinded Massachusetts' colonial charter.

By September of 1774, delegates of the 13 colonies met in Philadelphia at the first meeting of the Continental Congress. The attendees took the view that the Coercive Acts were specific to Massachusetts, not for all the colonies, and the idea of independence from Britain was raised and defeated. But the meeting did succeed in planting the notion that perhaps the colonies should be united as one country, not as separate colonies or loyalists to the Crown. The outcome of the congress, it seems, was to recommend colonists prepare for future conflicts by collecting and storing weapons and building the ranks of their militia. The Continental Congress also agreed to boycott British imports and discontinued trade with the West Indies.

The colonists' complaints, when lodged with the English Crown and Parliament, were met with a response from Britain that pointed out the colonists' hypocrisy to call for liberty for themselves while enslaving others. The colonists' claims of unjustified tyranny against free people seemed ludicrous to the British authorities.

The colonies had never been independent but had enjoyed a relatively hands-off oversight while the British Crown and government were preoccupied with other wars and conflicts, taking their attention away from the North American colonies. The colonists reacted with fear of losing their freedom given the renewed British attention, coupled with higher taxes and the arrival of the British army to enforce the laws. All of these served to remind the colonists of their subordination to British rule.

In 1775 the Second Continental Congress gathered, and the delegates agreed to form an army to defend the colonies. The congress attended to matters of defense since most colonists were still loyal to the Crown, and the issue of independence was yet unresolved. As the story of Attucks shows, Blacks joined whites in protesting against the British. Some colonists took the view that Blacks were citizens and should be free, and they believed Blacks also had civil rights. Some Blacks sought relief through petitions and legal suits submitted to the courts, the British government, and colonial authorities. Most of those who received these petitions denied the requests to free slaves. Yet it was not clear to Blacks who they should support, the English or colonial people; many were conflicted as to which side to take, or even whether they should stay neutral. The conflict turned into armed resistance and war:

> Thus, as American protest of British authority turned to military resistance, African Americans were divided over where they should stand in hostilities. Through most of the colonial period, regulations had generally barred slaves and even free blacks from inclusion in the militia, but during time of war these rules had often been disregarded.
>
> *(Horton & Horton, 2005, p. 57)*

George Washington took over the leadership of the American forces in 1775, and he and congress forbade Blacks, free or slave, to join the Americans in battle for fear that the British would use Blacks as well—and in fact they did. Many free Blacks and slaves joined British forces, along with poor whites, Native Americans, and others who were disenfranchised in the colonial world. This made Washington reverse his prior order, permitting Blacks, free and slave, to serve with American forces, except in some of the Southern colonies, where colonial leaders refused to use slaves in their militia to fight for the colonies.

During the conflict between the British and Americans, many slaves took the opportunity to flee while others remained to raid their former plantations. They effectively freed themselves. It is estimated that several thousand went to Canada, sought refuge in Indigenous lands, and settled in areas like Spanish Florida. The number of Blacks who were set free grew, some after being manumitted by owners who agreed that the ideals of the colonies and the Revolution should be honored and that to hold slaves was contrary to the principles they proclaimed. Bennett (1988, p. 69) states that one slave owner, Philip Graham of Maryland, wrote upon freeing his slaves "that the holding of his fellow men in bondage and slavery is repugnant to the golden law of God and the unalienable right of mankind as well as to every principle of the late glorious revolution which has taken place in America."

Establishing A New Nation

In June of 1776 the Continental Congress convened in Philadelphia and began to draft the Articles of Confederation. The first version referred to the collection of colonies or the confederacy as the United States of America (Kidd, 2019; Lepore, 2018). By the time the articles were completed and affirmed some 18 months later, the agreement was to establish a common defense for the "States" where each would be sovereign, and each should write a constitution about how it was to be governed. It was further proposed that the states would be free and independent, and a committee was formed to draft said declaration. While some were engaged in deliberations about what the country would look like and how it would operate, the colonists and settlers in North America remained divided with the war still raging; some were loyalists to the British, others were not sure, and others supported the colonists. In the meantime, the colonial political leaders were busy preparing and eventually circulating their justifications for independence. Slaves tried to get to locations held by British troops who said that if slaves fought with them, they would be freed (it was a false promise; Lepore, 2018).

The war, for the British, was difficult and was complicated by related events pressing upon the empire. To make things more challenging, there was no single place that could be taken that would have ended the war. The British lines were stretched thin, and supplies were hard to acquire from a long distance. To add to the Crown's worries was the reality that the British were engaged in war in many locations around the world, and in 1777 each British victory was matched by losses elsewhere (Kidd, 2019). They had a hard time making headway in the North America mainland, and other British colonies around the world were in jeopardy. Furthermore, other nations joined with the colonists, including the French, Spanish, and Germans in 1778 and 1779.

The conflict ended in 1782 as the British left North America. The Blacks who had fought with them and some who simply wanted to be free tried to reach cities the British held so they could leave the mainland with them. Colonists, however, scoured the cities trying to locate runaway slaves to prevent them from leaving.

In 1783 the Treaty of Paris was signed by American and British delegates. Britain agreed to recognize the independence and sovereignty of the United States, and Americans agreed to pay its debts to all they owed. Prisoners were exchanged, and those colonists who were loyal to the Crown were able to collect their property and possessions (Goldfield et al., 2014). By 1783 thousands of slaves were freed, and many more left with the British or allies to Canada, England, or other destinations. Those who departed to new lands were welcomed with the continuation of their slave status, under which they received harsh treatment and poor living conditions. In addition, the British created a settlement in Sierra Leone, Africa, in 1787 to relocate Blacks, and many were sent out of Canada to Sierra Leone in 1790. It is estimated that some 14,000 Blacks left with the British, and many were relocated to Jamaica or another West Indies colony to resume their bondage.

As the new nation was finding its footing and deciding upon its preferred form of government, its political and civic leaders could not resolve the clear contradictions inherent in the movement for independence and the continuation of slavery as an institution. The participants at the Constitutional Convention could not agree on what to do about slavery. South Carolina and Georgia refused to join the union if slavery was discontinued, a position which effectively silenced the debate on slavery. And the word "slavery" was not included in the final document. However, there was a section in the document about fugitive slaves being returned to their state(s) of origin, and prohibitions on the slave trade were introduced and passed as part of the new constitution but never acted upon. The framers of the Constitution in 1787, as Carter and Scheuermann (2020) note,

> formed a government and established a republic "for and by the people," but they did not agree on what to do about slavery. The economies of the southern colonies were more dependent on slave labor, while the north had fewer slaves and a more diverse economy. A central issue during the Constitutional Convention was how slaves were to be counted for representation in the Congress. An agreement was reached.... Slaves would be counted as three-fifths of a person. With Article I, Section 2 of the Constitution of the United States, the institution of slavery was embedded in our country's foundation. Efforts to dismantle slavery were successful in some states, but slavery's defenders rallied to erect barriers and rationales for its continuance. The US Constitution ... kept the system of slavery in place from the American Revolution to the Civil War. Not only did it count slaves as three-fifths of a person, ... the transatlantic trade was allowed to continue after being suspended by the colonies prior to the conflict with the British.
>
> *(p. 25)*

Finkelman (2018) notes that the Constitution was in fact a proslavery document. Based on the way slaves were counted, it gave the southern states considerable power. "The creation of the Electoral College was also directly tied to slavery" since the count of slaves increased congressional representation from the southern states. In fact, due to this provision, "southerners ... dominated the presidency from 1789 to 1861" (Finkelman 2018, p. 15).

The institution of slavery was maintained, and its supporters gained considerable political power and protection from provisions in the Constitution and the courts (Finkelman, 2018). It was not necessary until the 19th century to present an ideological justification for slavery, but an intellectual rationale was offered and promoted, operating as a significant barrier to freedom for Blacks. So the Constitution provided wealth and significant political power to slaveholders, which helped them defend the institution (Fredrickson, 1998).

The American founders proclaimed inherent rights to life, liberty, and the pursuit of happiness as the core principles of the new nation but did not extend those rights to Black people (or to women). The Declaration of Independence, Bill of Rights, and Constitution were remarkable achievements, ones that set the nation apart for the precedents they established. At the same time, the founders could not extricate themselves from exploiting others for their own gain. They could not apply the principles equally to all as they proclaimed, so they denied Blacks' humanity to justify maintaining human bondage, even in the face of their own struggle for freedom. Some state legislatures and citizens could not fully engage in the psychological deception employed by others and so rejected the idea that it was acceptable to continue slavery. In the same way that many individuals could not maintain the deception that slavery was justified while establishing their own independence as a nation, others could see no other path than to keep slavery in place. Horton and Horton (2005) state that

> during the war, many white Americans, particularly in the northern states, had become convinced that slavery had no place in a new nation being built on the principles of freedom. Vermont outlawed human bondage in its state constitution in 1777, echoing the Declaration of Independence in declaring "all men are created equally free and independent." Other New England states also wrote the abolition of slavery into their constitutions, but it sometimes took the determined action of slaves themselves to make it effective.... Slavery was abolished in Massachusetts in 1783. By 1784 when Rhode Island and Connecticut established emancipation programs, all of New England had prohibited slavery either by state constitution or by legislation providing for its gradual abolition. At the same time, New Jersey moved to ensure that owners free all slaves who had served the American cause in the Revolution, and a Congressional committee recommended ... that slavery be outlawed in the territory that would later become the states of Kentucky, Tennessee, Mississippi, and Alabama. Only one vote prevented Congress from adopting the measure that would have prevented the introduction of slavery in those areas after 1800.
>
> *(pp. 66–67)*

But the law failed to pass, and slavery was established in those new states. In 1778 Virginia stopped importing slaves and by 1782 encouraged manumission. In 1787 South Carolina closed trading in slaves, North Carolina levied taxes on slave trading, and Congress enacted legislation that outlawed slaves in the Northwest Territories.

The Age of Revolution had significant effects on the relationship between slaveholders and slaves in the North American mainland—now the United States. Events around the world had powerful reverberations in the mainland, bringing emigrees to North America from some of the locations that were disrupted by war, insurrections, and revolts. First the struggle for independence fractured the North American alliances and partnerships in such a way that slaveholders lost some power and influence and slaves gained some leverage to challenge some aspects of the institution of slavery and the related systems of white supremacy. Prior to the revolutionary conflict, slavery was supported by the planter class, the state or colonial authorities, and the nonslaveholding citizens. The movement for independence split slaveholders (some were patriots and others loyalists), and planters on both sides used their slaves in the struggle in ways that eroded state support, with many state officials turning against the interests of the planter class. A similar dynamic affected nonslaveholders, who found that they needed to set their own relationships with slaves and planters, many of which diverged from the old ways. These developments helped slaves find new pathways to ease their burdens or earn their freedom. Slaves benefited from the frequent and loud calls for liberty, coupled with the evangelical movement, which became louder and more passionate, with proclamations that all were equal in God's eyes.

The efforts to establish liberty and equality also spread to the non-English colonies on the mainland, to regions like the Florida Gulf Coast and the Mississippi Valley regions, areas held by the French and Spanish during the Revolutionary War. The Spanish wanted to offer slaves within their empire more humane treatment, but the planters objected, and the plans were not implemented. Nevertheless, slaves learned about the effort and took it as indications of their impending emancipation. Meanwhile, further worldwide unrest erupted in France when in 1789, with the fall of the Bastille, an assembly of French citizens who had revolted against the Crown promulgated its own Declaration of the Rights of Man. The new ruling assembly in 1792 rejected racial distinctions and in 1794 abolished slavery.

These events had powerful implications for French colonies, particularly Saint-Domingue, where people of color took up the cause for liberty and equality and pressed for recognition as full citizens. Island planters responded with fierce claims that people of color were no more than degenerates and arrested and jailed their leaders. So the free people there took up arms in 1790, and when it looked like they would not prevail, they armed their slaves, and the struggles turned into a slave insurrection that involved white against Black and free against slaves. The British and Spanish helped the slaves against the French planters and government. Berlin (1998) states that "by the time France tried to retake the colony and reimpose slavery, an independent Haiti had emerged under Toussaint L'Ouverture" (p. 221).

The events in Saint-Domingue struck the world and affected the French Louisiana colony as well as colonies in parts of Florida, all under Spanish rule;

as in other locations, slaves in those places tried to press for more liberty and possibly their freedom. Slaveholders dug in and pushed back against slaves' calls for more equality, and the slaves reacted with considerable resistance. But what seemed to matter most was the deeply set fear of what the Haitian Republic represented for slaves and mainly slaveholders. What also occurred that affected the mainland directly was the arrival of people from the island who had fled the revolt. These included planters of small and large estates, slaves, and free people of color. It has been estimated that more than 10,000 fled in 1793, and thousands more joined them over the next two decades. Most went to nearby islands, but some arrived on the mainland of North America. They landed in cities from Boston to New Orleans. They were witnesses of the perils and problems inherent in a slave society, for good or bad.

Berlin (1998) notes that despite the various forces and winds for change, slaves and free Blacks did not fare well:

> Despite the myriad forces assaulting slavery, freedom progressed slowly and unevenly. The Age of Revolution witnessed the liberation of only a small fraction of slaves in mainland North American. In many places, the advance toward freedom could hardly be noticed, and in others the process worked in the reverse, as slavery grew more rapidly than freedom during the late eighteenth and early nineteenth centuries. Far more black people lived in slavery at the end of the revolutionary age than at the beginning. Much of this increase derived from the reopening of the African trade.
>
> *(pp. 223–224)*

As it turned out, the number of Blacks who were freed was offset by the number of imported Africans. Added to the new arrivals was the twisted ideology promoted and promulgated by the slaveowners as they countered the arguments for abolition with the claim that, yes, all men were created equal, but some were slaves; then it followed that they could not be men, thus their status as property. Berlin (1998) notes that this perspective "moved some men and women from the body politic even as they incorporated others, inciting repression along with liberation" (p. 224).

Following the Revolution, Blacks chose many paths in reestablishing their lives—some in freedom, others as slaves. Some created new identities and names; some took up European Christianity and others created new religions; some moved to cities while others stayed in the country; and some remined on their masters' estates and farms. Some advocated for abolition, while others sought to serve their masters' interests. While Blacks chose varied paths during this time, whites were clear: Blacks were not worthy of any serious consideration, and "race" needed to be reconsidered and redefined.

At the same time, the states took varied actions with respect to slavery. Some stopped importation for a time; others levied taxes on importing slaves;

and some, like Pennsylvania (1780), changed slavery to indentured servitude with age limits. New York and New Jersey passed manumission acts that did not become effective until 1799 and 1804, respectively. Thus, the gradual and grudging shift away from slavery began. Berlin (1998) contends that the end of slavery in the North was in fact a slow and painful process wrought with indecision—and with outright rejection in the South. Recall that the populations of free Blacks and slaves in the northern region were small in relation to those in the South. Moreover, the economy of the North was far less dependent on slaves than was the case for Southern states and their plantations. Berlin (1998) points out that the process of freedom for slaves in the North was neither abrupt nor aimed at a clear end point. For instance,

> The New York abolition law of 1799 and the New Jersey act of 1804, like their Pennsylvania counterpart, mandated the eventual liquidation of slavery but actually freed no slaves. In New York, the children of slaves born after the law went into effect on July 4, 1799, would remain in the service of their mother's owner until age twenty-eight for males and twenty-five for females. It would take nearly another twenty years for New York to free the slaves [1820] who had been born before 1799. A similar formula delayed even longer the arrival of freedom in New Jersey. Still, by 1804 every northern state had committed itself to emancipation in one form or another [eventually].
>
> *(p. 234)*

So the actual reduction of slaves in the North was due to many factors, and some were beyond the colonists' enacting statutes to emancipate Blacks. Other factors included high mortality rates, low birth rates, the apparent closing of the slave trade, and slaveholders who sent or sold their slaves South or sent them to the back country. Freedom for Blacks did not come because the new Americans rejected slavery as an institution. In 1810, 27,000 Black slaves lived in so-called free states, but a generation passed before any of them were actually free (about thirty years—not until 1840), and more than two generations (1870—not until after the Civil War) passed before others could extricate themselves from the legal, social, and occasionally illegal traps that allowed former owners and other white people to control their labor and lives (Berlin, 1998, 2003). In essence, whites created situations in the North, for example, in New York and New Jersey, where Blacks were relegated to menial service roles and jobs, many of which were accompanied by laws and regulations aimed at limiting Blacks' rights and increasing their dependency.

Among the founding fathers of the new nation—the men who signed the documents creating the nation based on the principles of the rights of white men to be free and independent—one-third owned slaves. Yet it was also the case that the socioeconomic well-being of the new nation rested firmly on the backs of forced Black labor: there were 500,000 Blacks, free and slave, in the newly founded United States in 1776. Many must have been bewildered by these events and actions—how could people claim freedom and equality as a right while treating Blacks as beasts of burden? As Wright (2017) observes,

> The contradictions involved more than slavery and ideology. Among the results of the Revolution were paradoxical changes in African-American society and culture. The revolution helped make it possible for some blacks to gain their freedom. It played an important role in the ending of slavery north of Maryland and in considerable manumission in the Upper South.... Yet, the Revolutionary era did little to reduce the nation's reliance on slaves.... [Some] 500,000 slaves lived on the British North American mainland in 1776: nearly 700,000 were counted in the first United States census in 1790. Where emancipation did occur, in the North and Upper South, in almost every instance it came grudgingly, and in all areas white sons of the Revolution began circumscribing that freedom soon after more than a few blacks had gained it. North and South, white men in authority cut away at African-American rights, privileges, and opportunities, so that the black men and women who no longer were slaves remain separated and ostracized from the rest of American society.
>
> *(pp. 185–186)*

While freedom expanded in Maryland cities, the old forms of slave domination were steady and growing in both size and complexity. In many states class lines divided Blacks free and slave, but not so in the Upper South. Instead, a "two-caste system with ridged divisions between black and white came to exemplify the Upper South following the Age of Revolution" (Berlin, 1998, p. 256).

The slave populations grew by natural growth and through trade with the North and Lower South. The crop production was also varied; instead of growing tobacco, planters switched to crops like corn, wheat, and cereals, as well as dairy, which diversified the economy and the activities and duties of slaves. The planters moved into Kentucky, Tennessee, and Mississippi (which at the time were new to the nation and part of the Upper South region). They grew hemp in Kentucky and Tennessee. In 1790 Kentucky counted some 13,000 slaves, and by 1800 the general population had swelled to 40,000. It is estimated that by 1810 more than 115,000 Blacks were relocated to the Upper South, and their former lives, families, and communities were disrupted.

Settlements also spread to the Lower South or Low Country, which was composed of South Carolina, Georgia, and Florida and extended west to include Arkansas and Louisiana. The strictures of slavery held firm in the Lower South, and a three-tiered caste division existed among the free people of color, Black slaves, and whites in the Lower South. In this area, the war of independence was fiercer, and deeply fractured groups fought one another. There were also loyalists, patriots, and Tories who had not selected a side or claimed their cause; they took up arms against all parties, and all combatants engaged in guerrilla raids to promote their own interests. In this region the planters were split into three parts during the conflict. Planters also created armed militias to guard their borders, and Native American allies helped. These patrols also keep an eye out for any slaves who might try to flee or revolt. The planters enforced old laws with ruthlessness and acted with little hesitation to punish anyone—free or slave—suspected of violating their rules and prohibitions.

The region saw an increase in the cultivation of cotton, first as a staple in the slaves' own provisions and economy and then as an international and national crop, especially with the advent of the cotton gin, a new technology. The production of rice and cotton became staple crops, which increased the demand for slaves. Planters secured them from other states, the Caribbean, and Africa, thereby reestablishing the slave system and allowing the institution to thrive. But the addition of Africans also brought to Black American life the connections to their home country and to traditional practices and patterns that would help American-born Blacks connect to their ancestors and the culture that would give them strength.

Black Life and Ways Chosen to Survive in the Revolutionary Era

It could be said that the changes that took place during the revolutionary era occurred gradually, in a slow and steady way. Blacks responded to their status as slaves with acts of resistance and pushed back to reclaim their freedom and dignity. They took their names back, built their own homes (when set free), and sought paying jobs, even jobs with considerable limits. They created individual identities as free people, and built institutions aimed at expanding and maintaining their liberty as free people. They established and constructed churches, schools, and fraternal societies. Black leaders emerged who were dedicated to promoting the interests of Black people. There also were divisions and differences within and among Black society between slaves and former slaves, urban and rural, Blacks and mixed race (Bennett, 1988; Berlin, 2003; Wright, 2017).

Resistance: Pushing Back against Oppression

Some slaves reacted to racial oppression with acts of resistance while others accepted their status. In the Chesapeake (Virginia, Maryland, Delaware) and Low Country regions (North and South Carolina, Georgia, and part of Florida), some slaves in the 1760s took on African ways due to the lager number of "saltwater" Africans who came during this period, and this influx helped to reestablished some traditional practices such as polygamy. Some Blacks rejected the Anglican or European religious principles and church services, instead relying on spiritual practices they remembered or were taught in their country of origin. Other Blacks embraced European ways and beliefs so much that they sought to emulate Europeans. Another expression of Black life came about in the quarters, where they built homes for themselves that resembled African villages.

Some slaves found themselves living and working in urban centers in the Low Country serving white elites, and their lifestyles and experiences diverged from Blacks on the plantations, which usually were located in the far reaches of the counties.

> The incongruous prosperity of urban slaves and their attachment to Christianity, along with other manifestations of European-American society, also disturbed more than a few people of African descent, for the division between city and countryside marked a growing fissure within black society. On the plantations, the mass of black people, physically separated and psychologically estranged from the European-American world, had begun to create a new African-American culture, informed by the continued arrival of saltwater slaves. Urban slaves took a different course, perfecting their English, mimicking the planters' sartorial style, and welcoming Jesus. From their clothes, separate residences, and mastery of numerous artisanal skills, they were confident they could compete as equals on the planters' own ground. Barred from white society, this emerging colored elite wanted no part of life on the plantations. When they could not be part of white society, these skilled, privileged urbanites began to create a society of their own in which white people played little part.
>
> *(Berlin, 2003, pp. 80–81)*

Blacks created a world unto themselves, whether African-centered or European American focused, either way, Blacks lived in separate domains characterized by several aspects of their evolving culture. Many observers noted that Blacks behaved differently from what was assumed and expected because of the powerful influences of whites. The cultural practices that Blacks used during their enslavement were deeply held kinship bonds (beyond blood family), a work orientation, flexible family roles (no rigid male and female roles), prioritizing achievement and striving to do better, and spiritual practices to guide them through the rocky waters of the time (Webber, 1978).

Slaves showed determination to value and honor their former traditions and ways of living regardless of place and situation. While Africans had a wide range of languages, social practices, religions, beliefs, and psychological perspectives prior to being captives, many began to function as a group with common goals and objectives once they became captives and, later, slaves.

They used their core values and psychological orientations and resolutions as fuel to survive their new situations as low-caste slaves and restricted free people. More important, they taught the new generations the thoughts and behaviors that would aid in their survival. Blacks, regardless of location, were determined to be free. For the most part, they did not accept their subordination or their low-caste status. It was a formidable task to push back against, given that the majority of white colonists and, later, Americans shared the negative view of them and worked to keep them down.

It is also true that the centuries of harsh oppression resulted in significant damage to some members of the group, and many individuals were pressed into submission; some harmed themselves and others of the group. Nevertheless, many others held on and taught valuable lessons to those who followed, or left legacies that have guided them (Thornton, 2012).

Traditional Practices

Black people were successful at surviving slavery and racial oppression up to this point in history because many of them, with the aid of Africans who arrived directly from Africa or were brought from other colonies, allowed some Blacks to retain the beliefs and values, altered by their circumstances, that reflected and honored their ancestors. Honoring those who came before was a way of valuing the lives of those who had passed and a way of retaining African ways, such as the practice of being slow to move or respond or the practice of coming to events in one's own time, which came to be referred to as colored time, and the practice of expressing their sense of rhythm in movement, songs, and dances; another practice that can be traced to the ancestors and recognized as unique to Black people was their use of stories told through folk tales and by way of oral communication. Their cultural spirituality and myriad communal cultural practices were expressed through their psychological-based reference group identity or racial identity that placed a high value on individual action being related to the well-being of the group when the person identified positivity with their race.

Throughout the first century and a quarter of slavery, with its indignities and in the face of ever-growing and elaborate efforts to deny their humanity, free and enslaved Africans and their decedents found ways to establish and pass along the needed beliefs and psychological mechanisms necessary to maintain and create communities, families, and institutions. Even in the face of shifting locations and the harsh and degrading ways they were treated by owners and citizens alike, Berlin, Favreau, and Miller (1998) observe that

> slavery's brutality inhered less in the brutish and sadistic outbursts than in the routine, systematic violence of slaveowners found it necessary to reduce men and women to things....

> Violence called forth powerful resistance. Slavery's heroes and heroines should no more be forgotten than should the adversity they confronted.... It is equally important to appreciate the silent, everyday heroics of the men and women who stoically took the slaveholders' worst and quietly educated their children to take back piecemeal what the "masters" had appropriated.... In short, men and women recognizing their inability to overthrow slavery taught their children to survive until their moment arrived.
>
> *(pp. xxii–xxiii)*

Of Their Own Making: Black Organizations, Societies, Churches, and Schools

Blacks engaged in considerable efforts to build and develop community through organizations and institutions. Bennett (1988) tells about such efforts that occurred during the revolutionary era among both free and enslaved people. Bennett (1988) states that on

> Thursday, April 12, 1787 ... one month before the first session of the U.S. Constitutional Convention and two years before the election of George Washington ... eight [Black] men sat down in a room in Philadelphia and created a black social compact ... called the [Free] African Society, [a] prophetic step that marked a turning in the road that is critical to the history of Black America.... The founding of this seminal organization was only one wave in the tide of institution-building that rolled over the North in the 1780s and 1790s.
>
> *(pp. 55–56)*

Other groups and organizations were formed in other states as well. Blacks also formed independent churches, lodges, schools, and cultural organizations. Behind these efforts were, according to Bennett (1988, p. 56), two driving, contrasting forces: "a sense of identity and peoplehood that rejected black subordination and exclusion. The negative current, flowing with and out of white founding, was a campaign to exclude black Americans from the national social contract." The Black leaders set out to erect a Black political base that would push for equality and social participation. The organizational building that they began gave birth to a model for establishing such systems that others could use to form similar associations around the country, all self-defined and created by Black people.

> It was in the struggle surrounding the Revolution that the founders of Black America defined themselves and re-positioned themselves. It was the failure of that Revolution—it was the realization that the makers of

> the Revolution didn't believe what they said—that forced Black America to create itself.
>
> *(Bennett, 1988, pp. 56–57)*

The creation and content of the Declaration of Independence established for Blacks the rationale for their freedom (at that time, since they always knew they had a natural right to be free)—people were to be equal under the law—and the new governments, both federal and state, were to serve the will of the people. With these positions expressed as the basis for independence, some colonial leaders, like Thomas Paine, saw at once that slavery could not be justified and called for an end to its practice. Blacks, free and enslaved alike, pressed their case during this era to free themselves. They advocated for themselves and described their plight in the North and South by taking legal action. For example, in 1766 legal challenges to slavery were made in courts claiming unlawful detention, some cases were lodged in the Northern colonies soon to be states, like Connecticut and other locations. Blacks raised funds, hired legal counsel, and filed their lawsuits. Their legal challenges were aligned with protests, public meetings, collections of petitions, and testimony before state legislators. They also used the language and slogans of the independence movement to make their case; they joined—and, in some instances, led—protests and demonstrations like a confrontation, in 1768, with British troops in Boston to advocate for freedom from England and slave owners. All the while whites and Blacks advocated for the elimination of slavery so that the newly founded country could live up to its ideals and principles. The efforts of Blacks and whites who pressed for freedom by using their organizational skills resulted in dismantling some aspects and forms of slavery in the northern region. But the issue of ending slavery in other colonies often were debated, contested, and rejected. Most white males considered the Declaration of Independence and U.S. Constitution to apply only to them, not to Blacks, Native Americans, or women.

The revolutionary period was a time of reflection and ambiguity given that the new nation was being created and there was considerable unrest in the land. It provided opportunities for some Blacks to break through and be visible; for example, in some areas Blacks led churches, which were places of visibility. Some Blacks enjoyed freedom and recognition. Yet the vast majority, slowly and in different ways and at different times, began to be harshly excluded, regardless of their station. They were greeted with hostility, were assaulted and shamed throughout the North, and in the South new rules and laws were enacted to remove from Blacks any form of dignity; they were relegated to the lowest caste and regarded as less than human.

Some historians (Bennett, 1988; Berlin, 1998; Dodson, 2002; Franklin & Moss, 2000; Harms, 2018; Wright, 2017) contend that the new restrictions were sparked by the invention of the cotton gin, which made some aspects of growing cotton easier and extremely profitable; thus, planters wanted to grow more of it, which required more labor to harvest the cotton. This helped generate huge profits for planters, merchants, slave traders, and citizens in both the North and the South, which stopped the calls for social change and ended any further efforts to abolish slavery in southern or western states. So it could be argued that the question about slavery as an institution was settled. It would continue, just not in every state, and it would provide power and wealth to those involved in the slave trade and for those who held slaves. It was also settled that Blacks would not be treated as, nor recognized as, humans equal to whites. The reactions and regression that came with the post-Revolutionary War era, with the new cotton invention and the growing free Black population, sent whites into a frenzy of racial oppression.

Black people were left to establish their own institutions, many of which were clearly identified by the name "African"—whether a church, social club, or other association. Bennett (1988, p. 77) describes it this way: "Rebuffed, insulted, incessantly vilified, post-war blacks turned inward and formed their own social institutions and, in the process, created themselves. This act of self-generation created a community out of a collective of isolated individuals." Much of the activity of building and forming organizations and communities was undertaken by a small percentage of free Blacks in the North, many of whom were not slaves at the time but were former slaves. For instance, the Free African Society, formed by eight Black men, started as a church, then was a society to aid Blacks, then a political foundation for activism, and finally the seeds for a Black insurance company. The first organizations were followed by others in different cities in the North centered around New York and Philadelphia, and the memberships grew to encompass larger numbers. More importantly, these organizations were linked and connected to each other: "Through the medium of these organizations, blacks exchanged information, ideas, and programs.... They began to see their lives in a time-line extending from Africa to the Day of Judgement they believed would vindicate them" (Bennett, 1988, p. 80).

The Black church was part of the first group of social organizations, which started in the 1770s with the creation of the first African Baptist churches in Georgia, Virginia, and South Carolina. The churches helped Blacks establish social and fraternal organizations, the first of which started in Boston in 1787 as an African Lodge. These various organizations helped fuel the early efforts to promote Black equal rights (Horton & Horton, 2005). Following the efforts to organize, Black leaders set out to establish schools to educate their people. "All the while, on another level of existence, black leaders were pressing an increasingly sophisticated campaign against discrimination and segregation" (Bennett, 1988, p. 83).

As we move in time and place, to the South where most (90%) Blacks resided, and where Blacks were less able to move about and participate in organizations, we still find that the community was a core factor in Black people's lives. Much of the slave's life—day in and day out—was devoted to labor; from the morning horn (around 4:00 a.m.) until midnight, they labored either in the fields or the main house or in attending to their own needs and homes. Bennett (1988) and Webber (1978) note that this regimen was supposed to crush the slave's spirit and will. Yet Bennett (1988) notes that in fact the opposite was often true:

> For the slaves, in the most astonishingly creative act in our history transcended their environment, creating a new structure of meaning and putting their oppressors and the world in their debt. No one can read the record of that transcendence without a sense of awe at the audacity of the slaves' hope. This hope was clearly visible in the concentric circles of community that started in the family and radiated in larger and larger circles that enveloped the whole of the Slave Row. From that community came the rhythmic, spiritual, and psychic piles that bottomed the new synthesis called Black America. The results—the spirituals, the blues, the rhythmic tonality of Black America—point to and guarantee the medium, which was a community of passion and creativity.
>
> *(p. 96)*

The community was in part created by the establishment of the plantation, and the slave quarters were a product of it. At the same time, the community was not defined by the plantation, nor did it contain the Black's community or their spirit. "The community of the slaves was a communal entity characterized by a collective orientation stemming partly from the African past and partly from the exigencies of the situation" (Bennett, 1988, p. 96).

Bennett contends that the slave community mirrors Black communities of today and the recent past, but he also argues that the community of Blacks was not defined by geographic boundaries since the community was part of the person and not the situation or location. Each physical community nevertheless had leaders who were selected from among their own, and many looked to the community elders for guidance. Moreover, the community and its structure operated with several critical elements. People's roles and obligations in the community were arranged into what Bennett called proto-institutions, which dictated proper behavior and expectations and set standards for how relationships with slaveholders should be handled. There were standards and guides for how new people to the community should be brought along or included as part of the group. Some of these institutions represented translations of African practices while some were combined European and African forms. And still others were improvisations of European themes.

Three Foundational Points of Culture

The energies flowing through the forces of Black culture organized themselves around three foundational points:

> The first of course, was the axis of the spirit. In this realm, as in others the slaves reinterpreted white patterns, weaving a whole new universe around biblical images and giving a new dimension and new meaning to Christianity.... American slaves, with few exceptions, rejected [the] version of Christianity [promoted by slave owners]. Their God was the [one] that delivered the Israelites.... In a total and passionate quest for *this* God, the slaves, tempered and toughened by the annealing heat of adversity, turned American Christianity inside out, like a glove, infusing it with African-oriented melodies and rhythms and adding new patterns, such as the ring shoot, ecstatic seizure and communal, call-and-response patterns.
>
> *(Bennett, 1988, pp. 99–102)*

Some of the Africans and their descendants arranged to worship in private by stealing away into the woods or swamps, and they found ways to relay the message to others for when and where they would meet. In this setting they developed their own manner of worship and connection to one another. Their beliefs were twofold, one in God and the other in spirits who had power over the living. The second set of beliefs were visible in the use of taboos, charms, and other practices that were contrary to white Christian faith (Dodson, 2002). As Bennett points out, the religious element was a part of a more complex set of beliefs and practices.

The second factor in Black cultural forms that were created by slaves was music and rhythm. According to Jones (2003), rhythm was a core element of TRIOS—or time, rhythm, improvisation, orality, and spirituality—factors of Black culture he described. For Bennett and other historians (e.g., Berlin, 2003; Blassingame, 1972; Dodson, 2002; Horton & Horton, 2005; Webber, 1978), music, dance, and stories were a central aspect of Black people's lives both in and out of slavery. Bennett (1988) says that music and rhythm were

> this axis, which informed every element of slave life, ... characterized by the so-called "blues" tonality and a rhythmic, collective, and emotional orientation. The same elements are evident in slave folk lore and philosophy, especially the Brer Rabbit, Brer Fox and Old John cycles. The expression of this orientation was as varied as the people and included cries, hollers, work songs, devil songs, spirituals and blues.
>
> *(p. 102)*

Black musical forms such as the blues and spirituals are credited as original contributions of Black Americans. The music forms were used to communicate and to express the longing of their souls and spirits, both sorrows and, although less often experienced, joy and jubilation. The place where sounds of joy were most often expressed was during church services. These behaviors, in the beginning of plantation life, were often hidden from whites.

A third pillar of Black life was the family, merged with the spirit and the community (Berlin, 1998; Blassingame, 1972; Dodson, 2002; Horton & Horton, 2005). The slave family was not recognized and often had no legal status (Kulikoff, 1986). No matter the state or colony, husband, wife, and children could be separated at the will of the "owners." Moreover, multiple mates were often encouraged, for the sake of breeding and market sales. Even amid the brutal system of slavery, slaves established a way to mate and marry that helped them to survive and grow. Jumping the broom was one mechanism used for marriage ceremonies, which took place outside of the master's view and knowledge. But the couple had to take care not to touch the broom or that could be trouble for them, a bad omen for the marriage. Bennett (1988) and Sweet (2003) note that the manner of how these marriages occurred revealed that they were based on love and equality since the women could end the marriage when they desired, which was not so for the formal process undertaken by whites.

Stampp (1956) has suggested that Black people were of loose morals and engaged in unrestrained sexual behavior with no sense of family or kinship obligations, a common characterization of Black people, especially slaves. However, a comprehensive study by Gutman (1976) of the Black family from 1750 to 1925, both free and enslaved, reported family units that were headed by men and characterized by long-term marriages (of 30 or more years), where fathers were highly regarded and important and respected parts of the family system. Perhaps because they lived in proximity to one another, there was more openness about sex (a perspective shared by Africans). But when pregnancy happened before marriage, members of the Black community had strong expectations that marriage would follow. There was also the notion that, once married, one would not stray. And marriage was supported often by an extended family network, with and without blood relations, during and after slavery.

As we can see, the family was an important aspect of the community. It is also apparent that communalism consisted of several components. The belief in spirit as reflected in religious belief and practice that became particular to Black people, their unique use of music and rhythm, and the extended family and kinship networks, all contributed to Blacks' sense of self and the value placed of community. So, being group-focused may have been fostered in part by Blacks' circumstances, yet it was also something that came from their African ancestors.

The lives of Black Americans changed when the cry of revolution took hold across the Atlantic world. The time that passed from Africans' first arrival was considerable—recall that it was 1619 when the first Africans arrived in the North American mainland colonies. These were members of the Charter generation. Then came the Plantation generation. The lives of rural and urban Blacks diverged quite a bit in all time periods. But Black people were profoundly affected by the winds of revolution—in the colonies and the world. The ground regarding slavery began to shift and shake, and in the storms that followed some Blacks were released from bondage and others were set deeper in the pit of misery that was slavery.

> Largely because of the existence of the slave community, the struggle continued behind the lines of slavery until the end of slavery.
>
> Men and women nourished and sustained by the slave community pressed that struggle on several levels....
>
> The court records of this period yield ample evidence that a large number of slaves refused to play the game of slavery [that is, except as their masters desired that they believe they were helpless and had to obey]; they would neither smile nor bow. Other slaves bowed but would not smile. Still others, perhaps the majority, went through the ritual of obeisance. What about them? What did they think of slavery? What they thought can be inferred from what they did. Black and white historians have uncovered a mass of material on their passive "day-to-day resistance to slavery." These slaves who smiled sometimes and bowed sometimes used a variety of techniques to indicate their dissatisfaction with the system. They staged deliberate slowdowns and sit-down strikes. They broke implements and trampled the crops.... By resisting, maintaining, enduring and abiding, by holding on and holding fast and holding out, they provided one of the greatest examples in history of the strength of the human spirit in adversity.
>
> *(Bennett, 1988, pp. 107–111)*

To have a better sense of the slaves' experiences, in the following I refer to a few narratives that were published by former slaves about their lives and perceptions while being held in bondage.

Slave Narratives: In Their Own Words

Several things are revealed in the stories or narratives that relate to the themes of the current book. It becomes apparent that slaves lived in closed worlds usually consisting of the farm, estate, or plantation on which they resided. The estates or farms were populated by the slaveowners and their families, other slaves, and any other employed workers such as overseers. Most slaves were forbidden to learn to read or write, so in that sense they were ignorant and unaware. Many knew little of where they lived or the area surrounding them except for the short distances they could walk or travel with their owners.

Most knew that their lives depended upon pleasing their owners since they relied on them for food, shelter, and any possible protection. Owners varied from those who were cruel and abusive to those who were kind and humane. What slaves had, and this could be fleeting, were their family and connections to others who lived on the same property. These relationships tended to be their worlds. Some of the narratives tell of loyalty to the owners and the desire to be seen as a valuable worker; some made it their mission to do their tasks so they would benefit their owner. At the same time, those who earned some degree of status and responsibility as drivers or overseers also resolved to be productive so that the slaves on the property would have a better life, more and healthier foods, and nicer clothes to wear. The theme of poor diets and scant clothes is common in slave narratives. Many of the cultural practices discussed in this chapter are illustrated in the stories provided by some of the authors.

An example of the resistance employed by some slaves, mentioned by Bennett, is seen the demeanor of Ibrahima Rahman (Abraham), who was a West African prince of the Fulani people, raised as Muslim, highly educated, and wealthy prior to being taken captive. He was caught and transported in 1789 to the North American mainland and resided in the Natchez area of Mississippi where he was purchased by the Foster family and for more than a year refused to succumb to the expectations of a slave. In the early years of his bondage, he fled to the woods where he stayed for weeks. While hiding in the woods he deliberated about what course to take. It is said that

> when hunger and exposure forced him at length to decide what he was going to do, he chose against it [suicide]. It was not the fear of death; as a solider he had learned to ignore that fear as much as he could. Most possibly, Ibrahima strove to accommodate the will of God as he understood it.... [He] felt his misfortune came from God. No affliction befalls a person without divine permission....
>
> For Ibrahima it may well have been the reason why he chose to live.
>
> *(Alford, 2007, p. 47)*

After his stay in the woods and after his return to the property, he dedicated himself to being a loyal and industrious servant. In time, he married and had a family and was elevated to supervise the farm, where he oversaw the work and managed the crops and the livestock. He had experience and knowledge, which served the Fosters well as their property expanded. Yet as Alford (2007) notes,

> He remained a model of probity, hard-working and dependable at whatever he gave his attention. He never drank, he never cursed, he was never caught in a falsehood or dishonest act. He meant to survive, and he did, but the personal price was staggering. A man who knew him for two decades said that—despite the passage of the years, despite the love of his wife, the cheer of his family, despite the respect of his owner—in all the time he had known Ibrahima, he had never seen him smile.
>
> *(p. 65)*

Olaudah Equiano, or Gustavus Vassa, was born in 1745 in Africa in the area now known as Nigeria. He was taken from his home at the around the age of 11, so he started his years in bondage around 1757 or thereabouts, when he was sold in Virginia to a British navy officer. He lived in the West Indies after being sold again in 1762, but much of his life was spent in England (he thought of England as his home) or at sea on voyages to various ports and countries around the world. He seemed to have been treated fairly well as a slave. Yet he tells stories of instances of cruel and thoughtless behavior toward him and other Blacks. As time passed, Vassa was usually alone for the most part. There was not a group of slaves with him but mostly white sailors and mates, so he had to rely on his own devices to get through his bondage. His goal in life was to purchase his freedom, and he was allowed to earn small sums toward that end. He was not able during these periods to connect with other slaves or become involved in a community, so he relied on his spiritual beliefs to provide guidance and support in moments of distress and bewilderment. When such incidents happened, it was clear he could do nothing to stop them or seek any redress.

He tells of witnessing cruel acts committed upon the person of slaves who were being transported from islands to the mainland North America or other destinations. He observed that one constant practice whites engaged in was "violent depredations on the chastity of the female slaves" (Carretta, 1995, p. 104). He notes how helpless he was and that these acts, in his view, violated Christian morals. He thought that the Christian way was to treat others as you wished to be treated. He also thought that it was always best to be honest, even when others were not honest with him. He also observed, "I thought only slavery dreadful; but the state of a free Negro appeared ... equally so at least and in some respects even worse, for they live in constant alarm for their liberty, which is but nominal" (Carretta, 1995, p. 122).

Josiah Henson's story of slavery began in the year of his birth, which he says was 1789 as the youngest of six children. He had two brothers and three sisters in Maryland (Phelps, 1849). He tells of his first recollection when he was three or four years old: seeing his father with his ear cut off and his back covered in scars from being whipped. Apparently his father had beaten the white overseer for assaulting his wife and was punished and sold, never to be seen again. Three years later, his mother and siblings were put up for auction and sold. When he and his mother were separated at the sale, Henson describes how his mother begged the person who bought her to take him as well so she would not be separated from her youngest child. After his mother was purchased by Issac R.,

> she fell to her feet, and clung to his knees, entreating him in tones that a mother could command, to buy her baby as well as herself.... [He] turning a deaf ear to her supplications, but of disengaged himself from

> her with such violent blows and kicks, as to reduce her to the necessity of creeping out of his reach.
>
> *(Phelps, 1849, pp. 8–9)*

Josiah took ill shortly after the sale, and it was thought he would not recover, but his owner proposed to Mr. R, who had purchased Josiah's mother, that he take the child for a bargain price that R. did not refuse. His mother nursed him back to health, and he "grew up to be an uncommonly vigorous and healthy boy and man" (Phelps, 1849, p. 9).

A few of the slaves' narrative tell of the devotion and strong connection among family members even though it was common practice to separate families when the primary slaveholder died or had financial difficulties. Henson's (Phelps, 1849) life story also reflects the value and commitment to family that characterized Black families. In the course of this story there comes a time when he decides that it was in his and his family's interest to flee from their owner and seek freedom. He took action to purchase his freedom and was betrayed in this agreement. After receiving his manumission papers, his owner tried to sell him to acquire more income for him. The owner's effort failed, and Henson resolved to leave with his family. They left and headed to Canada, and through considerable peril and struggle they arrived at their destination. Once there, Henson, after several years, observed that the number of Blacks was growing and that they, as before, were working for hire, which helped the farmers but was not to the Black workers' advantage. They all were able to maintain a living but little else. He stated that "several hundreds of colored persons were in the neighborhood; and in the first joy of their deliverance, were going on in a way which, I could see, led to little or no progress in improvement" (Phelps, 1849, p. 84). He gathered some workers and addressed them about investing their earnings in land of their own. He pointed out that if they pooled their funds for this purpose then every tree cut and every ear of corn raised would be for themselves, so they could "secure all the profits of our own labor" (Phelps, 1849, p. 85). They looked for such land, found it, and settled there.

Henson's slave narrative reveals how core cultural practices of community and family operated and were aligned with education and spirituality. Henson's son was able to attend school and learn to read. Henson could not read or write, but he agreed, at his son's urging, to let his son teach him, and he did in time learn to read and write. Even without formal education, he achieved a great deal in part because he embodied the lessons and had the drive he learned from his people.

References

Alford, T. (2007). *Prince among slaves: The true story of an African prince sold into slavery in the American south.* Oxford University Press.

Bennett, L. (1988). *Before the Mayflower: A history of Black America.* Johnson Publishing.

Berlin, I. (1998). *Many thousands gone: The first two centuries of slavery on North America.* Belknap Press of Harvard University Press.

Berlin, I. (2003). *Generations of captivity: A history of African Americans slaves.* Belknap Press of Harvard University Press.

Berlin, I., Favreau, M., & Miller, S. F. (1998). *Remembering slavery.* New Press.

Blassingame, J. W. (1972). *The slave community: Plantation life in the anti-bellum South.* Oxford University Press.

Carretta, V. (1995). *Olaudah Equiano: The interesting narrative and other writings.* Penguin Classics.

Carter, R. T., & Scheuermann, T. D. (2020). *Confronting racism: Integrating mental health strategies with legal reform.* Routledge.

Dodson, H. (2002). *Jubilee: The emergence of African-American culture.* National Geographic.

Finkelman, P. (2018). *Supreme injustice: Slavery in the nation's highest court.* Harvard University Press.

Franklin, H. J., & Moss, A. A. (2000). *From slavery to freedom: A history of African Americans* (8th ed.). McGraw Hill.

Fredrickson, G. M. (1998). *The arrogance of race. Historical perspectives on slavery, racism and social inequity.* Wesleyan University Press.

Goldfield, D., Abbott, C., Anderson, V. D., Argersinger, J. E., Argersinger, P. H., & Barney, W. L. (2014). *The American journey: A history of the United States* (7th ed.), Vol. 1. Pearson.

Gutman, H. G. (1976). *The Black family in slavery and freedom: 1750–1925.* Vintage.

Harms, R. (2018). *Africa in global history with sources.* Norton.

Horton, J. O., & Horton, L. E. (2005). *Slavery and the making of America.* Oxford University Press.

Jones, J. M. (2003). TRIOS: A psychological theory of the African legacy in American culture. *Journal of Social Issues*, 39(1), 217–242.

Kidd, T. S. (2019). *American history: 1492 to the present.* B&N Academic.

Kulikoff, A. (1986). *Tobacco and slaves: The development of Southern cultures in the Chesapeake, 1680–1800.* University of North Carolina Press.

Lepore, J. (2018). *These truths: A history of the United States.* Norton.

Phelps, A. D. (1849). *The life of Josiah Henson: Formerly a slave, now an inhabitant of Canada.* Dover.

Stampp, K. M. (1956). *The peculiar institution: Slavery in the ante-bellum South.* Vintage.

Sweet, J. H. (2003). *Recreating Africa: Culture, kinship and religion in the African–Portuguese world, 1441–1770.* University of North Carolina Press.

Thornton, J. K. (2012). *A cultural history of the Atlantic world, 1250–1820.* Cambridge University Press.

Webber, T. L. (1978). *Deep like the rivers: Education in the slave quarter community, 1831–1865.* Norton.

Wright, D. R. (2017). *African Americans in the colonial era: From the Africans origins through the Americans revolution.* (4th ed.). Wiley.

PART 3

Africans' Conversion to American Life and Their Contributions to Its Prosperity

7

THE EXPANDED UNION AND BLACKS AS THE ENGINE FOR PROGRESS

We have seen in the last chapter that Black people reacted in myriad ways to the American struggle for independence from England and its aftermath. What describes the post-revolutionary era is fragmentation. In varied instances, the new nation was on fragile footing and struggled on numerous fronts, and the same could be said for Black people. Some Blacks found a path to freedom, while others were torn from all they knew—family and community—to reside in slave states. In this chapter I chart and describe some aspects of the post-revolutionary history and the changes that affected Blacks across the nation, altering their lives.

The Colonies Became States and the New Nation Expanded

The end of the 18th century and the early decades of the 19th century were marked by significant changes in government, politics, economics, education, geography, and technological advancement that dramatically altered how people lived, the social and work roles of men and women, and the standards and locations of work and home life as well as the lives of free and enslaved Blacks. It would help to recap the series of events that characterized the late 18th century and ushered in the 19th century.

The more significant event, some would argue, was the creation of a union of British colonies that declared their independence in 1776 (when the Declaration of Independence was signed and distributed); this declaration converted the 13 colonies to states of the United States. The colonist sent delegates to the Second Continental Congress where they approved the Articles of Confederation on November 15, 1777, to be fully recognized as the United States of America. Each state needed to ratify the Articles of

DOI: 10.4324/9781003111542-11

Confederation via their legislative bodies, with this process completed on March 1, 1781.

The 13 Confederated states and their dates of ratification, as well as the population of Blacks, both free and enslaved according to the 1790 census, were as follows:

TABLE 7.1 Ratification Dates and Populations of the 13 Confederated States

State	*Ratification date*	*Population of Blacks*	
		Free	*Enslaved*
Virginia	December 1777	12,866	292,627
South Carolina	February 1778	1,801	107,763
New York	February 1778	4,682	21,193
Rhode Island	February 1778	3,484	958
Connecticut	February 1778	2,771	2,648
Georgia	February 1778	398	29,364
New Hampshire	March 1778	630	157
Pennsylvania	March 1778	6,531	3,707
Massachusetts	March 1778	5,369	0
North Carolina	April 1778	5,041	100,763
New Jersey	November 1779	2,762	11,423
Delaware	February 1779	3,888	8,887
Maryland	February 1781	8,043	103,036

Source: Franklin & Moss, 2000, p. 98.

The next significant date was March 4, 1789, when the federal government was changed to one that was guided by the Constitution of the United States of America. The number of states slowly increased during the last decade of the 18th century and the first few years of the 19th, with four additional states being admitted into the union:

TABLE 7.2 Ratification Dates and Populations of the Next Four States

State	*Ratification date*	*Population of Blacks*	
		Free	*Enslaved*
Vermont	March 1791	269	0
Kentucky	June 1792	114	12,430
Tennessee	June 1796	361	3,417
Ohio	March 1803	—	—

Source: Franklin & Moss, 2000, p. 98.

These numbers show that Black people, slave and free, resided in greater numbers in the Southern states. By 1800 and during the early decades of the new century, the number of states rapidly grew to 17, along with numerous other changes in a wide range of areas, many of which had far-reaching consequences for the nation. In the course of the next two decades, seven more states joined the United States, bringing the number of states to 24, and by midcentury there would be 31 states, with the country extending from the East Coast to the West Coast.

Yet the story of the new United States and its people cannot be known from just the number of states and the population of Blacks. Goldfield et al. (2014) report, based upon the 1790 census, that the regions of the new nation were diverse in terms of religion, ethnicity, and class. The census reported that the total population was about 4 million presented in terms of four regions. The New England region had over 1 million residents, of whom 1.7% were Black (more were free than slave), and whites were mostly English (82%), with the remaining whites (16%) representing numerous ethnic groups (such as the Welsh, Irish, Scottish, and Dutch). Goldfield et al. (2014) state:

> The Puritan notions of religious liberty that prevailed in the region extended only to those who subscribed to the Calvinist orthodoxy of the dominant Congregationalist Church. Geography conspired with this religious exclusiveness to limit population diversity. New England's poor soils and long, cold winters made it an impractical place to cultivate cash crops like the tobacco and rice of the South. As a result New England farmers had little need for imported white servants or black slaves.
>
> *(pp. 200–201)*

The Mid-Atlantic's population (New York, New Jersey, and Pennsylvania) was counted to be slightly less than 1 million (959,000), of which 36.9% were English while white ethnics made up 57.8 percent of the population—German (20.9%), Dutch (9.3%), Scottish (5.4%), Irish (5.4%), and others. Black slaves accounted for 5.3% of the population, and free Blacks were 3.8%. The region was more diverse in terms of religion than New England. To settle this region and attract immigrants, freedom of religion was advertised as a feature of the region. The region was varied as to social class, and the environment and economic opportunities were greater and more promising as well. Thus, the demand for labor grew with the population and favorable agricultural markets. While for the most part the region did not rely on slave labor, it still was the case that as Blacks were slowly freed, they "had to confront enduring white racism" (Goldfield et al., 2014, p. 202) that held that Black people were inferior.

The South which consisted of Maryland, Delaware, Virginia, the Carolinas, and Georgia, had a population of more than 1.8 million people, with 35.7% English, 34.6% Black slaves, and 1.7% free Blacks. White ethnics were 8.4% Scots-Irish, 5.3% Irish, and 4.2% Scottish. Welsh and Germans each comprised 3.9%. The climate was ideal for staple crops that were sold in the international markets. White immigrants tended to avoid the grueling labor that the crops required; thus, Black slaves fulfilled that role. There were tensions in ideology between large and small planters in the region, but in the final analyses they all strove to protect their individual rights and to resist government intrusion.

The West region, an area between the Appalachian Mountains and the Mississippi River, had a population of about 109,000, and it was growing quickly after the Treaty of Paris added Kentucky and Tennessee. It was an area populated by Native Americans (about 150,000) from many tribes, and they resisted the presence of the white settlers, fighting to push back the new settlers arriving in the area. In 1780 the number of whites was around 10,000, yet that grew to about 200,000 by 1790.

> Indians strongly resented white claims on their land. A confederation of tribes in the Ohio Valley, led by the Miamis and supplied with firearms by the British in exchange for furs, kept whites out of the Old Northwest territory, the area north of the Ohio River. South of the Ohio, white settlements were largely limited to Kentucky and Tennessee. In what is today Alabama and Mississippi, the Creeks and their allies blocked American expansion.
>
> *(Goldfield et al., 2014, p. 204)*

The West region was an area with 45.1% English, and Black slaves composed 14.5% of the population (with 0.4% free Blacks). The largest white ethnic groups were Scots-Irish (14.3%) and nearly equal numbers of Irish and Scottish (7.5% and 7.2%, respectively), followed by Germans (4.6%), Welsh (3.4%), and others. Settlers were mostly poor rural whites, and they were mostly cut off from the east; most were squatters hoping to lay a stake to the land. The area turned into a contested territory in that the land was occupied by Native Americans who seemed to be ignored while whites settled the region. The area north of the Ohio River was claimed by eastern states, and the government issued the Northwest Ordinance in 1787 in an effort to organize the settlement of the area. Conflict over the course of the next decade ensued between the Western Indian Confederation and the United States over the territory.

The New Federal Government

Once the War of Independence concluded, it was necessary to form a working national government that was composed of multiple autonomous states. The national government was presumed to represent the interest of the people across the varied states and territories. There were those who wanted a strong federal government and those who sought the opposite. So in 1789, when George Washington assumed office as the nation's first president, he had to find a way to govern a widely disparate population.

The first Congress, assembled in 1789–1791, set out to erect a federal government from the U.S. Constitution, drafted in 1787 and ratified in 1788, which outlined the form of the federal system, but Congress and the president had to give it substance. They had to make the parts real and functional, meaning that the departments and parts of the executive and judiciary branches had to be established, not to mention the financial foundation of the new country also needed to be set in place. Added to these was the need for rules to guide international and foreign trade and diplomacy. And the first Congress had to set out the promised Bill of Rights, which would become part of the Constitution.

The Bill of Rights was written to ensure individual rights for many Americans and was not about the federal government. By 1791 the ten individual rights in the Bill of Rights were added to the Constitution, ratified, and became federal law. Most of us are familiar with some of these rights, such as the right of religious freedom and of freedom of expression, the right to property and protection from arbitrary legal proceedings, and several more. States had rights not granted to the federal government, and the remaining rights were vested in the people and the states.

The initial federal departments were also established and staffed as part of the executive branch, including the departments of State, Treasury, and Defense; the department heads constituted the president's Cabinet. For the judiciary, a tiered system was created to balance state and national interests, with 13 federal district courts and appeals handled in one of three circuit courts. Final decisions about the laws would rest with the Supreme Court. Tariffs were employed to generate revenue, a U.S. Bank was charted later, and the Treasury issued currency and stimulated and diversified the economy by encouraging various industries and manufacturing to develop, adding to the agrarian economy base that was already established.

Political life in the new nation became dominated by divisional factions between Federalists, many of whom were northerners who were pro-national government advocates, and Republicans, most of whom were southerners and farmers who wanted a weaker or smaller national government and promoted individual rights over that of the national system. The revolution in France, which turned violent and resulted in the ouster of aristocrats and the monarchy, led to war with Britain; Republicans supported the French, and Federalists wanted to remain neutral since Britain was the United States' main trading partner. George Washington, in his second term, took the neutral position regarding the conflict between France and Britain. The political landscape began to shift to groups that promoted the importance of the voices and interests of the people, not the political elite and wealthy, which characterized the Federalists. So the new political groups were known as Democratic-Republicans, and they began to grow in significance.

During his second term Washington met the challenge of settling part of the West for white immigrants when he was able to secure the Ohio area from Native American resistance in 1794. Meanwhile, in the East, the Whiskey Rebellion was met with force by the national government when citizens refused to pay the taxes imposed on the production of alcohol. And the new country continued to be threatened by other European nations that also had colonies in North America, like Spain.

The nation grew more partisan and divided during the election of the next president. John Adams was elected in 1796. He was the leader of the opposition party, and most who served with him were loyal to Hamilton and the French. Many people thought Adams was a British sympathizer at a time when the country was caught between significant conflict between Britain and France. These issues and Adams's efforts to promote peace led to more political conflict between the Federalists and Republicans. By 1800, upon the election of Thomas Jefferson as president, the ruling parties changed hands in a peaceful manner. Jefferson's administration supported the idea of the rights of the people and wanted to promote an agrarian society that provided equality for most white Americans. Goldfield et al. (2014) note that,

> Unlike the Hamiltonian Federalist, whose commercial vision of the United States accepted social and economic inequalities as inevitable, the Jeffersonians wanted a predominantly agrarian republic based on wide spread economic equality for white yeomen families to counter any threat posed by the privileged few to the people's liberties. Thus, they favored territorial expansion as a means of adding enough land to maintain self-reliant farmers as the guardians of republican freedoms. They also favored the spread of slavery. As long as racial slavery promoted a sense of unity among free white men.
>
> *(p. 226)*

The Nation Grows Westward

As fortune would have it, Jefferson's desire to expand the country was made possible in 1803 when Napoleon, the French leader, was willing to sell to the United States the area that became known as the Louisiana Purchase, a vast area of North America stretching from the Gulf of Mexico north and west to what is now Montana. Jefferson commissioned Meriwether Lewis and William Clark to explore and chart this region stretching from the Mississippi River to the Rocky Mountains. The purchase doubled the size of the United States and provided a new frontier for slaveholders in the Lower Mississippi Valley.

The next election in 1808 brought to the presidency James Madison, who declared war against Britain in 1812. The growing tension in the West between settlers and Native people, who wished to hold on to their land, led to more aggression and conflict in the Indiana Territory as well as in Spanish Florida and English Canada. This conflict was resolved during the course of the War of 1812, which raged on until a peace treaty was signed in 1814 but not ratified until later in 1815. The resolution of the treaty was affected by the Battle of New Orleans, which was a resounding victory for the United States under the command of Andrew Jackson.

The nation—and slavery—expanded. The country that had fought for its independence and freedom and established a national government had also expanded its institution of slavery and exploitation. Slaveholders were the main actors in the effort to devote more land to the production of staple crops, but their efforts were supported by federal authority and the military might of federal and state governments. Berlin (2003) states that

> federal soldiers and state militiamen forcibly expropriated millions of acres of land from the Indians through armed conquest and defended the slave regime from black insurrectionist and foreign invaders.... Federal soldiers turned their attention to sweeping aside Native people.
>
> *(p. 164)*

Advancing Freedom or Spreading Slavery?

Many people believe the War of 1812 was about expanding the boundaries of the new nation (Berlin, 2003; Goldfield et al., 2014). For some that meant an opportunity to advance freedom and equality, and for others it meant the spread of slavery to new fertile lands that were west of the old borders of the nation. The opportunities and profits to be made from cotton were enormous, and the southern and western lands offered extraordinary opportunities for large and more profitable plantations. Americans—both those who wanted to extend the institution of slavery and those who wanted to promote democracy and freedom—advanced the notion that the country should occupy all the land from coast to coast, which came to be known as manifest destiny (Kidd, 2019).

Another factor that pushed these developments was the transfer of people from the East Coast to the South and West, including European immigrants who hoped to benefit from the promise of land so they could start a new life on the American frontier. The Gulf region witnessed an astounding increase in population to the rich lands that were prime for growing cotton and sugar. Other states joined the union in the 19th century. Louisiana became a state in 1812, Mississippi in 1817, and Alabama in 1819. In 1810 the tristate area had some 40,000 people; by 1820 it had grown to 200,000; and by 1840 the population was about 1 million. And as the white population grew, so did the Black population, as slaves were needed to clear the land, plant, and harvest the crops. The amount of cotton that was grown on the Gulf region far exceeded that grown along the East Coast, producing three times what could be grown in the east.

> The emergence of the cotton kingdom, in which the work was carried on primarily by black slaves, had the effect of committing the Gulf region to

> a regime of slavery and unifying the South against any group or section that threatened to destroy those peculiar interests of the South and the cotton kingdom.
>
> *(Franklin & Moss, 2000, p. 126)*

Florida was a territory in 1819 after Andrew Jackson prevailed over the local Indigenous people, but it did not become a state (with slaves) until 1845. Missouri joined the union as a slave state in 1821, and Texas was added in 1845. Missouri's entrance set in motion the conflict about whether the nation would be a slave-oriented nation or free one. As Kidd (2019) notes,

> The question of *slavery on the expanding western frontier*, however, became arguably the most contested political issue in America from 1810 to the 1850s. The admission of states to the Union became tied to the question of whether the new states would foster the spread, or the restriction, of slavery.
>
> *(p. 145; italics in the original)*

When Missouri submitted an application to be a state in 1817, the debate began. The territory already had slaves, so it was assumed it would join the Union as a slave state, but its entrance in this fashion would have tipped the majority in the Senate to slave-holding states—thus the dilemma. Congress proposed, in 1819, that Missouri would be admitted but only if it ended slavery; the bill failed to pass Congress. The request from Maine (formerly a part of Massachusetts) to be admitted as a free state helped resolve the impasse: Missouri could be added as a slave state and the balance would be maintained if Maine were admitted as a free state, but there still was the matter of the remaining areas of the Louisiana Purchase territories. The compromise that Congress arrived at prohibited slavery above the southern border of Missouri. This meant that the northern two-thirds of the area of the Louisiana Purchase territories would be free, and the area that became Arkansas would be the only new slave state in the future. In 1821 the measure known as the Missouri Compromise barely passed Congress and became law.

The nation continued to be divided by those who supported a strong national government and those who advocated for states' rights. The core of the conflict between the various political factions was the ability to reject the dictates of the federal laws. The South was becoming weaker in the national arena, while the North was gaining strength. More importantly, the North was also becoming more industrial and relied more on wage laborers, while in the South and parts of the West slave labor in agriculture dominated. Thus, the regions' social, political, and economic interests and goals were in direct conflict. During this era, there were rumblings in the South that they should secede from the union in order to protect the South's customs and traditions and especially to maintain and expand the institution of slavery, upon which its social and economic structure depended.

Prior to the election of Andrew Jackson as president in 1828, politicians appealed to their political colleagues for election support, not the public (politicians voted for president, not the public). That changed in the 1820s when the mass electorate voted for candidates, and new political parties came into existence. The inclusion of the public in elections resulted in three times the number of people participating in elections during the 1824–1850 period. By the mid-1800s, two political parties vied for the support of the electorate. Goldfield et al. (2014) state that

> voters in favor of government aid for economic development and a social order based on Protestant moral controls turned to the Whigs. Conversely, those who saw an activist government as a threat to their economic and cultural equality turned to the Democrats.
>
> *(p. 277)*

At first the two parties took popular economic positions in 1844, so there was little sectional conflict or division, but soon the issue of slavery in Texas became a core and divisive issue in the election of 1844. "With this shift, party appeals began to focus on the place of slavery in U.S. society, creating an escalating politics of sectionalism.... Within a decade, the slavery issue would rip apart the second party system" (Goldfield et al., 2014, p. 277).

The institution of slavery was integral to the social, economic, and political life of the South. The foundation of daily life, well-being, and wealth rested on controlling the large numbers of Blacks; from this perspective, Southerners believed attacks on the enterprise and its functions had to be defended at all cost.

The Rise of the Cotton Kingdom

To fully understand the shift just discussed, consider how the institution of slavery changed and became concentrated in the South and West and declined significantly in the North and Upper South. The Lower South became the cotton kingdom because of a longer growing season, good rainfall, proximity to rivers, and new, viable, fertile land. In 1850 the Lower South consisted of South Carolina, Georgia, Florida, Alabama, Mississippi, Louisiana, and Texas.

The domestic slave market grew as prices rose twofold for male fieldhands between 1815 and 1850. The rising prices and demand for slaves between 1790 and 1860 resulted in the relocation of between 800,000 and 1 million Black people, most of whom were moved from the Upper South to the

Lower South. This trade activity was devastating to Black people as many families were once more torn apart and forever separated.

The profit margins planters realized with slave labor depressed incentives for them or other investors to pursue industrialization or urban development of the types that were taking place in the North. The idea of economic variety or diversification ran into a brick wall in the Lower South but gained considerable steam in the Upper South and North. Southern leaders also feared that urbanization and industrialization would weaken the slave regime. Slave labor declined in cities, where most slaves who resided there lived apart from their owners and many were artisans, domestics, or skilled workers who had somewhat more flexibility and ability to move about and interact with both Black and white people. Urban Blacks' lives were not tightly controlled as was the case on plantations.

The number of slaves in urban areas decreased by 50% between 1820 and 1860, dropping to a low of less than 10% of the urban population, in part due to the questions people had about slavery and whether it should continue. The profits that slavery generated in nonurban areas, and the rise of industry and technology in cities prompted even more inquiry. Most industries used paid labor since free labor would undermine its operating processes, making it more difficult to hire and fire at will. The manufacturing environment offered flexibility to workers, and they could earn and spend money as they pleased. Goldfield et al. (2014, p. 285) observe this about technological and manufacturing development: "Ever concerned to preserve slavery, planters would not risk slave discipline or the profits of cotton agriculture by embracing the unpredictable changes that industrialization was sure to bring."

Just as slavery declined in cities, it also did so in the Upper South, which consisted according to historians (e.g., Goldfield et al., 2014) of two zones, one made up of the northern-most states of Delaware, Maryland, Kentucky, and Missouri (each was in proximity to free states), and the second zone comprising the four states south of the first zone: Virginia, North Carolina, Tennessee, and Arkansas (states where slavery existed and was deeply embedded in its daily life, yet less so than in the Lower South). In comparison, the Lower South was more suitable for growing cotton and the use of gang slave labor, and the Lower South had a longer growing season and more fertile soil, so the demand for slaves shifted from the Upper to the Lower South, coupled with an economic downturn in the Upper South between 1812 and 1850.

The Upper South became less dependent on plantation agriculture, and its cities grew and related industrial economic activity increased. This changed their labor needs, which made it possible for people in the Upper South to provide the needed slave labor to the Lower South.

The Great Transformation in the Lives of Blacks

Several things happened to alter the lives of Black people, free and slave, much of which was triggered by the transformations and the change in location that came with the advances in technology. Blacks' lives were disrupted when members of families were sold down the river. Coupled with the abrupt changes of the culture and communities that had been established in the Chesapeake and Low Country regions, there were also losses in how slaves lived that had been negotiated over the course of many generations.

One change was that more Black people lived in the South, and the majority were native-born. The hardships and violence directed at them became more intense, and their ability to protect themselves was limited. Berlin, Favreau, and Miller (1998) note that the life Blacks created on the Eastern Seaboard that had lasted for some two centuries was grounded in kinship ties, friendships, and a community of shared values and beliefs. The movement of Blacks west and south for whatever reasons "tore that society asunder, exiling hundreds of thousands from their birthplace and traumatizing those who remained. Families and sometimes whole communities dissolved under the pressure of this Second Great Migration" (Berlin, Favreau, & Miller, 1998, p. xxv).

The new migration and relocation of Blacks also meant that race was being redefined both for whites and Blacks; Blacks were again deemed inferior regardless of whether they were free or slave, in the North or South. While slavery declined in the North, it did so slowly. And in the end, the North was a society with slaves and with Blacks who, while free, were severely restricted by custom and law. "Free black men and women sank to the base of northern society, marginalized, impoverished, and despised" (Berlin, 1998, p. 359). It took several decades for the antislavery movement in the North to take hold and to exert more force on the institution. Berlin (1998) puts it this way:

> Beginning in the 1830s, however, antislavery activists found new friends among the proponents of free labor, who conveniently suppressed the North's long commitment to chattel bondage. Whether they marched under the banner of radical abolition, Free Soil, or Republicanism, the opponents of slavery turned on the slave South as representative of everything they despised: ascribed status, unearned privilege, and rigid hierarchy.
>
> *(pp. 358–359)*

While the people in the north railed against the South, slaveholders built an ideology around slavery and upheld it as a model of how they were fulfilling their obligations to those who were dependent upon them, and as an honorable responsibility to care for their women, children, and slaves.

In the Lower South most Blacks lived on larger plantations with fifty or more slaves, most tending to cotton, which required little machinery or processing, just the labor of Blacks who worked from dawn to late in the night. The codes established to maintain control of slaves allowed for punishment for any manner of behavior deemed out of line, and any resistance was met with whipping or death. While slaveholders provided food, shelter, and clothes, these usually were allocated only to meet bare necessity. Clothes were distributed once a year—a garment for winter and one for summer, and usually these were coarse, rough garments, not intended for comfort. Shelter was one small room with a dirt floor in which multiple (four to five) people would live. Most Blacks worked on farms in large groups, and some lived on smaller properties with ten or fewer people working alongside their owners. On the larger plantations, family formation was possible; less so on the smaller farms. Food was rationed and was mostly cornmeal and salt pork, with few if any vegetables or other meats. Some slaves gardened, hunted, and fished, and these provisions supplemented their diets. But they often had inadequate nutrition, and many fell ill as a result. Goldfield et al. (2014) write:

> About 20 percent of the slaves on a typical plantation were sick at any given time. Infant mortality was twice as high among slaves as among white southerners in 1850; so was mortality among slave children up to age 14. According to one study life expectancy for slaves at birth was 21 or 22 years, roughly half the white expectancy.
>
> *(p. 291)*

Many historians (e.g., Bennett, 1988; Franklin & Moss, 2000; Goldfield et al., 2014; Kidd, 2019; Lepore, 2018; Webber, 1978) and scholars have documented that Black people responded to their oppression with veiled acts of defiance, yet they were persistent, and they sought means and methods to salvage their sense of humanity and dignity. Goldfield et al. (2014) state that

> by resisting an enslavement they could not prevent; they shaped a culture of their own that eased their pain and raised their hopes of someday being free. They retained their dignity in the face of continual humiliation and relied on their family life and religious beliefs as sources of strength under nearly intolerable circumstances.
>
> *(p. 290)*

In the renewed era of racial oppression with the transformation and migration south and west, researchers and scholars (e.g., Belgrave & Allison, 2019; Bennett, 1988; Blassingame, 1979; Webber, 1978) identified several elements of Black life that were sources of cultural strengths for the slaves, including their kinship bonds, a work orientation (many took pride in efficiency), flexible family roles (not living by rigid gender roles), the importance of achievement (pushing family to do better), and culturally based spiritual practices.

Psychologically, Blacks demonstrated a determination to use those who came before them as guides and to follow their ways of living. Slaves built upon the values and ways of their African forebears who taught them African social practices, religious and spiritual beliefs, and psychological perspectives. Blacks functioned as a group with common goals and objectives, and they used their connection to each other as their source of hope. They believed and prayed that someday they would be free and that God would provide. These notions helped to fuel their survival (Thornton, 2012).

In the face of shifting locations and the harsh and degrading ways they were treated, enslaved Blacks and their descendants found ways to establish and pass along the needed beliefs and psychological mechanisms necessary to maintain and create communities, families, and institutions. The transmission of the essential messages and ways of living were critical to the groups' continued existence and were sources of cultural strength that contributed to the people's psychological health. There is evidence to document some of the cultural practices, psychological mechanisms, and patterns that were used in the service of their continued existence. Narratives from former slaves and those who were free describe their lives and their community from 1831 to 1865, as captured by Webber (1978):

> Though the chains with which whites controlled black bodies were very real, try as they might, whites could not control black minds. These were molded from birth in an educational process created and managed by the [Black] quarter community. By passing their unique set of cultural themes from generation to generation, the members of the quarter community were able to resist most white teaching, set themselves apart from white society, and mold their own cultural norms and group identity. While still legally slaves, the black men, women, and children of the quarter community successfully protected their psychological freedom and celebrated their human dignity.
>
> *(p. 262)*

Webber documents and describes several cultural themes endemic to the slave quarter community. These slave quarters varied in size and type but were ubiquitous in American society. It is also where Black culture was nourished and prospered. Webber (1978) contends that by the time of the Civil War, Black culture was securely established and anchored in their African heritage. Elements of that culture were apparent in various forms and types of expressions, music, and art as well as religion and family life; Webber states that the slaves designed and constructed their way of life, irrespective of the barriers and obstacles in their path: "The [slaves] … nurtured the rites and beliefs of their community and religious life and … instilled in their children and other slaves the cultural themes of their community" (p. xiii).

There were other ways that characterized Black culture, in addition to the ways Webber (1978) and other historians (e.g., Bennett, 1988; Berlin 1998, 2003; Berlin, Favreau, & Miller 1998; Blassingame, 1972; Franklin & Moss,

2000; Jones, 2003; Stuckey, 2013; Thornton, 2012) have documented. Several additional cultural themes include a group identity that was formed by a commitment to solidarity, guided by moral and behavioral rules that members followed to maintain the trust of others, dictated by their deeds not their skin color. It was the code and practice of the Black slave community to share, protect, and care for each other as family. Bennett (1988) states also that Black people exhibited

> a sense of identity and peoplehood that rejected Black subordination and exclusion.... Blacks turned inward and formed their own social institutions and, in the process, created themselves. This act of self-generation created a community out of a collective of isolated individuals.
>
> *(pp. 56, 77)*

The community also held, as did their ancestors, strong spiritual beliefs, religious practices, and faith—not what was taught to them by whites but beliefs grounded in the Bible, which held that all people were equal and free. The core of the community was family, but not defined by blood. Webber (1978, p. 157) described the family in this way: "This larger family pattern included not only what is referred to as the 'extended family,' but also other persons not necessarily related by blood or marriage."

To transmit from one generation to the next the values, psychological principles, and cultural beliefs that Black people held dear and cherished involved using many mechanisms. The religious congregation, which at first met away from the slave quarters, was used to pass information to others. The community, family, and peers were also mechanisms used to convey critical cultural messages and to teach the rules used to endure. Songs and stories were used in the oral tradition and, due to prohibitions against learning to read and write, were the concrete tools for learning (even though forbidden, a small number of slaves were taught to read and write and shared what they knew with others). Regarding the songs and stories, Webber argues that while the songs and stories varied from region to region, they nevertheless shared themes and purpose. Webber (1978) states that

> the songs and stories of the quarter community expressed similar values, beliefs and attitudes.... In addition to giving voice to the themes of the quarter community, songs and stories were also the essential medium by which those themes were evoked, supported, and transmitted from generation to generation.
>
> *(p. 207)*

More important was the reality that while Blacks were property and lacked resources, they nevertheless were able to maintain psychological focus and develop and transmit their unique cultural values and beliefs. They fended off the teachings of whites, dismissed much of what they were being asked to believe, and rejected a lot of the expectations of how they should behave. Blacks were intelligent as well as inventive. Survival came at a high cost since many gave their lives or were harmed in ways that are unthinkable or horrific; some surrendered and others resisted (Bouie, 2019). Yet in the end,

> The conclusion suggested most strongly … is that white teaching failed because whites saw blacks as people without a culture, without themes and educational instruments of their own. Whites saw blacks as savages to be civilized; as children at best and animals at worst. As such, slaves were assumed to be without strong values or beliefs and certainly without a coherent culture or social organization of their own. For this reason, white teaching reflected an unstated attitude of filling up empty brains, of scratching white understandings upon the tabula rasa of limited black intelligence. That the content of white teaching directly contradicted understandings, attitudes, values and feelings which slaves had learned from birth in an educational process created and controlled by slaves themselves was a notion too incredible and too dangerous to entertain. To suggest that slaves were capable of molding their own culture, of fashioning and maintaining their own educational instruments would be to undermine the most fundamental arguments with which whites rationalized their enslavement of other human beings.
>
> *(Webber, 1978, pp. 249–250)*

Thus, the inferior people had a say in their lives in ways that went unseen by whites, and the controversy about being a slave or free nation raged on, erupting into armed conflict between the South and the North. Yet there would be the judgment of the highest court in the land, proclaiming the views of the times, that Blacks were indeed inferior and not citizens of the land.

The Court Speaks Loudly about Blacks

Blacks had to rely on themselves. Yet again, they were told, they did not matter as a people or as individuals after it became clear that the American leaders and authorities—not all, but many—and the courts did not have favorable views of them. The evidence was the Supreme Court's decision in *Dred Scott v. Sandford* in 1857. The Court ruled that Blacks were not U.S. citizens and therefore did not enjoy the same rights as citizens. Furthermore, the Fugitive Slave Act—which was passed by Congress in 1850 and legalized the capture of runaway slaves, dictating that they be returned to their owners—was affirmed. These legal victories appeased the South since the expansion of new slave states had slowed, even though new western lands had opened, such as California.

Historians take note of the Supreme Court's ruling in *Dred Scott v. Sandford* because it was a significantly powerful statement about the status of Black people in the nation, regardless of the claims made by those who advocated for ending slavery. For many white people, Blacks were inferior to them, but some whites thought Blacks should not be slaves and advocated for their freedom from bondage. The ideas promulgated in the decision set in place a negative perception of Black people that in some ways remains with the nation to this day.

The *Dred Scott v. Sandford* case was about whether a Black slave who lived in a free state could be held as a slave after being moved to another free area. The claim that Scott was free was challenged by his new owner on the grounds that Scott was a slave and not a citizen. The chief justice of the Court, Roger B. Taney, wrote the majority opinion in what has been described as a pro-slavery action by legal scholars (Bell, 2008; Finkelman, 2018). The opinion made several damming statements and took hurtful positions regarding Blacks in the United States. Taney noted that Blacks did not have the same status as Native Americans, who were accorded status of a foreign nation. Blacks, according to the Court, were never constitutionally intended to be American citizens. Taney further wrote that states cannot recognize citizens of the nation and that being a citizen of a state does not confer the same status as a citizen of the nation. Only Congress can confer the natural right of citizenship to all in the nation. Furthermore, the United States owed nothing to Blacks, no rights nor privileges. Thus Scott was not and could not be a citizen and had no standing to sue in Court. Moreover, according to the founding documents and public opinion, it was clear to the Court that Black people were

> regarded as beings of an inferior order, and altogether unfit to associate with the white race, either in social or political relations, and so far inferior, that they had no rights which the white man was bound to respect; and that the Negro might justly and lawfully be reduced to slavery for his benefit.
>
> *(U.S. Supreme Court, 1857)*

Taney went on to assert that the proof of his position could be found in the laws of the colonies that had proclaimed Blacks to be inferior. He noted that while all men are indeed created equal, as stated in the Declaration of Independence, that document excluded Blacks from the reference to "men" since Blacks were property. So even if Blacks were free, they still were not citizens according to state laws, and thus had no rights to be respected. This was so even if the Black person resided in a non-slave state. Federal law was limited to only apply to whites when citizens are naturalized.

At a time when slavery was reestablished and had grown in the Lower South, the highest court in the land had declared Blacks naturally inferior and devoid of rights. If they fled their masters, the law made it possible for them to be captured and returned, wherever they might go. These circumstances left Black people in the South isolated, but they were not alone. There were voices and organizations that continued to advocate for the abolition of slavery.

The Civil War: 1861–1865

There are many political and economic reasons and issues that led to the Civil War in 1861, including social, economic, political, and moral (religious) events and issues that had festered over the course of several decades. The Northern and Southern parts of the country had evolved in many different ways. For instance, the South was biracial in that 35% of the population was Black, while less than 2% of the northern population was Black.

The economy of the South was agriculturally based, with 84% of its economy based on crop production and little else, while the North had only 40% of its economy driven by agriculture; it had developed manufacturing and related industries and growing urban centers, unlike the South. The South accounted for only 15% of the nation's factories, while the North had 85%. In this era, railroads were being built, and the regions varied here as well. The South had about 10,000 miles of rail track with few links to other lines, while the North had twice the number of rail miles and considerably more links to lines that connected to the West. In addition, many more people in the South (17%) were illiterate than in the North (6%) (Goldfield et al., 2014; Kidd, 2019).

One might think that the majority of Southern whites held slaves, and that accounted for their strident support of the institution. However, in 1860 the majority of Southern whites (75%) did not own slaves; therefore, only 25% held slaves, and of those, only 1% had large plantations with 50 or more slaves, while about 3% had between 20 and 49 slaves on their plantations, and about 20–21% of whites held fewer than 20 slaves (sometimes fewer than five) on smaller farms or in city dwellings, and other whites worked and tended to their own land. "Both groups [those with or without slaves] sought to protect property rights from outside interference and to maintain a system of racial control in which white liberties rested on black degradation" (Goldfield et al., 2014, p. 298).

One major issue between the North and South centered on the desire of the North to limit the expansion of Southern influence and power in the west and in the federal government. In essence, the Civil War began over whether slavery would be brought to the western sections of the country. The nation in 1860 was divided between the two options: free or slave. Many schemes were instituted to address the matter, including letting the people in the territories decide the matter. This was tried in the Kansas territory, and the result was violent warfare between the two opposing sides. The Court's pro-slavery *Dred Scott v. Sandford* decision did not help decide the issues being contested; it just seemed to make matters worse. Each side took what was done or said by the other as a way to demean their position and perspective. Goldfield et al. (2014) contend that

> Americans in both sections [or sides] talked of freedom and self-determination, the black men and women in their midst had little of either. Lincoln went to war to preserve the Union; Davis, to defend a new nation. Slavery was the spark that ignited the conflict, but white America seemed more comfortable embracing abstract ideals than real people. Northerners and southerners would confront this irony during the bloodiest war in American history, but they would not resolve it.
>
> *(p. 401)*

Reconstruction and the Jim Crow Era

The Civil War raged for some four years and came to an end with the defeat of the South and considerable loss of life and innumerable injuries on both sides. Although slavery was officially abolished when the Thirteenth Amendment to the Constitution was passed in 1864 and ratified the following year, the reality was that Blacks' freedom was slow and gradual (Feagin, 2006).

Reconstruction (1865–1877), which followed the Civil War, intended to restore the South to the Union, but what occurred was establishing through legal means the imposition of racial oppression against Blacks in Southern states. This began immediately in 1865 by leaders of Southern states who enacted Black Codes, which were rescinded but then were used as guides for related laws (Foner, 1988; Packard, 2002). The customs and later laws of Jim Crow that were enacted resembled the previous world of slavery, but not formal slavery as property; instead, it was slavery as crime, in which the offenses (often minor) had exorbitant fees attached, and offenders who could not pay (mostly Blacks) had to serve time in a convict prison and then were leased out as laborers. So the world of separate and unequal accompanied these new racial rules and laws. Whites could not imagine a society where Blacks and whites were equals (Feagin, 2006; Foner, 1988; Silverstein, 2019). Blackmon (2009) states that what was done to Black people was a process of re-enslavement after the Civil War. The North did not fight in the Civil War to free slaves; rather, they fought to preserve the union and to maintain the strength and viability of the nation and federal government. However, it seems clear that the Southern states did go to war to maintain the right to hold slaves. Some historians report how reluctant President Lincoln was to intercede in the issue of slavery until it became clear that, to save the Union, he had to act to weaken the South's use of slave labor, which supported the South during the war. Moreover, the slaves who sought freedom through allegiance with the Northern troops also posed a continuous issue for the North and its campaigns.

In the South, the war left many wounds, and defeat brought with it the end of slavery and a dramatic change in race relations, so it seemed on the surface. For the most part, whites and Blacks pulled away from the close relationships they had during slavery and any mutual obligations they once shared. Many Blacks who now were free left the plantations and farms where they lived and roamed the country and cities. Blacks also left the churches to establish their own institutions. "In these and other ways the new order added physical distance to social distance between the races" (Woodward, 1974, p. 22). Whites panicked, fearing that Blacks would strike back at them and, worse, that Blacks could not be forced to work without being paid. Many Blacks wandered around the areas where Blacks once labored, drinking in their newfound freedom.

> In the presence of these conditions the provisional legislatures established by President [Andrew] Johnson in 1865 adopted the notorious Black Codes. Some of them were intended to establish systems of peonage [debt as slavery] or apprenticeships resembling slavery.
>
> *(Woodward, 1974, p. 23)*

Some states led the way in passing laws that separated whites and Blacks to different cars on railroads, prohibiting Blacks from first-class cars. According to Foner (1988),

> Mississippi and South Carolina enacted the first and most severe Black Codes toward the end of 1865. Mississippi required all blacks to possess ... written evidence of employment for the coming year. Laborers leaving their jobs before the contract expired would forfeit wages already earned, and, as under slavery, be subject to arrest by any white citizen.... To limit the freedmen's economic opportunity, they were forbidden to rent land in urban areas. Vagrancy, a crime whose definition included the idle, disorderly, and those who "mis-spend what they earn" ... could be punished by fines or involuntary plantation labor.... In case anything had been overlooked, the legislature declared all penal codes, defining crimes by slaves and free blacks "in full force" unless specifically altered in laws.
>
> *(pp. 199–200)*

Foner (1988) and other historians (e.g., Packard, 2002) point out that the Black Codes in many states were not enacted or actually became law, but the provisions and premise of these laws created a foundation upon which the post-Civil War South could reassert itself since it set up a plan for how Blacks would be dealt with and how their labor would be extracted. Most whites knew they needed Black labor and Blacks' knowledge and skills to survive, so instead of the explicit Black Codes, whites used laws and legal ordinances that enforced things like vagrancy, breach of contract, and apprenticeship—

things that did not refer to race but were racial in their effects. These were used to subjugate Blacks, when added to tax policies and all-white judiciary systems. The die was cast.

The State of Black Life After the Civil War

To set the stage, recall that Black people were denied education; they had little or no property or possessions; they knew only about where they lived and died; they worked the fields, farms, and homes of whites who regarded them as inferior beings; and at the end of the Civil War they were told that they were free to do as they pleased. Many did not know where they were, much less where to go or what was possible. Once they were untethered from their so-called owners, they had in an instant to decide how to shape and form their new lives as free men and women. Some left their local plantations, others demanded wages for their work. People from the North came to provide aid through the Freemen's Bureau, and others attached to the military assisted when they could. The aid and assistance rendered by some was halfhearted at best.

People in the North held Blacks in low esteem as well. So, once the war ended many lost interest in the plight of the wandering groups of the newly freed Black people. The newly freed people had little to use to construct new lives for themselves. Yet they set out to find loved ones and to locate, where possible, their own land to work. Blacks established organizations, including many churches, but now the church was Black only. Blacks left white churches in large numbers. Some sought to learn in the new schools for Blacks, while others served in elected offices in towns, states, and the U.S. Congress. Most Blacks looked for work and ached to use the skills they had acquired. The most significant failure of Emancipation was the empty promise of land and a stake for those denied a chance to fend for themselves. The lack of a stake in their new freedom left many to return to the farms and plantations they once worked on, but now they did so as contract workers or sharecroppers, arrangements that left them in basically the same place they had occupied during slavery. While no longer slaves, they lived and worked under similar conditions and circumstances.

Blacks' Efforts to Counter Negative Narratives

Many Blacks in America sought various ways to be independent and assert their individuality as well as ways to be seen as people of value in nonracial and racial terms. The contributions of Blacks have been documented in various ways; for instance, Franklin and Moss (2000) describe the work and contributions of Jupiter Hammond, a slave who wrote and published several works in the mid-1700s. He accepted his low status but proclaimed the system of slavery to be evil. There was also Phillis Wheatly, who had been born in Africa and brought to North America as a young servant girl. Her mistress taught her to read and write, and she introduced her to various subjects. In 1773 Wheatly was manumitted (set free) and sent to England, and she returned upon the publication of her first book of poems.

Franklin and Moss also describe the life of Gustavus Vassa, including his capture and subsequent life adventures, which were also published in a biography. He lived his life in bondage and when he returned to England, he was able to purchase his freedom. He took documenting the evils of slavery as his mission.

There were groups of Blacks who set out to establish institutions such as churches, schools, clubs, and other organizations. Much, if not most, of this activity of institution-building occurred in the North; less so in the South. Churches were common organizations that Blacks established. Franklin and Moss (2000) point out that an African Society was created in Boston in 1793 by 44 people. The society set as its goals to be a giving and caring organization and to adhere to the laws of the society.

> This organization and similar ones did much to bind blacks together and to give them the experience of leadership and cooperation that was to be significant in a later day. Blacks early sought out integration into the political, social, and economic life of the nation. Having been generally rejected, they had no alternative except to forge out of their limited background and training institutions of their own. It is significant, moreover, that in the case of these institutions, just as in the case of individuals, considerable effort was made to share in the general development of the country and to contribute to its growth. The African-American search for independence at the turn of the century, therefore, was essentially a struggle to achieve status in the evolving American civilization.
>
> *(Franklin & Moss, 2000, p. 117)*

References

Belgrave, F. Z., & Allison, K. W. (2019). *African American psychology: From Africa to America* (4th ed.). Sage.

Bell, D. (2008). *Race, racism, and American law* (6th ed.). Wolters Kluwer.

Bennett, L. (1988). *Before the Mayflower: A history of Black America*. Johnson Publishing.

Berlin, I. (1998). *Many thousands gone: The first two centuries of slavery in North America London, England*. Belknap Press of Harvard University Press.

Berlin, I. (2003). *Generations of captivity: London, England*. Belknap Press of Harvard University Press.

Berlin, I., Favreau, M., & Miller, S. F. (1998). *Remembering slavery: African Americans talk about their personal experiences of slavery and emancipation*. New Press.

Blackmon, D. A. (2009). *Slavery by another name.* Anchor.
Blassingame, J. W. (1972). *The slave community: Plantation life in ante-bellum South.* Oxford University Press.
Blassingame, J. W. (1979). *The slave community: Plantation life in ante-bellum South* (rev. & enlarged ed.). Oxford University Press.
Bouie, J. (2019, August 19). America holds onto an undemocratic assumption from its founding: That some people deserve more power than others. *The New York Times Magazine 1619 Project.*
Feagin, J. R. (2006). *Systemic racism: A theory of oppression.* Routledge.
Finkelman, P. (2018). *Supreme injustice: Slavery in the nation's highest court.* Harvard University Press.
Foner, E. (1988). *Reconstruction: America's unfinished revolution, 1863–1877.* Harper & Row.
Franklin, H. J., & Moss, A. A. (2000). *From slavery to freedom: A history of African Americans* (8th ed.). McGraw Hill.
Goldfield, D., Abbott, C., Anderson, V. D., Argersinger, J. E., Argersinger, P. H., & Barney, W. L. (2014). *The American journey: A history of the United States* (7th ed.), Vol. 1. Pearson.
Jones, J. M. (2003). TRIOS: A psychological theory of the African legacy in American culture. *Journal of Social Issues,* 39(1), 217–242.
Kidd, T. S. (2019). *American history: 1492 to the present.* B+N Academic.
Lepore, J. (2018). *These truths: A history of the United States.* Norton.
Packard, J. M. (2002). *American nightmare: The history of Jim Crow.* St. Martin's Press.
Silverstein, J. (2019). The 1619 Project: Introduction. *New York Times Magazine,* 4.
Stuckey, S. (2013). *Slave culture: Nationalist theory and the foundations of Black America* (25th anniversary ed.). Oxford University Press.
Thornton, J. K. (2012). *A cultural history of the Atlantic world, 1250–1820.* Cambridge University Press.
U.S. Supreme Court. (1857). Judgment in the U.S. Supreme Court Case Dred Scott v. John F. A. Sandford, 3/6/1857, Dred Scott, Plaintiff in Error, v. John F. A. Sandford, Appellate Jurisdiction Case Files, 1792–2010, Records of the Supreme Court of the United States, RG 267, National Archives Building, Washington, D. C., https://www.archives.gov/milestone-documents/dred-scott-v-sandford.
Webber, T. L. (1978). *Deep like the rivers: Education in the slave quarter community, 1831–1865.* Norton.
Woodward, C. V. (1974). *The strange career of Jim Crow* (3rd rev. ed.). Oxford University Press.

8

BLACK FREEDOM BLOCKED

The Churches, Land, and Schools

Black people in the post-Reconstruction era stepped out of bondage into a world of harsh racial oppression and segregation, hostility, and anti-Black violence. The door closed on Blacks and Reconstruction with the compromise reached in the contested 1876 election between Rutherford B. Hayes and Samuel J. Tilden for president of the United States. The outcome was to be decided by Congress because the election was so close, but Congress was deadlocked and a compromise was reached, which led to Hayes winning the presidency. It was agreed that, for supporting Hayes, federal troops still in Southern states would be removed. The outcome was devasting to Black people and those who supported Blacks' civil rights. As Franklin and Moss (2000, p. 281) put it, "when Hayes became president, the South was soon assuaged in its grief by his prompt withdrawal of troops. At last the South could rule itself without Northern interference or black influence."

Now whites could determine the fate of Blacks, and one way for the Southern leaders to do this was to remove Blacks' political and economic influences. Both legal means and extralegal methods were used to achieve whites' goals. Whites were aided by state codes that were designed to prevent Blacks from being involved in states' political processes. It took time to completely eliminate Blacks from political life, but in time the South eventually removed Blacks from any political participation in most Southern states. But they had to eliminate Blacks without also barring poor whites from voting. Mississippi led the way, a state with a majority Black population, when the state held a constitutional convention in 1890 with the aim of barring Blacks from voting. Mississippi legislators passed educational and economic poll tax requirements for voting and excluded from voting those who were convicted of certain crimes, which made more than 120,000 Blacks ineligible to vote. Other states followed Mississippi's lead and passed their

DOI: 10.4324/9781003111542-12

own versions of the voting requirements. The goal was to make white power supreme; Blacks and others protested and denounced the laws, to no avail.

Some have argued and stated flat out that Reconstruction in America was a failure, that it brought little to improve the lives of Black people. While they were no longer property, they also had fewer resources with which to build new lives. Their centuries of subjugation were not recognized, nor did they receive much of any compensation from any source for what they had endured. Some placed the blame on Blacks, arguing that Blacks were irresponsible when they held public offices. Some stole funds or violated other laws—evidence, whites said, that Blacks were not fit to have the right to vote or hold political office (Franklin & Moss, 2000).

Whites, for their part upon regaining power, could now deal with Blacks as they wished. Whites set out to return Blacks to their pre-Civil War status, or to get as close to it as possible. It began with the Black Codes, which were not laws but were used as guides for the creation of separate facilities as well as social and economic worlds for whites and Blacks. The idea was to make it appear that things were equal when they were not. Packard (2002) notes that

> within little more than a generation [by 1907] after Reconstruction's end [1877 or so], this kind of racial segregation [or Jim Crow laws and customs] would almost completely characterize the Southern and border-state life. To satisfy federal courts, Southerners built an overlay of "equality" into segregation, but it was rarely anything but a sham, a pretense that as long as the "same" was provided for both races, segregation would not offend the constitutional law or the judges who said what that law was.
>
> *(p. 63)*

While the separation of Blacks began in the South, it existed around the country, including in the North, where racial discrimination was directed at Blacks as fiercely as it was in the South. The difference was that more Blacks lived in the South. Nevertheless, there was little actual liberty or equality in other regions of the United States. Blacks were discriminated against in housing, education, the workplace, and the marketplace. Packard (2002, p. 64) states "everywhere in the North, black Americans were in this period treated with contempt, denied basic civil liberties, and subjected to lightning-fast, white-instigated violence."

Because most Blacks lived in the South, Jim Crow's effects were more acute and harmful in this region. It is suggested that from the end of 1896, with the Supreme Court's *Plessy v. Ferguson* ruling that separate facilities for Blacks and whites were permissible as long as they were "equal," the laws of segregation spread like a contagious disease, moving from community to community, from county to county, from state to state, until segregation characterized the entire Southern region. What began as unclear, foggy, unwritten rules and customs became "armored in the full force of statutory law, Jim Crow became what it meant to be Southern" (Packard, 2002, p. 65).

Some Blacks fled the region, seeking new lives and opportunities on the western frontiers only to find racial hostility there as well. The anti-Black sentiment was strong as they moved further west or north. The blocked paths they encountered would not abate until their labor was needed in the war effort that came a few decades later.

The nation had become deaf to the pleas of Blacks who called for recognition of their civil and human rights. Their voices and cries for help were seldom heard or acknowledged. Packard (2002) puts it this way:

> The quarter century prior to World War I had seen white America relentlessly consign the nation's 10 million black citizens to the outermost reaches of the national conscience. The result was that by the early years of the twentieth century the forces responsible for it—white power, white supremacy, and Jim Crow—had returned the large majority of African-Americans to a status not unrecognizably different from that they had suffered as slaves, and left the country in a position where racism provided the dominant social undertones of American life. Nowhere nearly as much so as in the South did the emphasis on maintaining white supremacy ensure that almost every facet of black Americans' lives was entangled on a daily, never-ending basis in racial bias.
>
> *(p. 108)*

The curtain of racial oppression and outright exclusion fell down upon the lives of Black people all around the country—unlike during slavery, when Blacks' relationships with whites were more intimate—this time the separation, exclusion, and denigration were harsh and complete. Blacks, yet again, were alone and isolated as a group and had to depend on themselves and the few in the nation who were willing, in small ways, to assist and support them. The support from allies came in specific ways and in accord with the rules of exclusion. But there were many ways Blacks engaged in self-help. One was to acquire and farm their own land; another was to build schools and provide for the education of their people; and a third form of self-help was to nourish their souls and spirits through religious and spiritual activities as they established and supported their own churches and community organizations. Each activity was related to the other, and together they slowly helped one another survive in their new state of social, economic, educational, and political exclusion.

Black people had little support and few advocates outside of their own community; it seemed that, on one hand, some whites believed slavery was immoral and wrong and thus advocated for it to end; yet, on the other hand, some antislavery advocates did believe Blacks were equals to whites. The centuries of depictions of them as lesser people had its effects, and when people came to their aid, it was to uplift them to a white standard. So in many respects Blacks, once free, had to rely on themselves for advancement and promotions of their goals and agendas. Blacks needed hope, with so much stacked against them, to be able to advance their own interests and goals. They had prevailed in changing their status from property to citizen, even though they were considered second-class citizens, but they knew it was possible to advance since they had the lessons from their ancestors, who had lived with hope and little else.

Farms and the Land

Most slaves and free Blacks labored on farms and plantations in various roles. Many were engaged in raising different types of crops, so they were familiar with the tasks and demands of farming. Their transition from slaves to free men and women did not change what they knew best, and many continued to labor on farms and plantations; although their status had changed, how they worked did not.

Many became sharecroppers or tenant farmers, and a small group worked to be independent farmers. Some focused on land acquisition so they could operate their own farms. For Black farmers, their independent status meant they made their own decisions about risks and rewards, which also made it possible for them to avoid the systems of control employed by many white planters, such as the credit practices that could result in the loss of their land. Some of the first efforts by Blacks to own land occurred as early as 1862, when Union generals seized farms and plantations and allowed Blacks to settle and tend the land. Some northerners also purchased land and hired freedmen to work these properties, and they arranged for the freedmen to purchase the land. The Freedmen's Bureau attempted to help Blacks acquire abandoned or unsettled land in 1865, but their efforts failed because few citizens were willing to allow Blacks to acquire the land in question. Instead, the Bureau helped establish contracts between planters and freedmen allowing the freedmen to operate farms. This arrangement meant that freedmen had tracts of land that they could operate, and they were allowed to build homes, raise crops, and share—to some extent—in profits from their labor. This way Black farmers were able to get a start. The Bureau also helped establish schools that educated the Black farmers about the business of farming.

Black people also established schools that provided general education, and churches helped many communities grow, as the churches were places that promoted and supported commerce and education. Membership in churches also helped farmers maintain a market and provided ways for the community to support farmers in the face of market pressures.

The situation changed between 1880 and 1920. Black farmers accounted for an estimated 3 million acres of land in 1875–1880 (Reynolds, 2002), which grew to 8 million acres by 1890, and to 12 million acres by 1900. Jim Crow's restrictive racial laws brought a decrease in Black farm ownership over time; in part, this was because many Blacks purchased farms and related supplies with credit that put them in debt. The heavy debt reduced them to the status of peons who could no longer afford to own land but were tenant farmers—sharecroppers who farmed land belonging to someone else. Much of this was backed by new racially based laws. From 1900 to 1930, the number of Black sharecroppers grew to 392,897. By 1930, the economy was in distress, which, coupled with the repressive segregation laws, further limited opportunities for Black farmers.

One mechanism employed by Black farmers to help them become self-sufficient and to meet other needs was to organize cooperatives. Following the example of Blacks in the northeast, who established improvement societies designed to improve homes and communities, a local Texas teacher and community leader, Robert L. Smith (Reynolds, 2002), started the Farmers Improvement Society of Texas (FIST). Its goals were to assist Black farmers in avoiding the debt associated with the credit system, help them operate on a cash basis, encourage them to pool their resources, enhance their farms, and increase their knowledge. The organization also established a bank in 1906. The improvement society helped Black farmers obtain agricultural education and learn ways to produce better crops and raise livestock. FIST also met various other needs of its members, helping to care for the sick, bury the dead, and improve homes.

Black churches organized similar associations to provide services for education and health and assistance for building homes. One of these organizations was the Good Samaritans. These associations had member dues and shared services to farmers. They, like the FIST group, helped with death benefits and burials. Even with the success of FIST, most cooperatives were informal, which reflects the limited market access Black farmers had during the first half of the 20th century.

Black leaders like Booker T. Washington helped set up the Southern Improvement Company, which helped Blacks acquire land for farming and related purposes (homes); the company was run by the Tuskegee Institute, but its success was limited and in time failed. What was more successful was when farmers diversified their crops, which meant Black farmers did not need to depend on growing cotton. This was aided by Black agents who worked for the U.S. Department of Agriculture, but the federal government, for the most part, did little to help Black farmers before 1960. Cotton prices decreased in the 1930s, and the Depression also took a toll on farming, impacting Black farmers negatively, with Black farm ownership declining during these years. During these years, newly established cooperatives promoted and sustained Black farmers, having an enduring effect. The size and scope of the cooperatives grew and expanded in the 1960s and 1970s, although they still encountered considerable resistance and hostility from white groups. Despite Black farmers' struggles, they persisted. With the leadership of Black churches, community building continued throughout the 20th century, including through new credit unions to support Black businesses.

The civil rights era brought more collaboration among Black farmers as well as more discrimination by whites. The white bias stimulated Black cooperation and collective action in purchasing supplies and equipment and in marketing goods. The farmers lacked sufficient leaders to run and organize their cooperatives, so as was true in the past, church leaders stepped in and led the way for Black farmers.

Blacks and Literacy: Education and Schools

Some historians contend that both attending schools and learning were activities that Blacks established while in bondage; even though these activities were forbidden, many Blacks sought to be literate and to understand and teach religious principles that were in line with their African beliefs and convictions.

Williams (2005) tells of how some slaves found ways to learn to read and write, and they sought to pass this knowledge on to other Blacks. Some owners' wives, inspired by their Christian faith, wanted to teach slaves the ways of God, so they taught them to read the Bible. Some states passed laws forbidding such behavior, but even with these prohibitions, many slaves would seek to be literate in covert ways, such as hiding spelling books in their hats until they could be used safely; or asking white children to teach them what they were learning, often when the white children were too young to know this was not allowed; or asking poor whites to provide lessons. Males took such actions more often than females, who had less mobility. Females did have access to young white children in their care and would use them as teachers for reading and writing. They could also learn from the people who lived in the main house by listening to their conversations. Some Blacks were able to memorize these exchanges and would relay them to the others in the Black community.

After emancipation millions of Blacks were poor, destitute, illiterate, and in need of education. Many white religious organizations from the North sent people to the South to help educate Blacks; these efforts laid the foundation for Black secondary schools and colleges, including many normal schools and colleges in several locations in the South, such as South Carolina, Alabama, Georgia, and Kentucky. Some of the colleges established in 1866–1877 grew into universities, including Fisk in Tennessee, Talladega College in Alabama, Howard in Washington, D.C., Hampton in Virginia, and other institutions (Mitchell, 2004). Primary schools were not overlooked; some of these were independent schools dating from the 1870s to 1920s.

The types of financial commitments Black people undertook while barely able to support themselves reveals, in important ways, their spirit and values.

> The freedmen were among the major financial supporters of the first Black institutions. Individual Blacks contributed nickels and dimes and carpentry skills, and Black communities organized suppers, excursions, and entertainment to raise money for the first Black schools and social agencies. There were 236 schools in Georgia in 1867; of these 152 were entirely supported by freedmen, who owned 39 of the buildings. By 1870, the freedmen of Virginia were supporting 215 schools and owned 111 school buildings ... Between 1865 and 1870 according to [one estimate], freedmen contributed $785,700 in cash to black schools.
>
> *(Simpkins & Simpkins, 2009, p. 31)*

Many Blacks did become literate, others were able to advance economically, and still others advanced their work skills from laborers to craftsmen. And while land grants were frequently contested, a significant number of Black farmers were able to acquire large plots of land, and some others "made small fortunes as cotton factors and directors of railroads, steamship companies, oil corporations and banks" (Bennett, 1988, p. 253). Bennett provides this written resolution from the Florida Black Methodist convention:

> We congratulate our people upon the rapid progress they have made in the past six years and upon the mixed industry, homesteads, and small farms, in opposition to the ruinous plantations system, and [we] consider those, together with the increase in school-houses and churches, and also the deposit of near three million dollars in the savings-banks, as a greater pledge of our progress to the friends of freedom throughout the world that can be found in the history of any people who sprang from as lowly a condition as ourselves.
>
> *(quoted in Bennett, 1988, p. 253)*

Blacks and Spirituality: Worship and the Bible

An African cultural ethos was always embedded in their religious beliefs; some were mixed in with Christian practices and others found expression in hidden and not so hidden ways. Some contend these emerged in the 18th and 19th centuries (Mitchell, 2004), while others argue that there were signs well before these times (Raboteau, 2001). I have indicated in earlier chapters what some of these beliefs and practices were and will repeat some of these points here. What is vital to comprehend is the fact that Blacks brought with them, and held on to, traditional African beliefs. Some Blacks who held these beliefs may not have been fully aware of their origins but used and believed in them nevertheless. In time many Blacks adapted and embraced Christian ideals and interjected their unique values into these accepted doctrines in part because the beliefs were accepted and practiced by whites and in part to be able to have and express their beliefs in the context of the existing religious denominations. Africans held beliefs that were flexible and capable of adaptation (Franklin & Moss, 2000; Gates, 2021).

Spirituality and religion, as reflected in churches, served as a vital and central Black institution for centuries, whether it operated in the woods during stolen time for worship or in the rickety buildings in which some were housed, these were often places in which Black people were free to express themselves, and it was time and space that was free of white interference. Many scholars have pointed to the "ring shout," which is a slave dance with African origins in which people would form a circle, move counterclockwise, and shout deeply felt emotions. The ring shout has existed in many African-based denominations (Stuckey, 2013). More so after Reconstruction, the church was the space that allowed leaders to emerge and for group action to be undertaken, where collectives could be formed to aid and assist people for various reasons. The Black church, in whatever form, was where their souls and hearts could find comfort and resolve.

Mitchell (2004) describes several indicators that show the roots of African culture in Black church life. He points to several things that reflect African roots, many of which were forbidden, such as the use of drums; these could be used to send messages, so white colonist stopped Blacks from using drums. Mitchell notes that Blacks replaced drumming with hand clapping and foot stomping, a practice that was also employed during religious worship.

In terms of music, the call and response that reflected African values of being spontaneous and improvising were joined with dance and singing. Blacks were known for singing songs that had rhythmic timing, which they used to relieve the strain of hard labor and to invite the spirits (Mitchell, 2004).

Gates (2021) draws on interviews with former slaves that were conducted in the 1930s to reveal important aspects of their religious lives. Respondents revealed that they were invisible institution participants and that sometimes people who had memorized parts of the Bible would preach the word from memory. Gates notes further that the enslaved who adopted Christianity

> found ways to make the new religion their own, infusing the religion of their captors with their own African spirituality. There is no Black church without music and dancing—never was, never will be—and the drum and dance would be unifying forces of Black forms of worship, expressing adulations and exaltation, signifying inheritance and belonging. One example of a carryover that enslaved Africans incorporated from their religious lives in Africa is the "ring shout."
>
> *(Gates, 2021, p. 33)*

For Black people, religion included notions of equality and justice that departed from the beliefs of many whites. Blacks seldom believed what whites taught, which tended to focus on obedience to them. Instead, Blacks took up notions of God, and their God stood up for the oppressed. They embraced the passages and parables of disciples who cried "let my people go". Gates (2021, p. 38) states that "despite the suffocating confines of slavery, African Americans found surreptitious ways to create sacred spaces in which they could worship God in their own voices and in their own image." They would gather in a cabin at night, or in a hastily made structure in the woods, or by the riverside, or in any place where Blacks could be alone with one another to create and express their spiritual selves in secret. While many could not read or write, some would remember what they heard and share it during these meeting, beyond the watchful eyes of whites.

Religious and lay leaders of the colonies were conflicted about teaching slaves Christianity; some argued it would make them rebellious, while others argued that it would render them docile and obedient. So as time passed there was more willingness to bring the words of God to the slaves. Before the American Revolution there came a religious movement that is referred to as the First Great Awakening, which took hold around the 1730s and 1740s and altered the customary practices of religious worship. It brought a vigorous and emotional form of worship that invited all—men and women, Black and white—into God's tent. Worship involved energetic preaching, shouting, dancing, and speaking out one's emotions. These elements mirrored African practices. To join the denomination, one needed only to have an inner connection with the Holy Spirit. So many Black people converted to or became Methodist or Baptist. The manner of worship provided by the Baptists and Methodists offered a new space that did not exist prior to this in white churches.

Blacks felt they were able to express themselves as never before, so many of them converted to the new groups in large numbers, which also brought along Black preachers. As Blacks were ordained and baptized in the new Methodist and Baptist churches, they were also allowed to become preachers, and they established churches. What took place in these early churches was a combination of African and American cultures. The early churches were controlled and monitored by whites for the most part, but Blacks brought to these churches what I call points of convergence from their African beliefs.

Mitchell (2004) and Raboteau (2001) point to several ways that traditional African spiritual, religious values, and beliefs operated for Black Americans during the colonial years and beyond, through to the post-Civil War era. These scholars contend that Blacks who converted to Christian religions seldom revealed what their actions meant to them. It seemed that if the enslaved could recite scripture, their conversion was accepted, which whites believed meant the Black person would be docile (Mitchell, 2004). Yet, some believe that Blacks converted to *appear* docile. In effect, according to

Mitchell (2004, p. 12), "It thus becomes clear that nothing can be said with certainty about any depths of slave conversions in the colonies, from the first arrivals until the spread of the influence of the First Great Awakening." Mitchell notes that, for Africans, their beliefs and religious faith was a natural part of their cultural ways and was grounded in their experiences and included some form of spiritual possession. Their religious conversion was an emotional and critical part of the religious experience for Africans and their descendants.

Other African beliefs helped Black Americans embrace Christian practices. Africans believed in the power and goodwill of God's love of justice. It was their core spiritual practices that served to support Black psychological survival during the many generations of racial oppression. Mitchell (2004, p. 16) writes, "They were also glad to find their ancient African credo in virtually pure form in the Bible." Enslaved people were clear that their owners would be judged by a just God when the time came. The deep well of spiritual conviction was partly responsible for keeping many sane. These beliefs and convictions were often expressed in spirituals, which were also forms of social protest.

African traditional religion was centered on the existence of an all-knowing, all-powerful God who also had intermediary deities with earthly functions. Again, these beliefs were revealed in spirituals such as the one Mitchell (2004, p. 18) quotes: "'God knows how much we can bear,' they sing about a God who will see and understand, maintain justice, and keep the load from being too heavy."

The church was not the only place where African spiritual ideas and convictions were shared; they were joined with biblical notions that were expressed in church, in the streets, in songs and speeches, and in preaching and daily conversations. Blacks' fundamental spiritual beliefs were also communicated by way of proverbs, according to many historians (e.g., Gates, 2021; Mitchell, 2004; Raboteau, 2001), but the ideas of "Jesus" and "hell" were new to Africans. Their God was extremely remote and unavailable except by way of bridges such as through ancestors or sub-deities (shrines were used to connect with them) and through the order of their social structures, which began with the immediate family, to extended members or elders, and to higher-level chiefs. So, for Africans, Jesus made God more accessible and personal.

Africans believed evil and wrongdoing was punished on earth, not in a realm like "hell." In African ways, honorable people who were held in high esteem upon their passing were honored by the living who offered them gifts of food and sought their guidance. In this instance, Africans' flexibility and beliefs allowed them to consider that evil deeds in life could be punished by sending a person to an invisible world after death where that person would be punished for cruel acts.

In a similar fashion, Africans and Black Americans were able to accept the Bible as the word of God in part because much of their folk wisdom and knowledge, held in proverbs, songs, tales, and dance, were shared by way of oral traditions. These had been restricted during the centuries of slavery, and much of this wisdom was lost over time, yet the core ideas of spiritual doctrines survived, and Blacks sought restoration in the words of God.

It was also common practice for Africans to adapt the gods and beliefs of other people to use as their own, as Mitchell (2004) notes, Africans

> on their own … found Moses and Jesus in the Bible. They stood for much that spoke to enslaved Africans' needs. Over time, there evolved a powerful adaptation of selected parallel portions of Holy Scriptures as a functional oral-replacement-in-English for their own revered traditional oral wisdom…. African traditional religious culture was very strong on memory, and once slaves heard a reading, they were well on their way to memorizing it. Their embrace of the Bible became so complete that illiterate ex-slaves, as late as the 1930s, were still able easily to recite and accurately interpret large sections of Scripture.
>
> *(p. 21)*

For Africans, the word of God came from ancestors and was shared through their words. The reliance and reference to ancestors occurred when someone would proclaim, "my mother would say," or "some other revered relative would say," and so on.

These many manifestations of their cultural ways operated prior to their ability to attend services in actual brick-and-mortar buildings, which at first housed praise settings and later churches. Between 1750 and 1800, according to Mitchell (2004), there were about 25 Black churches in the South and the North. After 1800 church growth continued. In various communities the Black church was the nerve center of the community. It helped nourish souls and bodies and was devoted to much more than spiritual matters. As Blacks took on more of the organizational needs and functions of the church, leaders emerged who spoke the word of God and tended to the secular needs of the congregation as well.

The first objective of church activism was to confront slavery and call out its evils. Many church leaders focused on abolitionist goals, most of which was done in the North. To bolster this effort, slaves and former slaves such as Fredrick Douglass and Sojourner Truth shared their experiences of the institution. Added to this was the covert effort to free slaves by aiding their escape through the Underground Railroad.

It was also through the church that many Blacks were recruited into the military, and some Blacks provided information about the enemy's activities during the Civil War. But these were far from the only secular work that church communities undertook. Mitchell (2004) notes, "From the beginning, African-American pastors and congregations rose to the occasion in times of disaster in need" (p. 136). They provided food for the hungry, clothes, shelter, education, and training. And they would help those who needed aid or to be laid to rest. Prior to the formation of churches, community societies took up the task of assisting with these basic needs. Mitchell (2004) states:

> The African-American belief system supporting this ready reception of responsibility for the needy was traceable to ethnic and religious roots, as opposed to popular social theories. To the call to what should I respond it was from the church as extended family. The common pattern of using familiar titles such as brother and sister came from the ethnic roots in those same extended family communities in Africa. Where they had no formal titles like Mr.; everybody was a relative, near or distant. Indeed, all the anti-slavery activity in other crusades were based, ultimately, on the deep-seated belief in justice going back to both African and Christian roots.
>
> *(p. 137)*

The churches were the seeds for many other Black organizations and institutions. The post-Civil War era was a time of growth and activism for Black people; in the face of unspeakable obstacles, they were able to establish more churches, schools, and businesses.

Black churches and communities supported and helped to establish and maintain Black family life. The family was intertwined with the church and its congregations. The majority of Blacks (90%) lived in the South and most resided in rural areas, which made it difficult for them to be educated or acquire skills they could use to find better working conditions or learn to run organizations. Mitchell (2004, p. 164) notes that Black churches "supported and facilitated the deep desire of ex-slaves to embrace the old African and Christian traditions of the sanctity of marriage."

Many communities and families had socially oriented societies that were devoted to charitable works. So the patterns of Black life surged forward during the Jim Crow era and were held together by Black institutions and organizations, made more essential by the high-pitched and all-encompassing racial segregation created by whites to limit opportunities for Blacks to participate in American society. The era is illustrated in the next chapter.

References

Bennett, L. (1988). *Before the Mayflower: A history of Black America*. Johnson Publishing.

Franklin, H. J., & Moss, A. A. (2000). *From slavery to freedom: A history of African Americans* (8th ed.). McGraw Hill.

Gates, L. H. (2021). *The Black church: This is our story, this is our song*. Penguin.

Mitchell, H. H. (2004). *Black church beginnings: The long-hidden realities of the first years*. Eerdmans.

Packard, J. M. (2002). *American nightmare: The history of Jim Crow*. St. Martin's Press.
Raboteau, A. J. (2001). *Canaan land: A religious history of African Americans*. Cambridge University Press.
Reynolds, B. J. (2002). *Black farmers in America, 1865–2000: The pursuit of independent farming and the role of cooperatives*. United States Department of Agriculture. RBS Research Report 194.
Simpkins, G., & Simpkins, F. (2009). *Between the rhetoric and reality*. Lauriat Press.
Stuckey, S. (2013). *Slave culture: Nationalist theory and the foundations of Black America* (25th anniversary edition). Oxford University Press.
Williams, H. A. (2005). *Self-taught: African American education in slavery and freedom*. University of North Carolina Press.

9

JIM CROW REALITY

Black people worked to create a life for themselves after they were set free, but their efforts were met with racial oppression and segregation as Jim Crow or the legal segregation era began. This time period is best described by racial hostility and anti-Black violence. It did not take long for whites to assert their dominance. Whites regained home rule, set their own state laws, and enforced their laws in the manner determined by their political leaders.

While whites in America were quite different from one another in background, beliefs, and experiences, many of them—regardless of their views, whether they were extremely liberal and open or were members of the far right extreme—upheld the notion that made Jim Crow accepted and vigorously maintained throughout the country: the conviction that white people were by nature superior to Blacks, and its corollary, that Blacks were inferior to whites. Some whites even held that Blacks were a subspecies and should be feared since they could mate with whites. Thus, Packard (2002) points out, "a hatred of Blacks furthered by religion, science, and history extended right across the wide American landscape" (p. 151). These beliefs were strongest in the South but nevertheless were present in the entire country. This belief in white superiority did not subside (somewhat) until the 1950s–1960s. Again Packard (2002) points out,

> The American social and intellectual mosaic lay buried under a blanket of racism that by its omnipresence gave whites a near seamless certainty of their superiority over blacks. In every generation and in every combination of whites—parent and child, pastor and parishioner, teacher and student—the principles of racism and white supremacism were almost effortlessly passed from the elder to the younger, from the formed mind

DOI: 10.4324/9781003111542-13

> to the unformed. Few places existed where one could hide from or be spared this fact of American life.
>
> *(pp. 153–154)*

To illustrate what American society, which was dominated by racism and white supremacy, was like for Blacks, I offer examples of the racial climates in Texas and California. First we examine how white supremacy was maintained.

How White Supremacy Was Maintained

Gates (2021) chronicles the ways and ideas that whites promoted to debase Blacks and to convince others that Blacks were subhuman. Whites, mostly in the South but not exclusively, were determined to convey that Blacks were unworthy of citizenship. This notion was promoted in many ways with myriad images and words. To comprehend the effort, consider that slavery fused race and class by forcing Blacks into a separate class. Its demise as a legal status after the Civil War led whites to construct a process of recreating that same class status for Blacks through other means. Since whites believed Black labor was essential to their survival, they could not accept that Blacks could be free and equal citizens. So, while no longer slaves, Blacks became sharecroppers mired in debt and in effect were placed in a new version of neo-slavery. Sharecropping was joined with segregation; thus, the old class and race status was recreated. Gates (2021) states that this

> neo-slavery … was justified by … an all-encompassing, suffocating, white supremacist discourse, which had a logic, a history, and a momentum of its own, one whose peculiar mode of reasoning and argumentation, with its own symbols and signs would carry on long after slavery.
>
> *(p. 17)*

It is important to provide an overview of the effort to inculcate into American society the crudest forms of anti-Black racism. It is equally important to discuss how Blacks responded to the campaigns that were aimed at holding them in caste and that purported to justify their second-class status as quasi-citizens.

At the conclusion of the Civil War, the confederate leaders, soldiers, supporters, and whites throughout the South, along with followers and sympathizers around the country, accepted their defeat as well as the loss of their human property. They accepted that their lives would change from what had been for centuries. Blacks were no longer slaves—yet regardless of the nation's efforts to elevate Blacks to the level of citizens, whites held firmly to the ideology of their superior status and Blacks' inferiority. Gates (2021) details the ways that white supremacy was promulgated and how it was spread throughout the nation, creating a walled-in existence and a separate world for Blacks. The goal was to get Blacks as close to their previous status of slaves as possible, and to do so with legal and extralegal authority. This way Blacks could be exploited and remain the source of cheap labor. The vehicles for communicating and debasing Blacks were (a) racial science that put forth presumed evidence of Blacks' inferior nature and their amoral character; (b) journalism; (c) political speeches and discourse; and (d) literature and visual images that Gates (2021) calls "fiction and folklore" (p. 56). He writes about the mechanisms that were employed, pointing out that they conveyed a view of rebirth in the South:

> Visions of the New South articulated by scientists, journalists, politicians, and academics of the post-Reconstruction era, portraying black people in a chronic state of childlike dependence, hinged on the continued vitality of the myths of the Old Negro whose devotion, labor and loyalty propped up the Old South. In response to that demand [the portrayal of Blacks], the era saw the flourishing of the genre of plantation literature, a kindred discourse to racial science, to musing about the so-called Negro Problem, and to the grotesque images circulating in American popular culture.
>
> *(p. 91)*

Fiction and folklore depicted Blacks—as did academics, scientists, and scholars using pseudo-science and myth as evidence—to be infantile, docile, and animal-like brutes. In novel after novel, white writers would characterize Blacks and their manners and speech using old-time dialects to depict their low mental state, their loyalty, and their devotion to their white betters. The writers in many of these efforts argued that it was a service to the country to show how Blacks and whites really were. It is difficult to comprehend that the stereotypes promulgated in this era still circulate today and still influence how many people view Blacks. The public discourse surrounding Blacks provides evidence of how people think Blacks live, how their grievances are understood, and how their perspectives are ignored and dismissed.

While words did hurt and have lasting effects, words pale in comparison to the effect of the visual images of Blacks that would depict them as less than human. Gates (2021) contends that these images were the most

> powerful weapon in the arsenal of white supremacist ideology because of the subliminal power of endless repetition. And their collective impact—in advertisements, postcards, and trade cards, in blackface minstrelsy on the stage, and ultimately in stereotyped black characters in moving pictures—would play a pivotal role in persuading American society that black human beings were not only fundamentally different from white people, but irreversibly different *in kind*, and dangerously so, necessitating the erection of rigid boundaries and walls that demanded constant

> vigilance, with transgressions justifying the severest forms of vigilante punishment.
>
> *(pp. 106–107)*

The images and discourse of white supremacy fueled the resistance throughout the country to Blacks receiving equal treatment and being accorded civil rights as citizens, and these efforts intensified as the 20th century began, even as Blacks contributed to the country by serving in the Spanish-American War and both world wars, worked in factories, and contributed to the war efforts by buying bonds. Whites took from these activities that Blacks were not "staying in their place," and frequent white race-riots and mob violence (often lynching) erupted with the aim of communicating to Blacks that they should stay in their place—which, for most whites, was under their boots.

The events between the First and Second World Wars bear out the contention that whites wanted to keep Blacks "in their place" and show how the foundation for Blacks' struggle for civil rights in the 1950s and1960s was laid—as well as how Blacks, in response, built psychological, social, political, and economic infrastructures upon which they were able to protest and advocate for being recognized as, and given full rights as, American citizens.

A key element of that infrastructure was education and their focus on becoming more literate as a people since education had been withheld from them. They knew it mattered whether they could read, write, and count. So people around the country, many of them in the North, invested in schools, and the schools became available to both whites and Blacks. Private foundations after the Civil War joined the effort to fund education at the primary and secondary levels, and some supported colleges and universities as well. Many Blacks also contributed to and supported schools and the training of Black teachers.

It was only natural that leaders among Blacks would surface and provide guidance in the early years of the 20th century. Several ascended to prominence, notably Booker T. Washington. He promoted, among other things, the notion that Blacks should acquire industrial education. He placed less emphasis on political and civil rights activism. Rather, he placed more focus on Blacks learning skills and abilities that fit their low social status, thus not threatening whites.

Washington was embraced by many white leaders and businesspeople. He believed Blacks needed to take small, measured steps toward full social participation, and in time they would be able to enter professional and business ranks. Opposition to Washington's views grew over time, including by W.E. B. Du Bois. It was Du Bois's contention that Washington's approach contributed to the creation of social inferiority for Blacks. Du Bois advocated for full political and civil rights for Blacks as well as full participation in American society. So he helped to found several organizations, such as the Negro

Business League in 1900, to promote fuller involvement and opportunities for Blacks.

Some Blacks began to learn how to operate their own businesses and enterprises. Franklin and Moss (2000, p. 312) observe that "at the end of the century African Americans were engaged in innumerable types and sizes of business. They operated grocery stores, general merchandise stores, and drug stores. They were restaurant keepers, caterers, confectioners, bakers, builders, and contractors." Black people were left alone, for the most part, to figure out on their own how best to survive in a hostile and demeaning country. The core institution that became the central nexus of Black life and spirit was the church. The church in many communities promoted literacy through Bible studies. It aided and encouraged its younger members to be educated, and it served as a social safety network for many. Franklin and Moss (2000) describe the church activities this way:

> Innumerable services were rendered to the community by the new institutional churches. Some [churches] worked in slums and jails, several established missions in slums in the North and South, while others established or supported homes for the aged and orphans.
>
> *(p. 315)*

In addition to the church, secular groups also contributed to Black life and betterment such as fraternal orders and related benefit groups and associations (Masons, Knights of Tabor, and so on). Black insurance companies and collectives were also established.

In the early years of the 20th century, Blacks met to address the things that made their lives difficult. One concrete outcome of these gatherings was the establishment, in 1910, of the National Association for the Advancement of Colored People (NAACP), which was officially formed as a biracial organization. Its actions and advocacy in its early years won some relief for Blacks in a series of court rulings against various forms of racial discrimination. The organization opened branches around the country and by 1920 had set up over 420 branches (Franklin & Moss, 2000).

The NAACP was not the only national organization to be established in this era; in 1911 the National Urban League was started with its focus on creating greater economic opportunity for Blacks, but, as Franklin and Moss (2000) state,

> the problems of African Americans in the United States at the opening of the twentieth century were so broad in scope and so deep in implication that only a large-scale, comprehensive attack on them could make more than a dent in solving them. The programs of the National Association for the Advancement of Colored People and the National Urban League were broadly conceived to meet this challenge, but there was no

> guarantee that these agencies had the right formula. In the difficult task of social reform and regeneration, science and reason together could scarcely keep the door of hope open if passion and prejudice were pressing with all their might to close it.
>
> (*p. 356*)

Another instance of Blacks trying to show their worth took place during World War I. In 1917 there were about 400,000 Blacks who had registered to serve in the military, yet their efforts were met with hostility and discrimination. Nevertheless, Blacks showed the world that they were capable of far more as soldiers than whites would have people believe. While some Blacks went to war to protect the country, back home during the war years many Blacks migrated from the South to relocate to urban centers in the North and West, pursuing social and economic opportunities. By 1920 some 1 million Blacks had moved, in part because the war industry made it possible for many to find employment in many war-related industries. Franklin and Moss (2000) make this observation:

> In the postwar racial strife the willingness of African Americans to fight and to die in their own defense injected a new factor into America's most perplexing social problem. It was no longer a case of one race intimidating another into submission. Now it was war in the full sense of the word, and blacks were as determined to win here as they had been in Europe.
>
> (*p. 389*)

It seemed that Blacks grew considerable self-respect by virtue of their moving away from the South; this, coupled with their increased level of group identity, was behind their determination to resist their oppressors. They learned more about the doctrine of democracy that they had fought to uphold, and they knew the odds of success were against them, yet they still resolved to stand their ground and give a good showing of themselves. Black activists also targeted many aspects of racial violence and racial discrimination. Black organization leaders spoke often and loudly, protesting the lack of fair treatment Blacks were accorded as citizens. Other organizations took on political exclusion and had some success, but their efforts did not capture the mass of Blacks who were struggling to get by, seeking ways to improve their lives.

Another segment of the Black community that took up the cause were literary people. Their numbers grew in the wake of the migration out of the South and to the North and West, where they found greater freedom to express themselves in art, music, and literature. They addressed the inequities inherent in the daily experiences of the mass of Blacks. They were part of the Black community determined to be silent no more about racial violence and rampant racial discrimination. Franklin and Moss (2000) state,

> In the riots and clashes that followed the war, blacks fought back with surprising audacity. By this time, moreover, they had achieved a level of articulation that made it possible for them to transform their feelings into a variety of literary forms. Despite their intense feeling of hate and hurt, they possessed enough restraint and objectivity to use their materials artistically. They were sufficiently in touch with the main currents of American literary thought, moreover, to adapt the accepted forms of expression to their own materials and therefore gain a wider readership. These two factors—the keener realization of injustice and the improvement of the capacity for expression—produced the crop of black writers who constituted the Harlem Renaissance.
>
> *(p. 402)*

Part of what the writers addressed was the fact that they were set apart, yet they recognized this status not as what whites thought—that they were exotic or inferior; instead, the writers knew that Blacks' experiences were evidence of their distinct, unique cultural heritage and well-established traditions. The cultural patterns come from the plantations; the slave quarters; the limits imposed on Blacks in the name of freedom; the public and often private manner in which Black men and women were lynched with impunity; the violent white groups that attacked Blacks, burned their homes, and took their lives; segregation in all its iterations and forms; and racial discrimination that infested all aspects of daily living—all of this fused a common experience that helped to establish and nurture the reality of a unique and distinct Black cultural community with its own leaders and selected spokespeople. The leaders and spokespeople raised their pens and voices to protest the numerous social and economic wrongs directed at Black citizens. Blacks wanted equality for all, not just themselves; at the same time, they took pride in their ways and dignity as a people. While they sought social and economic freedom, they held onto and valued their heritage, traditions, and cultural practices even if they came as a result of experiences of which they were not proud. They still cherished how they had forged a culture and way of being that gave them strength and hope.

The literary movement was centered in New York City in its Black community, Harlem, which was the core of intellectual and cultural life of Black America. Many Black authors, poets, and artisans contributed to the searing intellectual life of this period, which encouraged Blacks to share their lives and experiences. These artists also created, produced, and distributed primarily Black motion pictures.

In this postwar era, Blacks gained and Americans prospered. Due to the war effort, Black people were able to make inroads into many industries in both the North and South. The response from whites was to push Blacks out of their newly acquired jobs and make such employment white only. Added to this reaction was the Great Depression that began in late 1929 and continued into the 1930s, when a quarter of whites and 40% of Blacks needed welfare support, and by the mid-1930s the number of Blacks needing assistance grew to 80% in southern cities.

So times were bad, but all was not lost. The migration of Blacks to urban centers resulted in a renewed political strength in some northern cities and states. Black elected officials aimed to improve the conditions of Black life as they followed the lead of the literary crowd. Blacks' increased influence in political centers was reflected in their ability to elect representatives in state and local races, which in turn increased their leverage in national elections. They won seats in state houses in California, Illinois, Indiana, Kansas, Kentucky, New Jersey, New York, Ohio, Pennsylvania, and West Virginia (Franklin & Moss, 2000, p. 427). Beyond these offices, Blacks became judges and served as government officials, as members of school boards, and served on city councils. They were also law enforcement officers and lawyers who practiced in business and government.

To address the hardships brought by the Depression, the federal government enacted the New Deal, which established many programs to relieve the effects of the Depression on Americans. Some of these benefited Blacks in that the aid and policies, in some instances, cut through the hard walls of racial discrimination and bled through to Blacks.

While economic and political improvement were important, so was education. Responsibility for supporting education had shifted from private foundations and self-help groups to the public sector during the early years of the 20th century. But, as was true of most things that involved Blacks, there was little equality in school funding for whites and Blacks. Private sources for funding education were substantial and brought about a new era in the South. Grants given to citizens to aid and fund schools helped to drive self-help on the part of individuals, institutions, and states in the south. The funds provided by private organizations and individuals went to supplement teacher salaries, buy equipment, and build schools. Yet, during the late 19th and early 20th centuries, whites in the South objected to funding of private schools, with one church leader stating that the funds were dangerous and degrading handouts. Whites gave general support and approval to such funds only when they determined that the funders had little or no interest in creating racial equality or in any way disturbing or challenging white supremacy. The private support in no way affected the way public money for education was allocated. Public funds in the South benefited primarily whites. To illustrate how public funds were allocated, Franklin and Moss (2000) state that "the citizens of Adams County, Mississippi, were spending $22.25 for the education of each white child and $2.00 for the education of each black child" (p. 297).

Nevertheless, Blacks increased their level of literacy despite disparities in funding schools. In fact, private foundations helped build schools in the South for Blacks, with some 5,000 schools built between 1913 and 1932 with the combined aid of the Julius Rosenwald Foundation, state tax dollars, white supporters, and Black donors. With the onset of the Depression in the late 1920s and continuing into the 1930s, school construction for Blacks stopped and teaching staffs declined, as did their pay. Many schools in most states were segregated, yet there were positive outcomes due to segregation. One positive outcome was the creation of Black colleges. After World War I, in the 1920s, more Blacks sought out college educational opportunities. Blacks on many campuses protested for more freedom, greater academic rigor, and curricula that included Black history and culture, and Black faculty and administrators.

After World War II, some 20 or so years later, several trends in education became apparent. More Blacks in the second half of the 20th century attended white institutions, and Black administrators grew in numbers at both white and Black schools. Blacks also joined the ranks of professors at white colleges and universities, mostly in response to protests that called for greater Black presence in the halls and towers of higher education. These trends reached graduate and professional training as Blacks increased in large numbers in this area.

There was a struggle to break desegregation walls built into these higher-level educational centers. In the 1930s Blacks had to seek court relief to be admitted to graduate schools of law, pharmacy, and other disciplines. To avoid admitting Blacks, some universities actually agreed to pay for the Black students' out-of-state graduate school tuition, while other universities created separate graduate schools for their Black students.

The path to graduate and professional school admissions was through the federal courts. There were a series of Supreme Court rulings in the 1940s and 1950s that ordered that Blacks be admitted to professional or graduate schools in Southern states. "To white Southerners these rulings were a frightening departure from the separate but equal doctrine that had been laid down in *Plessy v. Ferguson* in 1896" (Franklin & Moss, 2000, p. 452).

Many whites accepted what they believed was inevitable. Instead, they turned their resistance to keeping public schools whites-only. At the same time, in the 1950s the NAACP targeted public school segregation as unconstitutional and brought several cases to the courts in an effort to strike a blow against such practices in the country. What followed was the *Brown v. Board of Education* decision, which struck down the separate but equal doctrine, at least in federal law. For a brief period, integration was attempted in some places. But as was the case with Reconstruction, support fell away and segregation was reasserted, yet this time it was done in the guise of geography or community boundaries (Franklin & Moss, 2000). It should be noted that a rose is still a rose even if it is given another name.

After the Second World War Blacks not only survived but they tried to participate more fully in American society. As their strides and efforts show, for three centuries they spoke in a clear and firm voice that they wanted respect and dignity as well as opportunity. They did not wish to live on others' terms or to emulate whites.

Throughout the 300 years in which Black Americans were set apart, to preserve their identity and community, they developed their own institutions. At the same time, they struggled to contribute and participate in mainstream American society. The demands of the two worlds, American society and Black life, were such that Blacks sought to lessen the burden and demands of the two separate worlds, by not duplicating life in every way and by seeking larger roles in mainstream society, since they were in reality citizens, irrespective of how they were treated and regarded by whites. Their inroads into mainstream society were minimal but significant. It became in this point in history more difficult for Black people to accept the status quo, in which they were held apart, since they observed the United States' officials and government leaders engage in international efforts to promote democracy, while also creating the United Nations. The new international body admitted several African countries, thus demonstrating that Black people around the world were given more regard than Blacks in the United States. At the same time, whites in the South were enraged at the efforts to desegregate schools, and they used considerable efforts to resist, often falling back on what worked in the past—violence.

Blacks' challenges to graduate and professional schools' admission policies paid dividends in that many more Blacks had entered professional disciplines and were able to provide needed services to Blacks and others. Said another way, by the 1950s a substantial Black middle class existed, populated by business and professional people, and the mass of Blacks shared the interests, social structure, goals, and preferences of this newly emerged middle class. Blacks built a strong infrastructure in their community, "with not just teachers and clergy, but also physicians, dentists, pharmacist, nurses, attorneys, social worker, recreation leaders, morticians, and others to perform a variety of personal service" (Franklin & Moss, 2000, p. 468). These professionals formed and created associations and affiliated groups to protect their interests and professional careers. And Black professionals in journalism and publishing helped raise attention to their causes (by the late 1970s there were over 350 Black publications, issued weekly or monthly).

Blacks' Experiences in Texas

Following the Civil War and until the First World War, many Black people remained in or close to the communities in which they had been enslaved (de Graaf, 1962). Texas, which had served as a safe haven for migrating Southern slaveholders, was no exception. Many slaveholders had sent their slaves to the state to prevent them from running away during the Civil War, and from being co-opted by the events surrounding the conflict and its aftermath. Already settled within agricultural communities, newly emancipated Blacks, "with their economic status little improved," continued to labor in the farm industry. Although the Black Codes that were enacted in Texas in 1866 permitted Black people to own and convey private property, other enacted sections of the legal scheme limited conveyance of public lands into Black hands and promoted "apprenticeship" and sharecropping as a new kind of servitude. Newly emancipated Black men were coerced into this new post-emancipation structure under threat of arrest for vagrancy and other freshly minted crimes that criminalized idleness and were enforced chiefly against Black people who were, in turn, largely excluded from participating in Texas's court processes as witnesses or jurors, meaning they were unable to defend any charges brought against them in court. Many freedmen in Texas and throughout the South faced few alternatives but to labor as sharecroppers.

Moreover, sharecropping was structured to hold the sharecroppers in a marginal status, a situation that lasted well into the 20th century. Sharecroppers would have to agree to share the proceeds of their crops with the landowners or landlords for use of the land. Additional payments accrued for supplies and food, often at inflated prices and high rates of interest. This kept sharecroppers always in debt. Added to this, laws related to liens on the property left Black tenant farmers in a state of near slavery and forced them to work until their obligations were paid, which, for most, was never (de Graaf, 1962).

The racial climate in the state of Texas also left Blacks in fear of being killed by mob violence. On February 28, 1908, the *Austin American Statesman* reported that a lynch mob hung 18-year-old Charley Scott from an elm tree near the Montgomery County courthouse in Conroe, Texas. The paper details that Mr. Scott, described as "not very strong mentally," was twice seen near the home of a white man who was known to be out of town. The circumstances behind the lynching are undocumented:

> no noise was made and no shots were fired and nothing was known of the lynching save by those taking part until Friday morning, when the sun revealed the gruesome sight of a dead body dangling and waving pendulum fashion by the breeze.

At Mr. Scott's feet the lynchers had placed a placard: "This is a warning to all negroes who are caught prowling around white folks houses." Blacks lived or died depending upon the whim and wishes of whites in the Jim Crow South.

As the United States began to experience an economic downturn following World War I, ultimately resulting in the Great Depression, Black Americans, particularly in the South, were disproportionately impacted. Agricultural prospects shifted as white farm owners transitioned from cotton to other crops or experienced significant erosion (from years of cotton growing), rendering the land less arable (de Graaf, 1962). Newer crops required less manual labor than cotton but more land—reducing the need for tenancy and rendering it less desirable. The shift to tractors and mechanization in the 1930s further led to fewer agricultural opportunities and a decreased need for year-round tenancy—a shortage more directly impacting Black people, who were routinely disfavored for employment over white competitors. The rural farming population declined by nearly half a million people during the 1920s, which started a migration toward urban centers (Barr, 1996; Truesdell, 1926). But with limited financial means, many Black people were unable to travel far and instead generally relocated short distances in the South. The urban migration continued through the Great Depression as previously agrarian Black people relocated into the crowded slums of the cities and towns, joining the ranks of the unemployed seeking to find work with the Works Project Administration.

In Texas one such area that saw substantial Black migration was Houston. Its population had begun to soar shortly after the end of the Civil War, when an influx of predominantly Black people, juxtaposed with segregation, necessitated relegating these new residents to the Fifth Ward. By 1870 the population of the ward was approximately evenly divided between whites and Blacks, with two schools corresponding to each racial group. This population influx continued into the beginning of the 19th century, as Houston and the surrounding area experienced a period of economic growth. In 1901 oil was discovered in nearby Beaumont, Texas. The city of Houston began constructing a ship channel, promising to bring economic growth that would identify the city as a commercial shipping center. In 1912, after a large fire occurred in the Fifth Ward, more Black families migrated to the community, seeking to rebuild homes in the city at a decreased cost. By the early 1920s the Fifth Ward was predominantly Black (Kleiner, 2020).

White communities expressed fear that migrating Black families would not remain segregated in wards 3, 4, and 5, and racial tensions were high. On November 27, 1920, 200 members of the Ku Klux Klan marched through downtown Houston and engaged in physically violent acts (Greene, 1988). On February 5, 1921, the Klan kidnapped B. I. Hobbs, a white divorce lawyer who represented Black and white clients alike. The Klan cut Mr. Hobbs's hair and tarred and feathered him before leaving him in the middle of San Jacinto Street. The Klan posted flyers to telephone poles throughout Houston, warning both Blacks and whites of the dangers of associating across the racial divide. When Mr. Hobbs later refused to heed the Klan's warnings to leave Houston, he was again abducted—this time from his sister's residence—and driven out of town. Approximately a month later the Klan kidnapped a Black man named A. V. Hopkins, who had supposedly insulted a group of white high school girls. After the Klan severely beat Mr. Hopkins, he left town for fear of further recrimination (Greene, 1988). In March 1921 the Klan then abducted William McGee, who had been accused of indecent exposure. Reports indicate the Klan drove Mr. McGee to a remote area and castrated him. A local Klan-sympathetic tabloid reported the incident, admonishing the public, "I know you will agree with me that under the circumstances that was the best thing that could have happened" (Bernstein, 2018). By 1940 these conditions were exacerbated when new highway construction in Houston cut through predominately Black neighborhoods and changed both their character and access to parts of the community.

At the same time, nearby Beaumont, Texas, was in the middle of significant growth due to booming war production. Blacks were able to find and secure well-paying jobs in plants and factories related to the war effort. The resulting overcrowded housing and transportation systems made it difficult to maintain the strict lines of separation required of racial segregation, and the situation led to many incidents that heightened racial tensions. As has been often true of the Southern racial violence, a mere allegation of rape by a Black man would trigger the usual white mob behavior. On June 4, 1943, a Black man who was drafted and afraid to report to the Army instead allegedly beat and raped a white woman. He was shot by the police while resisting arrest, and a small mob of 50 or so sought to lynch him but were turned back by the police chief. The Black man died a few days later. On June 15, 1943, another white woman alleged she had been raped by a Black man. Although this claim was later proven by a doctor to be false, a large mob formed with between 4,000–5,000 people demanding to see the person alleged to have committed the crime. When they were unable to locate him (because no one had been arrested), the mob turned its attention to the Black areas of town. They beat or killed any Black person they encountered and buried and ransacked Blacks' homes.

> Blacks suffered many causalities and witnessed much destruction during the riot. Rioters reportedly broke into over two hundred homes, many of which they fired. Probably at least three or four hundred blacks received injuries, and some were hospitalized.... Besides those injured about 2,500 blacks fled the city by foot or auto, some never to return.
>
> *(Burran, 1976, p. 44)*

The National Guard arrived after the violence ended. They, along with members of the state police and Texas Rangers, imposed a curfew to enforce order in Beaumont. And while there were some arrests of white rioters, no further action was taken. Martial law was declared, Black people were not allowed to go to work, and public gatherings were canceled (Burran, 1976).

Houston began to desegregate in the late 1950s and throughout the following decade. Integration carried with it numerous economic consequences, both intended and unintended. Black patrons began to take their business outside of Black communities, spending money for the first time in white-owned businesses and neighborhoods. Consequentially, Black communities and businesses received less economic support.

As Houston grew, it industrialized historically Black neighborhoods. Although these neighborhoods were now less attractive for residential use and were economically decimated, Black residents were still not fully welcomed in white communities or businesses. Many Blacks left Houston due to the economic downturn and lack of promise for Black residents. Some moved west to Los Angeles, California. Nevertheless, financial times remained difficult for many Black people, although the median household income in 1957 was approximately $5,000 (United States Census Bureau, 1958). By this time the civil rights movement had begun, as had the migration of Blacks out of the South.

The racial climate during this time in Texas remained a part of the spectrum of violence that characterized prior generations' experience. Around the time of the Supreme Court's 1954 ruling in *Brown v. Board of Education*, which ordered public schools to integrate, a white man drove by a section of the Black area of town where young Blacks were dancing and listening to music. The man, Perry Dean Ross, shot into a café killing Earl Reese and injuring the two girls. The shooter was arrested and 15 months later was put on trial for "murder with malice." His defense was that he wanted to scare Blacks away from integrating the schools. The district attorney asked the jury to call it a bad day for him; imploring the all-white jury to not send him to jail. After 90 minutes the jury came back with a judgment of guilty but without malice, recommending a five-year suspended sentence. The court sentenced Ross as recommended.

California's Racial Climate

The story of race relations in California, which was originally part of Mexico and became part of the United States in 1850, is somewhat different than in Texas. The issue of California statehood was intertwined with the congressional legislation known as the Missouri Compromise requiring a balance of free and slave states joining the Union—that is, for every newly admitted free state, a slave state also needed to be admitted. Unlike other regions of the country, California had a diverse racial history and heritage that included European, Spanish, Native American, Mexican, Chinese, other Asian, and Black people. The territory was spacious and offered opportunities that other locations did not. Some settlers in the territory nevertheless espoused racist sentiments that echoed in the debates surrounding California statehood. An article appearing in the *Californian* on March 15, 1848, argued that slavery should not be permitted in California upon its admittance to the Union. Although the article derided slavery as immoral, argued that the land was not good for slave labor, and proclaimed that Blacks should be equal to whites, it also revealed prejudice, saying that slavery should be prohibited because California desired to remain a white-only population. California entered the Union as the 31st state and was categorized as free (Hunt & Ramon, 2010).

Although initially regarded as the "untamed West," settlers rapidly flocked to California, particularly after transcontinental rail lines connected California's major cities, like San Francisco and Los Angeles, with the rest of the country in the 1870s. Many of these new settlers were white Midwesterners and Southerners. Whether poor, middle class, or upper class, these whites held firm to the notion that they were the superior racial group:

> Blacks were considered subhuman by most whites, simply not existing on the same plane as white Europeans. Whites thought blacks dirty, diseased, unable to reach white intellectual levels, with black males unable to control their "aggressive" and "brutalistic" sexual urges. That such creatures would and could bring down the white man in their undertow was the logic beyond any other for white antagonism to blacks and for white insistence on maintaining inviolate the barrier that Jim Crow represented.
>
> *(Packard, 2002, p. 100)*

These racial sentiments did not immediately resound against Black people traveling to the Golden State. At the turn of the century Black people were able to travel to California and live, unsegregated, throughout Los Angeles (United Way of Greater Los Angeles, 1991). But California's white-only perspective was echoed elsewhere. Residential restrictions, initially directed at Chinese people rather than Blacks, established racial segregation. San Francisco issued the state's first residential ordinance designed to maintain segregation by preventing Chinese immigrants from moving into white neighborhoods. Blacks migrated, largely by rail and mostly from Texas and Louisiana, to Southern California in the late 1880s. Many Blacks settled near downtown Los Angeles. At first blush, many things appeared different about Los Angeles from the other areas of the country where Black settlers had lived. Race relations in California seemed improved. Upon becoming a state, California prohibited legal racial segregation. The state enacted an anti-discrimination law in 1883, and the level of anti-Black violence was low. Blacks could also own homes in California. An estimated 40% of Blacks in Los Angeles had purchased homes around the turn of the century, as compared to 4% and 8% of Blacks in New York and Chicago, respectively (Sides, 2006).

On paper, California appeared to be the promised land of racial integration for Blacks coming from the South, but racial restrictions in practice remained prominent. In 1892 a California federal court affirmed that state and municipal governments could not discriminate against people on the basis of race but permitted individuals to perpetuate such discrimination in promulgating residential contracts (Kilgore, 2020). Although the number of Blacks in Los Angeles remained low, less than 5% of the overall population, white fears were heightened by the influx of Black people.

Real estate developers capitalized on this fear and marketed white-only property restrictions as key selling points in luxury developments (Sides, 2006; Slater, 2021). In 1902 the first racially restrictive covenant preventing property ownership by nonwhite people was filed in Los Angeles (Sides, 2006; Slater, 2021). The Los Angeles Realty Board, founded in 1903, went on to attach such covenants to as many new developments in the county as possible. The board financed litigation resulting in the California Supreme Court's 1919 decision that permitted a Black man to purchase a home but not live in it due to restrictive real estate covenants (Los Angeles Inv. Co. v. Gary, 1919). As Los Angeles entered a housing boom in the 1920s, the most desirable new construction featured racial restrictions on occupancy.

Meanwhile, because of outwardly promising opportunities, Blacks continued to flock to Los Angeles. A community grew along South Central Avenue, south of downtown Los Angeles. The Black population of Los Angeles grew from 2,131 in 1900, to 15,579 in 1920, to 38,898 in 1930 (Sides, 2006; Slater, 2021). Many white Angelenos feared that Black people would gain political power in Watts, an area in which Blacks were the majority (Bunch, 1988). Blacks had begun moving there early in the 1900s, when it was a separate city, but Los Angeles annexed Watts in 1926. The Klan had opposed this annexation.

By the 1930s restrictive covenants, white flight, and a burgeoning Black population created distinct, segregated districts with Black people predominantly congregating in the southeastern area of downtown Los Angeles (Tucker et al., 2010). This color line kept nonwhites in racially segregated areas. Thus, Blacks lived in proximity to other racial groups like Mexicans and Asians as well as some whites. As Black populations continued to expand, they remained hemmed by racist housing policies. The Great Depression further cemented these racial covenants and the long-lasting effects of such property restrictions on communities of color.

The Home Owners' Loan Corporation (HOLC) was established as part of the New Deal program intended to alleviate the greatest impacts of the Great Depression (Mitchell & Franco, 2018). In particular, HOLC purchased mortgages that were in default and offered families more favorable terms than those originally contracted. As part of this practice, HOLC created a series of "residential security maps" that outlined the desirability and, thus, the mortgage risk for particular residential areas. Although HOLC may have held these maps confidentially, these maps—whether viewed by private lenders or merely reflective of value judgments during this period about various property parcels—set the minimal equity value in predominately racial minority neighborhoods. The result was a practice that became to be known as "redlining," where residents in certain communities, predominately communities of color, were denied access to capital investment that could improve neighborhood housing and economic opportunities. Whereas predominately white communities received economic support from the federal government, redlining only further limited economic opportunity and undercut property values and community resources for minorities.

These residential restrictions isolated Black people within certain neighborhoods and limited interpersonal contact in other spheres of life, such as in schools, workplaces, and public spaces, as well as access to hospitals and leisure and business activities. The commitment to racial segregation was most evident in the schools. Liberal transfer policies worked as de facto segregation to establish and populate white-only schools and simultaneously create schools multiracially populated with Black, Mexican, and Asian students. Los Angeles's multiracial reality across minority groups made the city appear more accepting of Blacks. But this perception merely hid the tensions that existed among nonwhite populations.

As in the rest of the country, Black Angelenos also experienced barriers to employment. Blacks were often left out of the labor pools entirely or were hired near-exclusively as laborers, janitors, and porters. Black women were more often hired as domestic servants. These limited job opportunities were further curtailed because Black men competed with the Mexican labor force. Blacks were barred from joining unions or holding union jobs. Because of these limited avenues for employment, the Great Depression and resulting further unemployment waves hit the Black community particularly hard. According to one estimate, by 1934 half of Los Angeles's Black residents were unemployed. Not until white community members entered the bread lines in the late 1930s did the federal government begin to fund various programs aiming to employ the many hundreds of thousands of workers who lost employment during the Depression.

The Second World War and its industrial needs ushered in change for Blacks in Los Angeles. The war and resulting draft created labor shortages that, coupled with high labor demand in defense industries, forced employers to revisit the practice of hiring mainly white men. This trend was further aided by newly enacted federal laws that prohibited discrimination in employment. As the second-largest industrial center in the country, with airplane and ship building facilities as well as steel industries, Los Angeles attracted Black migrants in record numbers. Blacks increasingly migrated from the South—mostly from Texas and Louisiana and typically from southern urban centers (rather than rural areas)—to take advantage of the new opportunities. More than 200,000 Black Americans came to the city in search of work in the growing defense-driven and shipbuilding economy (Sides, 2006). The resulting changes in Los Angeles were dramatic. In 1940 Blacks composed 1% of California's population, but by 1970 they constituted approximately 8%. Although the city's white population increased by 41% in the 1940s, the Black population increased by 112% (United Way of Greater Los Angeles, 1991). This rapid Black migration highlighted the extensive costs of racial segregation.

> The Great Migration thoroughly transformed Los Angeles and other American cities because it forced white citizens and public officials to meet head-on the high social costs of segregation. Having long ignored the causes of residential segregation, Los Angeles city government was suddenly confronted by its debilitating effects, including the severely overcrowded neighborhoods of Central Avenue and the slums of Little Tokyo [occupied now by Blacks families], recently vacated by Japanese residents, who had been sent to wartime internment camps.
>
> *(Sides, 2006, p. 63)*

As the Black population grew, the community expanded from the Watts and West-Jefferson areas into surrounding neighborhoods (Sides, 2006). This influx of Blacks was met with racial hostility from whites who harbored fears of crime and illicit behavior. The negative perceptions and attribution of Blacks as drains on the state were common and persistent. Some whites thought Blacks were savages who were bringing the state down and draining its resources. Even when Blacks were not involved, public perceptions identified them as the root of racial violence. In 1943 white naval officers attacked young Mexican men, singling out those who wore outfits known as Zoot suits. Although Blacks were not involved, the community responded to the incident with increased fear of Black violence. Nearly simultaneously, other incidents and racial riots perpetrated by whites occurred throughout the South and around the country, yet fears of Black residents continued to rise (Flamming, 2005).

The post-world war years ushered in an era of prosperity and economic opportunity in California wherein many white families enjoyed a new middle-class standard of living. But most Black people still found many obstacles littering their paths to greater well-being. "African Americans encountered disheartening and capricious restrictions that made economic parity with whites virtually impossible" (Sides, 2006, p. 57). Job opportunities for Black people in Los Angeles dissipated. Most industrial employers continued to engage in racial discrimination, hiring Black workers only when whites moved on to lighter, less demanding, and higher-paid work. Many unions further supported and promoted white employment advantages.

Shortly after the end of the war, the Supreme Court struck down the racially restrictive covenants that had hemmed in communities of color in Los Angeles and elsewhere (Barrows v. Jackson, 346 U.S. 249, 1953). Those Blacks who experienced some benefit from the overall economic boon were able to now buy homes in sections of Southern California where prices were relatively low, outside of historically entrenched Black communities and in safe communities with good schools.

But Black "determination to further broaden the areas in which they could live generated an unprecedented wave of anti-black hostility and violence among white homeowners, forever undermining the relative racial peace that had characterized the prewar years" (Sides, 2006, p. 97). Although this hostility was less overt than that displayed in areas like Texas, it was nonetheless insistent and virulent. White Angelenos believed the influx of Black neighbors meant decreased property values and community morals and an increase in crime. In response to this hyperbole, most whites faced with new Black neighbors quietly sold and moved away. But for some blue-collar whites, this was not a viable option.

These remaining "white homeowners ... devised dozens of tactics to keep African Americans out of their neighborhoods" (Sides, 2006, p. 96), most notably those neighborhoods surrounding South Central (e.g., Inglewood, Hawthorne, Gardena, Compton, Lynwood, Huntington, Park, and South Gate). Whites used payoffs to real estate agents to discourage sales to Blacks, as well as using vandalism, cross-burning, bombing, and death threats. In 1951 a four-foot cross was set aflame on the lawn of a Black family who had moved into a home in Leimert Park near South Central. The following year a Black war veteran and teacher moved into a home northwest of South Central in a mostly white area. Their home was destroyed by a bomb. "Between 1950 and 1959, the County Commission on Human Relations reported six bombings and four incidents of arson against Black-owned homes in Los Angeles County" (Sides, 2006, p. 103).

Various institutions echoed these white homeowners' sentiments. "In the post-war era many individual white homeowners, and virtually all the public and private institutions in the housing market, did everything possible to prevent African Americans from living outside areas that were already predominantly black" (Sides, 2006, p. 108). Local real estate boards used an ethical code to forbid agents from introducing racial minorities to white neighborhoods. Police relied on an obscure city code to arrest real estate agents who sold homes in white neighborhoods to Black purchasers. Banks refused to violate the color lines set by white homeowners in financing mortgages for potential Black purchasers. Home builders joined with the banks to hold this color line. After white homeowners launched letter-writing campaigns to local and state leaders imploring them to intercede with "the Negro Problem" and to help maintain their neighborhoods as white enclaves, local police officers and politicians responded by campaigning with anti-Black and anti-Mexican sentiment to echo the cries of their white constituents.

Even the federal government contributed to the arc of racial segregation by refusing to defend integration. Instead, they demanded "that individual complainants provide proof of discrimination rather than creating an institutional mechanism to prevent it" (Sides, 2006, p. 107). The Federal Housing Administration (FHA) and the Department of Veterans Affairs (VA) financed numerous homes during this time, claiming to not discriminate, but they did not act to prevent Black buyers from being barred from home ownership. Of the 125,000 VA- or FHA-financed homes built in Los Angeles County between 1950 and 1954, only 2.4% (3,000) were open to nonwhite ownership. Simultaneously, whites expressed greater acceptance of other minority groups—namely, Mexicans, Asians, and Jews. These groups were able to move into predominantly white areas without the same difficulties Blacks faced. Once-multiracial communities in Los Angeles now became "hyper-segregated" as non-Black minorities departed. The poorest Blacks remained in the South Central region and created a new underclass at the bottom of Los Angeles's racial hierarchy (Sides, 2006).

As an example, consider the case of the previously all-white city of Compton. It was located south of Watts in Los Angeles County, and it had been an important industrial and residential center for Southern California's economy. It was a mostly blue-collar area with well-kept and attractive homes. In the 1940s the racial barriers were well-fortified; in 1948 there were approximately 50 Black people among the city's 45,000 residents. Because Compton was in proximity to two predominantly Black areas, Watts and Willowbrook, the white city residents and officials were vigilant in maintaining the racial boundaries. But Compton offered Black families who could afford to purchase a home prime land on which to relocate and develop.

Whites had strong reactions to Blacks moving into Compton. In the early 1950s white homeowners who listed or sold homes to Blacks were attacked and assaulted. Despite white resistance, the racial change in Compton was dramatic. In the 1950s Compton had about 48,000 white and 2,000 non-white residents. By 1960 Compton had about 38,000 white, 28,000 Black, and 6,500 Hispanic residents (Fecketter, 1979).

Press coverage shifted and began to report stories of gang violence, poverty, and physical, economic, and social decline in Compton (Smith, 1973). City leadership described community changes as not only negative but racially driven. Such spokespeople harped on an increase in transient working-class residents; shifting retail to poorer quality and discounted goods; an increase in crime and property damage, attributed to community youth; and a lack of planning and leadership structure in city governance. But city leadership tied each of these problems to the growing Black population. This political and media messaging both instigated and reinforced white community divestment and hostility at the local, state, and federal level as well as in private industry.

By the mid-1960s Black residents began to show frustration at the inescapable racism and marginalization across Los Angeles. Black political groups began to advocate for social change and promote unity and community. Some scholars contend that state and local government—namely, the governor of California; the Los Angeles district attorney; and the chief of police—were trying to disrupt Black community advocacy and engaged in illegal investigation methods, including entrapment and intimidation to infiltrate Black communities. The Black community and the Los Angeles Police Department grew to be at odds (Flamming, 2005; Sides, 2006).

In August 1965 Black residents in Watts reacted to a police encounter between Black Angelenos and white officers—namely, the arrests of a Black man and his mother, who protested her son's arrest. Although this event triggered the Watts disturbance, it was just one of countless incidents across the country wherein Black people were stopped and arrested without cause and sometimes were beaten in police custody (Hunt & Ramon, 2010). Many Watts protesters were native Angelenos who had firsthand experience of the county's legacy of white isolation and police mistreatment and abuse. Black youths, through their actions in Watts, expressed their overwhelming outrage with local, state, and federal officials and political leaders as well as Black elders and civil leaders, whom Black youths saw as accepting of snail-like racial progress.

Although similar incidents occurred in Black communities across the country around this time in response to frustration at the inescapable racism and constant threat of abuse and violence, the Watts disturbance resulted in more harm and destruction. The disturbance in Watts lasted six days and involved young men in Watts and South Central. Stores were looted and burned, people were beaten, and first responders were attacked. More than 30 people died and several thousand were injured. Many thousands were arrested. The property damage was estimated to be near $40 million (Hunt & Ramon, 2010; Sides, 2006).

The Watts disturbance resulted in the flight of many of the whites and more affluent Blacks who still lived in Watts and the surrounding community. Poor Blacks took their place, willing to take the vacated spaces, but they tended to be renters not owners. Compton then became a predominantly Black community. But the loss of income from taxes of these wealthier residents led to the decline of Watts, along with Willowbrook and Compton, which had experienced similar white flight. Accordingly, crime rates rose and only further discouraged businesses from locating in these areas. A 1967 survey reported that Compton had the highest rate of youth poverty in the county. Some Blacks formed political and social organizations to advocate for better conditions, but "for many others, no constructive outlet existed. Consequently, the economic problems of South Central contributed significantly to crime, drug addiction, rising rates of out-of-wedlock births, and the creation of a substantial and semi-permanent underclass of African Americans" (Sides, 2006, p. 185). But, despite its notoriety, Compton's demise and decline was no worse than that of other cities across the country.

Liberal whites also began to shy away from supporting Black rights following the Watts disturbance; at the same time, a right-wing conservative movement that resisted Black progress and integration gained momentum. In response to the Watts disturbance and increasing unemployment, Black organizations in Los Angeles became unified and mobilized through the Black Power movement. "After Watts, a sense of cohesiveness began to form among the various clubs, with members expressing an increased sense of self-worth and positive identification as pride pervaded the black community" (Alonso, 2010, p. 145). White resistance became more covert, and Blacks focused their attention on new issues and concerns in their efforts to seek social change. Black-on-Black crime, police brutality, and unemployment were key issues for members of the Black community, many of whom joined the Black Power movement.

An era of activism began for Blacks in the country, which was instrumental in moving the overall civil rights struggle.

References

Alonso, A. (2010). Out of the void: Street gangs in Black Los Angeles. In D. Hunt & A. Ramon (Eds.). *Black Los Angeles: American dreams and racial realities* (pp. 140–159). New York University Press.

Barr, A. (1996). *Black Texans: A history of African Americans in Texas 1528–1995.* University of Oklahoma Press.

Bernstein, P. (2018). *Ten dollars to hate: The Texas man who fought the Klan.* Texas A&M University Press.

Bunch, L. G., III. (1988). Black Angelenos: The Afro-American in Los Angeles, 1850–1950 [article written for an exhibit at the California Afro American Museum, 1988, June 11–1989, March 6].

Burran, J. A. (1976). Violence in an "arsenal of democracy": The Beaumont race riot, 1943. *East Texas Historical Journal,* 14(1), 294–308.

de Graaf, L. B. (1962). *Negro migration to Los Angeles, 1930 to 1950* (Publication No. 74–76563) [Doctoral dissertation, University of California, Los Angeles]. R&E Research Associates.

Fecketter, B. R. (1979). *A historical and socioeconomic analysis of Compton, California* [Unpublished doctoral dissertation]. University of Beverly Hills.

Flamming, D. (2005). *Bound for freedom: Black Los Angeles in Jim Crow America.* University of California Press.

Franklin, H. J., & Moss, A. A. (2000). *From slavery to freedom: A history of African Americans* (8th ed.). McGraw Hill.

Gates L. H. (2021). *The Black church: This is our story, this is our song.* Penguin.

Greene, C. (1988). Guardians against change: The Ku Klux Klan in Houston and Harris County, 1920–1925. *Houston Historical,* 8(1), 1–5.

Hunt, D., & Ramon, A. (Eds.). (2010). *Black Los Angeles: American dreams and racial realities.* New York University Press.

Kilgore, S. (2020, June 22). Los Angeles land covenants, redlining: Creation and effects. Los Angeles Public Library. https://lapl.org/collections-resources/blogs/lapl/los-angeles-land-covenants-redlining-creation-and-effects.

Kleiner, D. J. (2020, October 22). Fifth Ward, Houston. Texas Historical Society. https://www.tshaonline.org/handbook/entries/fifth-ward-houston.

Mitchell, B., & Franco, J. (2018). *HOLC "redlining" maps: The persistent structure of segregation and economic inequality.* National Community Reinvestment Coalition.

Packard, J. M. (2002). *American nightmare: The history of Jim Crow.* St. Martin's Press.

Sides, J. (2006). *L.A. city limits: African American Los Angeles from the Great Depression to the present.* University of California Press.

Slater, G. (2021, September 10). How Los Angeles pioneered the residential segregation that helped divide America. *Los Angeles Times.* www.latimes.com/opinion/story/2021-09-10/racial-covenants-los-angeles-pioneered.

Smith, S. C. (1973, November 11). Crime in Compton: Campaign to combat it intensifies. *Los Angeles Times*, SE1.
Truesdell, L. (1926). *Farm population of the United States.* Census Monographs.
Tucker, M. B., Pemberton, N., Weaver, M., Rivera, G., & Petrucci, C. (2010). Imprisoning the family: Incarceration in Black Los Angeles. In D. M. Hunt and A.-C. Ramón (Eds.). *Black Los Angeles: American dreams and racial realities* (pp. 168–187). New York University Press.
United States Census Bureau. (1958, December). Income of families and persons in the United States: 1957. www.census.gov/library/publications/1958/demo/p60-030.html.
United Way of Greater Los Angeles. (1991, October 16). The Black community.

10

A CENTURY OF BLACK ACTIVISM, 1920S–2020S

This chapter captures Blacks' experiences and stories and counternarratives that whites used to maintain Blacks' status as an inferior race. In this chapter I discuss the era of Black activism beginning from the world wars, through the civil rights movement of the late 1960s, and up to the Black Lives Matter movement of the 2020s. Most Black people in North America wanted to be regarded in the same way as others: with dignity, equality, and fairness. They wanted to care for themselves and their families and contribute equally to American society. These have always been motivating factors for Black activism.

Post-World War II Changes in American Life

The events and developments that followed the Second World War in the mid-1940s and beyond were dramatic and shifted American society in ways few thought possible. As part of the war effort, two things emerged: the creation of the atomic bomb, which the United States used on Japan, leading to Japan's surrender; and the creation of the computer, which was developed to provide an advantage to the Allied forces. Once the war ended, the computer was employed for uses in daily living. As Lepore (2018) notes, the computer of that era was hailed to be an electronic marvel operating at great speeds, so much so that it was believed that it eliminated time, yet

> the unintended consequences of the elimination of time would be felt for generations. But the great acceleration—the speeding up of every exchange—had begun. And so had the great atomization—the turning of citizens into pieces of data, fed into machines, tabulated, processed, and targeted, as the nation-state began to yield to the data-state.
>
> *(p. 527)*

DOI: 10.4324/9781003111542-14

Along with the nuclear and computer ages came the creation of the American middle class, with the notion that people from one generation can do better than their parents. Lepore describes this time as an age of affluence and American prosperity. It included beliefs that highlighted individual rights and freedom, which seem reasonable given the struggle during the war against oppressive political ideologies and systems. Yet, as was true of Americans historically, not all people were included in the new American well-being or were permitted to participate in the new prosperity. Part of the new prosperity was fueled by the passage and provisions of the GI Bill of Rights signed into law in 1944 by Franklin Roosevelt. It made benefits available to the 16 million Americans who served in the war, such as free four-year college educational opportunity, no-money-down low-interest loans to buy homes or businesses, and monthly payments for a year (52 weeks) to give veterans time to find and secure work. Lepore (2018, pp. 527–528) states that the GI Bill "created a new middle class, changed the arc of American colleges and universities, and convinced many Americans that the prospects for economic growth, for each generation achieving a standard of living higher than the generation before, might be limitless."

For all the benefits of the GI Bill, it excluded and continued the nation's long-standing inequities; for instance, women who served in the war in the auxiliary divisions of the military were not able to secure the benefits, and women were pushed aside when men began to crowd into colleges and universities. Servicemen who were suspected of being or were homosexual were denied benefits because of "blue discharges." Then, of course, Black people were excluded from the GI Bill's benefits, particularly its education and housing benefits. At the same time, the few Blacks who did receive some educational benefits were unable to use the educational awards since most predominately white colleges and universities would not admit Blacks, and Black colleges and universities had limited space. For example, Lepore notes that there were some 9,000 students at the University of Pennsylvania in 1946, with only 46 Black students. Homes for Black veterans were also hard to secure since banks would not loan them money, and they encountered restrictive covenants and redlining, which reflected the whites-only housing markets and neighborhoods. In cities in many parts of the country, Blacks and other minorities were restricted to segregated housing known as ghettos, usually in underdeveloped and undesirable urban areas. The courts prohibited housing restrictions—that had not existed prior to the postwar oppression of racial minorities—ruling that it was housing discrimination. Yet the practice continued unabated. The suburbs, located outside urban areas, were created by the large number of homes built and made available to mainly whites in the 1950s. In essence, cities became Black and the suburbs white; Lepore (2018, p. 531) observes that "the New Deal's unfinished business—its inattention to racial discrimination and racial violence—became the business of the postwar civil rights movement."

Black activists spoke out, as did Black veterans, against the persistence of Jim Crow laws and the denial of civil rights for Blacks as well as the lack of protection from white mob violence. The nature and means of activism after the Second World War were built on the efforts of millions of Blacks who set the stage and had the will to fight back in the years leading up to this era. They raised their voices and offered responses to oppression based on the belief that they should be free, just as they had done when they were property for more than two centuries. Blacks sought ways and spaces to express themselves, and they turned to one another for support and validation (Gates, 2019). More important, they created institutions and organizations and ways of being or cultural practices that advanced their struggle for recognition and acceptance. They pushed against the walls and barriers erected by whites. Blacks, wherever they lived, were not able to avoid the hostility and violence that marked their lives, no matter their station or status. Yet the walls did not extinguish the internal flame that was their spirit and collective humanity; they found ways to advance their agenda. They did so in a climate that was determined to keep them in their places and that held them down and portrayed them as subhuman. In many ways that process has continued even though the issues and manner of rejection have changed. Today, it is the denial of some voting rights, economic inequities, and police violence (Gates, 2021; Joseph, 2022).

The Civil Rights Movement

Regardless of Blacks' efforts, their acceptance as citizens without barriers or obstacles to participation in mainstream American life was not forthcoming and is still not fully achieved. Yet Blacks did not stop advocating for fair treatment and equal rights as American citizens. It is difficult to know exactly what events or series of events mark the onset of the civil rights movement of the 1950s and 1960s. Some contend that it was when a Black man in Mississippi, Moses Wright, testified in open court during a murder trial and pointed to three white men as the people who killed his nephew, Emmett Till, in 1955 (the men were acquitted), while others might point to the 1953 bus boycott in Baton Rouge, Louisiana, or the one in 1955 in Montgomery, Alabama; it could also have been Blacks' political lobbying that led to the passage of the 1957 Civil Rights Act or the student sit-ins in the 1950s. It is possible that all of these events led to the mass civil rights movement, but it is clear that all of these events reflected Blacks' impatience with race relations in the country as well as the fact that they seldom accepted their status; thus, they coalesced in various institutions and organizations to push back against the denial of their humanity.

Blacks' cultural traditions and practices served them well. They relied on religious and civic leaders who nurtured them in the churches and the social and civic institutions and organizations that were solely owned and operated by Blacks. Black people elevated other Blacks to lead them as pastors, church deacons, and activists, all of whom were accountable to the congregation or the organization. Congregations tended to be composed of people with similar experiences and means, so the various churches encompassed the strata of the Black community. Pastors also met with one another in related associations. In these ways, the vast and diverse Black community was held together by these interconnected relationships. Recall the cultural values of communalism and spirituality. These were combined and intertwined throughout Black communities and were self-reinforcing.

During the late 1940s and the 1950s the federal government made efforts to advance civil rights for Black Americans; in fact, between 1953 and 1957 the House of Representatives passed several bills granting Blacks civil rights, but the bills all failed to be considered in the Senate. In this climate civil rights advocates continued to press for change. President Dwight Eisenhower proposed a plan with multiple elements for Black civil rights that included a feature wherein the U.S. attorney general would be able to seek relief through the courts if people's constitutional rights were violated.

Finally, a civil rights bill was passed in 1957; the last such legislation had been passed in 1875. The NAACP was instrumental in advocating and lobbying for this bill. The new law provided that the federal government could bring action and lawsuits to obtain injunctive relief in federal courts. The civil rights section of the Justice Department was elevated to a division and the U.S. Commission on Civil Rights was established and given authority to investigate violations of people's right to vote or violations of equal protection under the law. Many argued that the 1957 civil rights bill had little meaning since it did not change conditions on the ground, while others noted that at least the federal government was no longer operating with its hands-off policy in civil rights matters. Observers believed that Congress, by passing the bill, was reacting to national and international concerns and pressures. Bell (2008) argues that Black progress occurs because it serves the interests of white Americans.

One important element that fueled the civil rights movement should be restated. Blacks' migration from rural to urban areas throughout the country, mainly from the South to the North and West, helped them experience different ways of living and removed some of the barriers imposed on them in the South. Added to this component were the Supreme Court decisions against school segregation; its rulings against limits placed on Blacks in regard to voting; the confrontations to states' bus segregation, marked by Rosa Parks's refusal to move to the back of the bus; coupled with the Baton Rouge, Louisiana, and Montgomery, Alabama, bus boycotts, all of which showed that Blacks had leverage, as emphasized and highlighted by the emergence of Black leaders like Dr. Martin Luther King Jr. and Malcom X. What these events began to reveal was that Blacks' view of themselves had changed, as had public policy. And as the landscape of race relations changed, people's thoughts and attitudes also began to be altered. Less attention has been given to the invaluable role of Black women in many organizations and their efforts to mobilize the Black community. This point is important because it reflects more flexible gender roles in Black culture (Franklin & Moss, 2000).

Blacks and like-minded whites who objected to Blacks being denied civil rights participated in sit-ins and freedom rides to protest equal access to dining facilities and interstate transportation due to segregation policies and laws. They marched in nonviolent ways and confronted authorities throughout the South; in time, they took the struggle North. They sought to integrate white schools. Blacks and whites who joined the protest were met with law enforcement, who arrested them and held them in jail; they encountered assaults by law enforcement in the form of fire hoses used to disperse them; police attack dogs were also employed to slow their advance; and police assaulted Blacks with clubs. Blacks were also put upon by white citizens, both men and women, who threw bricks and rocks and wielded clubs in an attempt to stop or dissuade the protesters. Black children who sought to attend white schools required police or, more commonly, military escorts for protections from white mobs, who were enraged by the presence of Black students and did not want Blacks in their public schools and communities (Bennett, 1988).

Technology of this era captured these struggles, which shamed the nation. The advent of television and wire news dispatchers were able to show how these events unfold in real time. Black protesters prepared themselves in advance not to react or strike back when assaulted. This way they were shown to be put upon by law enforcement personnel or white citizens. Blacks and white supporters were punched, kicked, hit with clubs, thrown about by fire hoses, and jailed simply for walking along peacefully protesting. The attacks by officials and their actions to stop the protests and nonviolent demonstrations were broadcast to the nation.

To slow or stop Blacks' struggle for civil rights, two Black leaders, Medger Evers and Martin Luther King Jr., were assassinated, and between these killings several activists and volunteers were also found dead. In 1963 President John F. Kennedy and, five years later, his brother Robert Kennedy were assassinated. Lyndon Johnson became president upon Kennedy's assassination and was instrumental in gathering congressional votes to pass the 1964 Civil Rights Act. Then Malcolm X was gunned down in 1965.

Overall, some things did change for Blacks. There was somewhat less overt racial discrimination; organizations employed affirmative action programs and became equal opportunity employers; and antipoverty programs were created with federal funds. The political and economic climate shifted somewhat. Schools were less hostile to Black students, and some integrated.

But the progress on the ground was slow to change between 1955 and 1970, and there was discontent with the nonviolent stance, a perspective that

Malcolm X and other younger Black leaders rejected. The civil rights protests also brought considerable backlash. Over time, whites simply moved away from cities into predominantly white suburbs. At the same time, Blacks rediscovered their African roots.

The murder of Martin Luther King Jr. triggered significant unrest in Black communities across the country, which was reflected in riots and vandalism in many major cities such as New York City, Los Angeles, Baltimore, and Newark, New Jersey. Blacks' reactions and their violently expressed outrage troubled the authorities, who responded by calling out the National Guard and larger contingents of law enforcement to quell and patrol the hot spots of Black anger (Bennett, 1988).

The Outcome of Black Activism

Black activism could be considered successful by some measures, as legal obstacles to Blacks' social participation were removed due to challenges by Blacks, and Blacks had many breakthroughs and experienced many firsts. Some Black people became the first to hold a position or enter a field, such as being members of the president's Cabinet or serving on the Supreme Court. There were gains netted by the masses of Blacks in that more were able to vote, earn higher incomes, gain access to educational opportunities, have better health care, and find employment. Black activism also opened opportunities for white women and people in general, regardless of race. However, irrespective of the gains, there were larger losses and a "turning within" among the mass of Blacks. Bennett (1988) notes that

> by 1972 Blacks had been struggling in the streets of America for seventeen years. They had tried everything or almost everything. They had marched, demonstrated, boycotted, protested, petitioned, dreamed, prayed, rioted—and they had not overcome. So, inevitably there was a turning within and a turning away and a groping for new avenues of escape and assertion.
>
> *(p. 436)*

Amid the struggle, segments of the Black community who had been blocked from work and not provided aid relied on the underground economy to survive and earn income. Involvement in the underground economy came with the risk of being swept up by drug use and related illegal activities, which led to jail or arrests, leaving many families disrupted and in disarray.

At the same time, whites came to believe they had done enough—and that the country needed to return to the principal of individualism. A clear expression of these views was reflected in the election in 1968 of President Richard Nixon, who aggressively promoted policies and programs that echoed the "enough with Black demands" point of view. He supported positions such as the notion that racial integration was forced, and he established policies and programs that penalized poor people in general, most of whom were white, but many were also Black. Nixon encouraged efforts to investigate and criminalize civil rights and Black power leaders and organizations, and he stopped efforts to address racial inequality.

The Nixon era ended badly for him; he resigned from office after it was revealed that he had been involved in the illegal activities of members of his administration. The election of Jimmy Carter did not bring much change or relief for Blacks during this time, and Carter was followed by eight years of the conservative Ronald Reagan, who was president from 1981 to 1989. The 1980s were the onset of the global economy in the United States, which meant that foreign goods were more numerous and American-made products started to decline. This was apparent in the automobile industry with the growing presence in the American market of German and Japanese cars. There was an effort to stem the tide of foreign products by emphasizing "buy American," yet American automakers were struggling against Honda and Toyota, and in 1982 the auto industry, centered in Detroit, Michigan, was laying off workers. Hostile feelings were directed at Asians, blaming them for the success of Japanese auto companies.

In one case of anti-Asian hostility, two white men—one a supervisor, Ronald Ebens, and the other, Michael Nitz, an auto industry employee—encountered Vincent Chin, a Chinese American man who the white men believed to be Japanese. They blamed Chin for the layoffs and were so enraged that they beat him to death. They were arrested the same night the assault took place and released the next day after being charged with second-degree murder. They pled guilty to manslaughter and were sentenced to three years' probation and a $3,000 fine. The judge stated that the men were not the types you send to jail. The Asian American community across the country reacted strongly to this miscarriage of justice.

It is a familiar theme in America to blame the nonwhites for society's ills. In this climate, the Japanese were accused of unfair trade practices by politicians, so they established manufacturing plants in the United States. As a result, more than 250,000 Americans worked for U.S.-based Japanese businesses, and by 1989 Honda was the best-selling make of vehicle in the country.

American technology also advanced as Apple and IBM introduced personal computers. These developments led to numerous other advances that dramatically changed personal and business life in the nation. Another significant technological change was the cell phone, which appeared in the 1990s.

The country also moved away from the racial progress of the 1960s–1970s and made distinct movements to the political right with conservative leaders picking up the mantle. These changes were evidenced by the election of Ronald Reagan, who used racially charged ads in his political campaigns in 1980 and 1984. One ad references a "welfare queen" who was alleged to have more than 80 names under which she collected benefits, milking the government out of some $150,000—at least, that is how he told it on the campaign trail. The person in question had defrauded the government for about $8,000 in welfare payments (Alexander, 2012; Lepore, 2018).

Reagan's two terms in office were followed by George H. W. Bush, who served one term as president, 1989–1993. The Republican political leader lost to Bill Clinton, who was elected in 1993 and served until 2001. Clinton was not a far-right leader, but some of his policies had extremely negative impacts on Black people, even as he tried to present a pro-Black agenda. For instance, while a candidate for the presidency, he made a point of attending the execution of a mentally impaired Black man. The man asked that his dessert at his last meal be saved so he could have it the next day, showing that he did not comprehend what was happening. Clinton flew to his home state to show how tough he was on crime, wanting to be perceived as being tougher than any Republican (Alexander, 2012). During his 1994 State of the Union address, President Clinton—again, to show how tough he was on crime—indicated his support for a proposed federal crime bill, the "three strikes and you are out" law. He signed the new law in August 1994, again demonstrating that Democrats were able to take the mantle of fighting crime away from Republicans. The bill that Clinton signed into law provided $30 billion in new funds for a range of crime-fighting initiatives. The crime bill also established more than a dozen federal capital crimes and made it so that, if convicted on the three-strike provisions, defendants would be sentenced to mandatory life terms. The bill also provided for funds to state and local prison and police forces so they could expand. He was recognized as being the president that oversaw the largest increase in federal and state prison inmates in American history (Alexander, 2012). The increase in prison population included a considerable number of Black men and women.

Yet he was not done; he also outdid conservatives when he turned his attention to welfare reform, which many considered to be a conservative racial agenda. The welfare reform policies undertaken by the Clinton administration were "part of a grand strategy articulated by the 'new Democrats' to appeal to the elusive white swing voters. Clinton—more than any other president—created the current racial underclass" (Alexander, 2012, pp. 56–57). Clinton signed into law a bill that replaced Aid to Families with Dependent Children with block grants to states called temporary assistance to needy families. The state grants imposed a five-year limit on welfare aid and a lifetime ban for anyone who was convicted of a felony, like possession of marijuana. While these laws did not exclusively impact Blacks, it is safe to say they were disproportionally affected. Clinton's two terms were followed by another move to the right in the election of George W. Bush, who took office in 2001 and served until 2009.

Then the country witnessed a historic event in the election of Barack Obama as president. His election brought about a sense of hope and dignity for Black people in this country. At the same time, he was less able to direct programs to aid Blacks, given the state of the nation when he took office. He had been elected to oversee a nation in decline. His signature legislation was the Affordable Care Act, which provided health care insurance that many Blacks had been unable to get prior to the act's passage. Yet, many of his policies and action bypassed ordinary Americans who had lost jobs, homes, and savings in the financial collapse, yet wealthy businessmen and businesswomen were offered bailouts and loans.

Obama's term in office ended in 2016. Some would argue that the country was not pleased by his presidency and elected Donald Trump as president in 2016 in response. Trump served one term, and Joe Biden, Obama's vice president was elected president in 2020.

Increase in Racial Tensions and Open Expressions of Racist Sentiments: The Obama and Trump Years

Over the past few decades, there has been a documented rise in racial tensions. The election of Barack Obama produced an increase in racial animosity with a proliferation of negative racial stereotypes and hate websites (Costello, 2016; Williams, 2018). The combination of the Black Lives Matter movement, the murder of George Floyd, and the COVID-19 pandemic highlighted and contributed to ongoing racist behavior and expressions of racial hostility toward Black people (Chae et al., 2021; Dubey, 2020; Elias et al., 2021; Flores-González & Salgado, 2022; McCoy, 2020; Stolberg, 2020; Wright & Thomas, 2023).

Drakulich and colleagues (2021) describe how Black Lives Matter (BLM) activity revealed a racial polarity in the United States, with white Americans disapproving of and most Black Americans supporting BLM. Data reveals a disturbing rise in domestic terrorism perpetrated by right-wing extremists during the presidency of Donald Trump, more so than during Obama's term (Fortunato et al., 2022). Racial resentment toward people of color was thought to have been an instrumental factor in the 2016 election of Donald Trump (Abramowitz & McCoy, 2019; Clayton, Moore, & Jones-Eversley, 2021). These events triggered an increase in racial dialogues—some to combat racism and others to express overt negative racial sentiments. There have been more documented racial confrontations, expressed racial hostility, and incidents of hate crimes across the country.

Hate crimes instill a sense of fear and victimization in community members and lead to fear and a sense of harm among individuals in the group being targeted (Farrell & Lockwood, 2023). The general sense is that, although racial resentment has varied over the years from state to state, with some regions reflecting improvement and other regions reflecting stagnation, racial resentment directed at Black Americans continues to be a very real phenomenon across the Unites states and occurs in every region of the country

(Smith, Kreitzer, & Suo, 2020). Based on Federal Bureau of Investigation reports, hate crimes continue in the United States, and Black Americans continue to be targeted by such crimes at the highest rate, representing 63% of single incidents in 2021 (Department of Justice, 2023). Furthermore, hate/bias crime data in 2020 showed a 6% increase over data reported in 2019, the highest level reported for hate/bias crime since 2008. In addition, such race-based hate crimes occurred in all regions of the country.

Ruisch and Ferguson (2022) conducted 13 investigations with a total of 10,000 American adults, and they found significant increases in acts of blatant racism among those who were supporters of former president Trump, with the largest proportion of these acts being directed at Black Americans. In addition, between 2015 and 2021 there have been several events reported by national news outlets that involved hostility directed at Black people, including the murders of Breonna Taylor by officers from the Louisville Metro Police Department; the murder of George Floyd by the police officers from the Minneapolis Police Department; the murders of nine Black churchgoers in Charleston, South Carolina, by a white man; and the murder of Ahmad Arbury by three white males in Glynn County, Georgia. There is also evidence to suggest that hate crimes increased during Trump's presidency compared to the number of hate crimes during Obama's presidency (Koski & Bantley, 2020; Malazada, 2020).

The Political Shift as a Response to Racial Activism

Part of what drove the conservative and Republican political agenda was what they attributed to the cultural changes brought about by racial activism of the 1960s and 1970s. For members of the political Right, these changes led to suffering, turmoil, and, they argued, breakdowns in traditional family structures. The acceptance of gay rights and disease that was connected to men having sex with men, known as HIV-AIDS, were examples of the turmoil. HIV-AIDS was discovered in the 1980s and over time, health officials learned that HIV could also be transmitted through unsafe use of needles by drug users and via blood transfusions. Many drug users who contracted AIDS were Black and Brown. In the 1990s hundreds of thousands died from AIDS or HIV infections. Americans' understanding of how HIV was contracted changed when a well-known professional basketball player named Ervin "Magic" Johnson announced that he had contracted HIV, and he was not gay. Perceptions of the disease were altered and more was done to find treatments for the disease and help people survive.

Before the 1980s and Reagan's presidency, Blacks had progressed in some areas, but there remained significant social and economic problems as well as obvious racial discrimination. Some Blacks were elected to political offices in large cities, and Rev. Jesse Jackson ran a campaign for president. But the masses of Black people still struggled. Some contend that the frustration of

Black people was expressed in a style of music known as rap, which was thought to be an element of a wider culture known as hip-hop. This art form included art, dance, and music, and it emerged in the 1970s in New York City and other centers of Black life. Blacks' visibility seemed to be centered in music and sports, where Black entertainers and athletes became well known.

In March of 1991 a group of friends were out socializing, and while returning home they took the 210 Freeway in Los Angeles. Rodney King, Bryant Allen, and Freddie Helms were in the vehicle driven by King. Mr. King had been drinking and was speeding when he was approached by California Highway Patrol officers, Tim and Melanie Singer (a married couple). King failed to stop out of fear of being cited for driving under the influence, which would have violated his parole. So he fled and led the police on an eight-mile chase. During the chase, at least three other officers joined as well as a chopper. Once stopped, the three men were ordered out of the car. Allen and Helms complied, and they were beaten by officers, but King was slow to get out of the car. He was defiant, according to the officers. Officers claimed he was high on PCP, which was not supported when he was later tested. Four officers set about subduing Mr. King. As fate would have it, a nearby resident heard the commotion and began filming the events that took place. The officers claimed that King resisted arrest, although those present denied this claim. The officers tased King, and others beat him with their batons, with more officers joining the beating. The neighbor's video recorded some 53 baton strikes and kicks by the eight officers involved in the beating. King was finally cuffed and taken away. He suffered from a fractured facial bone, broken right ankle, broken teeth, and neurological damage. The neighbor, George Holliday, provided the video to news outlets, which aired it on the nightly news. Some 92% of those who viewed the beating believed the officers had used excessive force. After the incident four of the officers were charged with assault and excessive force, and others were disciplined but not charged. Evidence at the trial indicated that the officers' actions were racially motivated as one was heard saying during the beating "I am going to kill you nigger." Because of the publicity, the trial was moved out of Los Angeles to Simi Valley to avoid a biased jury. The jury was composed of 10 white people, one bi-racial person, a Latino, and an Asian. The trial lasted about three weeks and it took the jury one week to deliberate and return a verdict of not guilty on all charges. The rage was so intense that the protesters attacked store owners and motorists, and the police did not act to stop the violence that erupted. The police chief had in fact told the department not to respond to 911 calls about rioting and looting. To quell the protesters, the governor called out the National Guard. Five days passed before the disturbance stopped. Fifty people were killed, some by police; 2,000 people were injured; and more than 6,000 people were arrested, close to 40% Black and 51% Latino. Property damage was estimated to be around $1 billion.

The mayor established a commission to investigate the LAPD, and the chief of police, Daryl Gates, retired a year after the incident with Mr. King. The Justice Department brought charges against the officers for violating Mr. King's civil rights; two were convicted after the 1993 trial and sentenced to 30 months in jail, and two were acquitted but were fired from the LAPD. Rodney King was awarded $3.8 million by the City of Los Angeles for his medical bills and pain and suffering. The verdict seemed to say that what people saw was not real; it did not happen as was captured on the video. People in Los Angeles were angry, and they took to the streets to protest (Bush, 2023). Similar, highly watched racial incidents took place in the early years of the 1990s, some involving racial profiling or "driving while Black."

Bill Clinton took office as a moderate Democrat in 1993 (Kidd, 2019). Clinton's election was in part a response to the sociopolitical and racial climate that was established by the multiple presidential terms of Republicans. So people sought a political shift by electing someone who was considered to be a centrist or moderate Democrat, hoping that he would push back against right-affirming political positions, but that turned out not to be the case. Lepore (2018) states that "Clinton … moved to the right even before the mid-terms and much of his agenda amounted to a continuation of work begun by Reagan and Bush."

During the Clinton years a series of bills were passed and signed into law dealing with combating crime, criminalizing drug use, and reducing assistance for poor people. Clinton, with Democratic support, took the position to eliminate welfare or Aid to Families with Dependent Children. The welfare bill that was passed shifted responsibility for welfare to the states. The change to state control had negative effects on Black people, who often were unable to find employment and relied on public assistance. For many, that support ended, as did their ability to keep their apartments and homes.

Clinton left many on both sides of the political aisle unhappy. He pushed a health care bill, led by his wife, Hillary, that failed and made his leadership more complicated. To win back support, he passed bills that pleased few Democrats. For instance, he endorsed the drug war by signing the 1994 Anti-Drug Abuse Act, and he signed a crime bill that made it legal to punish possession of crack (a rock-like version of cocaine common in Black and poor communities, 100 times more powerful than powder cocaine). This act was directed for the most part at Blacks. Lepore (2018) states that

> these … measures contributed to a social catastrophe, an era of mass incarceration, in which nearly one in every hundred American adults were in prison.… Two-thirds of the rise in the prison population between 1985 and 2000 involved drug convictions. The overwhelming majority of Americans convicted of drug offenses are black men.
>
> *(pp. 699–700)*

According to Alexander (2012), mass incarceration of Black and Brown people was possible under the guise of President Reagan's War on Drugs (discussed in the next section) with its rationale to reduce crime. Research evidence indicates that crime rates were expected to decrease as more resources were allocated to the War on Drugs and drug offenders were sent to jail. In fact, crime rates did not decrease. Saadatmand, Toma, and Choquette (2012) say their empirical analysis shows that the War on Drugs has not reduced crime rates. Yet, laws were passed, court rulings handed down, and resources were provided to police departments that allowed millions of poor Black and Brown men and women to be incarcerated. Once labeled as felons, their rights were stripped away, resembling the status of Blacks during the era of legal segregation.

Black activism had slowed in the 1990s and 2000s, and many Black communities were hollowed out with the large numbers of men and women in jail or on parole or probation, living under the thumb of state and local authorities, who were free to isolate them and render them unable to ward off the walls, barriers, and assaults visited upon them and their families. In the new political climate, both the Left and Right changed and adopted what some called "identity politics." Yet what was "new" actually was not since, in fact, the nation was founded on identity politics.

The Constitution identified white men as the only people able to vote and Blacks as lesser people (three-fifths of a person)—in essence, the nation was founded upon white supremacy. The racial superiority notion was argued in the mid-1860s by Stephen Douglas, while debating Abraham Lincoln, when he stated that the nation was "made by the white men, for the benefit of white men and their posterity forever." Lincoln took the position that Negros were entitled to all the rights in the Declaration of Independence. Lepore (2018, p. 701) writes that "Overthrowing the Stephen Douglas's brand of identity politics—the identity politics of slaveholders and, later, of the Klan, and of immigrant restrictionists, had been the work of more than a century struggle, for abolition, emancipation, suffrage, and Civil Rights."

The counter to the right in the 20th century arose from multiple sources: the Black Power movement, the gay pride movement, and from feminism groups. Because all these groups had encountered various forms of oppression, they joined together as a political force. To oppose the Left, people on the Right embraced the National Rifle Association to express white male resentments of Blacks and immigrants; thus, the politics of this era became characterized by cultural styles that reflected "indictment and indignation" (Lepore, 2018, p. 702).

The dialogue and discourse in the coming new century became more divisive, and the political climate had serious and distinct outcomes. Dreams of being able to live well and surpass the preceding generation had withered and were dying, in part due to conflicting political agendas. On the one hand, during the 1990s there was prosperity for start-up dot-com companies and hedge fund executives as well as entertainment leaders and global traders. On the other hand, the middle class, particularly rural whites, were in economic and social decline. Members of different racial (i.e., Black and Brown versus white) and political groups (i.e., Right-leaning Republicans and conservatives versus Democrats) blamed other opposing groups for the economic and social decline, while others blamed the government, employing conspiracy theories often from right-wing groups or put forth by new radio personalities like Alex Jones. So what emerged was, in effect, intolerance for differences. For conservatives when they objected to a position taken by Left-leaning liberals, it was called "political correctness." Black activists responded by going after hate speech while placing less emphasis on protecting free speech.

The political climate was changing to a more divided one where truth was not at the core of discourse, and the rules and principles of fairness changed as well. These developments fueled a partisan and conflicted environment in the country.

The War on Drugs and the New Racial Caste System

Meanwhile Black and Brown people were being assaulted under the guise of fighting crime and drug use. But according to some scholars, the effort to reduce crime and drug use was focused on Black and Brown people. Several developments contributed to the state of affairs in the 1990s, some of which preceded the last decade of the 20th century. For instance, shortly after being elected president, Reagan wanted to be more involved in fighting street crime, but that was the purview of local and state law enforcement. But in time, during his administration, the Department of Justice was reconfigured to focus less on white-collar crime so it could attend more to street-level offenses. Reagan started what he called a War on Drugs, in the early 1980s. He made this a pressing and urgent matter for the nation, even though only about 2% of the public believed drugs were a concern. But Alexander (2012) argues that public support was not the focus for Reagan, and the lack of public support did not matter:

> This fact [little public concern about drugs] was no deterrent to Reagan, for the drug war from the outset had little to do with public concern about drugs and much to do with public concern about race. By waging a war on drug users and dealers, Reagan made good on his promise to crack down on the racially defined "others"—the undeserving.
>
> *(p. 49)*

The federal budget for law enforcement agencies doubled between 1980 and 1984. Alongside the drug war was economic decline in Black and Brown communities as the economy changed from being industrially centered to being service-oriented. In the new service-oriented economic reality, educated and technology trained employees did well, while those with less advanced skills and education fared poorly. Added to this change was globalization (jobs moving out of the country) and fewer industrial opportunities that hit Black communities the hardest. The jobs that did remain in the country were moved out of cities to suburbs. What was left for many Black people was the underground economy. Alexander (2012) observes:

> The decline in legitimate employment opportunities among inner-city residents increased incentives to sell drugs—most notably crack cocaine. Crack is pharmacologically almost identical to powder cocaine, but it has been converted into a form that can be vaporized and inhaled for a faster, more intense (though shorter) high using less of the drug—making it possible to sell small doses at more affordable prices. Crack hit the streets in 1985, a few years after Reagan's drug war was announced, leading to a spike in violence as drug markets struggled to stabilize, and the anger and frustration associated with joblessness boiled. Joblessness and crack swept inner cities precisely at the moment that a fierce backlash against the Civil Rights Movement was manifesting itself through the War on Drugs.
>
> *(p. 51)*

The impact from crack was real and painful and created large-scale suffering in Black communities. It was possible to respond to the events with care and compassion, rather than with punishment and isolation. It was possible to provide treatment and prevention, as was done by other countries faced with similar problems with drug use and addictions. Portugal faced a similar epidemic of drug use and addiction, yet it responded with treatment, prevention, and educational programs along with economic investments in the affected communities. They also changed the laws to reduce the criminal offenses associated with drug use and possession. The result was a decline in drug use and offenses a decade later.

The approach in the United States appealed most to pivotal white voters since it blunted the progress of Blacks, much of which had come about through affirmative action policies and civil rights advances and enforcements. Actions and policies that stopped and slowed Black progress were welcomed and supported. In effect, those people who advocated being tough on crime were found in research cited by Alexander (2012) to be the same people who endorsed anti-Black racial attitudes. The bottom line was that the War on Drugs offered a way for whites to support reductions in racial progress while not referring to race, yet they could endorse harsh and punitive measures as a veiled way to express their anti-Black sentiments.

George Bush Sr. followed Reagan as president in 1989, and he used racial divisions to secure his election and continued to employ race-based messages and policies that appealed to poor and working-class white voters. Bush, once in office, opposed Black progress by not supporting affirmative action, weakening civil rights enforcement, and continuing the War on Drugs. In a CBS News/New York Times poll, some 74% of respondents believed that the most pressing issue in the country was illegal drug trafficking and use. No poll had found higher numbers expressing these views. "The surge of public concern did not correspond to a dramatic shift in illegal drug activity, but instead was the product of a carefully orchestrated political campaign" (Alexander, 2012, p. 55). The actions taken regarding the crime and drug problem by political leaders were unsupported by direct evidence. Researchers were not able to establish any strong connection between actual crime and drug use (Beckett, 1997). But that fact was not visible if you followed the words and actions of political leaders. Thus, segments of the society, especially Black people, were yet again being demonized and regarded as unworthy to participate fully in American society.

By the 1990s, there was little meaningful pushback against the new system of racial control. The new "racial caste system—mass incarceration—was taking hold" (Alexander, 2012, p. 55). The prize for politicians was the support and votes of working-class and poor whites, who, like Blacks, were struggling in the new global economy. At the same time, it seemed expedient to concentrate on seeing racial reforms as threats. Allies of Blacks also wanted to demonstrate that they too could be tough on "them"—people of color. Since breaking the law was difficult or impossible to defend for Black leaders, activists, or the masses, their voices fell silent. The result of the new political path was felt in Black communities where, by 1991, one-quarter of Black men were under the control of the criminal justice system.

Even Bill Clinton took up the cause of being tough on crime during his presidency. He supported the federal law that created the "three strikes and you're out"—you stay in prison—rule in 1994. The bill allocated some $30 billion to fight crime, and now Democrats could take credit for being hard on crime. Alexander (2012) notes that

> the bill created dozens of new federal capital crimes, mandated life sentences for some three-time offenders, and authorized more than $16 billion for state prison grants and expansion of state and local police forces. ... As the Justice Policy Institute has observed, "the Clinton Administration's 'tough on crime' policies" resulted in the largest increases in federal and state prison inmates of any president in American history.
>
> *(p. 56)*

The law-and-order position that first came into being during the height of the civil rights movement by staunch and committed segregationists became nearly hegemonic two decades later. The sad point is that by the mid-1990s there was no viable alternative to the War on Drugs and the harsh stance on crime. Political leaders could not now say that the drug and crime issues were not as they had proclaimed, so they had to follow through with the legal, enforcement, and political stance they had undertaken.

Scholars have noted that several million people were behind bars as the new century began, and millions of others were shunted to the outer limits of society, outside of meaningful political and social spaces in ways that resembled Jim Crow (Alexander, 2012). In this instance, the discrimination in employment, housing, and education were legal, as was their removal from the rolls of eligible voters. What is astonishing about this new system is how well and automatically it functioned. In fact, its racial aspects appear to be natural since "ninety percent of those admitted to prison for drug offenses in many states were black or Latino, yet the mass incarceration of communities of color was explained in race-neutral terms" (Alexander, 2012, p. 58).

How was the process of race-neutral or color-blind mass incarceration accomplished? How did the War on Drugs operate? The prevailing beliefs are that our society is based on the rule of law, that citizens have rights of due process, and that citizens are protected from invasive searches and seizures. We are taught that these principles are applied with the assumption that a person is innocent until proven guilty. We are taught to believe that we all have the right to legal representation. All forms of literature and entertainment depict the inner workings of the justice system in this manner. Most television and movie dramas show how people are told their rights and depict how the police and law enforcement must have a valid reason to surveil or search a person or home. They show how a lawyer will be assigned to all who are arrested and charged with crime. Movies and television programs emphasize the adversarial legal system to highlight how people's rights are protected.

There are two parts of the criminal justice system, the police or law enforcement agencies who investigate and charge people for suspected crimes and offenses, and the legal segment in which prosecutors act on the charges brought in court. All defendants have the right to a lawyer and other rights that, at least according to TV and movies, are a central feature of our criminal justice system.

Yet, as was the case with slavery, when the constitutional amendment was passed abolishing slavery, it also included an exception for criminal convictions. So, too, did laws associated with drug use and crime. The courts and legislators included an exception for drug-related cases and thus changed how people's rights were to be regarded. For instance, provisions of constitutional protections, such as the Fourth Amendment, were not applied to drug cases, which prohibits unlawful search and seizures. Yet one Supreme Court justice, in a dissent, noted that between 1982 and 1991 the Court ruled in over 30 Fourth Amendment drug cases, and the majority involved search and seizure without a valid warrant, and in most of these matters the Court upheld the police actions in apparent violation of the Fourth

Amendment—thus the exceptions made in cases involving drugs. The justice acknowledged that the Court had become a foot soldier in the administrations' fight against crime.

The prime objective in the War on Drugs was to end the flow of illegal drugs into local communities. Accomplishing that goal of preventing drugs from getting into vulnerable communities would mean targeting and arresting kingpins, or high-level smugglers and dealers. With the goal of stopping the availability of drugs and reducing harm to citizens, one would assume that there would have been considerable attention and effort directed at reducing the more harmful illegal substances like heroin and cocaine. And related to taking down the high-level people who were central to establishing distribution systems and who sold harmful substances, law enforcement efforts and vast economic resources would be expected to focus on those who commit violent crimes since it was argued that such crimes fueled drug use and the sale and distribution of drugs, and these activities caused related crimes, so the arguments went.

> Yet it turns out that the vast majority of those arrested are *not* charged with serious offenses. In 2005, for example, four out of five drug arrests were for possession, and only one out of five was for sales. Moreover, most people in state prison for drug offenses [had] *no* history of violence or significant selling activity.
>
> *(Alexander, 2012, p. 60)*

Furthermore, most drug arrests were for possession of marijuana, considered a less harmful substance. It also was the case that the preponderance of arrests was for nonviolent minor offenses. So harmful and dangerous substances were not the focus, nor was violent behavior. People in possession of marijuana were the people most often arrested, charged, and sent to prison. The War on Drugs resulted in a huge increase in people being sentenced to prison, which in turn funded a prison industrial complex. The number of people involved with the criminal justice system or who were incarcerated between 1980 and 2000 went from 300,000 to 2 million, and by 2007 the number increased to some 7 million in prison or on probation or parole.

As I have shown through the chapters of this volume, the principles and beliefs promoted as the American way were not available to Black people over the last few centuries. It turns out that this was—and still is—true with respect to the notion that citizens are afforded the right to legal counsel when charged with a crime or offense. The stories about how the criminal justice system works is as far from this reality as possible; in fact, TV and movies are fictions when the justice system is being portrayed. What happens in real life is seldom portrayed.

According to Alexander (2012) and other scholars, the typical practice by law enforcement has been to sweep an area or place suspected of drug activity and arrest and charge most if not all the people they encounter. Mind you, the courts had eliminated constitutional protections under the Fourth Amendment for most citizens suspected of drug activity, meaning that the police could stop anyone, anywhere, without notice and seize their property, belongings, and person. People who committed no crime or offenses were often put in situations where they were held in jail awaiting legal action. They were separated from their families and livelihoods without recourse. They were often charged and faced, based on established law, frightening mandatory sentences if found guilty at trial. Yet many would be offered plea bargains. Their options were limited, and remaining in jail with no income or anyone to care for your family has a cost, and legal representation is also expensive. For many low-income or working-class people, waiting for a trial that could clear one's name is out of the question, and they could not afford to wage a legal battle or assert their rights. Many others want to avoid the risk of a trial.

Alexander (2012) tells the story of a single mother of two young children who was arrested in a drug sweep and charged with drug activity. She was held in detention and after some time was offered a deal to plead guilty, even though she was innocent and was not involved in any drug activity; she just happened to be in the place where drug offenses were suspected. She was nevertheless taken away from her children and was unable to work. The single mother turned down the plea deal presented by her court-appointed attorney. But as the weeks become months in detention waiting for her trial, she relented and agreed to plead guilty so she can return to her children.

She pled guilty to distribution of drugs in exchange for probation, a fine of $1,000, and additional probation and court costs. She was released from jail and now is a convicted felon. In her mind, she had avoided the possible outcome of a trial and a longer term in prison. However, as a felon she is now not able to receive food stamps, and she could be denied employment (she had to reveal her conviction to potential employers). She was ineligible to vote for more than a decade, and she can no longer live in public housing. These outcomes rendered her homeless, which resulted in the loss of her children, who were placed in foster care. Sometime later she learned that those who did not plea bargain had their cases dismissed by a judge who ruled that the sweep and arrests were based on an unnamed source who provided false information. But the life outcome for the single mother—and for other similar Black and poor defendants who often have outcomes like hers—is dismal. Most of the people swept up, arrested, and jailed for drug offenses have been Black and Brown.

In 2000 it was reported that in many states Blacks were 80–90% of all drug offenders sent to prison. In more than 15 states the rate of Blacks being sent to prison on drug charges was 20 to 57 times greater than that of whites. What stands out in these numbers is that Blacks constitute only 10–12% of the general population. According to survey research evidence provided by the federal government, such as the National Household Survey on Drug Abuse (2000), the majority of illegal drug users and dealers in the country are white, yet three-fourths of all people arrested and jailed for drug charges were Black and Latino (U.S. Department of Health and Human Services, 2001).

However, not all Black people have been caught up in the law enforcement activity. Many took advantage of the nation's civil rights reforms in years past and were able to establish better lives for themselves and their families. Yet, as a group, Blacks have been buffeted by myriad forces that have created a roller coaster existence. Some were able to buy homes only to lose them when the real estate market's bubble burst as the result of the collapsing subprime mortgage market, leading to a global financial crisis in 2007–2008. Many Black people were victims of this crisis, falling behind after thinking they had gained a footing.

The Next Generation of Black Activism

It was in this period that Barack Obama, a Black man and senator, gave public notice and ran for election for the office of president (Joseph, 2022). Black people were energized by his candidacy for the Democratic nomination for president in 2006 and 2007, and they were also moved by his election to the post. Obama served two terms between 2008 and 2016, and it was during this time that the next generation of Black activism emerged, becoming known as the Black Lives Matter movement (BLM). The movement was triggered by the unprovoked murders of Black people by citizens and law enforcement officers. Most of the killings resulted in no charges being filed or, if filed, few convictions for these acts were handed down. For the most part, people and police officers were not held accountable for their actions. It seemed that time had been frozen and we were not living in the 21st century but in the 19th or 20th centuries (Joseph, 2022).

The BLM movement used technology to aid in organizing, and it drew upon the core values of Black culture to fuel its activities and its manner of functioning. The movement's leaders formed community coalitions and reached low to offer a hand and voice to those who were believed to be oppressed in multiple ways (e.g., the queer community, women, other minorities). They found common ground with others in similar circumstances and integrated their issues with the goals of BLM. Yet, in the decades of the new century, the social, economic, and political landscape changed and became more divided and hostile to Blacks.

While in many instances Blacks functioned as a group and as communities, it should not be believed that Blacks were a monolith; to the contrary, Black individuals' psychological orientations to their racial group membership and culture has considerable variation (Joseph, 2022). It is important to understand that aspect of Black life and culture since the culture is reflected in a range of psychological perspectives. All too often commentators and public figures talk as if there is one Black community and one voice and one view that reflects Blacks beliefs and experiences. This is not so. The next chapter turns to a discussion of Black psychological and cultural elements.

References

Abramowitz, A., & McCoy, J. (2019). United States: Racial resentment, negative partisanship, and polarization in Trump's America. *The ANNALS of the American Academy of Political and Social Science*, 681(1), 137–156. doi:10.1177/0002716218811.

Alexander, M. (2012). *The new Jim Crow: Mass incarceration in the age of colorblindness* (rev. ed.). New Press.

Beckett, K. (1997). *Making crime pay: Law and order in contemporary politics.* Oxford University Press.

Bell, D. (2008). *Race, racism, and American law* (6th ed.). Wolters Kluwer.

Bennett, L. (1988). *Before the Mayflower: A history of Black America.* Johnson Publishing.

Bush. K. (2023). *Rodney King, the L.A. riots, and the aftermath.* Portland Center Stage. https://www.pcs.org/features/rodney-king.

Chae, D. H., Yip, T., Martz, C. D., Chung, K., Richeson, J. A., Hajat, A., Curtis, D. S., Rogers, L. O., & LaVeist, T. A. (2021). Vicarious racism and vigilance during the COVID-19 pandemic: Mental health implications among Asian and Black Americans. *Public Health Reports*, 136(4), 508–517.

Clayton, D. M., Moore, S. E., & Jones-Eversley, S. D. (2021). A historical analysis of racism within the US presidency: Implications for African Americans and the political process. *Journal of African American Studies*, 25(3), 383–401. doi:10.1007/s12111-021-09543-5.

Costello, M. B. (2016). The Trump effect: The impact of the presidential campaign on our nation's schools. Report for Southern Poverty Law Center. https://www.splcenter.org/sites/default/files/splc_the_trump_effect.pdf.

Department of Justice. (2023, February 14). 2021 hate crimes statistics. https://www.justice.gov/crs/highlights/2021-hate-crime-statistics.

Drakulich, K., Wozniak, K. H., Hagan, J., & Johnson, D. (2021). Whose lives mattered? How white and black Americans felt about Black Lives Matter in 2016. *Law & Society Review*, 55(2), 227–251. doi:10.1111/lasr.12552.

Dubey, A. D. (2020). The resurgence of cyber racism during the COVID-19 pandemic and its aftereffects: Analysis of sentiments and emotions in tweets. *JMIR Public Health and Surveillance*, 6(4), e19833.

Elias, A., Ben, J., Mansouri, F., & Paradies, Y. (2021). Racism and nationalism during and beyond the COVID-19 pandemic. *Ethnic and Racial Studies*, 44(5), 783–793. doi:10.1080/01419870.2020.1851382.

Farrell, A., & Lockwood, S. (2023). Addressing hate crime in the 21st century: Trends, threats, and opportunities for intervention. *Annual Review of Criminology*, 6, 107–130.

Flores-González, N., & Salgado, C. D. (2022). Shifting racial schemas: From post-racial to new "old-fashioned" racism. *Sociological Inquiry*, 92(2), 341–363.

Fortunato, O., Dierenfeldt, R., Basham, S., & McGuffee, K. (2022). Examining the impact of the Obama and Trump candidacies on right-wing domestic terrorism in the United States: A time-series analysis. *Journal of interpersonal violence*, 37(23–24), NP23397–NP23418. doi:10.1177/088626052210788.

Franklin, H. J., & Moss, A. A. (2000). *From slavery to freedom: A history of African Americans* (8th ed.). McGraw Hill.

Gates, L. H. (2019). *Stony the road: Reconstruction, white supremacy, and the rise of Jim Crow*. Penguin.

Gates, L. H. (2021). *The Black church: This is our story, this is our song*. Penguin.

Joseph, P. E. (2022). *The third reconstruction: America's struggle for racial justice in the twenty-first century*. Basic Books.

Kidd, T. S. (2019). *American history: 1492 to the present*. B+N Academic.

Koski, S. V., & Bantley, K. (2020). Dog whistle politics: The Trump administration's influence on hate crimes. *Seton Hall Legis. J.*, 44(1), 39–60.

Lepore, J. (2018). *These truths: A history of the United States*. Norton.

Malazada, S. A. (2020). *Hate crime explained through UCR data during the eras of Barack Obama's and Donald Trump's political power* [Unpublished doctoral dissertation]. University of Colorado.

McCoy, H. (2020). Black lives matter, and yes, you are racist: The parallelism of the twentieth and twenty-first centuries. *Child and adolescent social work journal*, 37 (5), 463–475. doi:10.1007/s10560-020-00690-4.

Ruisch, B. C., & Ferguson, M. J. (2022). Changes in Americans' prejudices during the presidency of Donald Trump. *Nature Human Behaviour*, 6(5), 656–665. doi:10.1038/s41562-021-01287-2.

Saadatmand, Y., Toma, M., & Choquette, J. (2012). The war on drugs and crime rates. *Journal of Business and Economic Research*, 10(2), 285–290.

Smith, C. W., Kreitzer, R. J., & Suo, F. (2020). The dynamics of racial resentment across the 50 US states. *Perspectives on Politics*, 18(2), 527–538. doi:10.1017/S153759271900268.

Stolberg, S. (2020, June 7). "Pandemic within a pandemic": Coronavirus and police brutality roil Black communities. *New York Times*, https://www.nytimes.com/2020/06/07/us/politics/blacks-coronavirus-police-brutality.html.

U.S. Department of Health and Human Services, Substance Abuse and Mental Health Services Administration. (2001). *Summary of findings from 2000 National Household Survey on Drug Abuse*, NHSDA series H-13, DHHS pub. No. SMA 01–3549.

Williams, D. R. (2018). Stress and the mental health of populations of color: Advancing our understanding of race-related stressors. *Journal of health and social behavior*, 59(4),

Wright, J. E., & Thomas, M. B. (2023). The erosion of the administrative state under President Trump: Citizens' pushback against individual and institutional racism. *Public Administration Review*, 83(1), 210–214.

PART 4

Integrating Black Cultural Strengths into Psychological Practice

11

ELEMENTS OF BLACK CULTURE

In this chapter, I describe some aspects of Black cultural values and practices that emerged over the centuries of racial oppression. Many qualities of Black culture have been touched upon in previous chapters, and here I review and discuss how the cultural practices evolved and changed with time and circumstance. While there are many elements and expressions of Black life and culture, there are also central themes and core principles that served as foundations for the many forms and styles of African ways and their varied expressions. I organize the review by cultural pattern or belief, such as spirituality, community, family and kinship, music and dance, and so on. I begin with what I call foundational beliefs, the intersections of family and spirituality, which can be expressed through religious practices. Please note that family interacts and is bound-up with other cultural practices, so it will appear in other sections as well.

Foundational Beliefs: Spirituality and Family

My analysis of Black cultural strengths started in Africa, the homeland, long before contact with Europeans. Contact with Europeans that impacted Africans adversely came later, along the west coast of the continent. What we know about the ancient prehistory and Common Era is that the people across the continent spoke many languages, had numerous beliefs, and had cultural ways on which to draw. Some have suggested (e.g., Webber, 1978) there were also some common cultural elements across the continent, and others believe (e.g., Horton & Horton, 2005) that Africans' beliefs, values, and practices came with those taken from their homeland to the New World colonies. Those beliefs and cultural ways were reestablished in the colonies of the North American mainland by Africans who were relocated or shipped

DOI: 10.4324/9781003111542-16

directly to the mainland regions. Gates (2021) states, regarding the Africans brought to North America, that the people were

> Igbo, Mandinka, Fulbe, Kongo, Akan, and Wolof, that were the most numerous and each brought with them their own belief systems. Out of this diverse blend of customs, religious faiths, and practices the African American people arose.
>
> *(p. 16)*

Africans had different notions about the world and God. Africans' beliefs about the universe set the foundation for how they organized their lives before and after enslavement, and their connection to the natural world contributed to how they came to perceive their surroundings and drove their need for some particular beliefs and practices. Like all people, Africans had to manage in the environments in which they found themselves, and this adaptation gave them information about the nature of things; they believed it was vital to live in harmony with one's environment and to honor the life forces that existed and were hard to deny.

Africans, prior to and after being captured and enslaved, believed that supreme and divine beings were responsible for life's vital forces. At the same time, Africans' God was not a singular person but instead was part of all life and all things. For them, God created particular people. Usually, God was held to be the ancestor of specific people linked to a cherished elder, as were all things—to family and to those who came before, the ancestors, looked after the living. The spirits of the departed were also responsible for good and evil, for good fortune and bad luck; the spirits had characteristics and attributes that gave each unique personalities that the living could discern and understand.

The vital forces that came from the supreme being were distinct (Sweet, 2003) from the God of European beliefs. Thus, the creator could shape and be shaped by the events and needs of the people, in the present. So there existed many spirits and deities that were responsible for daily events, actions, and decisions. There was no location where God existed since God was all around. The past and present were guides to the future. The guides were the ancestors in the form of spirits.

Sweet (2003) states that the spirits who mattered to Africans were often those who had recently passed and had the most say about those still living. African people knew their deities by name, location, personal attributes, and, more importantly, the action they could take for good or ill. Africans employed their spirituality and its principles for managing and solving day-to-day issues. Their spiritual beliefs were used to explain, predict, and control daily life events. Rather than focus on an afterlife, as in other religious practices, Africans' beliefs and, in some cases, their form of Christian beliefs were converted to and communicated through their rituals, which were aimed at dealing with the everyday world, with its bounty, misfortunes, diseases, droughts, and so on (Aderajew, 2019; Horton, 1967). Thus, knowledge and the spiritual were at all times related and bound together; said another way, science and religion were one and the same (Sweet, 2003).

Their deeply held spiritual orientation offered another view and course of action: hope and perseverance. Another factor of African religion was that they had no desire to promote their views or get others to follow them; this meant that Africans were willing to accept new deities, usually from outside of their clan or tribe or ones that others followed. Africans practiced Christianity based on their cosmology, Islam, and traditional religions.

Africans used music and art to communicate with the spirits and let them know they were being taken seriously; music and art were used as an expression of life. Men and women danced because it had social and spiritual meanings to value and honor the ancestors as well as the living. From their spiritual/religious bases, Africans focused on the present and past. Their African spiritual orientation had embedded communalistic beliefs because they valued the group (i.e., family, village) and because the needs of the group mattered over the wishes, wants, and needs of individuals or personal obligations. A guiding principle was that the people must follow the ways of the ancestors and must maintain balance with all things.

Blassingame (1979) observes that there were similarities in European and African cultures such that it was possible to blend or re-create aspects of the African ways; this way Africans were able to use European forms to serve African customs:

> Most Africans believed in a Creator, or all-powerful God whom one addresses directly through prayers, sacrifices, rituals, songs, and dances....
>
> Christian forms were so similar to Africans religious patterns that it was relatively easy for early slaves to incorporate them ... with their traditional practices and beliefs. In America, Jehovah replaced the Creator, and Jesus, the Holy Ghost, and Saints replaced lesser gods. The Africans preserved many of their sacred ceremonies in the conventional Christian ritual and ceremonies.
>
> *(pp. 20–21)*

The retention of African forms appears in the songs and burial practices; in particular, the spirituals created by slaves contained African elements and evoked strong emotions, as intended.

> Not only did Southern slaves [and Black Americans] decorate graves like their African ancestor, they also retained the practice of celebrating the journey of the deceased to his "home" by dancing, singing, and drinking.
>
> *(Blassingame, 1979, p. 45)*

White Christians wanted Blacks to learn from scripture that they should be submissive and obedient and accept their status as slaves. Slaves essentially rejected the messages from whites when they were taught to accept their lot. Dodson (2002) writes that in the 1700s,

> allies of the slaveholders in their attempts to "civilize the heathen" Africans and make them better, more loyal servants, … tried to teach the enslaved that they were born to be slaves, that they should work and serve their masters faithfully, and that they should never disobey their master or lie or steal.
>
> *(p. 138)*

Of the various denominations presented to Blacks, the ones that offered more autonomy had the greatest appeal. For instance, Catholicism's structure and process removed the worshipper from direct communication with God and the spirit world, a situation that was contrary to Blacks spiritual preferences and beliefs, but Baptists, Methodist, and Episcopalians offered a religion that allowed Africans to

> invent their own Afro-Christian religious practices. Fusing remnants of their traditional African worship … with their own interpretations of the Christian faith, [Blacks'] praise meetings became unique New World African religious experiences. African-American oratory, music, and religious and theological worldviews are all rooted in the African Christian religious experience invented by enslaved Africans during the era of slavery.
>
> *(Dodson, 2002, p. 138)*

The unique elements of the Africans' belief system are what makes it stand apart from traditional forms of Christianity. For instance, the conviction that the people and community were regularly interacting with the spirit world and that spirits were also part of daily life were two of their core spiritual principles. Observers attributed Blacks' beliefs to primitive superstition and witchcraft; Africans' beliefs were considered to be a "perversion of the natural revelations of God" (Dodson, 2002, p. 141). Many Blacks in the South and other parts of the country elected to participate in the Baptist, Methodist, and Presbyterian churches. Dodson notes that the

> black faith that evolved from the coming together of diverse religious influences became … something distinctly different from any of its major contributors. Both the slave congregations of the South—"the invisible institutions" (religious meetings held away from Whites) and the more or less free black churches of the North developed a religion that masked

> a subliminal outrage balanced with patience, cheerfulness, and a boundless confidence in the ultimate justice of God.
>
> *(p. 147)*

Belgrave and Allison (2019) point out that while free and enslaved Africans adopted Christian beliefs, nevertheless, their perspectives on their faith were formed mostly by their African-based spiritual convictions and principles. The slaves' religious activities outside the reach of whites allowed them to incorporate many of their African cultural religious ideals and perspectives and to retain their views of the Supreme Being, nature, and the power of the ancestors and spirits. They were also able to establish independent institutions in the North, and later in the South, that went beyond just tending to the people's souls.

At the center of many African societies, wherever they evolved, was the family unit. Most societies formed social groups around family and lineage. Daily life was centered on the village, usually small ones headed by a chief and elder council as its leaders.

In some locations, written communication evolved, and yet in others the spoken word was the primary means of communication, and oral traditions were used to pass on the group's history and practices. As noted previously, the groups formed around family or lineage were also used to construct governing systems as the people grew and settled into larger bodies and as they adapted to environmental conditions to survive.

The family unit was central to many African people, and the community followed in importance since families formed the basis of villages, and the villages were the basis for the districts. Family ties connected people to one another, so their traditions were grounded in the protection and well-being of the family. Alongside family was the belief in God and the ancestors. In this realm of the spirit, as in others,

> the slaves reinterpreted White patterns, weaving a whole new universe around biblical images and giving a new dimension and new meaning to Christianity.... American slaves, with few exceptions, rejected [the] version of Christianity [promoted by slave owners]. Their God was the [one] that delivered the Israelites.... In a total and passionate quest for *this* God, the slaves, tempered and toughened by the annealing heat of adversity, turned American Christianity inside out, like a glove, infusing it with African-oriented melodies and rhythms and adding new patterns, such as the ring shout, ecstatic seizure and communal, call-and-response patterns.
>
> *(Bennett, 1988, pp. 99–102)*

Throughout the period of slavery from the 18th to 19th centuries, with all their restrictions, it did not dampen the slaves' vitality and thus did not render them childlike and dependent. Rather, slaves were able to establish independent cultural forms as seen in their spirituals. Levine (2007) points out that the secular and sacred were joined in the way songs were presented and in how they reached back to past times and upward to reach toward a world beyond. In their music, Blacks were able to affirm their individual creativity and communal life. Levine (2007) observes:

> In fact, the form and structure of slave music presented the slave with a potential outlet for his individual feelings even while it continually drew him back into the communal presence and permitted him the comfort of basking in the warmth of the shared assumptions of those around him.
>
> *(p. 33)*

Slaves found a way to vent their feelings in a way that affirmed their community life. They did not sing only at certain times and places but sang during many activities and chores that they were required to undertake. The slaves sang about many things, but one theme was consistent in their spirituals: that they were chosen to be saved. Mothers sang to their children, and workers sang while they labored. They sang while they relaxed and while they celebrated events in their lives. Through singing, they held to the notion that they were the chosen people—irrespective of their harsh reality—for their God and their ancestors were real and present, as they were for those from whom they descended in Africa.

One effect of the limited world in which slaves were forced to reside was that it left them to their own cultural themes and beliefs since they were shut off from all aspects of American society. They relied on what they knew to feed their consciousness and worldview and to set their emotional states. Levine (2007) notes that

> true acculturation was denied to most slaves. The alternatives were either to remain in a state of cultural limbo, divested of the old cultural patterns, but not allowed to adapt those of the new homeland—which in the long run is no alternative at all—or to cling to as many as possible of the old ways of thinking and acting. The slaves' oral tradition, their music, and their religious outlook served this latter function and constituted a cultural refuge at least potentially capable of protecting their personalities from some of the worst ravages of the slave system.
>
> *(p. 54)*

In the 17th century, North American colonists were deeply religious people, yet they were ambivalent about teaching Africans their faith; some did so but at the same time enacted laws so that Africans, once they became Christian, would remain slaves, even though it was the custom and part of Christian doctrine that Christians should not be enslaved (Reiss, 1997). From the arrival of Africans until the Great Awakening in the 1750s, Africans did not embrace nor accept Christian faiths in total. Gates (2021) states,

> So perhaps, it should not surprise us that enslaved Africans in North America did not accept Christianity—when finally offered a chance to embrace it—exactly as white Americans practiced it or pictured it. Instead they reshaped it in their own images, to satisfy their own spiritual and practical needs.
>
> *(p. 16)*

Later, American mainland Blacks began to follow the Christian faith. Africans and Black Americans joined a number of denominations; as Gates (2021) notes some of the religious groups to which Blacks belonged were Methodist, Baptist, and Pentecostal as well as the African Methodist Episcopal Church (AME) and the Church of God in Christ (COGIC). There were also other denominations that Blacks belonged to such as Roman Catholic, Seventh-Day Adventists, Jehovah's Witnesses, and Muslim. In the 21st century many Blacks have moved away from the church, yet Gates (2021) notes that when asked how important religion is in their lives, 80% of Blacks responded that it is very important, more than any other racial group.

Yet family has always been a central concern. Blacks have historically struggled to maintain family ties and connections, a dynamic that continues to this day as families are separated by mass incarceration, economic inequality, and health disparities (Alexander, 2012; Joseph, 2022; Villarosa, 2022). The struggles that characterize Black families today date back into the slave era. Kulikoff (1986) outlines the forces that shaped the Black family on plantations and small farms in the Chesapeake region, noting that Black families were often separated due to the death, misfortunes, and decisions of owners. Slave owners would sell or bequeath their human property to relatives or others upon their deaths. Sometimes the slaves were used to pay debts incurred while the person was living, wherein the ownership of property was given to the person holding the debt. Each time slaves were sold, they had to re-create family wherever they landed.

Some American-born slaves understood their plight and circumstances with respect to family—so much so that they lobbied for more family rights. Once some rights were secured, other concessions followed; women wanted more time with newborns and wanted relief from field work when expecting children and caring for newborns. Blacks also asserted their right to name their children, which was once the domain of the planters, and Black slaves who had skills would pass them on to their young. As part of establishing families, they lobbied for cabins. Thus, slaves wrestled for recognition that they were entitled to privacy. Black family life was established to some extent, and its existence was contrary to the core tenets of slavery, which held that the slave was not human. But Blacks' actions forced recognition of their humanity. Yet when the migration to the Lower South began, these hard-won rights were lost and had to be reestablished, which was a tremendous challenge.

African kinship systems were not re-created. Blacks, however, took what they knew from their former lives and the situation they were in and redefined family to fit their new lives and their new reality, the same way that kinship had been simulated during the Middle Passage. Children were taught to respect elders and adults by employing terms of authority and respect like "aunt" and "uncle" when appropriate. Since parents and even grandparents could be separated from children, it was customary for members of the community to take up the responsibility of caring for these unrelated children and adults.

The practice of caring for the unrelated and adding them to the current re-created family is an example of one of the ways family was redefined and how it operated in contrast to the European American nuclear family. For many Blacks, living together as a family was not possible. Blacks would marry by mating with men or women on nearby plantations, which they called being "married abroad." Family ties were strong among Black people, as evidenced in publications for runaway slaves who were trying to reconnect with family members who had been sold away. Mitchell (2004) states:

> The spontaneous family formation already seen in the slave community and then the extended family … continued in full bloom after the Civil War. What had been mostly a means of emotional and spiritual support could now become more nearly a replica of the African extended-family society, even without blood ties. No detached female or male, young or old, need be an orphan in a relational vacuum. An instant "kin" now had resources, though meager, which could be shared to meet real needs. One didn't have to wait years for the tie to become binding enough to involve a sense of familiar obligation.
>
> *(pp. 167–168)*

So the patterns of Black life surged forward during the Jim Crow era and were held together by Black institutions and organizations made more essential by the high-pitched and all-encompassing racial segregation that whites created to limit opportunities for Blacks to participate in American society. The ancient beliefs in the life force aided the process of adopting and creating a spiritual ethos from the biblical images and scriptures of Christianity to which they were exposed and to which they adapted and found comfort and guidance in the notion that God would free the people. What they needed to do was stay focused and together.

Community and Kinship Networks

Most Blacks resided in the South, before and after the Civil War, where they were less able to move about and participate in organizations like the National Association for the Advancement of Colored People, yet we still find that the community was a core factor in Black people's lives. Much of the slaves' and poor Blacks' lives—day in and day out—was devoted to labor; from the morning horn (around 4:00 a.m.) until midnight, they labored either in the fields or the main house, or they attended to their own needs and homes. Bennett (1988) and Webber (1978) note that this regimen was supposed to crush the slaves' spirit and will. Yet Bennett (1988) notes that in fact the opposite was true:

> The slaves [and poor Blacks, during and after the Jim Crow years], in the most astonishingly creative act in our history, transcended their environment, creating a new structure of meaning and putting their oppressors and the world in their debt. No one can read the record of that transcendence without a sense of awe at the audacity of the slaves' hope. This hope was clearly visible in the concentric circles of community that started in the family and radiated in larger and larger circles that enveloped the whole of the Slave Row. From that community came the rhythmic, spiritual, and psychic piles that bottomed the new synthesis called Black America. The results—the spirituals, the blues, the rhythmic tonality of Black America—point to and guarantee the medium, which was a community of passion and creativity.
>
> *(p. 96)*

The community was in part created by the establishment of the plantation and as such the slave quarters were a product of it; at the same time, the community was not defined by it, nor did it contain the Blacks' community or their spirit. "The community of the slaves was a communal entity characterized by a collective orientation stemming partly from the African past and partly from the exigencies of the situation" (Bennett, 1988, p. 96).

Bennett argues that the slave community was much like the Black communities of today; both are not defined by geographic boundaries since the community is part of the person. Black communities had leaders selected from their own. The community, during slavery and the Jim Crow era, was structured around several critical elements. Community members' roles were arranged into quasi-institutions dictated by proper behavior and expectations, and there were set standards for how relationships with slaveholders and landlords should be handled. There were guides on how people new to the community should be included. Some of these institutions represented translations of African practices, while some were combined European and African forms. And still others were improvisations of European themes.

Blacks invested in family and community. Even when the stability of family was tenuous and often disrupted or destroyed, they would re-create what they could when possible. Their commitment to family was often the means by which whites forced their cooperation and obedience during and after slavery. Threats of selling off family members were commonly used to keep slaves in line. While the family was important to Black life, it was considerably difficult to maintain family ties to one another in the face of white oppression and while being treated as property. As the communities became more stable, family life was more feasible, as were extended kinship lines. Cultural practices are apparent in settled Black slave and nonslave communities in that they were structured around family and kinship ties.

Many observers (Levine, 2007; Stuckey, 2013) note that Blacks behaved differently from what was assumed and expected, from the powerful influences of whites. The cultural practices that Blacks used during their enslavement and segregation were deeply held nonblood kinship bonds, a work-hard orientation, flexible family roles (rejection of rigid male and female roles), the importance of achievement or striving to do better, and spiritual practices to guide them through the rocky waters of the time (Johnson & Carter, 2020; Webber, 1978).

Black churches and communities supported and helped to establish and maintain Black family life. The family and the church were intertwined. Mitchell (2004, p. 164) notes that Black churches "supported and facilitated the deep desire of ex-slaves to embrace the old African and Christian traditions of the sanctity of marriage." Many Black communities had societies that were devoted to charitable giving. Another cultural practice that lasted over the centuries is found in Blacks use of songs and stories.

Songs and Stories: Expressive Cultural Styles

Africans and their descendants retained emotional lifestyles reflected in songs and stories, which became their unique cultural signature. Levine (1977) documents how music, movement, songs, and stories reflected continuity over centuries and constituted a way to psychologically release tension, frustration, joy, and hope for Africans and their descendants. Levine (2007) states:

> Black slaves [and Black Americans] engaged in widespread music exchanges and cross-culturation with whites among whom they lived, yet throughout the centuries of slavery and long after emancipation their song style, with its over-riding antiphony [call-and-response or interactive style], its group nature, its pervasive functionality, its improvisational character, its strong relationship in performance to dance and bodily movement and expression, remained closer to the musical styles and performances of West Africa and the Afro-American music of the

> West Indies and South America than to the musical style of Western Europe. In their songs, as in their tales, aphorisms, proverbs, anecdotes and jokes, Afro-American slaves, following the practices of the African cultures they had been forced to leave behind them, assigned a central role to the spoken arts, encouraged and rewarded verbal improvisation, maintained the participatory nature of their expressive culture, and utilized the spoken arts to voice criticism as well as to uphold traditional values and group cohesion.
>
> *(p. 6)*

Levine (2007) documents the relationship between African practices in terms of songs and dance and that of slaves. He shows how similar patterns and practices characterize both groups, and he highlights elements of their behavior and actions that show how the African and slave practices were related and connected one to the other. He points out that Black people's songs had many functions, both in Africa and America. Verbal expressions in tales, songs, and verbal games served multiple purposes. One purpose was to preserve community values and cohesion while allowing the individual to move beyond social conventions and environmental limits, thus permitting the individual to share deeply held feelings about others and leaders, which in most instances could not be shared or verbalized without negative consequences. But among African people, periods were designated such that a person could, through song, dance, and tales shared with the social group, express thoughts and feelings that would otherwise be prohibited. Levine (2007) presents examples of these rituals that were observed in Africa spanning more than two centuries. He shows these same practices being enacted in slave communities, also over centuries, in which songs and related activities were used to release psychological pain and discomfort as well as to affirm Blacks' dignity.

With songs, there was dancing, and the way Blacks moved when they danced stood out to observers. Both in Africa and the Americas, Black music, both vocal and instrumental, was intertwined with dance or bodily movements. It was said that Blacks would plan for opportunities to go about, sometimes miles away, to dance and frolic. Levine (2007) argues that African dance had particular characteristics such as gliding, dragging, and shuffling steps and fluid bodily movements, which were contrasted with the erect dancing styles of Europeans. For centuries, African dance emphasized flexibility and improvisation. Between secular songs and spirituals, Blacks found more value and expression in spirituals. The spirituals afforded them the ability to adapt and transcend their circumstances.

Scholars and historians have debated the origins of Black spirituals, with some contending that spirituals derived from whites' hymns, while others insisted that Blacks were responsible for the songs they sang. For Levine (2007), the fact that Blacks created and re-created spirituals reflected a communal process revealing a distinct Black awareness. Such creations provided slaves an emotional release and an opportunity for suppressed expression.

Alongside the songs were folktales and stories, many of which were not collected until after the Civil War but were clearly used and told throughout the slave era. The origins of Black folktales are debated, but that they existed is not. Like songs that expressed the oral traditions, tales and stories served several functions, one of which was to relay and document historical events, many of which involved Africans being captured and their journey to the New World. Allegorical stories told the exploits of various smart animals who would trick the more powerful animals and evade deadly outcomes. Then, of course, there was the manner and style of storytelling, which included variations in delivery and prompted listeners to chime in, making the exercise communal and participatory, a unique feature of Black life.

As was true of their African ancestors, the enslaved and, later, free Black people used words and stories as educational tools to convey information about life and moral actions. The stories taught the listeners, children and adults alike, how to live and behave. It is vital to highlight this reality for most Black people; they went about their days and years enmeshed in the tasks and activities of living, irrespective of their situations. They sought to make the best of their lives, families, and friends and, thus, to make each day all they could. Their stories and tales often spoke to issues they encountered in daily living, and the stories also spoke about dealing with important relationships. Many tales were not grounded in religious guidance or teachings. Levine (2007) points out that human connections were often the subject of tales told and shared—like the story of the buzzard who could fly high as an eagle, but, as the story goes, he still had to come down to earth to eat. The moral of the story was to be kind to others—no matter what you have, be kind to others because we all have to live on the same level. Stories stressed the importance and value of friendship as well as the dangers of being dishonest. Responsibilities were also conveyed in the tales told. In a story about a chick that failed to follow its mother's warnings and was eaten by a hawk, the moral was to obey your parents. The rites of passage to adulthood were also themes of many tales. Levine (2007) states that many moral tales have been dismissed or ignored, but they are important because their content provides a glimpse into the minds and thoughts of Blacks as they entered emancipation. According to Levine, the stories reinforced Blacks' religious values and set a vision for the people of what was good and moral by placing significant emphasis on the ideals of friendship, cooperation, productive activity, and commitment to family. Blacks made it a point to highlight the dangers of going too high or pushing too far or going beyond your place. "It was dangerous for black men and women to forget who or where they were, and this danger constituted a motif running through Negro tales" (Levine, 2007, p. 97).

Another source of psychological release and resolution employed by Blacks were the stories of various types of tricksters, which have been linked to Africa. These stories served as a mechanism and means to relieve psyche tension when they were subjugated to the whimsical authority of whites and were a way to, at least symbolically, strike back at the powerful whites in their lives. These stories often had the same structure. The animal who was most powerful (a fox or wolf) would attack the weaker animal (a rabbit), who in turn would fight back with whatever they could find. The stories relied on intimate knowledge of both actors of the other. In essence, the stories are about how the weak evade the will and power of the strong. In the course of the conflict, the weak learn the ways of the strong. Brer Rabbit, in these stories, was humanized to the point where the Rabbit fought to survive. The Rabbit wanted to be wealthy, successful, and honored and to exhibit sexual prowess.

Levine (2007) states that there is evidence that Blacks identified with the trickster in the tales. In effect, Brer Rabbit's victories were theirs as well. It was this sort of imagery and symbolism that helped or contributed to the Blacks being able to outlive slavery.

> So as long as the perilous situation and psyche needs of slaves continued to characterize larger numbers of freedmen as well, the imagery of the old slave tales remained both aesthetically and functionally satisfying. By ascribing actions to semi-mythical actors, Negros were able to overcome the external and internal censorship that their hostile surroundings imposed upon them.
>
> *(Levine, 2007, pp. 113–114)*

For Levine (2007), Blacks' identification with animals in their stories indicated a mechanism they employed to separate their emotional and psychological worlds from whites as well as to reveal a reality they believed was unified and included humans, animals, spirits, and nonhuman objects as essential aspects of the natural world.

Music and Rhythm

According to Jones (2003), rhythm was—and still is—a core element of Black culture. For Bennett (1988) and other historians (e.g., Berlin, 2003; Blassingame, 1972; Dodson, 2002; Horton & Horton, 2005; Levine, 2007; Stuckey, 2013; Webber, 1978), music, dance, and rhythm were central components of Black people's lives both in and out of slavery. Pasteur and Toldson (1982) contend that rhythm is a natural part of behavior, that living beings and animals reveal a pattern or rhythm in their behavior. They also argue that rhythm is a foundational component of Black expressiveness. They state that rhythm

> is most easily transmitted in aesthetic forms that become tangible enclosures for the waves of force (rhythm) that are nourished by that which is "spiritual" in the universe. Clearly a human characteristic, rhythm's vibratory nature pulsates throughout the universe. In human behavior it is expressed sensually, through lines, surfaces, colors, languages, music, and movements in dance and other motor responses. Blacks walk, talk, dance, prance, look, cook, play and pray in marvelous harmony to, and with, this rhythm of the universe.
>
> *(p. 63)*

Bennett (1988) describes music and rhythm as a part of the lives of African and Black people,

> which informed every element of slave [and Black American] life, was characterized by the so-called "blues" tonality and a rhythmic, collective, and emotional orientation. The same elements are evident in slave [and Black American] folklore and philosophy, especially the Brer Rabbit, Brer Fox and Old John cycles [and tales]. The expression of this orientation was as varied as the people and included cries, hollers, work songs, devil songs, spirituals and blues.
>
> *(p. 102)*

Black musical forms such as the blues, jazz, hip-hop, and spirituals are credited as original contributions of Black Americans (Gates, 2021). The music forms were used to communicate and to express the longing of their hearts and spirits, both sorrow and—although less often experienced—joy and jubilation. Sounds of joy were most often expressed during church services but then moved outside of the church to the streets and communities. These behaviors and beliefs, in the beginning of plantation life and later in the 21st century, were often hidden from whites and mainly things that took place among Black people. Gates (2021) describes hip-hop's contributions this way:

> It reflected secular-based responses that were not offered in the churches, it was the youth who took the microphone and spoke where they felt there was silence and invisibility, they wished to be seen and heard "Hip-hop seizes the microphone to amplify the urgent drama of Black dispossession.... Rappers are secular preachers."
>
> *(p. 168)*

The spirituals and stories emphasized the notion that the weak could prevail over the strong and powerful since the power was not permanent. Blacks exhibited a consistent belief in the possibility that they would transcend their status, that things would change. These elements tell us that, while songs, spirituals, and folktales told and sung by slaves and people who were free had differences, they were not distinct expressions but were, in effect, part of a continuum that gave voice subconsciously and consciously to their worldview.

Slaves and Black Americans, later, had to balance ideals with the practical reality so they could find ways to instill hope and optimism for the future without forgetting the facts of the present. It was a present full of unjust, unwarranted actions, and of judgments, all of which had to be dealt with in the moment. Levine (2007) says of Black folk tales, "their tales prepared the slaves [and the general Black population] to do this by identifying the forces which shaped their lives and by giving prescriptions for overcoming or at least surviving them" (p. 134).

The combination of their songs, stories, and tales could lighten the moment, and applying the folk beliefs during their lives helped them feel less out of control. The telling of their tales aided in their efforts to live as fulfilling a life as was possible. The sum of the songs, folk beliefs, and stories reflected a distinct cultural style that came about as a creative blend of African, white, and Black cultural patterns. This style was held on to as the emancipation era dawned and remained into the future. The music of the 1950s–1960s, known as soul and rhythm and blues, were distinctively Black, as were jazz and blues, then came rap and hip-hop, musical forms that are said to blend various elements of Black culture. In 2023 rap and hip-hop celebrated its 50th anniversary. In some ways rap can be seen as an extension of the stories and folktales of the past. The music is a form of resistance and protest, speaking to the struggles of Black and Brown people.

Communalism: Organizational and Institutional Development

Black churches, as independent institutions were started in the 1770s with the creation of the first African Baptist churches in Georgia, Virginia, and South Carolina. The churches helped Blacks establish myriad other social, fraternal, and business organizations. One of the first of social societies started in Boston in 1787, the African Lodge. The various organizations helped drive efforts to promote Black equal rights (Horton & Horton, 2005). Coupled with the activity of the churches was the effort to educate its people, so Black leaders endeavored to establish schools (Bennett, 1988). The efforts by free Blacks, however, did not reach into the South, where 90% of Blacks were located, and they were not able to benefit from or participate in these efforts. The slaves were, following the plantation model, held in quarters so they could work the fields or tend to the main house. Blacks were shut off from social interactions and were isolated in their respective communities or slave quarters.

Black people were left to their own devices, and they needed to depend on themselves. Those who were able, mostly free Blacks in the North and Upper

South, organized and established social institutions to improve the lives of Blacks in the nation. Organizations like the Free African Society, begun by a group of eight free Black men, were formed to aid Blacks. Groups in Philadelphia and New York followed these men's lead and created related social, religious, civic, and business organizations.

Blacks' organizational efforts took on more urgency following the world wars because many of them experienced different treatment away from the United States—for example, European whites' interactions with Blacks were respectful and fair—and this motivated Blacks in the United States to act and organize. Their actions and organizational building were demonstrated during the civil rights movement and beyond, mobilizing community members. Black people stunned the nation with their ability to gather and move their issues forward, perhaps even making white authority nervous both in the Black Power era of the 1970s and in the Black Lives Matter activism of the 2020s.

In response to racial oppression over time, Blacks attempted to reject and deny inequality or to transcend obstacles and barriers that walled and isolated them. Blacks also created new structures and assigned new meaning to their social status. More than anything, Blacks have maintained their vision and prayers for a better and more just life. They kept hope, expressed in several ways, for how they elected to live and what they chose to value (Blackmon, 2008)—for instance, fairness for all, public school education for all, voting rights for all, not just for themselves. Blacks' hope is visible in the life, rhythm, and feelings of the communities that started in the family or on the plantations and slave quarters and circulated in larger and larger ripples throughout towns, counties, and states, and into the Black national ethos. The ripples of hope and striving were sent via Blacks' struggles for change that were erected upon the foundation of their cultural values and reflected in their movement and motion, in songs and stories, driven on by their passion.

While in many instances Blacks have functioned as a community, Blacks are not a monolith—to the contrary. Black people's psychological orientations to their racial group membership and culture have always had considerable diversity (Joseph, 2022). It is important to understand this aspect of Black life and culture since the culture encompasses a range of psychological perspectives. All too often commentators, pundits, journalists, and public figures speak as if there is one Black community, with one voice and one view, that reflects all Blacks' beliefs and experiences. This is not so; there never has been one and only one Black viewpoint. Rather, psychological and cultural diversity is a more accurate description of Black life and culture, with a number of racial identity ego statuses and cultural values that illustrate that variation.

Black people used their core values and psychological orientations and resolutions as fuel to survive their new situations as low-caste slaves and restricted free people. More important, they taught the new generations by way of tales, folk stories, and songs the thoughts and behaviors that would aid in their survival. Clearly, Blacks regardless of location were determined to be free. For the most part, they did not accept their subornation or their low-caste status. It was a formidable task to push back against, given that most white colonists and Americans shared the negative view of Blacks and worked to keep them down.

Many Black cultural patterns came from Africa to North America and the United States, while others were formed from Blacks' experiences with racial oppression. In particular, racial identity ego statuses as a psychological orientation have varied perspectives associated with what it means to be a Black person. A topic for the next chapter. But know that the experiences of racial oppression and the denigration of Blacks as a people created a psychological need to learn how to value oneself and one's people and culture in an environment that rewarded rejection of African or Black American beliefs and practice. The literature and conceptualization of racial identity emerged in the 20th century, with empirical evidence about it in the same era and in the beginning of the 20st century.

It is also the case that racial identity had to be passed on through the developmental process of racial socialization, which is the active effort of family and the community to teach children how to navigate a racially hostile social world, including how to cope with racial oppression and how to believe in one's people (racial identity) (Belgrave & Allison, 2019; Bell, 2000, 2008). The transmission of the essential messages and ways of living were critical to the groups' survival and were sources of cultural strength that contributed to the people's psychological well-being.

Members of the Black community created ways and means to aid one another and established organizations and institutions that contributed to their well-being and eventual survival. It was also true that Black "families nurture each other and especially their children" (Chafe, Gavins, & Korstad, 2001, p. xxx). Parents taught their children what to expect and what to do while also teaching racial and personal pride and self-worth. Their work lives were double-edged swords, providing the essential means and the prospect of further and deeper levels of humiliation. Chafe and colleagues (2001, p. xxxi) observe that "the workplace was a perennially contested ground, potentially a source of pride and accomplishment, but just as often, a site of threat, danger, and unpredictable cruelty." Blacks turned to their own institutions for hope and investment, they supported schools and teachers, and they aligned with the churches as core organizations that sustained the people and held them together. The church and its leaders also sustained the struggle for a better life and equal rights and bolstered personal and racial pride. In short, Blacks—in the face of unimageable hostility—mounted considerable resistance to racial oppression by way of their cultural practices: community, family, religion, and personal and cultural pride. A developed and culturally focused racial identity was needed for there to be constructive messages about racial socialization.

A positive racial identity is, first and foremost, a necessity in maintaining Black cultural strengths through generations. Once a Black person has developed a positive racial identity, they can pass on Black cultural values and beliefs onto the next generation. It is also possible that as the individual matures, she can come to grasp the meaning of their race and group membership. The process by which racial practices are encouraged and by which racial orientations are fostered is racial socialization. Stevenson (1994) states that the

> phenomena of family socialization processes that contribute to the healthy racial identity development of African American men, women, and children have been and continue to be of clinical and research interest.
>
> *(p. 445)*

When parents teach their children to prepare for racism, those children are more likely to exhibit stronger feelings of closeness to other Blacks. Stevenson (1995) defines racial socialization as the "process of communicating messages and behaviors to children to bolster their sense of identity given the possibility and reality that their life experiences may include racially hostile encounters" (p. 51). He argues that it is important to consider racial socialization as comprising cultural interaction that exceeds reactions to racial oppression and includes creative adaptations as well. He states that racial socialization should be considered more than responses to racial hostility:

> It is proposed that reactive and creative racial socialization messages and behaviors are relevant for different contexts and that the flexible application of both messages by youth should result in greater interpersonal competence and coping. This is, instead of viewing racial socialization as preparing the child only for oppressive experiences (e.g., protective African American culture), it is proposed that these processes also include teaching children how to be proud of their culture because its substance is historic, African derived, culturally empowering, and not dependent on oppressive experiences. A second perspective … about … a socialized identity is the view of self as extended and interactional as opposed to individualistic.… We can improve our understanding of Black adolescent identity development by knowing what the individual thinks of self in context through the activities, experiences and interactions that happen outside himself or herself and through experiences that represent the group. This definition is akin to the concept of reference group orientation.
>
> *(Stevenson, 1995, pp. 51–52)*

Racial socialization offers a way to examine the Black cultural orientation to social relations since it is defined as teachings about race relations and protection against racism as well as the process of learning about how to function as a member of the Black cultural group. Overall, racial socialization is aimed at instructing Blacks about their individual and social realities and how to navigate the world with this knowledge. Racial socialization is communicated through the direct and indirect messages an individual receives *or* through the beliefs a person holds as a result of receiving race-related messages. Elmore and Gaylord-Harden (2013) emphasize the importance of racial socialization as the process of rearing children toward a positive racial identity and often involves preparing children for racial encounters. Peters (1985, p. 161) notes that Black parents have the additional task of "raising physically and emotionally healthy children who are Black in a society in which being Black has negative connotations." Lesane-Brown (2006) thinks racial socialization involves both verbal and nonverbal messages sent to younger generations for the purpose of imparting values, attitudes, behaviors, and beliefs associated with race and racial stratification, between- and within-group interactions, and personal and group identity. For Blacks in general over time, racial socialization has been one mechanism through which generations pass down instructions about the rules and meaning of being a member of the Black racial group as well as how to exist and flourish as a Black person in U.S. society.

What can be gathered about racial socialization is that it exists within a system beyond the nuclear family and can involve the interaction of social issues, direct and indirect messages, the influence of others besides parents, and the impact of the views and behaviors of their targets. Current racial socialization literature aims to understand and address the full complexity of this process and the many factors, such as time, deliverer of messages, and the composition of an individual's environment (Barr & Neville, 2014).

It is in the context of racism in North America that Black parents and families must raise their children, yet the reality is that many Black parents may not wish to address race during the process of socialization. Stevenson and colleagues (1996) point out that there is considerable variation in attitudes about whether to teach about race and if so how. Thornton and colleagues (1990) reported from the National Survey of Black Americans that 64% of parents did teach about race during socialization of their children while 36% did not. These researchers point out that some Black parents did not want their children to be aware of racism. Some parents believed that teaching about race would discourage their children before their lives began. Other reasons parents gave for not wanting to teach their children about race include believing that such teaching would make their children bitter and angry, considering the matter of racism to be too big an issue for children to grasp, and thinking racism was not a big problem.

Race and racial socialization theorists (see Belgrave & Allison, 2019) thought early on that identity development was influenced by race and that, for a healthy Black identity, a person had to address the matter of race, thus the link between racial identity, personal identity, and socialization in a racial context. Recent events and protests for racial equality in reaction to the killings of Black men in the United States have raised renewed concerns about racial issues and racial socialization practices. Turner (2020) found that low-income Black mothers harbored the same concerns as middle-class mothers of Black children: they worried about their children's safety and taught them to behave in ways that were contrary to the stereotypes of Blacks being criminals. Umana-Taylor and Hill (2020) conducted a 10-year review of research focused on racial and ethnic socialization; the authors touched on many issues but confirmed the importance of using multiple racial socialization messages for optimal outcomes. They note that several racial messages, coupled together, work better for youth adjustment than focusing on a single message.

References

Aderajew, A. (2019). African systems of thought: Whether they fit scientific knowledge. *Journal of Philosophy and Culture*, 7(2), 14–25.

Alexander, M. (2012). *The new Jim Crow: Mass incarceration in the age of colorblindness* (rev. ed.). New Press.

Barr, S. C., & Neville, H. A. (2014). Racial socialization, color-blind racial ideology, and mental health among Black college students: An examination of an ecological model. *Journal of Black Psychology*, 40(2), 138–165.

Belgrave, F. Z., & Allison, K. W. (2019). *African American psychology: From Africa to America* (4th ed.). Sage.

Bell, D. (2000). *Race, racism, and American law* (4th ed.). Aspen Law & Business.

Bell, D. (2008). *Race, racism, and American law* (6th ed.). Wolters Kluwer.

Bennett, L. (1988). *Before the Mayflower: A history of Black America.* Johnson Publishing.

Berlin, I. (2003). *Generations of captivity: A history of African Americans slaves.* Belknap Press of Harvard University Press.

Blackmon, D. A. (2008). *Slavery by another name.* Anchor.

Blassingame, J. W. (1972). *The slave community: Plantation life in the antebellum South.* Oxford University Press.

Blassingame, J. W. (1979). *The slave community: Plantation life in the antebellum South.* Oxford University Press.

Chafe, W. H., Gavins, R., & Korstad, R. (2001). *Remembering Jim Crow.* New Press.

Dodson, H. (2002). *Jubilee: The emergence of African-American culture.* National Geographic.

Elmore, C. A., & Gaylord-Harden, N. K. (2013). The influence of supportive parenting and racial socialization messages on African American youth behavioral outcomes. *Journal of Child and Family Studies*, 22(1), 63–75.

Gates, L. H., Jr. (2021). *The Black church: This is our story, this is our song.* Penguin.

Horton, J. O., & Horton, L. E. (2005). *Slavery and the making of America.* Oxford University Press.

Horton, R. (1967). African traditional thought and Western science. *Africa*, 37, 155–187. doi:10.2307/1158253.

Johnson, V., & Carter, R. T. (2020). Black cultural strengths and psychological well-being: An empirical analysis with Black American adults. *Journal of Black Psychology*, 46(1), 55–89.
Jones, J. M. (2003). TRIOS: A psychological theory of the African legacy in American culture. *Journal of Social Issues*, 39(1), 217–242.
Joseph, P. E. (2022). *The third reconstruction: America's struggle for racial justice in the twenty-first century*. Basic Books.
Kulikoff, A. (1986). *Tobacco and slaves: The development of Southern cultures in the Chesapeake, 1680–1800*. University of North Carolina Press.
Lesane-Brown, C. L. (2006). A review of race socialization within Black families. *Developmental Review*, 26(4), 400–426.
Levine, L. W. (1977). *Black culture and black consciousness: Afro-American folk thought from slavery to freedom*. Oxford University Press.
Levine, L. W. (2007). *Black culture and black consciousness: Afro-American folk thought from slavery to freedom* (30th anniversary ed.). Oxford University Press.
Mitchell, H. H. (2004). *Black church beginnings: The long-hidden realities of the first years*. Eerdmans.
Pasteur, A. B., & Toldson, I. L. (1982). *Roots of soul: The psychology of Black expressiveness*. Anchor.
Peters, M. F. (1985). Racial socialization of young Black children. In H. P. McAdoo (Ed.). *Black children: Social, educational, and parental environments* (pp. 159–173). Sage.
Reiss, O. (1997). *Blacks in colonial America*. McFarland.
Stevenson, H. C. (1994). Validation of the scale of racial socialization for African American adolescents: Steps toward multidimensionality. *Journal of Black Psychology*, 20(4), 445–468.
Stevenson, H. C. (1995). Relationship of adolescent perceptions of racial socialization to racial identity. *Journal of Black Psychology*, 21(1), 49–70.
Stevenson, H. C., Reed, J., Bodison, P., & Bishop, A. (1996). Kinship social support and adolescent racial socialization beliefs: Extending the self to family. *Journal of Black Psychology*, 22(4), 498–508.
Stuckey, S. (2013). *Slave culture: Nationalist theory and the foundations of Black America* (25th anniversary edition). Oxford.
Sweet, J. H. (2003). *Recreating Africa: Culture, kinship and religion in the African-Portuguese world, 1441–1770*. University of North Carolina Press.
Thornton, M. C., Chatters, L. M., Taylor, R. J., & Allen, W. R. (1990). Sociodemographic and environmental correlates of racial socialization by Black parents. *Child Development*, 61(2), 401–409. doi:10.2307/1131101.
Turner, J. L. (2020). Black mothering in action: The racial-class socialization practices of low-income Black single mothers. *Sociology of Race and Ethnicity*. doi:10.1177/23332649219889683.
Umana-Taylor, A. J., & Hill, N. E. (2020). Ethnic-racial socialization in the family: A decade's advance on precursors and outcomes. *Journal of Marriage and Family*, 82 (1), 244–271. doi:10.1111/jomf.12622.
Villarosa, L. (2022). *Under the skin: The hidden toll of racism on health in America*. Anchor.
Webber, T. L. (1978). *Deep like the rivers: Education in the slave quarter community, 1831–1865*. Norton.

12

CRITICAL DIFFERENCES AMONG BLACKS AND OTHERS REGARDING RACE AND CULTURAL VALUE PREFERENCES

During the middle years of the 20th century, a vital change took place in the minds and hearts of Black people, and it happened in plain sight as the social movement for civil rights unfolded. Blacks experienced a psychological and emotional shift away from thinking of themselves as colored people with all the negative characteristic that came with that reference (although not all Blacks had accepted that negative self-concept). The visible change in self-perception and identity came about when "colored" became "Negros," and that reference was a source of pride and dignity. But what also changed was that Negros who took as an insult—being called "Black"—they embraced Black as their self-proclaimed group reference. They gave the group reference new and powerful meaning, by connecting it to their roots as Africans. They declared themselves to be Black and proud. They openly and publicly recovered their roots as Africans and expressed reverence for their ancestors; they rejected many aspects of white European cultural ways, like names, dress styles, and personal grooming. Many "went natural" and began to value their natural hair, speech, and mannerisms. This chapter endeavors to describe this psychological and emotional transformation.

To do so I return to a discussion of human development that I began in the earlier chapters. All people create meaningful, personal, and related identities from the interaction between their environment and their internal consciousness. What we learn about ourselves comes from those around us, from family, and from others as we grow up, as well as from our own understanding of our circumstances and through our own analyses of ourselves and others around us.

Carter (1995) argues that race and, thus, personal and racial identity issues are salient when a person selects a mate or spouse—provided that the person is able to make such a choice (for many Black women during slavery and the

DOI: 10.4324/9781003111542-17

Jim Crow years, there was no choice). Many enslaved Black women were raped, and many gave birth to the children of their white owners or rapists, who often denied or rejected the child as their own. The child often was not accepted into the white family. But how they came to see themselves was influenced by what they looked like since racial group membership was (and is) defined by skin color, physical features, and language. Each individual, irrespective of their race, comes to some psychological resolution about the meaning and significance of their racial group membership to oneself and in turn to others, a process called racial identity status development. That process also aids and connects to particular racial groups' cultural values and ways of living. Blacks' psychological resolutions to their racial group or their racial identity status is very significant, but not well understood. There is a range of possible resolutions or ways of understanding one's racial group membership. Said another way, not all Black people think of race in the same way. The notions of "Oreos" or "Sambas" capture the idea that Black people for generations have had varied ways of seeing themselves in racial terms.

Embedded in the selection of a mate is a decision, when choice is involved, that has bearing on the children the couple has. Thus, the issue of the children's race and, in time, their possible racial identity status, which may change as the children mature, is influenced by their appearance and skin color. While the number of interracial unions has grown since the period of American history when they were outlawed, there is still considerable social pressure to marry and mate within one's own race. Carter (1995), states:

> A person's worldview, through the lens of racial identity, has implications for how he or she processes information, forms perceptions, understands behavior, and selects and understands what is important. Stewart and Bennett ... argue that racial and cultural assumptions have powerful influences on how a person interprets himself or herself and others. Additionally, a person from any racial/ethnic group who psychologically identifies with traditional White American cultural values uses this orientation to guide his or her thoughts, behaviors, and feelings. Therefore, one's racial identity operates as a filter for one's thoughts, feelings, and behaviors and shapes his or her worldview. Race, racial identity, personality, and one's worldview are ultimately connected and intertwined. If this is the case, then each participant in a therapeutic [or social] relationship brings a particular mental framework that originates from his or her racial identity.
>
> *(pp. 113–114)*

Even within racial groups, skin color issues often are an aspect of mate selection such that a child's potential looks and skin color influence such decisions; while these factors are not always acknowledged consciously, they nevertheless occur even when there was no choice in one's mate or the parent of one's child.

Upon the birth of a child, the process of socialization begins. Much has been written about various aspects of development and socialization such as gender role, cognitive maturation, intellectual functioning, social characteristics, and other aspects of development. Less has been written about racial socialization as it relates to personal and racial identity development. When looking at the importance of race in American history and sociopolitical life, the developmental processes and the life paths of all Americans are affected by race or one's ascribed racial group membership. Just as there is gender role learning that affects one's personal identity and self-concept, so there is racial role socialization, and it influences one's development. Everyone, irrespective of their ascribed racial group, receives messages about the appropriateness or inappropriateness of their racially based behavior, thoughts, and emotions (Carter, 1995, 2005). The messages received by Black people are such that they may have to devote considerable psychic energy attempting to overcome or navigate society's evaluations, which for Blacks has been and is still generally negative; thus, the mental energy becomes a central theme for one's personal identity development and therefore is related to their racial group membership and its personal meaning.

As stated earlier, development begins with birth and is accompanied by characteristics and attributes that inform one's developmental process. Markers such as skin color and physical features are biologically determined and at the same time inform one's social makeup. As children begin to mature physically, emotionally, socially, and psychologically, they do so in the context of their family structure. What this means is that children begin to learn about their identity, personal and racial, through the modeling of their parents and other adults around them, which Carter (1995) says begins within the first few months of life.

Research (Carter, 1995, 2005; Helms, 1995; Thompson & Carter, 2013) has focused on the development of healthy racial identity. Young Black children are said to internalize the prevailing deprecating and demeaning perspectives about them because of their race and might begin to challenge these negative aspects of their personal and racial identity only as they mature, perhaps as teenagers (Thomson & Carter, 2013) or after maturing to a level at which logical thinking is available. We have seen that the negative views of Black people have been and are being transmitted in effective ways such that most whites and many Blacks adopted, communicated, and lived according to these portrayals. When Blacks attend schools or are engaged in any form that is in essence their educational process, the lessons therein contribute to communicating important notions about Black people's abilities and their characters. Educators or care providers were and are clearly perpetrators of this vast and daunting race-based injustice, operating as cultural educators (Helms & Piper, 1994; Webber, 1978). The notion of a racial role as an aspect of development is consistent with Bronfenbrenner's ecological model of human development.

Racial Identity Attitudes: Concepts and Evidence

Racial identity status refers to the fact that all people, regardless of their race, ascribe different psychological meanings and cultural investment to their presummed racial group membership. It is this meaning and cultural value preferences that determine how an individual makes sense of the world and themselves as racial beings (Helms, 1990). Racial identity is composed of a person's thoughts (cognitions), feelings (affective states), behaviors, and cultural worldview (Carter, 1995; Helms, 1990; Thompson & Carter, 2013). This is why racial identity status is important in understanding Black cultural strengths and psychological variation since it goes beyond one's skin color and physical features and includes psychological perspectives, emotional states, and cultural worldviews.

Racial identity theorists argue that one's race alone does not determine the type of resolution one adopts (Helms, 1990; Sue et al., 2019). The variability in racial identity statuses is reflected in the range of behaviors and thoughts people hold. To illustrate, some individuals believe race does not matter, others are confused about the importance of race, while some think and act in ways to suggest that race is all that matters and, therefore, they maintain racial inequality. Still others regard race as a complex aspect of their personality and behave accordingly. Given the variation in how people understand the meaning of their race, this can influence a person's personal development, interpersonal interactions, and social relationships. Racial identity is not specific to Black people, but it was observed in them prior to its application to other racial groups (e.g., whites and people of color; see Helms, 1984; Helms & Carter, 1990). As such, an understanding of racial identity theory and a method to directly apply that understanding is highly meaningful in mental health service and treatment interventions. As well as for economic and socio-political activies (Carter & Johnson, 2019; Carter & Pieterse, 2020).

It is important to note that while many scholars wrote explicitly about racial identity in the years after the civil rights movement, I contend that the psychological variation that became more evident in that time has always existed from the time Africans were subjected to racial slavery. The psychological stances were more apparent during the civil rights movement because a psychological and emotional transformation was visible and took place in public view as an entire people changed their self-identification from the imposed label of "colored" to proclaiming themselves to be "Black"—a term that was deeply offensive when directed at a Negro or colored person. Black people took an insult that had led to within-group fights and anger and converted it to a label that was embraced as a source of pride, honor, and dignity. Seeing these psychological and cultural issues unfold in the context of the social movement for civil rights and Black power helped scholars to document something that existed but was less visible before the civil rights era. These events and the way Blacks transformed their group identity—as well as their individual psychology and cultural preferences surrounding race—served as the basis for the theories, research, and measures of racial identity that emerged initially in the 1960s and 1970s but have grown since that time to encompass a wider range of racial groups and experiences. What makes the racial identity work valuable is that, in time, theorists rejected the notion that Black people were devoid of culture, and many scholars observing the group identity transformation that occurred during the decades of the civil rights and Black Power movements (1950s–1970s) described how some Black people reclaimed their cultural roots and heritage in the face of a hostile societal reaction. Yet, even as Blacks struggled for recognition, they had to live with racial oppression and had to manage the developmental processes associated with nurturing their families and maintaining their communities.

Racial Identity in the Psychological Literature

Scholars have described behavioral and psychological variation among Blacks (e.g., Black, 2007; Du Bois, 1903/1965; Fanon, 1952/1967). For instance, Du Bois (1903/1965) introduced the notion of double consciousness in his book *Souls of Black Folk* in 1903. He described double consciousness, according to Black (2007), as the Negro in America having a veil that gifted him with second sight. The veil prevented the Negro from having true self-consciousness; rather, the Negro saw himself through the lens of the other world. The double consciousness functioned as a sensation in that one looked at oneself through the eyes of the others. The view offered a perspective of one's soul, and of a world that saw the Negro with amused contempt and pity. The feeling of twoness was constant—one was an American and a Negro: two souls, two thoughts, two conflicting ideals in one body, a body that was held together by sheer strength of effort and will (Black, 2007). So, for Du Bois and other scholars, there was psychological complexity associated with being Black. However, what became more apparent in the 1960s was deeper and more nuanced, and it also revealed cultural value perspectives in which a Black person could select a psychological status that meant she endorsed white cultural values, or he could be confused and move between both white and Black values, and it was possible to have Black/African-centered cultural values. These variations were—and are—possible and applicable to Black individuals, but this variation had not been as clearly addressed in the past.

Psychologists and racial scholars, as a reaction to the public transformation that occurred, presented several models to capture the various ways that Blacks thought about themselves and others. Vontress (1970) suggested that mental health professionals should be aware that there could be three types of Black clients: (1) the "colored" client, who was white-identified and thought of themselves from the perspective of a white cultural worldview and standards; (2) the "Negro" client, who was confused about their and others' race; and (3) the "Black" client, who was described as no longer ashamed of their African heritage and asserted their African beliefs and cultural worldview. For Vontress, each client would present, as a result of their race identity, with a markedly distinct orientation in life, and he warned mental health professionals of the potential variation these race identity perspectives would mean in their interactions with clients. Other scholars observing the social movement and the psychological and cultural transformation in the behavior and attitudes of Blacks proposed types, and some introduced stages of the Black identity development processes. One of the most influential models was called Nigrescence, which follows the Negro-to-Black conversion process (Cross, 1971). Nigrescence is defined as ideas that describe the developmental course that occurs in the process of becoming and being a Black-identified person.

For most scholars of Black identity, being Black was not about one's skin color alone; rather, being Black referred to how one thought about and judged oneself and one's social or reference group as well as one's opposing racial group. Scholars (see Helms, 1990) stated that racial identity or one's reference group was distinct but related to one's personal identity. In fact, the notion that personal identity merged with reference group identity was believed to occur only at the highest level of Black identity. It was suggested that for healthy racial and personal development to occur, Black people needed to reject identification with white culture and white standards, and it was posited by some that being white-identified was unhealthy even if it was seen as a survival mechanism. The position that being white-identified was not healthy was a direct departure from the notion of assimilation promoted by B. T. Washington and others like him, which had prevailed in American society as the appropriate path for Blacks to follow to be accepted members of mainstream society.

Yet there were differences in how Black identity scholars thought about the link between reference group and personal identity. Some argued that they were separate, and others held that the two were intertwined. In the beginning, for the most part, theorists working independently of one another put forth similar Black racial identity models in which one moved from one racial identity level to another. In essence, this progression meant moving from white-identified to a Black-oriented racial and cultural identity, and some believe that this progression reflects movement from unhealthy to healthy psychological and emotional resolutions of racial identity. As Helms (1990) points out, theorists varied in how they named and described this process, and each differed from the other.

For instance, Thomas (1971) suggested that there were two white-oriented phases, while Jackson (1975) argued that there was only one. There was also variation in the sequence of the phases. Each theorist proposed that Black people's psychological resolution regarding their race and racial group and that of others' race transformed from negative to positive about their racial group membership, and with this shift came a change in cultural worldview and values.

A variety of theorists presented models, but the theories presented by Thomas (1971), Cross (1971), and Parham and Helms (1981) were used in the mental health literature and, moreover, were subjected to the most empirical research inquiry and investigations. Cross's initial model was later revised and changed by Helms and colleagues, and it was tested empirically. Later, Cross and colleagues (Vandiver et al., 2001) updated and revised his original model and introduced an instrument for empirical analysis called the Cross Racial Identity Scale. These scholars and researchers identified and described the important transformation that occurs in Black people.

Thomas (1971) thought there was a phase he called *negromachy*, which refers to an identity that was approved and affirmed by whites and a self-concept that was devoid of race and likely dominated during the slave era and beyond. He believed that Black people had to retreat into themselves to locate their Black identity. Thomas's second phase was Blacks *testifying* about their self-denial and rejection of Blackness, and he believed that Blacks had to confront their distress surrounding becoming Black; with *information* regarding Black heritage and culture, they would be led toward *processing* and withdrawal into a worldview that was grounded in the experiences and values of the Black community. This would trigger the *activity* phase, which involved being Black through social action. In time, Blacks would move to what he called a *transcendental* phase, which described a state of transition and where they move beyond using social and cultural meaning; they are now emotionally and psychologically centered in Black identity and cultural values (Hall, Cross, & Freedle, 1972).

Cross presented his notions about the Negro-to-Black process in 1970 and 1971 when he proposed a stage model of the changes he observed. His ideas and model were similar to that of Thomas even though they had worked independently from one another. Cross proposed four stepwise stages. The first *Pre-encounter* involves the idealization of white American worldviews and acceptance of them as the dominant sociocultural status. At the same time, people with this worldview do not see themselves as racial beings but rather as people absent of race; thus, they are colorblind or human beings who happen to be Black. The other phases are called *Encounter*, *Immersion-Emersion*, and *Internalization*. The four stages describe a process in which a person discovers their Blackness, thus, once they embrace their Blackness, it is possible for them to believe that they are Black and not inferior.

Pre-encounter refers to the old Negro worldview that rejects Blackness, while *Encounter* involves two steps, a jolting experience or series of experiences that lead to questions about the old Black worldview and tests of the new perceptions about the previous non-racial identity. The result of the Encounter is that the old views fail to work, and the person searches for new ways of viewing one's Blackness, which triggers movement to *Immersion-Emersion*, where the psychological, emotional, and cultural transformations occur along with an effort to dismantle the old identity. It is necessary to withdraw into a Black world either physically or, if this is not possible, psychologically. Several thoughts and behaviors emerge during this phase. As the transition from the old non-racial view to the Black person begins, this process requires that aspects of the former identity be replaced with the new Black-African-centered perspective. In this phase,

> the person's level of Blackness is high, but the degree of internalization of the new identity is minimal. This period of emergent identity or "just discovered Blackness" is manifested in the construction of the correct ideology and/or world view, glorification of African heritage, either/or thinking, blacker-than-thou attitudes, unrealistic expectations concerning the efficacy of Black Power, and the tendency to denigrate White people and White culture while simultaneously deifying Black people and Black culture.
>
> *(Cross, 1980, p. 85)*

Immersion is followed by an emergence characterized by a leveling off of intense emotions and thoughts, and one experiences "affective and cognitive openness" (Cross, 1980, p. 85); thus, the person is able to be more critical in her analysis of race and cultural differences. It is possible to see both the pluses and minuses of Black society, and psychological and emotional control returns, marking the end of the period and the beginning of *Internalization*. Conflicts between the worldviews of the old non-racial identity and the Black aspects of one's identity are resolved, and one is able to use one's race as their main reference group.

Theory is important, but such complex experiences require empirical evidence that shows how people actually function. In an empirical investigation, Parham and Helms (1981) used a Black racial identity attitude scale to predict Black people's preferences for the race of their counselors. In this groundbreaking study several things were done. Parham and Helms contrasted studies that used race as a demographic variable for racial self-designation and compared that with a measure of internal psychological variation of racial identity attitudes regarding how Blacks thought of themselves in racial terms. They applied the comparison to Black college students' preferences for Black or white counselors; thus, they introduced psychological variation of Blacks into the area of mental health. Parham and Helms (1981) stated that

> racial identity refers to a person's beliefs or attitudes about her or his own race, whereas racial self-designation refers to one's own racial group

> membership. Self-designation need not reflect one's own racial attitudes but more likely reflects the zeitgeist.
>
> *(p. 251)*

Parham and Helms (1981) constructed the Black racial identity attitudes scale for the study and found evidence that Black racial identity attitudes were related to Black clients' preferences for Black and white counselors in a manner consistent with theory. Pre-encounter attitudes were related to preferences for white and not Black counselors, while Encounter and Immersion-Emersion attitudes were related to preferences for Black counselors, and Internalization did not reveal any racial preferences. Thus, the study established the merit of within-group psychological differences among Black Americans.

Helms (1990) restated and revised the Black racial identity model to emphasize that it was an aspect of personality and part of one's racial self-concept. She also proposed at least two phases for each racial identity attitude or status and provided more detailed descriptions of each level as well as the transitions from one to the other. The view of racial identity as a component of self is based on the notion that it is also related to one's cultural values and group preferences. Carter and Helms (1987), in a related study, tested that notion empirically, reporting that Black

> racial identity attitudes predicted three of the five Afro-centric values [Harmony with Nature, Doing Activity, and Collateral Social Relations] and none of the Euro-centric [based on Euro-American philosophy] alternatives. Immersion-Emersion and Internalization attitudes significantly predicted belief in Collateral Social Relations ... [meaning that social relations are governed by the will of the group over the wishes of individuals]. In addition ... Internalization attitudes were also predictive of a belief in Harmony with Nature and Doing Activity orientations.... Empirical support for Boykin's (1983) and Nobles' (1980) contentions that vestiges of African philosophy beliefs have been retained by Afro-American culture and are expressed by the self-actualizing Afro-American.
>
> *(p. 193)*

Cross, Parham, and Helms (1991) reviewed multiple Black racial identity models and sought to show similarities and differences between them. The review illustrated how the descriptions of the phases of identity varied little. The early phase, Pre-encounter, was described as being related to rejection of group identity or of racial group membership. Theorists like Thomas (1971) thought that this identity was associated with subservience, extreme anger, and maladaptive emotions and behavior, while other theorists attributed issues of worldview and generic values to this identity phase. The movement from this first phase or status is a transitional period is marked by experiences that challenge the prior beliefs. In other words, people learn that race does matter to them. The event(s) that communicate that race does matter often come as a shock, and adjustment to the disruption is necessary, which begins the process of identity change and reevaluation.

The third phase is the one with the most abrupt and intense changes to a person's identity as a Black person. It is the level when the person transitions from the old to the new identity—in a sequential manner. These changes need to be fed by knowledge and must be fueled by energy and social support. The person then constructs a desired self-image and works to erect the desired and fantasized self. This process requires considerable support from like-minded group members, and it helps if the person can withdraw into an exclusively Black world, either in physical or psychological ways. This phase goes from withdrawal to emersion from the isolation, and the intensity of learning a new identity wanes, so an evenness is achieved in psychological and emotional terms. This new level of awareness allows for more openness in thoughts and feelings as well as a more balanced understanding of Black society, past and present, and of whites.

The last step in the transformation is marked by the process of integration and synthesis in which the person must get the parts of his identity to work in concert; thus, the person is Black, male, middle class, a Christian, an urban dweller. It is no longer necessary to split off part of oneself to fit in a hostile society; at the same time, cultural considerations come to the fore and must be acknowledged and integrated.

That is, Blacks live in two cultural worlds—in some instances, separate, and in others, interwoven. Blacks in the United States are American and were socialized as such and are Black, which involves cultural beliefs and behaviors that are distinct and apart from those of mainstream Americans. We see from the descriptions that Black identity is part of personal identity and thus would influence socialization beliefs and other possible cultural practices. Internalization also functions as a defense against racism and arms the person with the ability and awareness to monitor the social environment for potential racial acts. The person's primary reference group is Black American, and yet she still can view the world from various perspectives and is open to a range of viewpoints. Furthermore, some contend that internalization assists people in being proactive and rising above the previous identity outlooks and is therefore able to connect to other aspects of self-identity (i.e., gender, age, class) and that of others.

Parham and Helms (1981) discussed the idea that people can cycle through the stage over their lifespans, and they discussed Helms's notion of worldviews. In essence, Helms contends that each stage represents a distinct worldview or identity. For racial identity scholars, "the racial identity stages refer to that portion of the person's (internal) and society's (external) definition of the worth and salience of the group to which one is ascribed" (Cross, Parham, & Helms, 1991, p. 334).

Helms (1990) and colleagues proposed that racial identity development was not a stagewise or linear process; rather, they (e.g., Carter, 1995; Carter & Johnson, 2019; Cross, Parham, & Helms, 1991; Helms, 1996) described statuses wherein a person possessed all the racial identity statuses but to varying degrees of influence. The status that was used more than others tends to be more dominant and thus occupies more psyche space. If information was not processed well or effectively by the dominant status, then one might begin to rely on other statuses; then that status would grow to have more influence.

The revised thinking also meant that measurement procedures needed to be revised and instruments had to be used differently to capture the complexity of racial identity status attitudes. But there were two debates occurring among scholars regarding racial identity. One had to do with whether development was linear or sequential. The other point of debate centered around the issue of whether racial identity was primarily a group orientation, set apart from one's personal identity or if personal and group racial identity were intertwined. Cross, Parham, and Helms (1998) and Cross (1991) argued that personal identity (PI) and reference group orientation (RGO) were distinct and not related. While Helms and her colleagues took the position that racial and personal identity were psychologically connected and not separate, they also believed that racial identity development was sequential, not linear or stagewise.

Cross, Parham, and Helms (1998) reviewed the empirical literature associated with racial identity, and they examined two bodies of research investigations, one that focused on RGO issues (i.e., group characteristics such as ideology) and another that looked into PI issues. In particular, the researchers looked for correlates between racial identity and PI, such as anxiety or self-esteem.

From their examination of the literature of RGO and PI, Cross, Parham, and Helms (1998) found that RGO and PI were not predictive of one another, meaning that one's personal identity as measured by self-esteem and related characteristics was unrelated to group orientation as measured by ideology or related constructs. They also found that there was little change in one's PI for those who experience the Nigrescence process—going through the Negro-to-Black conversion. This does not mean there is no relationship between RGO and PI, just that no relationship was found when looking at the available literature. Yet they also noted that there was some evidence to suggest that indirect measures of the RGO and PI relationship did reveal some connections between the two states:

> Pre-encounter types did enter the Nigrescence process with PI deficits directly linked to the dynamics of their negative racial identity. More specifically, when characterized by (1) a Eurocentric perspective, (2) a tendency to feel distant, unsupported and unaffiliated with other Blacks, and (3) a tendency to hold negative stereotypes about other Blacks, the Pre-encounter profile has been linked to problems of low self-esteem, hypersensitivity,

> hostility, increased anxiety, tension, a defeatist attitude and a diminished level of self-actualization. Since such a pattern accounts for very little variance, it appears that although oppression has, in far too many cases, succeed in promoting a Eurocentric orientation and identity in Pre-encounter Negros, it is equally true that most Pre-encounter types have not internalized racist thinking about other Blacks, they nurture and relish the support of Black friends and associates and they feel good about themselves, personally.
>
> *(Cross, Parham, & Helms, 1998, p. 49)*

Moreover, studies reviewed also showed that the Negro-to-Black conversion process was more likely to have an impact on RGO than PI spheres of a Black person's self-image. These researchers found evidence that, unlike what earlier scholars would have us believe (e.g., the Clarks' doll studies that linked RGO preferences to self-esteem when the two seemed unrelated; see Cross, 1991), PI and RGO are not necessarily merged or related. In the doll studies, the Clarks, husband-and-wife psychologists, conducted studies using dolls with Black children and found that Black preschoolers preferred white dolls over Blacks ones when offered a chance, leading the Clarks to infer that the Black children lacked self-esteem. Their results were cited in the *Brown v. Board of Education* Supreme Court decision in 1954, which altered racial segregation in schools. The research about RGO and PI indicated that a person with Pre-encounter attitudes, or pro-white/anti-Black views, does not suffer from poor mental health or hates themselves, as suggested in the Clarks' doll studies, where Black children seemed to hold negative views of themselves that could raise to self-hatred.

In other words, one's RGO can change without there being a corresponding shift in PI. Furthermore, these scholars noted in their review that racial identity should not be thought of as stages or types but as aspects of people that are continuous and multifaceted.

> Our repeated emphasis on "process" is not accidental, for we believe that the development of racial identity attitudes is a phenomenon which occurs over time. In attempting to isolate the correlates of nigrescence, however, our discussion does allow the reader to construct a profile of the "typical" Black person whose racial attitudes correspond to one of the four identity stages. While the typology approach we adopted was necessary to facilitate our outline and discussion of the material, it in no way was it intended to imply that we believe "typing" or classifying people by stage is the most appropriate use of the model. On the contrary, classifying according to a single stage may lead to less appropriate interpretations, because such a procedure connotes rigidity and stagnation, and clouds the potential for change and growth which more accurately characterizes the nigrescence process.
>
> *(Cross, Parham, & Helms, 1998, p. 61)*

Helms and Piper (1994) described the nature of how racial identity operates as a continuous part of one's ego or personality and should be considered a circumplex, or circle, as a way to illustrate how racial identity occupies cognitive space and shifts from one status to another depending upon what the person needs to process racial information. Helms (1996) restated the distinctions between race and ethnicity. Where race and ethnicity are not interchangeable, ethnicity reflects one's country of origin and is associated with cultural patterns to maintain one's cultural connection, which can change; race, however, was established by law and custom and is not changeable. Helms (1996) pointed out that race and ethnicity are not the same even though people use the terms as if they have the same meaning. She also highlighted how racial identity is an ego status, not a fixed type or stage; rather, she contended that racial identity ego statuses influence how people process race-related information.

Since our society is structured on the basis of race, that includes a considerable amount of information. Helms pointed out that "identity" involves both perceptions of self and community in that people strive for a healthy identity, a means coming to terms with personal continuity that aligns with one's collective context or culture. Thus, one seeks to be "integrated into that community by adequately fulfilling social roles given the relevant historical circumstances" (Helms, 1996, p. 152). The purpose of the Helms (1996) article was to address both conceptual and measurement issues in the application of racial identity theory and to illustrate how best to use measurement instruments.

In that vein, she reviewed what she called general principles of racial identity—namely, that racial identity pertains to the psychological results of being raised in a racially oppressive social system where some are advantaged and others disadvantaged due to the racial group membership of each. Furthermore, the presumed biological nature of race is not relevant since race is a social construct. What matters more is how a person reacts internally to the notion that she belongs to a so-called racial group. This internal process operates because people in the United States are treated as if they belong to separate racial groups, where little or no overlap is allowed. If a person is in fact racially mixed, their physical appearance drives how they are perceived and classified. The implication of racial group membership is that members of some groups are presumed superior and as such hold the favored socio-political positions in society, and those thought to be unworthy are people of color who hold lower positions in the social order, usually with Blacks at the bottom and other people of color in the middle. Thus, there is a contrast group for racial identity; for whites, it is usually Blacks or people of color, and for Blacks, it is whites. Helms pointed out that her models of Black, people of color, and white racial identity have some points in common. The development of racial identity involves one's contrast group, and healthy development is reflected in letting go of the socially imposed racial definition in exchange for one's own self-identity. The process of racial identity is sequential, in which "increasingly more sophisticated differentiation of the ego evolves from earlier or less mature statuses" (Helms, 1996, p. 155), and there are variations in how racial identity is expressed, which can be measured.

As is clear, aspects of Black racial identity serve to the betterment of Blacks' psychological functioning. In addition to having a profound impact on an individual's functioning, Black racial identity impacts the behaviors one undertakes. For African-centered practices and orientations to have lasted through centuries in a society that devalues them, there must have been an appreciation and an evolutionary need for them. Those who possess positive views of their racial group and of other racial groups have been shown to be the most psychologically healthy (Pieterse & Carter, 2010). These individuals inherently appreciate Black culture and thus may communicate the need for others, especially their offspring, to appreciate these cultural practices and values.

Historians, sociologists, and educators have written about the unwavering importance of the Black family (Gutman & Berlin, 1987). The racial identities of the elders (grandparents, parents, uncles, and aunts) have historically been important mechanisms by which information and stories were, and still are, passed down from generation to generation. The absence of a developed Black racial identity in these individuals may foreclose the transmission of important lessons and messages about one's race to Black children, thus creating a deficit in the children's ability to reach a developed and positive Black racial identity. A positive racial identity is first and foremost a necessity in maintaining Black cultural strength through generations. Once a person has developed a positive racial identity, they can pass on Black cultural values and beliefs to younger Blacks. The process by which racial practices are encouraged and by which racial orientations are fostered is *racial socialization*.

Racial socialization fosters racial identity in generations of Black people. Many Blacks have taken to protesting, while others have asserted themselves in other ways, including those who silently behaved in ways that represented Blacks and the group's values. Others rejected the same path and focused on being accepted and valued as a person who happens to be Black, and they achieve from that vantage point.

Practice Implications

Racial identity status attitudes have been incorporated into models of racial inclusion and relationship types (Carter, 1995; Carter & Helms, 1992; Carter & Johnson, 2019). Carter and Johnson have also presented measurements and an assessment method that allow clinicians and researchers to determine the relative strength of a person's statuses. They reported on three possibilities. Before I get to that, I first offer a brief review of relationship types.

To date, racial identity development models and measures have been used in empirical research for all racial groups. Models created for whites are characterized by abandonment of racism and the development of a nonracist identity, while models for people of color describe a process characterized by the abandonment of reliance on white culture for self-definition to an acceptance of a positive racial-cultural identity as a member of a non-dominant racial group (Helms, 1995). Patterns of resolutions, however, are similar across racial groups and exist in a circle where a status may have more space than another, not in stages (Helms & Piper, 1994). The following is a summary of the models of whites and people of color (POC) and major empirical findings related to these models and their scales. The least mature and more external racial identity status attitudes are *Contact* (whites), *Conformity* (Asians, Native Americans, and Latinx), and *Pre-encounter* (Blacks)—statuses associated with the denial of racism or endorsement of a colorblind worldview. *Disintegration* (whites), *Dissonance* (POC), and *Encounter* (Blacks) are also externally defined statuses characterized by conflict or confusion about the meaning of one's race, as are *Reintegration* and *Pseudo-Independence* (whites). These statuses are characterized by in-racial-group idealization and active out-racial-group rejection, while *Immersion-Emersion* (own-group idealization and less out group rejection during the emersion phase) or *Resistance* (POC) status attitudes reflect recognition of one race and group membership and the accompanying emotions. Emotional reflection makes it possible to integrate race into one's personal identity structure. This leads to the more mature and internal racial identity status attitudes of *Internalization* (POC) and *Autonomy* (whites), which are generally associated with the resolution of conflict regarding racial differences, the acceptance of race and of self as a racial being, and the development of racial identity that is not based on notions of inferiority or supremacy.

Helms's (1984) Interaction model for therapy process and outcome and Carter's (1995) racially inclusive model of therapy identified four different types of interaction (i.e., *Parallel, Crossed, Progressive*, and *Regressive*) in therapist-client dyads or groups or social interactions that are determined by the pairing of patient-therapist (less and more powerful) racial identity status attitudes, regardless of their respective demographic racial groups (Helms, 1990). The pairings create the dynamics, both as processes and as outcomes, of the clinical encounters or social interaction. Each distinct pairing is described as a relationship type, for it is not the therapy participant's race or skin color that characterizes the relationship type but how the participant's and therapist's racial identity status attitudes combine. Moreover, Carter (1995) suggested that varied cognitive processes, affective states, actions, and reactions to the therapy relationship characterize the different types of relationships, and he presents evidence of how the therapy process is in fact so affected. A *Parallel* relationship is one in which the counselor and clients are similar in their racial identity development. Thus, both may hold the same attitudes, or both may be confused or immersed in their respective racial groups. A *Crossed* relationship occurs when the therapist and patient hold basically opposite attitudes about racial groups. For instance, if, in a Black/white therapy dyad, the therapist held anti-Black/pro-white attitudes and the patient held pro-Black/anti-white attitudes, this dyad would be crossed. These are rare, and we expect the relationship would not last long, if at all. A *Progressive* relationship involves a therapist whose racial identity status attitudes are more mature than the patient's. For instance, an Asian therapist (*Immersion-Emersion*) working with a Native American patient who was characterized by *Dissonance* status attitudes and was confused about his racial identity. A progressive relationship may be associated with the therapist's ability to recognize race and racial issues and is able to express genuine race-based empathy and acceptance (having had a similar experiences). The therapist would be able to guide the client's self-exploration. In a progressive type of relationship, one would expect the session to be perceived as positive and perhaps beneficial by both parties, and one might also find moderate levels of anger and anxiety (Carter & Helms, 1992). In a *Regressive* relationship the patient has a more mature racial identity status development than the therapist, and therefore the regressive relationship is conflictual; the parties have more negative perceptions about the sessions and have higher levels of anxiety and hostility due to both of them struggling for control of the session when racial issues are the topic (Carter, 1995).

Several scholars have contributed to the literature on racial identity by offering models and measures (e.g., Cross & Vandiver, 2001; Helms & Carter, 1990; Sellers et al., 1997). The theory and measures put forth by Helms and her colleagues (Helms, 1990, 1996; Thompson & Carter, 2013) are a focus in this discussion because they apply to all racial groups (whites, POC; see Carter & Johnson, 2019) in the United States, not just Blacks (the focus of the other theories and measures). What follows are guidelines for a way to use the instruments for an individual and apply the results directly to clients and inform practice. We recommend that the person-centered method of assessing racial identity be employed (Carter & Johnson, 2019).

The personal or individual approach is based on assessing the relative strength of endorsement of a particular racial identity status for an individual compared to its adjacent status and how they can be understood as a racial identity profile (see Carter & Johnson, 2019, for scoring steps). The profile scoring procedure produces three sets of profiles (and when done for a sample, the profiles can be arranged into groups). The status attitudes are compared to assess whether they differ significantly from one another, which is called strength of endorsement. There are three strength-of-endorsement profile types: *Undifferentiated or Flat,* wherein there are no significant differences between the contiguous status comparisons; *Dominant,* where one status is high (greater than 1 standard error of difference) or very high (2 standard errors of difference) and all others are equal; or *Blended*, when more than one status is either high or very high.

The various profile configurations reveal some of the complexity that previous studies that used subscale mean scores did not reveal and thereby can help the clinician in their understanding of the influence of racial identity statuses on an individual's psychological functioning. Since racial identity is an aspect of the personality and occupies space in the ego structure as statuses, it can vary in terms of how much space each status occupies. Racial identity involves maturation from an externally defined meaning of one's race, to an internally defined and more differentiated ego status, which is not a matter of levels or developmental stages. Moreover, one can assume that the profile configuration can be associated with unique emotional and behavioral expressions, thus helping therapists and clients fully grasp all of the nuances of racial identity status expressions. Carter and Johnson (2019) state that

> in order to work from a racially inclusive model, clinicians should heed the following steps; …
>
> … Assessment at the outset of treatment should examine the systemic (e.g., ideologies, social climate), psychosocial (e.g., parents, family, friends), psychological (e.g., coping mechanisms), and personal (e.g., skin color) aspects of race for the client.
>
> *(p. 53)*

To do so, clinicians need not *ask* about the significance of race for the client. Clinicians give a racial identity measure to generate the strength of endorsement profile for a client or their own racial identity configuration. Clinicians should not attribute issues of race to resistance. The therapist's racial identity is as important to therapy outcomes as that of the clients. Clinicians should consider their own racial identity and determine if their dyad is *Parallel, Crossed, Progressive*, or *Regressive*, and they should be conscious of the barriers to the therapy process (e.g. hostility from the therapist or client) and outcomes (e.g., abrupt or early termination).

References

Black, M. (2007, Summer). Fanon and DuBoisian double consciousness. *Human Architecture: Journal of Sociological of Self-Knowledge*, V, Special Double Issue, 393–403.

Boykin, W. A., (1983). The academic performance of Afro-American children. In J. T. Spence (Ed.). *Achievement and achievement motives: Psychological and sociological approaches* (pp. 321–372). W. H. Freeman.

Carter, R. T. (1995). *The influence of race and racial identity in psychotherapy*. Wiley.

Carter, R. T. (Ed.). (2005). *Handbook of racial-cultural psychology and counseling*, Vol. 1, *Theory and research*. Wiley.
Carter, R. T., & Helms, J. E. (1987). The relationship of Black value-orientations to racial identity attitudes. *Measurement and Evaluation in Counseling and Development*, 19, 185–195.
Carter, R. T., & Helms, J. E. (1992). The counseling process defined by relationship types: A test of Helms' interactional model. *Journal of Multicultural Counseling and Development*, 20(4), 181–201.
Carter, R. T., & Johnson, V. (2019). Racial identity statuses: Applications to practice. *Practice Innovations*, 4(1), 42–58.
Carter, R. T., & Pieterse, A. (2020). *Measuring the effects of racism: Guidelines for the assessment and treatment of race-based traumatic stress injury*. Columbia University Press.
Cross, W. E., Jr. (1971). The Negro-to-Black conversion experience: Toward a psychology of Black liberation. *Black World*, 20(9), 13–27.
Cross, W. E., Jr. (1980). Models of psychological Nigrescence: A literature review. In R. L. Jones (Ed.). *Black psychology* (2nd ed., pp. 81–98). Harper & Row.
Cross, W. E., Jr. (1991). *Shades of Black: Diversity in African-American identity*. Temple University Press.
Cross, W. E., Parham, T. A., & Helms, J. A. (1991). The stages of Black identity development: Nigrescence models. In R. L. Jones (Ed.). *Black psychology* (3rd ed., pp. 319–338). Cobb & Henry.
Cross, W. E., Parham, T. A., & Helms, J. A. (1998). Nigrescence revisited: Theory and research. In R. L. Jones (Ed.). *African American identity development* (pp. 3–73). Cobb & Henry.
Cross, W. E., Jr., & Vandiver, B. J. (2001). Nigrescence theory and measurement: Introducing the Cross Racial Identity Scale (CRIS). In J. G. Ponterotto, J. M. Casas, L. A. Suzuki, & C. M. Alexander (Eds.). *Handbook of multicultural counseling* (pp. 93–112). Sage.
Du Bois, W. E. B. (1965). *The souls of Black folks: In three Negro classics*. Avon Books.
Fanon, F. (1967). *Black skin, white masks*. (C. L. Markmann, Trans.) Grove Weidenfeld.
Gutman, H. G., & Berlin, I. (1987). *Power and culture: Essays on the American working class*. Pantheon.
Hall, W. S., Cross, W. E., & Freedle, R. (1972). *Stages in the development of Black awareness: An exploratory investigation*. In R. L. Jones (Ed.). *Black psychology* (pp. 156–165). Harper & Row.
Helms, J. E. (1984). Toward a theoretical explanation of the effects of race on counseling: A Black and White model. *Counseling Psychologist*, 12(3–4), 153–165. doi:10.1177/0011000084124013.
Helms, J. E. (1990). *Black and white racial identity: Theory, research, and practice*. Greenwood.
Helms, J. E. (1995). An update of Helms's white and people of color racial identity models. In J. G. Ponterotto, J. M. Casas, L. A. Suzuki, & C. M. Alexander (Eds.). *Handbook of multicultural counseling* (pp. 181–198). Sage.
Helms, J. E. (1996). Toward a methodology for measuring and assessing racial as distinguished from ethnic identity. In G. Roysircar Sodowsky & J. Impara (Eds.). *Multicultural assessment in counseling and clinical psychology*. Buros Institute of Mental Measurement University of Nebraska-Lincoln.

Helms, J. E., & Carter, R. T. (1990). The development of the white racial identity inventory. In J. E. Helms (Ed.). *Black and white racial identity attitudes: Theory, research, and practice* (pp. 67–80). Greenwood.

Helms, J. E., & Piper, R. E. (1994). Implications of racial identity theory for vocational psychology. *Journal of Vocational Behavior*, 44(2), 124–138. doi:10.1006/jvbe.1994.1009.

Jackson, B. (1975). Black identity development. In L. H. Golubchick & B. Persky (Eds.). *Urban, social, and educational issues* (pp. 158–164). A Doctorate Association of New York Educators series. Kendal Hall.

Nobles, W. E. (1980). African philosophy: Foundations for Black psychology. In R. L. Jones (Ed.). *Black psychology* (2nd ed., pp. 23–36). Harper & Row.

Parham, T. A., & Helms, J. E. (1981). The influence of Blacks students: Racial identity attitudes on preference for counselor's race. *Journal of Counseling Psychology*, 28, 250–257.

Pieterse, A. L., & Carter, R. T. (2010). The role of racial identity in perceived racism and psychological stress among Black American adults: Exploring traditional and alternative approaches. *Journal of Applied Social Psychology*, 40(5), 1028–1063.

Sellers, R. M., Rowley, S. A. J., Chavous, T. M., Shelton, J. N., & Smith, M. A. (1997). Multidimensional inventory of Black identity: A preliminary investigation of reliability and construct validity. *Journal of Personality and Social Psychology*, 3 (1), 805–815.

Sue, D. W., Sue, D., Neville, H., & Smith, L. (2019). *Counseling the culturally diverse: Theory and practice* (8th ed.). Wiley.

Thomas, C. (1971). *Boys no more: A Black psychologist's view of community*. Glencoe Press.

Thompson, C. E., & Carter, R. T. (Eds.). (2013). *Racial identity development theory: Applications to individual, group and organizational interventions*. Erlbaum.

Vandiver, B. J., Fhagen-Smith, P. E., Cokley, K. O., Cross, W. E., Jr., & Worrell, F. C. (2001). Crosses' Nigrescence model: From theory to scale to theory. *Journal of Multicultural Counseling and Development*, 29, 174–200.

Vontress, C. E. (1970). Counseling Blacks. *Personnel and Guidance Journal*, 48, 713–719.

Webber, T. L. (1978). *Deep like the rivers: Education in the slave quarter community, 1831–1865*. Norton.

13

APPLICATIONS FOR BLACK CULTURAL STRENGTHS IN TRAINING AND PRACTICE

In this chapter I discuss the application of cultural strengths to mental health teaching, training, and practice. In doing so, I undertake a survey of the educational landscape to locate evidence of the foundations of educational practices and activities to which mental health professionals are exposed. I offer guidance so those who might wish to use the strength-based perspective in teaching and training of mental health professionals may do so.

Mental Health Training for Racial-Cultural Competency

Training and mental health practices are shaped by several interrelated factors. One significant factor is the worldview or the cultural patterns and beliefs of the dominant group in the society. The dominant group's cultural beliefs shape the norms and structure of institutions and organizations. In this way all institutions and organizations are linked in that they exist to serve the goals and to pass on the teachings and values of the society as reflected in the worldview of the dominant white racial-cultural group (Carter, 1995).

These institutions and organizations include schools, colleges and universities, hospitals, mental health systems, families, and communities. Families socialize their members to participate in the structure of society and teach the values, communication patterns, behaviors, attitudes, and beliefs that are congruent with the sociocultural context in which they live.

The Eurocentric view dominates theory and practice in mental health professions and in society in general. This dominance has not allowed for consideration that other cultural worldviews may exist or should be understood. The prevailing view is that mental health professionals assume that the dominant racial-cultural worldview is universal. Differing worldviews are not taught or used in practice, so mental health professionals may not be racially and culturally competent or effective.

DOI: 10.4324/9781003111542-18

By racial-cultural competency, I do not mean being able to work primarily with nonwhite or immigrant group members. Racial-cultural competence as I define it is broad and encompasses conscious knowledge of one's own racial-cultural group; it means recognizing the versatility of knowing, feeling, and behaving in particular ways due to one's reference group within one's own racial-cultural worldview (i.e., gender, ethnicity, social class, religion); and it means having knowledge about people who belong to groups other than one's own, including factual information about each group's social-political history and how that history influences the group's current status and participation in the country. To achieve racial-cultural competency, self-knowledge coupled with knowledge of one's racial-cultural group must be enhanced by individual racial-cultural self-exploration and development (Carter, 2005). One must evolve an identity that is free of bias or in which the existence of bias is recognized and monitored. Said another way, effective and competent mental health professionals have evolved an advanced racial identity such that they are able to facilitate growth and exploration in others as educators, advocates, policymakers, or practitioners.

Yet, unlike other scholars, I contend that the knowledge of one's reference groups comes through the lens of racial group membership and one's racial identity ego status—that is, how one understands one's ethnic or gender group membership is determined by one's racial group and one's corresponding racial identity ego status (Carter & Pieterse, 2005).

The approach that I advocate treats all racial-cultural groups as important to understand and to focus on in our teaching and practice. We should avoid the practice of describing the ills of our social system and the outcomes of exploitation and oppression by focusing on the victims of oppression as if that is all to know about their experiences. Emphasis on the victims of oppression is a limited and fragmented view. We do not fully understand the role of racial-cultural worldview, sociocultural norms, and institutional policies in the development of illness or in notions of abnormality and health or as sources of cultural strengths.

Rather, mental health professionals must make a conscious effort to keep in the foreground the context of their racial-cultural worldview and remember how it sets and shapes their perceptions, thinking, feelings, interaction patterns, communication styles, and beliefs about what is normal and what is not. It is easier to see racial-cultural difference in those who are immigrants to the United States but somewhat more difficult to see the role of race and culture among people who belong to groups that have been here for many centuries. Furthermore, we must always remember that, while it is true that skin color, physical features, and language are primary sources of difference in our society, there are other sources of difference that also need to be understood.

Cultural Strengths in the Mental Health Care Setting

The mental health profession has begun to alter its identity from a mental health-oriented discipline to that of a health care profession, with a larger role in the health care system. In the last few decades there is greater recognition that mental health plays a role in health with respect to stress, wellness, and disease prevention. The new ways of providing mental health care have meant that there are demands for mental health treatments to be evidence-based, and there are also calls for better services to people of color (Phelps, Bray, & Kearney, 2017; Washburn, 2019).

The shift from a concentration on mental health to health care as the focus of psychology means that the medical model has more importance in mental health practices, and there is more reliance on research evidence typical in medicine, like clinical trials, to demonstrate that treatment approaches are effective. This new trend is problematic in that the medical profession and social scientific applied practices (e.g., psychiatry, psychology, counseling, and social work) have histories of racism and racial oppression regarding people of color (see Carter, 1995; Washington, 2006).

The American Psychiatric Association's assembly and board of trustees approved a statement and resolution against racism (American Psychiatric Association [APA], 2021; see Paradies et al., 2015). In the statement the group acknowledges that racism and racial discrimination adversely affect mental health in that racism and racial discrimination operate to reduce the targets—self-worth, confidence, and mental functioning. Racism also diminishes the perpetrator's ability to live in a multicultural and multiracial society. The psychiatric association, the oldest national physicians' organization (established in 1844), is attempting to address racism in psychiatry. It pledges to rectify past acts and inherent injustices associated with the treatment of people of color and its racist practices enacted against them. The apology goes on to note the various injustices and atrocities directed at people of color in the name of psychiatric treatment.

The national organization of medical professionals, the American Medical Association (AMA) also issued a statement that racism was a threat to public health. In 2021 the AMA issued statements about racism, saying it would "confront systemic racism in medicine" (AMA, 2021). They pledged to define racism and racial bias and attempt to reduce its effects in the practice of medicine.

The American Psychological Association (APA) issued several policy statements, resolutions, and apologies about its role in promoting and maintaining racism in the United States, irrespective of its many policy statements to the contrary. One issued in 2012 addressed preventing discrimination (American Psychological Association Presidential Task Force, 2012). It was followed in 2017 by an updated ethical code and general multicultural guidelines (APA, 2017a, 2017b). More were presented in 2021, according to Najdowski and Stevenson (2023):

> On October 29, 2021, American Psychological Association (APA) council of Representatives approved a resolution regrading APA's role in

> dismantling systemic racism in criminal legal systems as well as other critical area (education, science, health care, work and economic opportunities, early childhood development and government and public policy)… . APA adopted this resolution along with two others ("Apology to People of Color") … ; ("Advancing Health Equity in Psychology") … to acknowledge and apologize for its role in racism in the discipline and to commit to efforts to apply psychological theory and scientific methods toward remedying systemic racism within various areas of concern.
>
> *(p. 398)*

The apologies and admissions of racism on the part of these organizations indicates that there is little reason to believe that treatment guidelines will include much about racial issues or race-related stress/trauma or Black cultural strengths. I take this view because racial-cultural considerations have not been important, despite the policy statements, but have received considerable rhetoric in mental health professions. It has been the practice in mental health to assume universal human principles, engage in hurtful racist practices and policies according to their own statements, and not rely on racial-cultural group-specific characteristics to guide treatment and interventions (see Carter & Pieterse, 2020).

In the same way that mental health professionals have difficulty with race and racism, I suspect that they will have trouble with understanding and using Black cultural strengths in treatment with Black clients. (To be clear, *race* is defined in terms of skin color, language, and physical features and its sociopolitical use, whereas *ethnicity* is defined as one's country of origin and is connected to one's heritage and family background, and *culture* is defined as patterns of behavior and thought learned through socialization.) The issues arise in several ways, one from the perspective of the client/patient, who is less likely to discuss their cultural patterns and practices with therapists. A complication here is that many may not be aware that they are using or living according to these deeply embedded cultural values. Even if they knew, most would not disclose these details to their therapist, irrespective of the therapist's race.

Therapists have little training that would aid them in understanding or considering that Black people have cultural strengths, and they would not have been taught to apply such knowledge if they had it. To illustrate this point, consider the work of Hemmings and Evans (2018), who created a survey to examine professional counselor experiences when dealing with race-based stress and trauma in the counselors' work with clients. Respondents to the survey were 106 mostly white, middle-aged, licensed professional counselors, three-quarters of whom reported they had worked with clients who presented with race-based issues while the remainder had not. They were asked what factors (from among nine choices) had contributed to their clients' racial trauma. The list and the reported frequencies were as follows:

covert acts of racism (88.7%), hate crimes (84%), institutional racism (84%), microaggressions (80%), out-group comments (76%), overt racist acts (86.5%), racial discrimination (86%), racial profiling (83%), and own-group racial comments (71%). Participants were asked whether they were trained to deal with race-related stress and trauma issues that clients might present. Of the 106 counselors, 19% said they had received training to treat race-based trauma and 81% had not. For those who were trained, their training had taken place during continuing education activities or after their formal education and training.

Counselors reported working with clients who had distressing racial experiences, but these counselors had received no training to assess or treat, nor were there any professional policies on race-related or cultural stress/trauma with treatment recommendations. More important—the policies, training, and treatment associated with race-related stress/trauma were found to be inversely related to competencies, meaning that when counselors reported being trained in providing treatment, applying policy regarding race-related therapy issues, they also were found to be less competent, which indicated that the counselors knew they were ill equipped to deal with clients' racism-related issues (Hemmings & Evans, 2018). Even when the issues and events pertaining to how mental health care is delivered and the policy statements about attending to racial-cultural differences have challenged mental health professionals to act, less has been accomplished, as researchers have documented, to include consideration of the effects of culture and racism in mental health care service delivery.

Another researcher's work is more revealing. Benuto and colleagues (2019) examined, using mixed-methods (i.e., interviews and surveys), the cultural competency–training experiences of 143 psychologists. Most reported that their training included a class (out of some 40 that are required) on diversity (85%), and most had supervised clinical experience with diverse populations (i.e., meaning they treated people from other racial-cultural groups; 83%), and had didactic training about cultural competency (i.e., the one class mentioned above; 82%). More important, most of the participants (76%) reported that exploring personal biases, in supervision or in a class, was a part of their training, yet how this was done is not clear. However, fewer had experiential activities (67%) or cultural immersion (38%), so it is hard to know what diversity training actually meant. Much of what was reported was cognitive learning rather than direct practice or application. I contend that it is not possible to address an issue in treatment in the absence of any assessment or identification of that issue. Said another way, assessment precedes any intervention.

Traditional assessment practices are insufficient to aid therapists in how to use Black cultural strengths (Johnson & Carter, 2020). To assess for such practices, the practitioner must understand Blacks' cultural variation and the person's racial identity status to determine how these might influence the client's thoughts and behaviors. At the same time, this assessment is not possible if the therapist is unaware of their own cultural and racial perceptions and behavior (Thompson & Carter, 2012). Carter and Pieterse (2020) note that, at its core, assessment is about how well the therapist engages the patient. Eliacin and colleagues (2016) note that client engagement is crucial to health care, and the actions taken in health care delivery are influenced by the characteristics of the respective actors. They found in their investigation that communication and mental health treatment decisions for Black people were less collaborative and that Black people were more likely to terminate treatment early (Eliacin et al., 2016; Villatoro et al., 2018). Eliacin and colleagues (2016, p. 3) contend that factors contributing to a low level of client engagement in mental health care were "distrustful interactions, and weak working alliances between minority patients and their providers." A positive working alliance, in contrast, would be associated with positive therapy outcomes and symptom relief (Davis, Ancis, & Ashby, 2015; Dixon, Holoshitz, & Nossel, 2016; Eliacin et al., 2016).

Matter (2010), writing about the state of racial-cultural considerations in psychology, observes that

> training models prevalent in the United States emphasize traditional clinical approaches and the objective stance of the therapist and researcher. There are very few [psychology or mental health training] programs in the United States that teach and include ethnographic training as well as an emphasis on cultural self-awareness and self-examination as a training tool for psychologists.
>
> *(p. 50)*

Moreover, she states,

> Narrow notions of culture in the scientific literature emphasize demographic variables at the expense of explorations of power dynamics, immigration, historical legacies of slavery, societal violence, systemized discrimination against nondominant groups and the implications of the interactions of patient-clinician demographics among others.

She believes training should go beyond the "us versus them" approaches used by many multicultural educators. The clinician is often not prepared for clients with race-cultural issues. This perspective indicates that most mental health professionals would not be equipped to be able to see the cultural values that guide the lives of many Black people; they would be blinded by their own cultural teachings and the negative and cultural deprivation views held regarding Black lives. So it would be necessary for mental health professionals to be conscious of their own cultural values and practices in order for them to be able to see cultural values and practices in others, particularly in Black people.

Malott and Schaefle (2015) offer a four-stage approach that includes therapist racial-cultural competence, which suggests that the therapist should begin the conversation with clients with what they called "counseling frameworks" that recognize racism and racial group culture in the etiology of the clients' concerns. They note that the mental health professional must have acquired racial-cultural competence, particularly the awareness, knowledge, and skills to engage in racial-culturally focused therapy. Awareness means that the mental health professional knows about her own race and culture and knows something about the worldview or cultural practices of her clients. Specific to understanding race and culture, the therapist must know historical and current racial-cultural sociopolitical dynamics directed at Blacks in the United States. Additional racial-cultural competencies needed before any assessment related to the clients' racial-cultural experiences can take place include skills in racial-cultural case conceptualizations and knowledge and awareness of white norms and of personal and systemic forms of cultural, institutional, and individual racism. The racial identity statuses of both parties would also influence the process and outcome of their interactions (Carter & Johnson, 2019).

Assessing the role and impact of racial-cultural experiences of Black clients must be done throughout the therapeutic encounter. This assessment of the interaction is affected by what Malott and Schaefle (2015) call the counseling framework or theoretical orientation—a traditional or westernized, mostly intrapsychic perspective—that could lead clinicians to inadvertently view Black clients' behavior as pathological rather than a culturally embedded coping response to racism or oppression that has been taught and passed on from one generation to the next (Sue et al., 2022). Traditional mental health approaches often overemphasize the client's role in developing and maintaining symptoms rather than recognize the need for a wider contextual lens that considers the role of racial-cultural learning and socialization and related environmental stressors in the client's presenting issues. Which theory is used with interventions may be less important than the therapist's ability and capacity to grasp the complex racial-cultural issues.

Although addressing Black cultural strengths in treatment requires the same fundamental therapy skills common to psychotherapy, clinicians' effectiveness in applying these skills when addressing racial-cultural practices that may operate in less conscious ways hinges on the clinicians' ability to understand their own personal and cultural ways, irrespective of the racial or cultural group to which they belong. They would also need to identify as racial beings within a racialized society and locate their and the patient's racial identity status so they can better gauge the person's racial socialization experiences (Bryant-Davis & Ocampo, 2006; Carter & Johnson, 2019; Comas-Diaz, 2016; Hemmings & Evans, 2018). Researchers have shown that raising awareness of one's cultural and racial experiences is associated with a range of strong emotional reactions including guilt, shame, confusion, and anger that may hamper growth and the clinician's ability to see and grasp the client's cultural worldview (Johnson & Carter, 2020; Sue & Sue, 2016; Sue et al., 2022; Utsey, Gernat, & Hammer, 2005). It is imperative, however, that the clinician learn about these essential emotional processes both within themselves and with the client, and that they bring this level of racial-cultural awareness and self-understanding to their role within the therapeutic encounter. It seems too much to ask someone to work with a person's cultural strengths when they are oblivious to their own practices and how these function in their lives as well as how these values influence their own behavior and emotional reactions.

Clinical interviews could include a focus on cultural teachings in the context of one's race and socialization. It is likely that what was taught was not explicit or was not always done with conscious awareness. Many cultural lessons could be communicated in actions and experiences and thus would need to be discussed after a process of learning about one's range of experiences. A key factor in the clinical assessment would be to explore the client's racial identity process since it is the vehicle that would indicate how much or in what ways racial-cultural issues may have occurred and when in the patient's life.

Racial Identity Statuses for Non-Blacks

To date, racial identity development models and measures have been used in empirical research for all racial groups in the United States, as noted in the previous chapter. As has been discussed previously, racial identity ego statuses vary from less mature (that is, ego statuses that rely on identification with the external dominant racial-cultural group) to statuses that are more mature as reflected in an identification that is internal and associated with one's own racial-cultural group. Racial identity applies to whites, Blacks, and all other people of color (POC). A discussion follows of the racial identity statuses for people who are not Black (Carter, 1995; Carter et al., 2017; Carter & Johnson, 2019; Thompson & Carter, 2012).

Racial identity for whites is characterized by abandonment of racism and the development of a nonracist identity, while models for POC describe a process characterized by the abandonment of reliance on white culture for self-definition to an acceptance of a positive racial-cultural identity as a person of color (Helms, 1984, 1995). The sequential resolutions are similar across racial groups.

The least mature and more externally derived racial identity status attitudes are Contact (whites) and Conformity (POC), which are associated with the denial of racism or endorsement of a colorblind worldview. Disintegration (white), and Dissonance (POC) statuses are also externally derived yet internally questioned; thus, these statuses are characterized by conflict or confusion about the meaning of one's race.

Resistance (POC), Reintegration, and Pseudo-independence (all three white) are characterized by idealized notions of the power and superiority of one's racial group as well as using in-group standards to understand their racial-cultural selves and group membership. A person may conclude that it is best to idealize their racial group and to actively reject other racial-cultural groups. In contrast, Immersion/Emersion (POC and whites) status attitudes reflect a conscious, internally focused recognition of one's membership as part of a racial and cultural group and any accompanying emotions associated with said membership.

Emotional awareness makes it possible to integrate race and culture into one's unique personal identity structure, leading to the more mature and internally derived racial identity status attitudes of Internalization (POC) and Autonomy (whites), which are associated with the end of conflicts regarding the meaning of race for self and others. Internalization and Autonomy reflect an acceptance of self as a racial being and the development of a racial identity status that is free from notions of inferiority or superiority.

What is important, among other things, about incorporating racial identity in mental health practice and training is understanding how one's attitudes influence therapy interactions and determine how interactions evolve and what outcomes occur based on how the two parties' racial identity statuses combine and affect one another. Thus, the interactional or racially inclusive model of therapy process and outcome informs how attitudes about race influence the treatment dyad.

Interactional Dynamics of Racial Identity Statuses

Racial identity statuses can be used to understand interactions between people in therapy and in social relationships, and it can guide mental health professionals in understanding the circumstances in which to use Black cultural practices in the treatment interaction. I describe the interactional dynamics associated with racial identity statuses, and then I present how cultural strengths can be used in therapy. I contend that there is a relationship between one's racial identity status and their cultural preferences. The interactional model aids in that discussion.

Helms's (1984, 1995) interaction model and Carter's (1995) racially inclusive model of therapy identify four pairings of patient-therapist racial identity status attitudes. Regardless of their respective demographic racial groups, the pairings (e.g., parallel and crossed, progressive and regressive) set the context for how racial-cultural factors enter into the psychological treatment dyad (Carter & Helms, 1992; Carter & Johnson, 2019).

The two models focus on how racial identity status attitudes interact in therapy relationships and how the interaction affects clinical encounters. Each pairing and combination of racial identity attitudes form a distinct relationship type. Thus, in Helms's (1995) and Carter's (1995) models, it is not the participants' race that characterizes relationship types but how their racial identity status attitudes combine. Moreover, Carter presents evidence about the different types of relationships. He shows how the relationship types vary in terms of thought processes, affective states, behaviors, and reactions. A detailed discussion about this aspect of relationship types is beyond the scope of the current discussion (Carter, 1995).

As was discussed in the last chapter, in a *parallel* relationship, both parties may hold the same attitudes, or both may be confused or immersed in their respective racial groups. In a *progressive* relationship the therapist is more advanced than the client. In a *regressive* pair the patient's racial identity status development is more mature than the therapist's, so the interaction and process in therapy is conflictual.

The most effective relationship type is progressive, yet the interactional models emphasize the exchanges that occur between both parties in the therapy process and consider how both contribute to its outcomes. Currently, however, medical and mental health professionals seldom see therapy as interactional in this way; rather, the medical view and model of treatment is focused on the clinician as expert and usually considers how the clinician's behavior and emotions impact the client, not the other way around. Therefore, the medical approach to understanding treatment interactions has been one-sided. In this instance, aspects of Blacks' cultural lives would be obscured.

Medical and mental health treatment approaches focus less on the dyad as being interactional. To consider the interaction from both the client's and counselor's sides challenges the white, European American, culturally bound nature of psychotherapy, which seldom includes the client's perspective in interventions and treatment protocols.

The application in training and practice of racial identity and the interaction model reveals several important points that need to be grasped before a mental health professional can use knowledge of Black cultural strengths in therapy and treatment. It is not possible to understand a Black person's cultural strengths if the therapist believes that race is not salient to himself or herself or to the client. This situation would be present if the therapist is operating at a low or less mature racial identity status and is in a parallel, crossed, or regressive relationship with the client. If this is the case, there would not be much symptom relief, nor would there be much recognition of the client's cultural strengths, regardless of the race of the therapist. Nor would the therapist be able to see or grasp the client's worldview; instead, it is likely that the therapist would attribute white cultural practices to the client and judge him or her on that basis.

A prerequisite for therapists to be able to use Black cultural strengths is for therapists to have evolved a racial identity status that would allow them to see themselves as racial beings and to in turn understand their own cultural values; this way they would see where there are racial-cultural differences between themselves and their clients, if any exist, and perhaps to also recognize the areas in the clients' lives that reflect strengths that could be highlighted in therapy.

In my teaching, training, and clinical practice, issues of race offer more of a challenge than other types of differences, like gender, social class, or religion. I have seen how people, including mental health professionals, struggle more with race. I suspect their struggle is related to how race has been treated and addressed in our society. The advocacy for people to be colorblind complicates efforts to address race directly. The social taboos that are attached to discourse about race adds to the difficulty.

In teaching and training, even when I did not focus on or introduce race as the primary subject, it was brought in and used as a proxy for culture or it was ignored. Students and participants (regardless of race) often assumed that only POC were members of racial groups, or they ignored race as an aspect of difference. So it seems to me that a race-based approach to cultural understanding and building competency in counseling and psychology is essential and imperative. It is one of the things we think we know about a person on sight, and from that visible marker we make automatic assumptions about qualities and group memberships. It is my view that mental health professionals should adopt a perspective on cultural difference such that they are able to see Black cultural patterns that use race as the context for understanding culture. However, it does not mean that one should focus on a specific racial group. Rather, the focus should be on how race—and through race, culture—effects psychological and social functioning. As discussed earlier, race is defined in terms of skin color, language, and physical features and its sociopolitical use as well as one's racial identity status, whereas ethnicity is defined as one's country of origin and is connected to one's heritage and family background, and culture is defined as patterns of behavior and thought learned through socialization.

Mental health professionals must consider all that is possible in a group's or individual's life and family. Therefore, accepting the possibility that those from your racial group, or from another racial group, might operate psychologically and behaviorally from a worldview that you are not familiar with is a starting point for racial-cultural competence. Furthermore, grasping the cultural strengths of Black people is a challenge since one must look past all the real and negative disparities that are well documented and that we are reminded about on a regular basis.

Helping professionals do not provide treatments and interventions to groups of people; they assist individuals, usually people who are in some or many ways struggling emotionally or psychologically (Marcelin et al., 2019). In the United States, the training that mental health providers receive is focused on the individual who seeks or is made to receive mental health treatment. At the same time, as has been pointed out throughout this volume, individuals do not raise themselves. Each person develops in a context, usually in a family but not always. Assuming that there was a family and community, then the therapist can begin to build an understanding of the Black person with consideration of his or her family life and to assess the manner in which that group embraced the dominant racial group's culture, or if they also invested in their racial group's cultural beliefs, values, and practice. Consider the guidance offered by Johnson and Carter (2020):

> Some cultural practices and beliefs of their African ancestors have become customs and traditions of Blacks in America.... A belief that the survival of the individual is dependent on the survival of the group (i.e., communalism) and an interconnectedness between a person, nature, and others (i.e., spirituality) are among these cultural practices. Furthermore, additional practices and beliefs have emerged within the Black American collective identity. First, racial identity broadly refers to the process of developing an understanding of oneself as a member of the Black racial group. This process can encompass varying levels of engagement with other Blacks, endorsement of Africultural values, and beliefs about the importance of race.... Additionally, part of the Black collective experience is the need to orient younger generations regarding the role of race and racism in the lives of Black Americans, as well as how to cope with racism (i.e., racial socialization and racism-related coping).
>
> *(p. 59)*

During the assessment of the presenting problems and issues and in the process of building background knowledge of the client, the therapist would need to determine the extent to which the patient knows about these customs and traditions. There is a possibility that the client may not hold this information in conscious awareness or know if asked directly. The lesson, if offered, may have taken a form that is particular to the patient's family. This means the lessons could have been passed on; what needs to be discovered next is how and in what forms. How were the cultural values and strengths of communalism and spirituality communicated in the patient's family system? There could have been lessons taught outside the family; recall the ecological developmental model that was presented in the first section of the book. It is possible that such lessons could be learned in the larger community or from extended family members. The therapist should take her time in building this store of information. In the same way that the presence of collective identity should be explored, the client should be aware of having an identity in which they feel connected to the larger group of Black people. One way to explore this aspect of the person's psyche could be to discuss their reactions to news stories and events that affect Black people in general. For instance, in the last few years there have been media and social media posts of incidents involving Black people being assaulted, killed, or harmed in some way. Some Black have reported feeling stressed and traumatized by such incidents. What does the client say about such experiences? How they respond would be a cue to their collective identity. Research evidence provides some guidance about how such information can impact people.

Race-Related Stress and Racial Trauma from Social Media: Implications for practice

Indirect exposure to traumatic events, also referred to as vicarious or secondary trauma, is recognized in the *Diagnostic and Statistical Manual of Mental Disorders* (DSM-5; APA, 2013). Defined as "repeated or extreme exposure to aversive details" (p. 271) of a traumatic event, the DSM-5 also recognizes the association between media exposure to traumatic events and the development of trauma symptoms (APA, 2013). Research has found that traumatic events do not need to be experienced personally and directly in order for people to be psychologically impacted. Researchers have also found associations between media reports of highly publicized acts of violence (e.g., school shootings, terrorist attacks, police killings) and trauma-related symptoms (Bor et al., 2018; Garfin, Holman, & Silver, 2015). For example, a study of college students who were not personally exposed to the 2007 Virginia Tech shooting found that as hours of viewing television or internet coverage of the incident increased, there was a significant increase in intrusive thoughts, distraction, sleep disturbance, stomach upset, fear, and appetite disturbance (Fallahi & Lesik, 2009). While these studies demonstrate that exposure to media about traumatic events that one was not directly exposed to but that have some personal significance can have a significant psychological impact, other research has shown that even those who have no personal connection to an event can experience symptoms as a result of exposure to media. Research of a large sample of American adults immediately following the Boston Marathon bombing found that greater exposure to both traditional and social media about the bombing was associated with increased acute stress symptoms, and viewing six or more hours per day of media about the event was associated with greater acute stress symptoms than direct exposure to the actual event (Holman, Garfin, & Silver, 2014). Another study also found that 20% of participants across four clinical studies who had no history of previous trauma exposure and who only witnessed traumatic events via social media scored high on clinical measures of post-traumatic stress disorder (Ramsden, 2017).

Over the last decade there has been much greater media and social media coverage of the harassment and murders of Black men, women, and children primarily, but not exclusively, by police, starting with the widely publicized killing of Trayvon Martin by George Zimmerman in 2012, followed by Zimmerman's acquittal in 2013, which spurred the use of the #BlackLivesMatter hashtag across the internet and social media (Pew Research Center, 2016). The Black Lives Matter movement, which leverages viral videos of the harassment and killing of Black people by police, began to gain prominence following the murder of unarmed teenager Michael Brown in Ferguson, Missouri, in 2014 and with subsequent protests (Foran, 2015). Over nearly a decade that followed, cell phone cameras have captured many incidents that in turn have been posted online. Many of the stories posted online were about racial hostility against Black people, including instances of anti-Black violence and even murder. What is alarming is that many of these situations in which Blacks were attacked were as innocuous as the person asking for directions. Many of these incidents have been reported in the traditional media, and some were accompanied by eyewitness videos that were posted at an alarming rate on social media. A *New York Times* article documented 27 viral videos depicting racially charged murders and hostile encounters between June 2013 and April 2017 (Benzaquen, Cave, & Oliver, 2018).

The increasing prevalence of viral videos depicting violence against Black people, both on social media and in traditional media, was accompanied by considerable popular media coverage speculating about the potential psychological impact of exposure to the sheer volume of raw videos as early as the summer of 2015, following the murders of nine Black churchgoers in Charlotte, South Carolina, on June 17, 2015 (Attiah, 2015; Williams, 2015; Wortham, 2015), and again in the summer of 2016 (Downs, 2016; Lewis, 2016; Westman & Intagliata, 2016) following video of the immediate aftermath of the shootings of Alton Sterling and Philando Castile, which was transmitted live on Facebook. The articles just cited include descriptions by journalists and laypeople recounting the Black community's reactions to media coverage of incidents of racial harassment as well as mental health clinicians and researchers theorizing about the psychological impact of this chronic exposure to vicarious racism. Responses described in the articles included a range of emotional reactions from sadness, anger, shock, disgust, stress, exhaustion, and anxiety, to fear, anguish, and terror as well as a general sense of lack of safety, and people described symptoms such as difficulty sleeping or eating and increased impulsivity.

The widespread sharing of videos detailing the killing of unarmed Black individuals has increased the exposure of Black Americans to race-related traumatic events (Maxie-Moreman & Tynes, 2022). Research also indicates that, on average, Black American adolescents are exposed to five racial discrimination events daily, with the majority of these occurring online (English et al., 2020). A number of studies have examined the psychological impact of vicarious exposure to racist violence against Black people through social and traditional media using correlational, population-based, quasi-experimental, and experimental studies, all of which have found a negative psychological and emotional impact on Black Americans. One population-based study using data from 696 Black and 6,707 white participants from the Behavioral Risk Factor Surveillance System (BRFSS) found that exposure to highly publicized incidents of racial violence targeting Black people, including police killings of unarmed Black people, decisions not to prosecute police involved in these incidents, and hate crime murders of Black people were followed by significant increases in poor mental health days for Black people but not for white people (Curtis et al., 2021). Similarly, in a study of 103,710 Black Americans using the BRFSS data, Bor and colleagues (2018) found that exposure to police brutality and violence against unarmed Black people via word of mouth and both traditional and social media were significantly associated with an increase in poor mental health days within the two months following the incident for Black Americans living in the same state where the incidents occurred. Another study found significantly greater increases in anger and sadness following the murder of George Floyd among Black as compared to white Americans in a Gallup data set of 47,355 people (Eichstadt et al., 2021). The same study found significant increases in anxiety and depression severity for both Black and white Americans in a U.S. Census data set of 319,471 people, with the increase being significantly greater for Black than white people.

Two studies of African American adults found that simply reading about the Zimmerman trial and acquittal was associated with negative affect including feelings of depression, anxiety, and hostility as well as intrusive thoughts (Mason et al., 2016) and feeling unsafe (Blackmon & Thomas, 2015). Another study found that reading a description of racially biased shootings of African Americans was associated with increased feelings of personal threat and psychological distress among Black college students who identified strongly with their race (Roberts et al., 2017). Utilizing self-report measures of exposure to online discrimination and witnessing of traumatic racial events, Maxie-Moreman and Tynes (2022) surveyed a sample of 245 emerging Black adults (age range 18–25) and found that participants who reported more experiences with individual online racial discrimination and traumatic events online also reported higher trauma symptoms of discrimination. These findings have been supported by other investigations identifying the negative psychological and trauma-related responses to social media exposure of race-related incidents of violence and harm (Curtis et al., 2021; Donaldson, 2021; Rowan-Kenyon et al., 2021).

Quasi-experimental studies have found that exposure to videos of racism-related violence is associated with negative outcomes. Vine (2022) investigated the impact of exposure to an online video of racism-related violence in a sample of 209 Black American adults. Results indicated that an increased length of time spent viewing racism-related social media content was associated with higher levels of race-based traumatic stress (RBTS) symptoms. Furthermore, utilizing an experimental setting, Vine reported that individuals exposed to a video of the police killing of a Black individual evidenced higher rates of RBTS symptoms than those exposed to a video of the police killing a white individual. Similar results were found in a quasi-experimental study of 217 college students of color that found that those who were exposed to media clips depicting a variety of racial and ethnic injustice and discrimination against POC experienced a significantly greater increase in negative affect as compared to those who were exposed to a neutral video (Giordano et al., 2021).

The results of population-based, correlational, and quasi-experimental studies have also been confirmed via qualitative studies. Hurd and colleagues (2022) conducted a series of investigations including the use of survey research and focus groups examining the experience of online racial discrimination among Black American college students studying at predominantly white institutions. Participants endorsed an increase in racism witnessed and encountered on social media platforms, and the types of racist experience included both blatant racial hostility and more indirect racial discrimination such as dismissing the experiences of Black students or providing a justification of racially based police violence. Furthermore, participants also endorsed harm associated with exposure to online racism, identifying a range of negative emotions (e.g., frustrated, infuriated, disappointed, irritated, isolated, overwhelmed, and exhausted) and indicating an experience of mistrust. In a qualitative examination of how Black people feel after viewing or hearing about incidents of police brutality against Blacks, reactions included hyperarousal and chronic fear of dying; a constant sense of helplessness; and debilitating sadness. Participants in the study described identifying with the victim or identifying their own family members with the victim; experiencing sadness compounded by frustration when having to deal with white people in the workplace who were unable to understand or appreciate the psychological and emotional impact these incidents had on them; and difficulty completing daily tasks as a result of their emotional reactions (Hawkins, 2022).

At least two studies have examined the impact of vicarious exposure to large-scale, well-publicized, racial trauma on employees of color at work. Ruggs and colleagues (2023) explored cognitive and affective reactions of 114 Black and White workers following the highly publicized shooting of Black man by police in 2016. They found that exposure was associated with significantly greater negative affect, rumination, and anger for Black workers as compared to white workers, and that Black workers avoided discussing incidents with white co-workers for fear of not feeling supported.

Leigh and Melwani (2022) used the concept of mega-threats (i.e., negative, identity-relevant occurrences that receive significant media attention) to examine the impact of exposure to vicarious racial trauma on workers. They defined three necessary characteristics of mega-threats as (1) overwhelmingly adverse events that involve attacks, threats, or violence directed toward an individual(s); which are (2) identity-related in that observers make the attribution that the event was motivated by bias, hostility, or prejudice against a specific identity group that has been historically devalued in society; and (3) are highly publicized through both traditional news outlets and social media. They argued that anti-Black mega-threats (e.g., police brutality/killings of Black people; hate crime murders of Black people) elicit visceral emotional and cognitive reactions from Black people, impacting their psychological well-being and increasing embodied threats (i.e., heightened awareness of increased likelihood of experiencing harm because of their identity). As such, vicarious victims of mega-threats are likely to become more vigilant to similar cues of potential harm in their own environment. In two studies, they found significant associations between mega-threats and embodied threat among Asian employees following the March 2021 murder of six Asian spa workers in Atlanta (study of 332 participants); Black employees following the October 2019 police killings of Black civilians Botham Jean and Atatiana Jefferson by police (study of 401 participants, 50% Black); and the May 2020 police killing of Black civilian George Floyd (study of 61 Black and 51 white participants). Thus, their results suggest that anti-Black mega-threats are likely to make Black workers feel an increased sense of vigilance in anticipation of themselves being victims of anti-Black violence.

Research evidence shows there is quite a bit of support for being concerned about how Black clients might be impacted by media and social media reports; the extent to which they report symptoms from such exposure reveals the level of investment in Black collective identity. Furthermore, their reaction and potential symptoms might be an indication of their level of racial identity development. The indicators revealed in the clients' responses about how they might have been impacted by media and social media posts and videos could also be valuable in assessing their racial socialization experiences as well as in learning how they were taught to cope with racism. What is important about the Black cultural values presented are that many have been found to promote psychological well-being in addition to facilitating generational and present-day survival.

The Empirical Evidence for Black Cultural Strenghts

Johnson and Carter (2020) also explored whether two types of Black racial identity constructs would be associated with psychological health and well-being or a general sense of wellness. Helms's (1995) internalization status attitude scale and Sellers and colleagues' (2006) centrality scale were used to assess the importance of being Black to oneself, and a measure of private regard was included, which refers to one's positive or negative feelings toward Blacks and about being Black. The construct employed by Johnson and Carter was called "central-internalized racial identity" since it comprised scales from the Black racial identity attitude scale and the multidimensional measure of Black identity.

One of the other Black cultural strengths tested by Johnson and Carter is communalism, which is the belief that the success of the individual and the group are inseparable, which is expressed through preserving and valuing extended family systems (i.e., beyond blood ties), as shown in the practice of shared child-rearing beyond family members. The other foundational cultural value, which is sometimes conflated with religiosity, is Black American spirituality, which encompasses a sense of connection with one's ancestors and family and the group as a whole; it also includes the idea that things in nature have a force that directs life events. This cultural value exists in tandem with or separate from one's religious practices. Spirituality, as a cultural belief, has been found to be positively associated with quality of life and optimism (Underwood & Teresi, 2002) and negatively associated with depression and stress disorders (Watlington & Murphy, 2006). These were tested by way of related instruments by Johnson and Carter (2020). Other aspects of Black cultural practices that were tested by Johnson and Carter were related to racial oppression, such as racial socialization and racism-related coping. In their study the instrument measured only some aspects of racial socialization. One aspect that was measured was preparation for bias (i.e., teaching about group differences and explaining racial bias), and the other was cultural socialization, which involves lessons about one's cultural heritage so the student or family member is knowledgeable and aware. There are eight forms of race-related coping Blacks use, as reported by Forsyth and Carter (2014), of which they used in their study Confrontation, the direct interaction with the person involved in the racial incident; Empowered Action, the use of community and legal means to address racism; Spiritual, seeking religious guidance through prayer or mediation; and Constrained Resistance, coping that combines passive and more active efforts to address racial incidents.

Therapists would need to engage in considerable information gathering to learn about how these cultural factors function in the lives of their clients. Johnson and Carter (2020) have investigated whether these cultural values do function as strengths for Black people and found that these values combined help to reduce the levels of stress that comes from being subjected to racism and racial discrimination. It is apparent from media and social media research that there are many sources of potential stress for Black people, and this reality should not be overlooked when they seek help from mental health professionals. At the same time, mental health professionals will need to overcome their own socialization and cultural worldviews so they do not obscure their perception and ability to understand Black clients and block their ability to see Black clients' cultural perspectives.

Dominant Cultural and Social Environments

Many professionals accept that the dominant cultural and social environments shape who we are and how we behave and feel in the world. And this applies to some extent to Black Americans, given that they have been part of the society for several centuries, yet they were also set apart, which allowed for the development of a unique set of cultural practices and beliefs. Often our culture is reflected in our neighborhoods and communities. Many racial communities have historically been segregated; today many are still subject to external forces that maintain their social separation, while other communities may exist as distinct enclaves by choice. Nevertheless, our experiences as members of racial-cultural groups in society, as well as our personal understanding of that experience (i.e., one's racial-cultural identity), affect our mental health and how we come to know and understand others who are like and who are not like us.

Our cultural context (race, ethnic group, gender, religion, language, social class, etc.) influences how we understand health and mental wellness. Our culture also determines what is considered normal and abnormal. The circumstances we encounter in society, such as access to work, shelter, and health care, also influence our understanding of our experiences and those of others as well as how we and—we assume—others function in our and their communities and in society.

It is important to acknowledge the elements of American culture or worldview that characterize our society and dominate our belief systems, behaviors, and expectations. American culture has evolved from white, ethnic, upper- and middle-class values and beliefs. American cultural systems are superordinate to ethnic group values. According to Carter (2005), white American cultural patterns include individualism, expressed through personal preferences; self-expression, reflected in a combination of conformity to social expectations and achievement of goals based on external criteria (e.g., good grades, good job); authority and power that is hierarchical; communication patterns that are verbal and normal only if standard English forms are used; a future time orientation; a Judeo-Christian religious system; belief that the nuclear family structure is ideal; and standards of music and beauty and social traditions (holidays, monuments, etc.) that are based on European cultures. It is a way of knowing that is practical and technical and that reduces ideas to their simplest terms and discusses ideas in terms of common elements.

Members of racial-cultural groups vary in the level of identification and investment they make in their racial-cultural group. Cultural investment in the dominant racial-cultural group and psychological identification with one's racial group vary by individual, and the variation influences the meaning and significance of the group and its culture for the person. Socioeconomic resources also influence the vulnerability one has to stressors or life events. Fewer resources and lower social status are associated with greater vulnerability to life event stressors. One's community and its organizations can have both positive and negative effects on mental health. Support systems and organizations that seek to reduce the effects of social, personal, and economic problems can protect people from the harm of stressors and reduce the incidence and prevalence of negative mental and physical health outcomes. And they can promote the value of employing constructive cultural values and protect and guard against harmful experiences and actions.

It is easy for anyone to see differences when someone speaks a different language, wears different clothes, or when they are physically different. It is harder to see and understand differences grounded in culture that influence perceptions of the world, in thinking patterns, and in interpersonal relationships when there are greater levels of similarity. It is even more difficult in the context of American society, where many racial groups have been in the country for hundreds of years and are American but not part of mainstream society but know its cultural patterns. Under these circumstances, it is difficult to discern less obvious racial-cultural variation among Americans.

Moreover, the process of learning about and understanding racial-cultural differences in training and practice conflicts with dominant American cultural patterns; what I call dynamic cultural conflicts arise and need to be acknowledged and addressed (Carter, 2005). Dynamic cultural conflicts occur when two cultural styles are operating at the same time but in contradiction to one another. For example, an American cultural norm is to reduce an issue to its simplest terms. Thus, when Americans are attempting to understand a different culture, they do so by trying to reduce the other culture to its bare essentials. But cultures are complex, not simple; understanding a different racial-cultural person requires accounting for that complexity. Therein lies a conflict: We either allow complexity or we strive for simplicity. We must allow complexity to exist to learn about racial-cultural influences, and so we must suspend our style of reducing things to simple terms. That is, we cannot reduce a racial-cultural group to general characteristics or understand a person through statistical or historical information about the group alone. Mental health professionals will need to allow Blacks' lives to be presented in all their complexity in order to see and build upon the person's cultural strengths.

Furthermore, people who are part of the dominant culture are generally taught to be professional, which usually means to leave personal beliefs out of work; this is explicitly taught to mental health professionals. Culturally, added to the separation of personal and professional selves, people are encouraged to fragment other parts of themselves, like keeping religion and politics out of social interactions or friendships. Consider this process and how it might work for American mental health care professionals, who are told to separate their professional and personal lives. Yet, there is an issue that might prevent the professional from being able to see and use Black cultural strengths: to learn about race and culture, we must explore personal experiences and beliefs regarding race and culture, yet at the same time, to do so is a violation of the dominant racial-cultural norms and thus is a dynamic cultural conflict (Carter, 2005). Americans are not accustomed to revealing ourselves or being the focal point of learning. Nevertheless, racial-cultural learning is most effective when it is grounded in self-exploration. The more aware you are of your racial-cultural norms, values, and communication styles, the easier it is for you to grasp another person's racial-cultural way of seeing and experiencing the world. A fish doesn't know that it is in water. From the perspective of the fish, there is no other way to be. And it is likely that the fish does not see the world as water but simply as the world. If you believe that the world is as you see it without variation and you use your worldview to understand those who seek your help, then it will not be possible to discern their use of cultural practices other than the ones that guide your actions and perceptions (Carter, 2005). It will be impossible to acknowledge that another worldview exists and to see the world through another racial or cultural lens. It will be difficult to learn and understand another person's racial-cultural worldview, another's way to communicate, another's way to behave if you are not aware that your perceptions and ways of knowing and being are bound by your unique, unexamined racial-cultural worldview, and you are not aware that other ways also exist.

References

American Medical Association (AMA). (2021, November 16). AMA: Racism is a threat to public health. https://www.ama-assn.org/delivering-care/health-equity/ama-racism-threat-public-health.

American Psychiatric Association (APA). (2013). *Diagnostic and statistical manual of mental disorders* (5th ed.), Text revision. American Psychiatric Association.

American Psychiatric Association (APA). (2021, January 18). APA's apology to Black, Indigenous, and people of color for its support of structural racism in psychiatry. American Psychiatric Association. https://www.psychiatry.org/news-room/apa-apology-for-its-support-of-structural-racism.

American Psychological Association (APA). (2017a). Ethical principles of psychologists and code of conduct. https://www.apa.org/ethics/code.

American Psychological Association (APA). (2017b). Multicultural guidelines: An ecological approach to context, identity, and intersectionality. https://www.apa.org/about/policy/multicultural-guidelines.pdf.

American Psychological Association (APA). (2021, October 29). Apology to people of color for APA's role in promoting, perpetuating, and failing to challenge racism, racial discrimination, and human hierarchy in U.S. https://www.apa.org/about/policy/racism-apology.

American Psychological Association Presidential Task Force on Preventing Discrimination and Promoting Diversity. (2012). Dual pathways to a better America: Preventing discrimination and promoting diversity. https://www.apa.org/pubs/info/reports/dual-pathways-report.pdf.

Attiah, K. (2015, July 24). How black people can emotionally protect themselves in the age of #BlackLivesMatter. *Washington Post*. https://www.washingtonpost.com/blogs/post-partisan/wp/2015/07/24/how-black-people-can-emotionally-protect-themselves-in-the-age-of-blacklivesmatter/?utm_term=.aa07c9994a2.

Benuto, L. T., Singer, J., Newlands, R. T., & Casas, J. B. (2019). Training culturally competent psychologists: Where are we and where do we need to go? *Training and Education in Professional Psychology*, 13(1), 56–63. doi:10.1037/tep0000214.

Benzaquen, M., Cave, D., & Oliver, R. (2018, March 28). The raw videos that have sparked outrage over police treatment of blacks. *New York Times*. https://www.nytimes.com/interactive/2017/08/19/us/police-videos-race.html.

Blackmon, S. K., & Thomas, A. J. (2015). African Americans and Trayvon Martin: Black racial identity profiles and emotional responding. *Journal of African American Studies*, 19, 279–297.

Bor, J., Venkataramani, A. S., Williams, D. R., & Tsai, A. C. (2018). Police killings and their spillover effects on the mental health of black Americans: A population based, quasi-experimental study. *Lancet*, 392(10144), 302–310. doi:10.1016/S0140-6736(18)31130–31139.

Bryant-Davis, T., & Ocampo, C. (2006). A therapeutic approach to the treatment of racist-incident-based trauma. *Journal of Emotional Abuse*, 6(4), 1–22. doi:10.1300/J135v06n04_01.

Carter, R. T. (1995). *The influence of race and racial identity in psychotherapy*. Wiley.

Carter, R. T. (Ed.). (2005). *Handbook of racial-cultural psychology and counseling*, Vol. 2, *Training and practice*. Wiley.

Carter, R. T., & Helms, J. E. (1992). The counseling process defined by relationship types: A test of Helms' interactional model. *Journal of Multicultural Counseling and Development*, 20(4), 181–201.

Carter, R. T., & Johnson, V. (2019). Racial identity statuses: Applications to practice. *Practice Innovations*, 4(1), 42–58.

Carter, R. T., Johnson, V., Roberson, K., Mazzula, S. M., Kirkinis, K., & Sant-Barket, S. (2017). Race-based traumatic stress, racial identity status, and psychological functioning: An exploratory investigation. *Professional Psychology: Research and Practice*, 48(1), 20–37.

Carter, R. T., & Pieterse, A. L. (2005). Race: A social and psychological analysis of the term and its meaning. In R. T. Carter (Ed.). *Handbook of racial-cultural psychology and counseling: Theory and research*, Vol. 1 (pp. 41–63). Wiley.

Carter, R. T., & Pieterse, A. (2020). *Measuring the effects of racism: Guidelines for the assessment and treatment of race-based traumatic stress injury*. Columbia University Press.

Comas-Diaz, L. (2016). Racial trauma recovery: A race informed therapeutic approach to racial wounds. In A. N. Alvarez, C. T. H. Liang, & H. A. Neville (Eds.). *The cost of racism for people of color: Contextualizing experiences of discrimination* (pp. 249–271). American Psychological Association. doi:10.1037/14852-012.

Curtis, D. S., Washburn, T., Lee, H., Smith, K. R., Kim, J., Martz, C. D., Kramer, M. R., & Chae, D. H. (2021). Highly public anti-Black violence is associated with poor mental health days for Black Americans. *Proceedings of the National Academy of Sciences*, 118(17), e2019624118. doi:10.1073/pnas.2019624118.

Davis, T. A., Ancis, J. R., & Ashby, J. S. (2015). Therapist effect, working alliance, and African American women substance users. *Cultural Diversity and Ethnic Minority Psychology*, 21(3), 126–135. doi:10.1037/a0036944.

Dixon, L. B., Holoshitz, Y., & Nossel, I. (2016). Treatment engagement of individuals experiencing mental illness: Review and update. *World Psychiatry*, 15(1), 13–20. doi:10.1002/wps.20306.

Donaldson, M. R. (2021). *Circulating racial trauma: How Black college-age students experience and cope with police brutality on social media* (Unpublished doctoral dissertation, Arizona State University).

Downs, K. (2016, July 22). When black death goes viral it can trigger PTSD-like trauma. *PBS News Hour*. https://www.pbs.org/newshour/nation/black-pain-gone-viral-racism-graphic-videos-can-create-ptsd-like-trauma.

Eichstadt, J. C., Sherman, G. T., Giorgi, S., Roberts, S. O., Reynolds, M. E., Ungar, L. E., & Guntuku, S. C. (2021). The emotional and mental health impact of the murder of George Floyd on the U.S. population. *Proceedings of the National Academy of Sciences*, 118(39), 1–5.

Eliacin, J., Coffing, J. M., Matthias, M. S., Burgess, D. J., Bair, M. J., & Rollins, A. L. (2016). The relationship between race, patient activation, and working alliance:

Implications for patient engagement in mental health care. *Administration and Policy in Mental Health and Mental Health Services Research*, 45(1), 186–192. doi:10.1007/s10488-016-0779-5.
English, D., Lambert, S. F., Tynes, B. M., Bowleg, L., Zea, M. C., & Howard, L. C. (2020). Daily multidimensional racial discrimination among Black U.S. American adolescents. *Journal of Applied Developmental Psychology*, 66, 101068. doi:10.1016/j.appdev.2019.101068.
Fallahi, C. R., & Lesik, S. A. (2009). The effects of vicarious exposure to the recent massacre at Virginia Tech. *Psychological Trauma: Theory, Research, Practice and Policy*, 1(3), 220–230.
Foran, C. (2015, December 31). A year of Black Lives Matter. *Atlantic*. https://www.theatlantic.com/politics/archive/2015/12/black-lives-matter/421839/.
Forsyth, J., & Carter, R. T. (2014). The development and preliminary validation of the racism-related coping scale. *Psychological Trauma: Theory, Policy, Research, and Practice*, 6(6), 632–643.
Garfin, D. R., Holman, E. A., & Silver, R. C. (2015). Cumulative exposure to prior collective trauma and acute stress responses to the Boston Marathon bombings. *Psychological Science*, 26(6), 675–683. doi:10.1177/0956797614561043.
Giordano, A. L., Prosek, E. A., Henson, R. K., Silveus, S., Beijan, L., Reyes, A., Molina, C., & Agarwal, S. M. (2021). Effects of vicarious racism exposure via the media on college students of color: Exploring affect and substance abuse. *Journal of College Counseling*, 24, 1–17.
Hawkins, D. S. (2022). "After Philando, I had to take a sick day to recover": Psychological distress, trauma and police brutality in the Black community. *Health Communication*, 37(9), 1113–1122.
Helms, J. E. (1984). Toward a theoretical explanation of the effects of race on counseling: A Black and white model. *Counseling Psychologist*, 12(3–4), 153–165. doi:10.1177/0011000084124013.
Helms, J. E. (1995). An update of Helms's white and people of color racial identity models. In J. G. Ponterotto, J. M. Casas, L. A. Suzuki, & C. M. Alexander (Eds.). *Handbook of multicultural counseling* (pp. 181–198). Sage.
Hemmings, C., & Evans, A. M. (2018). Identifying and treating race-based trauma in counseling. *Journal of Multicultural Counseling and Development*, 46(1), 20–39. doi:10.1002/jmcd.12090.
Holman, E. A., Garfin, D. R., & Silver, R. C. (2014). Media's role in broadcasting acute stress following the Boston Marathon bombings. *Proceedings of the National Academy of Sciences*, 111(1), 93–98.
Hurd, N. M., Trawalter, S., Jakubow, A., Johnson, H. E., & Billingsley, J. T. (2022). Online racial discrimination and the role of white bystanders. *American Psychologist*, 77 (1), 39–55. doi:10.1037/amp0000603.
Johnson, V., & Carter, R. T. (2020). Black cultural strengths and psychological well-being: An empirical analysis with Black American adults. *Journal of Black Psychology*, 46(1), 55–89.
Leigh, A., & Melwani, S. (2022). "Am I next?" The spillover effects of mega-threats on avoidant behaviors at work. *Academy of Management Journal*, 65(3), 720–748.
Lewis, C. (2016, July 12). Videos of police brutality are everywhere. What does watching them do to us? *Vox*. https://www.vox.com/2016/7/12/12147290/police-brutality-racial-trauma-castile-sterling.
Malott, K. M., & Schaefle, S. (2015). Addressing clients' experiences of racism: A model for clinical practice. *Journal of Counseling & Development* 93, 361–369. doi:10.1002/jcad.12034.

Marcelin, J. R., Siraj, D. W., Victor, R., Kotadia, S., & Maldonado, Y. A. (2019). The impact of unconscious bias in healthcare: How to recognize and mitigate it. *Journal of Infectious Disease*, 220, S62–S73.

Mason, T. B., Maduro, R. S., Derlega, V. J., Hacker, D. S., Winstead, B. A., & Haywood, J. E. (2016). Individual differences in the impact of vicarious racism: African American students react to the George Zimmerman trial. *Cultural Diversity and Ethnic Minority Psychology*, 23(2), 174–184.

Matter, S. (2010). Cultural considerations in trauma psychology, education, research and training. *Traumatology*, 16(4), 48–52. doi:10.1177/1534765610388305.

Maxie-Moreman, A. D., & Tynes, B. M. (2022). Exposure to online racial discrimination and traumatic events online in Black adolescents and emerging adults. *Journal of Research on Adolescence*, 32(1), 254–269. doi:10.1111/jora.12732.

Najdowski, C. J., & Stevenson, M. C. (2023). A call to dismantle systemic racism in criminal legal systems. *Law and Human Behavior*, 46(9), 398–414.

Paradies, Y., Ben, J., Denson, N., Elias, A., Priest, N., Pieterse, A., Gupta, A., Kelaher, M., & Gee, G. (2015). Racism as a determinant of health: A systematic review and meta-analysis. *PLoS ONE*, 10(9), e0138511. doi:10.1371/journal.pone.0138511.

Pew Research Center. (2016, August). Social media conversations about race. http://www.pewinternet.org/2016/08/15/social-media-conversations-about-race.

Phelps, R., Bray, J. H., & Kearney, L. K. (2017). A quarter century of psychological practice in the mental health and health care: 1990–2016. *American Psychologist*, 72(8), 822–836. http://psycnet.apa.org/doi/10.1037/amp0000192.

Ramsden, P. (2017). Vicarious trauma, PTSD and social media: Does watching graphic videos cause trauma? *Journal of Depression and Anxiety*, 6(3), suppl, 54.

Roberts, L. B., Maduro, R. S., Derlega, V. J., Peterkin, A. L., & Ellis, K. T. (2017). Race-based rejection sensitivity and racial identity predict African American students' reactions to the fatal shooting of other African Americans: Personal threat and identification with shooting victims as mediators. *Journal of Loss & Trauma*, 22(6), 472–486.

Rowan-Kenyon, H. T., McCready, A. M., Alemán, A. M. M., & Barone, N. (2021). Measuring racist aggressions on social media and the effects on US college students of color: An instrument validation. *Measurement and Evaluation in Counseling and Development*, 54(3), 156–172.

Ruggs, E. N., Marshburn, C. K., Summerville, K. M., & Grenier, K. (2023). The struggle is real: Employee reactions to indirect trauma from anti-Black policing. *Journal of Business and Psychology*, 38(25), 25–44.

Sellers, R. M., Copeland-Linder, N., Martin, P. P., & Lewis, R. L. (2006). Racial identity matters: The relationship between racial discrimination and psychological functioning in African American adolescents. *Journal of Research on Adolescence*, 16, 187–216. doi:10.1111/j.1532-7795.2006.00128.x.

Sue, D. W., & Sue, D. (2016). *Counseling the culturally diverse: Theory and practice* (7th ed.). Wiley.

Sue, D. W., Sue, D., Neville, H. A., & Smith, L. (2022). *Counseling the culturally diverse* (9th ed.). Wiley.

Thompson, C. E., & Carter, R. T. (Eds.). (2012). *Racial identity development theory: Applications to individual, group and organizational interventions*. Routledge.

Underwood, L. G., & Teresi, J. A. (2002). The daily spiritual experience scale. *Annals of Behavioral Medicine*, 24, 22–33. doi:10.1037/t01587-000.

Utsey, S. O., Gernat, C. A., & Hammer, L. (2005). Examining white counselor trainees' reactions to racial issues in counseling and supervision dyads. *Counseling Psychologist*, 33(4), 449–478. doi:10.1177/0011000004269058.

Villatoro, A. P., Mays, V. M., Ponce, N. A., & Aneshensel, C. S. (2018). Perceived need for mental health care: The intersection of race, ethnicity, gender, and socioeconomic status. *Society and Mental Health*, 8(1), 1–24. doi:10.1177/2156869317718889.

Vine, K. (2022). *When Black death goes viral: The relationship between social media exposure to vicarious racism and Black Americans' race-based traumatic stress* (Unpublished doctoral dissertation, Marquette University).

Washburn, J. J. (2019). Master's level providers in health service psychology: An idea that has come and passed, and now must come again. *Training and Education in Professional Psychology*, 13(2), 92–99. doi:10.1037/tep0000228.

Washington, H. A. (2006). *Medical apartheid: The dark history of medical experimentation on Black Americans from colonial times to the present.* Doubleday.

Watlington, C. G., & Murphy, C. M. (2006). The roles of religion and spirituality among African American survivors of domestic violence. *Journal of Clinical Psychology*, 62, 837–857. doi:10.1002/jclp.20268.

Westman, N. & Intagliata, C. (Producers) (2016, July 15). The health costs of racism. *Science Friday.* https://www.sciencefriday.com/segments/the-health-costs-of-racism/.

Williams, M. (2015, September 6). The link between racism and PTSD. *Psychology Today.* https://www.psychologytoday.com/us/blog/culturally-speaking/201509/the-link-between-racism-and-ptsd.

Wortham, J. (2015, June 24). Racism's psychological toll. *New York Times Magazine.* https://www.nytimes.com/2015/06/24/magazine/racisms-psychological-toll.html.

14

APPLICATIONS TO PROGRAMMING AND POLICY

In this chapter, I discuss several issues associated with applying Black cultural strengths, but the overarching focus of the chapter is the application of strengths to policy and programming in mental health. To grasp the issues, I survey the policy and organizational landscape for recognition of Black cultural strengths in policy and program activities used by those who help implement mental health services and programs. Then the discussion provides guidance to those who might wish to use the strength perspective in developing programs and setting policy in mental health service delivery.

Mental Health Services and Black Americans

Mental health service systems in the United States have not been directed at the well-being or treatment for Black Americans. In my early published work, I wrote about how race and racial identity influence the psychotherapy process and outcomes (Carter, 1995). I advocated for what I called a racially inclusive model, and my concluding chapter focused on how to assess race from a racially inclusive framework in clinical treatment. I find myself returning to that work now since the policy in mental health service delivery and in programs for mental health treatment have struggled to meet the needs of Black people, and people of color in general. The cultural, diversity, and multicultural movements have made some inroads, but I would argue that little in terms of how therapy is delivered has changed over the last several decades. Consider the number of guidelines that have been issued and published by the American Psychological Association (APA). Some have been for specialty areas like forensic and clinical psychology, but they all represent statements rather than substantive changes in how mental health services are delivered. There are the APA's ethical guidelines (2015); APA's multicultural

DOI: 10.4324/9781003111542-19

guidelines (2017); APA's resolution against racism (2021a); APA's equity, diversity, and inclusion framework (2021b); APA's statement about its role in dismantling systemic racism (2021c); and APA's Guidelines from the Task Force on Race and Ethnicity (2019). I have also pointed out that in the context of diversity and multicultural efforts in mental health, issues of race and racism have received less attention. Only recently has the APA made statements about race and racism exclusive of general diversity, which indicates that race has been regarded as less important for the organization to address. The association's public apology to people of color for their role and participation in systemic racism supports my claims (APA, 2021c).

Blacks' mental health as stated by the APA has not been effectively or adequately addressed; thus, one can conclude that Black people's needs are less important when mental health services are offered and when programs and policies are devised and implemented. Moreover, for many who provide mental health services, whether publicly or privately funded, there is an oversized emphasis on funding and income generation. Funding health and mental health is driven by the Diagnostic and Statistical Manual of Mental Disorders (DSM-5, APA, 2013) that insurance companies use to justify paying for mental health services. So, to the extent that the issues Black clients bring to treatment do not conform to DSM criteria, it is more difficult to have their services covered by health insurance. In this climate, mental health providers would be focused on generating a diagnosis that is acceptable to the insurance companies, or the client would have to pay for services out of pocket. It is likely that considerations in treating Blacks might not lead to examining their worldviews in part due to training and the involvement of the discipline in systemic racism and in part due to incentives of the insurance industry. Keep in mind, the insurance industry relies on mental health and medical associations for guidance and standards for practice. And as was noted in the last chapter, the psychological, psychiatric, and medical associations have admitted that they also have been deeply involved in the country's system of racism. Yet mental health services are provided by individual therapists who operate within society's system of mental health and health care.

The therapist should begin with the intake and assessment aimed at learning about the person's background and family history; this way race and racism can be integrated into that process and procedure. In my view, it should be the policy of service providers who work with Black Americans to consider the person's race and culture, and the intake or initial sessions be used to gather information that would provide some perspective about the person's race, racial identity status, and cultural preferences. My recommendation is that these be gathered as part of the clinical assessment procedures and processes.

It is common practice to provide a physical description of the client that includes information about their emotional and cognitive presentation. The initial meeting also is focused on the person's presenting issues or a statement about why they are seeking help. However, overlooked in this procedure is the way in which the racial identity statuses of the parties affect their perceptions and information processing, emotional states, and actions. The role of racial identity is critical in how the parties relate to one another. Evidence indicates that many therapists are trained to perceive Blacks as more disturbed than whites, which might lead the clinician to interpret what the client says in a way that is inconsistent with what was actually meant. The therapist may also be invested in mainstream cultural patterns and as such would look for these patterns in the client and be unaware that other cultural patterns may be endorsed by the client. For example, the client may not strive for independence and separation from their families or loved ones, as is the practice among white Americans. This deviation from norms could be seen as an indication of psychological issues rather than as a potential cultural strength.

For an effective racial-cultural assessment, personal, systemic, and psychosocial factors—or, said another way, a systems-focused perspective—should be employed and integrated into the assessment process. Doing so requires policy and program changes to the service delivery system.

A system-level assessment looks at the client's personal identity and psychological functioning, assessing it at several levels with the understanding that the various levels interact to influence each other. As is standard practice, the physical description of the client is provided but with more detail than just noting the person's presumed racial group. Attention is given to personal factors such as skin color, hair type, and related physical characteristics as well as how the person describes themselves in racial terms. Psychological factors also need to be assessed, including coping style, maturity, and manner of interacting. The evaluator could attempt to learn how the person incorporates race into their personality, so their racial identity status and cultural preferences would be critical to determine. These facts might come out as the person is discussing their presenting issues or in the process of establishing rapport with the clinician. However, it may be necessary to learn about how the client was taught about their personal identity, whether it was strongly influenced by others or mainly intrapsychic, and how their psychosocial development progressed; these would be valuable questions to explore.

Psychosocial Factors and Cultural Preferences

Psychosocial influences are derived from parents, family, friends, peers, schools, churches, and other social institutions like social media, television, and so on. These are in turn shaped by systemic or macrosystems and related forces that are expressed through beliefs systems, ideologies, political perspectives, and sociopolitical actions and forces as well as economic situations and circumstances. Personal and psychosocial factors are shaped by intrapsychic dispositions, psychosocial factors, and systems influences that together form one's racial-cultural worldview. One's worldview serves as the primary vehicle for information processing because it aids in sorting internal and external data, makes sense of it, and guides actions, feelings, and perspectives. The data works to provide consistency to the person about the self and others in general and in specific ways as well as provides guidance about one's racial group and that of others.

What is important to keep in mind is that these processes are subconscious and are not always available to the person's conscious mind. So it should not be expected that the person can relay how all these factors work in their lives, but they should be able to convey their life experiences and their reactions to them. The assessment must proceed slowly and with a focused effort to learn about the inner life and external influences that the client is aware of, and the clinician must make connections about these and the factors that operated and impacted the client.

Psychosocial factors can function in several ways to impact one's life and worldview. One major element is the way race and racism affects one's development since race or racial group membership can be valued or not, nor can race be avoided. It is possible to learn through socialization that your racial group—and you, as a member—are devalued and denigrated. A person can be seen as less than human and, thus, treated in a manner that reflects that devalued perspective. In this case, society communicates messages about racial groups in general ways that reveal little about the individual and more about group qualities. So the social environment indicates the relative worth of any person based on the racial group they are presumed to belong to, a judgment that bypasses individual or personal qualities. In the United States, if the person appears to be white, then all the qualities attributed to the white group are assigned to that person. For instance, such a person would be considered superior, to have greater abilities and intelligence, to be more capable, and so on. And the opposite would be true if one is presumed to be Black; in that case, less intelligence and less ability are attributed to this person. These beliefs about one's qualities are communicated early in one's life and determine the circumstances to which one is subjected.

The circumstances for Blacks have shifted and changed over the centuries and yet the essential messages about Black people have not changed. Their social status has been altered considerably through the efforts of some whites and many Blacks, yet the legacy of being Black in American society remains. It is this reality, for Blacks, that clinicians must grasp in order to conduct assessments designed to uncover the embedded cultural patterns that are a source of strength and well-being for many Black people. The challenge comes about when neither the client nor the clinician knows that the strengths exist or are even possible.

Here is an illustration of what I mean by being unaware of one's own cultural preferences. In the introduction I talked about the journey I took that led me to the study of cultural practices of Blacks. While working on my doctorate, there was a requirement that students take a comprehensive exam once course work and related clinical training was completed. The exam was designed to assess the depth and breadth of the students' learning from the beginning to that juncture in their training. After the exam, students would complete the final stages of training, which were usually internship and dissertation. The exam was administered over two full days, in which the student had to answer five questions in essay form. Each had to be completed in two- to three-hour segments, three questions the first day and two the second day. It was the custom that students in the same cohort would study for the exam as a group. There were four students in my class, me and three white women.

I advocated for a group-study arrangement, but the women did not want to work as a group, at least not with me as a member. I was left to prepare on my own. I was disturbed by this rejection, and at the same time I could not understand why working as a group was so important to me. I got over the rejection and was able to prepare, and I passed the exam. After the written phase, there was an oral portion in which I had to defend my answers in front of a faculty committee. Clearly, this was not group-based, yet here again having others to prepare for this task, in my mind, would have made the task easier to bear.

In previous years Black students in the department who had classes together would usually work in study groups, so the expectation seemed reasonable, given the importance of the comprehensive exam and how demanding studying for it was. Even so, I did not understand the depth of my anger and upset with my classmates at the time. I felt betrayed in a way that stayed with me for many years. I came to recognize that my expectation was grounded in a value I held that I had, up to that point, not named. It was clear to me that it was one that I expected, that some things are handled best with the group. I had failed to see how that belief was contrary to what my white classmates had learned and expected. They were taught to be individuals, not to be group oriented. I was able to pinpoint this cultural value and how it worked for me during my time in doctoral study and later in my life. My anger subsided, and I was struck with an awareness of how cultural values can operate outside of one's conscious awareness.

The point is, it is more likely that clinicians, regardless of their race, will find out about cultural values in their clients through indirect methods of inquiry, which is why it would be important that agencies have policies and programs that facilitate the type of assessment that I recommend. Assessments should explore the person's experiences and background from multiple perspectives—the personal, psychosocial, and systemic—and there be consideration for one's race, racial identity status, and cultural patterns as well as their presenting issues.

Clinicians should push past the myriad obstacles that exist to seeing Black people as having aspects of themselves and their racial group that are constructive and positive and that contribute to their psychological well-being. Layers of negative and harmful stereotypes and images will make this task challenging and difficult, particularly since many of these perceptions are evoked automatically, given the centuries of such messages sent in ways that make it hard to discern when they are present.

Theories of Personality and Human Development That Hinder Racial-Cultural Understanding

Another obstacle is what mental health professionals are taught about human development and personality. The theories and models often assume that human experience is universal, and they seldom integrate or consider racial-cultural variation. More important, race and culturally based aspects of development are often not addressed in such theories; most assume white, European American cultural foundations without stating so but by implication. Several theories are used to understand human personality and development: Psychoanalytic, Cognitive-Behavioral, Humanistic, Person-Centered, Eclectic, and various combinations.

Psychoanalytic oriented clinicians focus on varied issues, mostly centered on inner conflicts that shape self-worth, while humanists have centered their focus on relational interactions, and cognitive-behavioral clinicians concentrate on reinforcement and social learning as the critical forces that shapes one's self-concept. The theories share the notion that the self is shaped from interactions that are mostly internal with some recognition of the role of key relationships. Ecological theories have also been presented, which includes the systemic influence of the macro environment. Yet the macro world and society, in many theories, seem to play a lesser role in forming and understanding personality.

I have argued that there needs to be recognition of the role of race and culture. Messages from the larger social structure and its institutions and people contribute to how a person comes to see themselves. To a large extent, systemic forces help determine the social and physical environment and influences not only through direct messages about one's worth but also via metacommunications (unspoken communications).

The messages from the sociocultural environment determine and are driven by societal and systemic forces such as political positions, economic circumstances, and social movements and beliefs that are promoted. The combined power of these forces—sociopolitical, economic, and ideological patterns, historical realities, and institutionalized racism—creates numerous obstacles and problems that people in our society must face. So those who set and formulate policy, devise programs, and determine how services are delivered need to devise mental health policies and design programs to reduce said obstacles and to promote psychological well-being and healing for all clients who seek mental health services.

The process could begin by examining the embedded cultural assumptions in existing policy, such as the notion that the focus of treatment should be primarily on the person as an individual rather than the person as part of a system of interacting relationships. The assumption that psychological health is the absence of disorder could also be examined and questioned, as could the notion that the family is nuclear and not extended. The false idea that Black people are damaged and devoid of strengths points to the need for agencies and clinicians to learn about aspects of Black life that could be present but hidden under layers of mental and emotional protective walls and barriers since it has been necessary for generations for Blacks to keep some parts of themselves from public view in order to survive. At the same time, it does not mean that the Black strengths are not there operating in conscious and subconscious ways.

Unfortunately, we are living in a time of backward social and racial progress regarding race relations and perceptions and treatment of Black Americans. This is illustrated by the events and effects of the worldwide COVID-19 pandemic, which harmed and killed Blacks and other marginal Americans at a higher rate than whites, coupled with the frequent killings of unarmed Black men and women, a stark example was the murder of George Floyd on May 25, 2020, by police officers in Minnesota, which brought attention to race and racism and triggered global protests against racial injustice. The focus of the protests after the Floyd killing was on police racial bias directed at Black men and women, but the protests also highlighted the negative effects of racism on the mental health of Black people. These events revealed the harm inflicted on Blacks in America. Many have been led to believe that Blacks have psychological and mental health issues that need attention. But is this accurate?

The State of Black Mental Health

The current picture of Black mental health is one that is both surprising and hopeful, considering the relative functioning of Blacks in other areas of American life. Research conducted since the mid-20th century has found that Black Americans had poor self-images (e.g., Kardiner & Ovesey, 1951), but starting in the 1970s, during and after the civil rights movement, research evidence changed and was reporting that Blacks had higher self-esteem than white Americans (Gray-Little & Hafdahl, 2000; Twenge & Crocker, 2002). Furthermore, the rise in self-esteem among Black people was associated with the transformation from the Negro identity to the Black and Proud, or Black Is Beautiful, movement that characterized the Black Power era of the 1970s, that followed the biracial civil rights movement and protests (Twenge & Crocker, 2002). In fact, in the face of persistent racism and racial oppression that resulted in racial disparities in virtually all areas of American life, coupled with the higher levels of exposure to stress associated with these disparities both in daily activities and across time and generations, three decades of research has documented that Black Americans report the same or better mental health when compared to white Americans, where better is defined as lower rates of mental disorder. The lower rates reported in empirical studies of mental health is known as the Black-white mental health paradox, which has been evident in rates of major depression. However, when investigators have expanded their research beyond that particular disorder to some 16 other different mental health disorders, including mood, anxiety, and substance use disorders, measured both in the past year and across the lifetime, Blacks are found to have lower incidence and prevalence than whites even when socioeconomic status and age were controlled (Erving, Thomas, & Frazier, 2019; Gibbs et al., 2013).

Research has found evidence suggesting that the Black-white mental health paradox may be explained at least in part by higher rates of flourishing or overall positive mental health among Blacks when compared to whites (Keyes, 2009). Flourishing was defined as having generally positive affect (i.e., feeling happy, calm, peaceful, and satisfied); self-acceptance (i.e., positive attitudes toward self, including accepting both positive and negative aspects of oneself); social acceptance (i.e., positive attitudes toward others while accepting differences and complexity); personal growth (i.e., understanding of one's own potential and openness to challenging experiences); social actualization (i.e., belief that people, social groups, and society have the potential to grow in a positive direction); purpose in life (i.e., belief that life has purpose and direction); social contribution (i.e., perception of one's life as useful to society and valued/valuable to society); environmental mastery (i.e., ability to manage a complex environment and mold the environment to suit one's needs); social coherence (i.e., an interest in society and social life and belief that society and culture are meaningful); autonomy (i.e., self-direction guided by internal standards and resisting negative social pressures); positive relations with others (i.e., warm and trusting interpersonal relations and capacity for empathy and intimacy); and social integration (i.e., sense of belonging to, comfort in, and support from community).

In examining the Black-white mental health paradox, Keyes (2009) found that more Black people than white people were found to be flourishing and free of mental disorders, and when racial discrimination was controlled for, rates of flourishing increased for Black people. This investigation reveals the substance of Black Americans' strengths in their perceptions of self, community, and ways of dealing with adversity and racial discrimination that promote psychological health and well-being.

Louie and colleagues (2022) noted in their study that self-esteem and church attendance were found to explain racial differences in depressive symptoms and mental health disorders in that those with high levels of self-esteem explained the observed differences in depressive symptoms between Black and white Americans. There is also evidence that racial identity status contributes to increased self-esteem and mastery for Blacks as compared to whites, and that Black people who had more mature levels of racial identity were less likely to have mental health and substance use disorders than white people (Hughes, Kiecolt, & Keith, 2022). Louie and colleagues (2022) also found that higher levels of religiosity and spirituality reduced depression disorders for Black people as compared to white people. Upeneiks, Louie, and Hill (2023) also found that Black people experience fewer religious and spiritual struggles than white people and that these struggles contributed to greater distress among white people. They suggested that Black people may experience greater spiritual support from their religious congregations than do white people, providing Blacks with greater strength and less conflict. Research has also found that there are protective effects on mental health for Black people living in predominantly Black neighborhoods, with up to 84% Black residents (Becares, Nazroo, & Jackson, 2014), suggesting that the social cohesion, sense of community, and social support of predominantly Black—although not racially segregated and isolated—neighborhoods may help reduce rates of depression. Taken together, the results of these studies on flourishing, self-esteem and racial identity, religiosity and spirituality, and ethnic density provide strong support for the notion that the Black cultural strengths described in this book, including racial identity, racial socialization, communalism, cultural spirituality, and racism-related coping, contribute to the ability of Black Americans to thrive in the face of centuries of significant and unrelenting adversity.

Scholars and researchers (Alegría et al., 2013; Erving, Thomas, & Frazier, 2019; Himle et al., 2009; McLaughlin et al., 2019; Roberts et al., 2011) have found some exceptions to the Black-white mental health paradox: Black people have higher rates of posttraumatic stress disorder (PTSD) and are significantly more likely to be diagnosed with schizophrenia. Over the last 20 years, suicide appears to be yet another emerging exception to the Black-white mental health paradox. These three trends tell a story about the impact of the interaction between structural racism, interpersonal racism, and poor access to mental health care in Black communities.

An area of concern is the underutilization of mental health services by Black adolescents, which may be linked to the rising rates of Black youth suicide. Their rates of suicide (ages 10–19) were historically quite low, yet the rates rose dramatically between 1980 and 1995 (Price & Khubchandani, 2019, 2022). As of 2020, suicide was the second-leading cause of death for Black adolescents. Between 2001 and 2017, suicide rates for Black adolescents rose by 60% for boys and 182% for girls. These findings are quite notable in the context of opposing findings for adults. It appears that Black children and adolescents are particularly vulnerable to mental health struggles (Price & Khubchandani, 2019). Yet it is important not to think of Blacks as a monolith, since they can vary in how they understand their race. Another possibility is that youths are impacted by their exposure to social media, as reported in chapter 13.

Explanations of the Harm Blacks Have Suffered from Racial Oppression

Some people believe that Blacks have been mentally damaged by racism and their marginal social status, and that the harm has occurred across generations (e.g., Kardiner & Ovesey, 1951). These viewpoints invoke a fatalistic and self-hating explanation that suggests Black people were destined to suffer psychological problems due to racial oppression and their lack of culture, their poverty, and their dysfunctional families. Yet, Blacks pushed back and stated that Black people were culturally different from other racial-cultural groups.

Most mainstream characterizations of Black people's psychological functioning seek to understand or explain mental *illness, disorder, and dysfunction* (Griffith, Jones, & Stewart, 2019). There have been three primary paradigms employed regarding Black mental health: Blacks are inferior, disadvantaged, and culturally different.

The formal apology by the American Psychological Association issued to people of color for its "role in promoting, perpetuating, and failing to challenge racism, racial discrimination, and human hierarchy" in the United States (APA, 2021c) also documented a chronological statement of the history of racism in the formal discipline of psychology (Cummings Center, 2021). This catalog presented historical evidence of structural and systemic racism as well as how paradigms of racial inferiority and deficiency were woven into the development of the research, profession, and practice of psychology in the United States in a way that has generated, spread, and is intricately tied to the racial mental health disparities evident today. From the origins of the discipline in the United States in the 18th century to the present, psychology has been complicit in endorsing and delivering false scientific evidence to support the belief in an innate biologically based racial hierarchy, with Black people as the inferior race and white people as the superior race.

As was just pointed out, writings and scholarship in psychology regarding Blacks have been, among other things, centered on the negative mental health effects of racism, particularly Blacks' predisposition toward anger, paranoia, and hostility, which causes mental health issues. Scholars (e.g., Grier & Cobbs, 1992) have written about the *historical hostility* that Black clients exhibit as a result of their unequal treatment. These authors asserted that this hostility leads to rage, protest, substance use, and excessive violence. Further they suggest that historical hostility was part of the collective unconscious of Blacks as a group. Regarding the destructiveness of historical hostility, these scholars think that hostility is a reasonable defense mechanism against daily discrimination; that Blacks' hostility explains violence, substance abuse, and sexual promiscuity among Blacks; and that violence, substance abuse, and promiscuity could be forms of escapism from depression (Vontress & Epp, 1997). This theory, and others like it, attempts to acknowledge the influence of hundreds of years of slavery, oppression, and violence toward Blacks, yet it appears to discuss Blacks as only negatively impacted and suffering as a result of their interactions with whites. Aspects of Black consciousness that have been adaptive and protective of Black mental health are missing from the discussion. In fact, we learned that Blacks were less likely to have debilitating mental health disorders, including major depression (U.S. Department of Health and Human Services, 2001).

Theories of Racial Differences

Now I turn to the three principle ways that have been used to understand Black people's social, psychological, and cultural states and statuses—biological inferiority, cultural deprivation, and cultural difference. When a particular perspective is ascendant, it is used to explain situations and circumstances people find themselves in, and it is used instead of other viewpoints. More important, when people use a particular perspective, they seldom look for alternative viewpoints. Instead, they use the concepts and beliefs of that point of view to problem solve and to create and establish policies, procedures, programs, and interventions (Carter, 1995). It is important to remember that while each theory is primarily associated with a particular period in the nation's history, none of the three are confined to that era. Therefore, the viewpoints overlap; they have been employed simultaneously, and the assumptions derived from each are embedded, to varying degrees, in current health and educational beliefs, institutions, policies, and practices. Remember that psychiatry is a subspeciality of medicine that has its own legacy of racism (see Blackstock, 2024; Hylton, 2024)

Many members of American society believe that whites are superior and their culture is normative. As far as Blacks people were concerned, and for some this is still the viewpoint, people believed they had no distinct culture, which cemented the notion of their biological inferiority and justified their low-caste status. Nevertheless, "uncivilized" was the core notion about Black people, so their low status was seen as natural. Yet their inferior state also meant that they were not able to experience mental distress. But, Black people had to adapt to white culture and society to obtain any measure of social participation. The theory of Blacks' inferiority was taken for granted and was based on presumed biological and genetic limits that made Black people deficient compared to whites. Therefore, any differences—including the ones structured into society that limited Blacks' movement, educational access, and work options—in behavior, culture, and mental status between whites and Blacks can be attributed to the inherent inferiority of Blacks (Carter, 1995). From a mental health perspective, the inferior view led many to see Black people as not mentally sophisticated enough to suffer from mental disorders since they were "an uncivilized race"; thus, they had less or almost no mental illness (Faber et al., 2023).

The focus on biological and genetic explanations for racial group differences declined, and scholars and policymakers took up the idea that social class disparities and the caste structure of the United States was the source of Blacks' problems since they lacked family structure and cohesion. The family system was not the same as that of white families and, thus, was judged to be a system that was damaged and harmed its members. The term "disadvantaged" and its derivative terms "deprived" and "underprivileged" began to appear with reference to Blacks. The cultural deprivation notions used the social and biological meaning of race to create a criterion whereby racial group members are compared to a white normative standard in order to demonstrate the various ways in which they were deprived or deviant (Harrington, 1963). In fact, this new emphasis seemed like a shift in perspective from that of inborn inferiority since it was centered on social conditions. Yet the shift, while real, was subtle at best. In both points of view, white culture and social structure are the norms to be attained. The cultural deprivation view attributes the differences between white and Black to cultural disadvantage, which affects not only social position but also variation in behavior, personality, and mental health. Therefore, advocates of this perspective assert that inequality in economic, social, and cultural experiences are the basis for any psychiatric or psychosocial differences between the "races." While structural barriers are noted, these are given less emphasis or importance.

The emphasis on the characteristics of social disadvantage led to investigations that continue to this day, documenting the presumed abnormal effects of poverty and racial discrimination. Consequently, most investigations typically report on such issues as juvenile delinquency, crime, poverty, dysfunction, mental disturbance, and so forth. The focus on the outcomes surrounding a group's sociopolitical, economic, and psychosocial life presents a distorted picture of Black people that has become ubiquitous in the social and behavioral sciences and has persisted over time. As Black scholars have noted, the literature on Black people and families is focused on the negative. It is fair to argue that for those who live in poverty, encounter racial discrimination, and are excluded from social institutions (e.g., schools), this has an adverse effect. Yet it is probably wrong to assume that all Black people have been permanently psychologically destroyed or crippled by the destructive influences of racism and have no cultural moorings. It is important to identify the social obstacles that obstruct and hamper a group's or an individual's potential. Yet this does not mean that the obstacles "crippled" the individual.

Given the social-political-historical and contemporary salience of race in our society, it is reasonable to conclude that it is not possible to be socialized into this society without being presented with myriad opportunities to internalize beliefs and attitudes about racial groups. In the sciences and popular culture, the message is that anything other than white culture is unacceptable. Blacks have for centuries been the repository of negative projections, distortions, and destructive myths about their race and culture (Williams & Mohammed, 2013).

Such myths and beliefs have been internalized by most Americans; consequently, these messages and the boundaries due to race are maintained to this day. No person or professional group—including mental health professionals—are immune to the infectious influence of racism. Few training programs adequately equip their developing professionals with the knowledge, attitudes, and skills that allow them to work with the racial obstacles that exist in our society. Consequently, much of what is known about Blacks is overwhelmingly negative. More important, Black culture evolved because of the same conditions that brought about the ideas that Black people had no culture. The truth is, Black culture has always been visible, but it has always been devalued and denigrated (Belgrave & Allison, 2019).

The cultural difference perspective holds that psychological and behavioral differences between whites and Blacks are best explained in terms of the various influences related to racial and cultural background. Difference advocates reject the notion that race and culture for Black people is lacking. The argument is that Black people retained and developed their own unique cultural patterns in part due to their isolation and segregation from mainstream society.

In terms of mental health, the cultural difference perspective influenced training and practice such that some have begun to develop interventions and instructional guidelines that reflect the racial-cultural experience of Black Americans to some extent. Much of the cultural difference literature has involved awareness building, increasing knowledge regarding particular racial groups' cultures, and building skills to enhance cross-racial effectiveness (Sue et al., 2019). There is now some recognition that Blacks have a culture that differs from whites, yet in some respects, the belief that social conditions dictate the cultural patterns of Blacks remains.

The Truth about Black Cultural Values and Beliefs

Writers have argued that therapists and mental health professionals must understand their patients' culture if they are going to provide appropriate services. More specifically, Carter and Pieterse (2020) describe several aspects of the psychotherapy relationship that are influenced by the participants' race and culture: (a) the therapist's and patient's racial-cultural backgrounds; (b) the assumptions that each in the therapy dyad make about the nature of illness, helping, relationships, and the source of their problems; and (c) how the environment where therapy takes place is influenced by cultural beliefs and practices. As can be seen, many elements of the therapeutic relationship are subject to racial-cultural socialization factors and professional training. People's expectations, perceptions, feelings, thoughts, behaviors, and the way they organize information represent their racial-cultural learning and training. The family and the social context are the primary sources of racial-cultural learning.

Some scholars (e.g., Jensen, 1968) believe that Blacks, because of their low social status, develop negative attitudes and beliefs about themselves and their racial group. However, Jones (2003) states that this is not so; he contends that oppressed people can have positive regard for themselves and their group. And he presents an African-based cultural worldview associated with positive psychological well-being for Black Americans, which consists of both existential propositions, which are guides to behavior and attitudes, and psychological components, where one's culture is reflected in ways of thinking, emotional expression, and behavioral actions that are shared and communicated through symbols, ideas, and values.

As a cultural group, Black people coped and adapted to their circumstances as oppressed captives and had to do so over time. They had to learn how to handle the loss of their freedom and how to deal with being dehumanized, yet they held on to their core African cultural ethos.

Black American cultural values are characterized by beliefs in a group orientation, sharing, spirituality, present time, improvisation, rhythm, emotional expressiveness, and harmony with nature (Carter & Helms, 1987). Hill (1972) suggests that while racial oppression attempted to destroy the Black family, it survived because of its strong kinship bonds, flexibility of family roles, and high value placed on spirituality/religion, education, and work. Black families, according to Boyd-Franklin (1989, 2006), are organized around extended kinship networks, which includes blood and unrelated persons. Family roles and responsibilities, jobs, and functions are often interchanged among family members, as was the case in the past and, strangely enough, were noted and deemed signs of pathology. This sharing of roles and functions occurs across generational and gender roles. These activities are used by Blacks to reinforce their self-worth.

The cultural themes established in the 19th century remain active into the 21st century. Black American cultural values are characterized by beliefs in a group focus (Carter & Helms, 1987) as well as several other cultural patterns and practices such as the valuing of rhythm, improvisation, orality, communalism, racial socialization, racism-related coping, and racial identity status development (i.e., psychological orientation to one's race). As one historian (Webber, 1978) observed, the limits and controls used to keep Blacks in line were quite real. But the devices and methods used against them did not reach into their minds, nor did the oppression they endured prevent Blacks from educating their young and imparting to them their cultural beliefs and practices. Blacks still were able to create social norms and expectations that they held one another to abide by and that set the framework for their unique cultural and psychological perspectives. They held on to hope and to their belief in what was right and just. As many scholars (e.g., Belgrave & Allison,

2019; Bennett, 1988; Franklin & Moss, 2000; Gates, 2021; Horton & Horton, 2005; Jones, 2003; Webber, 1978) have noted, the cultural practices of Blacks was well established by the time of the Civil War and were centered in family, community, spirituality/religion, artistic and musical expression, and improvisation, rhythm, and oral traditions, which were shared and passed on to the succeeding generation.

Blacks' experiences with and lack of regard by medical and mental health professionals tend to lead them away from mental health professionals or, if they do seek help, they enter with low levels of trust (Thompson, Bazile, & Akbar, 2004). The Black client may enter therapy with a number of defenses associated with race. She may have anxieties about the therapist, regardless of the race of the therapist. Thompson and colleagues (2004) noted that Blacks view therapists, no matter their race, as reflecting the perspectives of mainstream society. Thus, the Black client may be less forthcoming, not as verbal, and less likely to self-disclose. They may perceive their therapists as being distant and unable to relate to Black experiences. More importantly, many Black clients may simply desire a therapy relationship in which they can self-disclose without educating their therapists about race and racism. The Black client may also be beset with anxieties associated with Blackness and status in society. Consequently, the client may tend to be less active and involved and may react negatively to counseling interventions attempted by the therapist. In such instances, one would expect that the client would either terminate therapy early or leave with little symptom relief. Therefore, program developers, policymakers, and service providers need to examine their current practices if they want to create a more welcoming environment for Black people.

Pitfalls and Problems in the Therapy Setting

Some authors (e.g., Faber et al., 2023; Sue et al., 2019) have argued that Black therapists, because of their shared experience of oppression and discrimination and their shared racial background, are better suited to treat Black clients. However, this may not be so since Blacks differ from one another in how they view their race. A criticism of mental health training programs is that they do not train mental health professionals to be racially culturally effective or knowledgeable. Black therapists are usually trained to work with white clients (Carter, 2005), meaning that Black therapists are trained in programs that employ universal methods of interventions and treatment techniques and assume all people react and relate in similar ways. So racial-cultural differences and specific problems of Black people are seldom included in the techniques and theory of human development offered in mental health training programs. Therefore, Black therapists are subject to the same pitfalls as white therapists when working with Black clients.

Clinicians today may know more about the pitfalls attendant with a lack of cultural knowledge, a failure to examine one's own racial background, and gaps in professional training. However, most mental health professionals are still poorly equipped to handle race and Black culture in psychotherapy (Belgrave & Allison, 2019). Thus, cultural factors that lead to misunderstandings by the therapist can hamper the therapy relationship. Therapists who operate from a worldview with relatively fixed expectations and role behaviors expect self-disclosure from patients; the patient is presumed to be autonomous from family and other ties. It is expected that the past, present, and future will be appropriately distinguished such that the client will strive for a life focused on the future. The client is supposed to see the therapist as a powerful, knowledgeable expert. The therapist also sees himself or herself as responsible, able to judge what is real for the patient, capable of objectivity or neutrality, and using a nonjudgmental stance. The expectation is that the therapist will not bring their own personal values into treatment and can therefore aid the client to uncover important aspects about past and present in the service of the client's future. Yet when cultural values conflict, as reflected in racial dynamics, then therapists and patients encounter innumerable problems such as ruptures or disruptions in the therapeutic alliance, when interactions become so difficult that little progress can occur and termination often is the best option (Liu & Pope-Davis, 2005). Under these circumstances, race and culture introduce difficulties that must be overcome or resolved before effective therapeutic work can occur.

Race and culture as discussed in the therapy literature suggests that racial attitudes of both the therapist and the client affect therapy (Thompson, Bazile, & Akbar, 2004). What we know from the literature is how the race and culture of clients creates problems in treatment (Liu & Pope-Davis, 2005). What is unclear from the literature is what characteristics of patients and therapists predict or determine specific types of influences. How does one determine if a client is operating from a particular cultural or psychological perspective?

Another obstacle to effective treatment of Black clients in psychology and mental health is the absence of theory and race's marginal status in human development and personality theory. The lack of theory-based models keeps the discourse about race speculative and emotional and prevents insight. The tendency to use racial-cultural group categories or membership as the primary unit of analysis is also an obstacle to effective treatment. This practice implicitly promotes a belief that racial issues are the exclusive province of Black people, while most whites deny or are unaware of the racial-cultural context in which they live. Therefore, when conflicts or cultural differences arise, racial issues are generally construed as marginal or as a "Black" concern. The assumption seems to be that whites do not as individuals need to consider racial issues as important to them. Yet, if race is one-sided, how do we understand the influence of race and culture in our work as helping professionals?

The psychological significance of race and culture for each individual varies as a function of the individual's interpretation of their socialization and psychosocial developmental processes. The psychological significance of race and one's culture affects how one thinks, feels, acts, and, consequently, sees the world and others in the same and in different racial groups. Because race has personal meaning for each individual, it follows that race would matter in interpersonal and helping relationships.

Mental health professionals and other helpers continue to perpetuate the sociocultural milieu surrounding culture and race. One reason for perpetuating racial-cultural barriers is the tendency of most people to approach these issues as absent history and without any theoretical basis. Considering the confessions of health and mental health associations, perhaps the denial and rejection of race and culture might subside. And more programs and policies will be developed that will enhance mental health professionals' ability to use and build upon Blacks' cultural strengths.

Black Cultural Strengths and Psychological Well-Being

Despite the view of Blacks as culturally deficient and psychologically damaged, the work of many scholars has shifted this perspective on Black culture from it being inferior to being culturally different (Sue et al., 2019). Contemporary work has uncovered aspects of Black culture that enabled Blacks to both survive the ongoing racial oppression in the United States and to maintain psychological health. Blacks have not lost their minds due to racial oppression.

I have described several cultural strengths associated with Blacks that contribute to their psychological health and well-being. Recall that culture is defined as a system of meaning with values, norms, behaviors, language, and history that is passed on from one generation to the next through socialization and participation in the group's organizations and institutions (Stewart & Bennett, 2011).

Scholars have asserted that it is important to examine Black culture from an African-centered perspective, to look at Black culture as separate and distinct from white culture (Belgrave & Allison, 2019). Given the promising yet minimal empirical findings associating the Afrocultural expression with prosocial values and behaviors (e.g., decreased delinquency), it remains important to work from an African-centered viewpoint but also to explore other Black cultural values that may promote psychological and social functioning (Johnson & Carter, 2020), including increased overall well-being and satisfaction with life.

Most Blacks have maintained a sense of connectedness to each other and a sense of self-worth even while being racially oppressed. They have employed racial socialization practices to pass these beliefs to new generations. Other values and beliefs that Blacks hold and express are expressive individualism as well as being community-oriented, being invested in cultural spirituality, religious worship, racism-related coping, and racial identity development (psychological orientation to one's race) (Johnson & Carter, 2020). These elements of Black culture are sources of Black cultural strength that allow for growth and progression as well as psychological health. I have discussed several of these, particularly racial identity, racial socialization, communalism, cultural spirituality, and racism-related coping, and I have presented evidence to show that these are related to psychological well-being and demonstrate cultural strength in the face of racial oppression.

Racial identity theorists (Cross & Vandiver, 2001; Helms, 1990; Sellers et al., 1998) contend that how one thinks and feels about being Black matters, but each theorist conveys this in different ways.

Johnson and Carter (2020) used measures of Black cultural practices and behaviors in their empirical study to determine whether the cultural practices or beliefs would, in a statistical model, predict the construct of Black cultural strengths. In essence, they used instruments administered to a Black adult participant group. The participants' scores on parts of the instruments captured the respective variable. For instance, two racial identity models and measures were one by Sellers and colleagues (1998), a multidimensional model of Black identity, and another by Helms (1990), a model and measure of racial identity statuses. Sellers's model and measure captures four qualitative dimensions of being Black: *salience*, which refers to how relevant race is to self-concept; *centrality*, which is one's normative perception of self; *regard*, which includes feelings of negativity or positivity about being Black in both public (others' view) and private (one's own feelings about being Black); and *ideology*, which is one's beliefs about how Blacks should interact in society.

Helms (1990) proposed multiple statuses ranging from Pre-encounter (rejection of one's own racial group) to Internalization (acceptance and investment in one's race and culture). While many domains exist to understand Black racial identity, only some of them have been positively associated with psychological health. Investigators in numerous studies and with varying methods have found that psychosocial well-being is associated with racial identity that reflects Black pride and investment in Black culture, in addition to tolerance for other racial groups. For instance, scholars have reported that Internalization status attitudes, high centrality, and high private regard are positively related to psychological well-being. Therefore, the construct employed in the study was central internalization, which consisted of Internalization status attitudes from Helms's Black racial identity attitudes (BRIAS) measures and centrality and private regard from the Sellers and colleagues' Multidimensional Inventory of Black Identity (MIBI).

Connected to racial identity development is racial socialization. Thus, as researchers did with racial identity, they looked for how best to measure this cultural practice. More important, they considered what aspects of racial socialization would be more positively related to racial identity.

Racial socialization involves intergenerational transmission of attitudes and values accomplished by way of direct and indirect messages about being aware of racial oppression and being taught racial-cultural pride from parents, family members, or people in the community, or by being self-taught.

Studies show that parental racial identity influences the degree to which parents talk or care about race, what types of racial messages they transmit, and the resulting racial identity development of family members. Higher salience and positive evaluation of one's Black identity (e.g., centrality, private regard, Internalization attitudes, or centralized-Internalization) are positively related to transmitting messages of racial pride, cultural socialization, and preparation for bias. So the subscales from racial socialization instruments that assessed preparation for bias and cultural socialization were used in the study as measures of positive racial socialization as a cultural practice.

The Black cultural attitudes and practices known as racial identity and racial socialization were possible, and could have only been maintained, in a context that placed value on the interconnectedness among Black Americans, known as communalism—the belief that the success of the individual and group are interrelated (Boykin et al., 1997; Brown et al., 2013). Communalism is expressed in Black cultural customs such as upholding the importance of the extended family, (beyond blood ties) and the practice of sharing resources and assisting one another. Scholars have found communalism to be related to positive emotions and a sense of purpose and achievement that come about through cooperation and collaboration, as can be seen in Black churches and social and fraternal organizations. Johnson and Carter (2020) used measures of collective African identity and a measure constructed to assess communalism; together the scores of the two instruments served as the variables in the model for the group orientation, indicating it to be a Black cultural strength. Community was intertwined with spirituality and religious practices.

Scholars contend that Black spirituality is a cultural practice that encompasses a sense of connection with one's ancestors and contains the idea that things in nature have a life force that directs life events. This belief is contained in Blacks' religious practices. Spirituality, as a cultural belief, has been found to be positively associated with quality of life and optimism (Underwood & Teresi, 2002) and negatively associated with depression and stress, meaning that high levels of spirituality are related to low levels of depression and stress. Like the other cultural practices and beliefs, there needed to be a way to assess spirituality, and it needed to be specific to the concepts of it that were characteristic to Black Americans. Johnson and Carter found a spirituality instrument designed to measure African American-based beliefs. This was used with an instrument that was designed to assess spiritual beliefs in general. So there were—like with the other cultural practices—two instruments were used to capture this aspect of Black beliefs and practices. Related to spiritualty and religion is racism-related coping, and spirituality was one coping options that researchers found for Blacks.

Forsyth and Carter (2014) found that spirituality is an important form of racism-related coping that works with other cultural practices, attitudes, and beliefs such as racial identity and communalism. The various coping strategies are Bargaining, in which one looks to oneself for explanations of racial incidents;

Hypervigilance, where one becomes more cautious with whites; Social Support, where one looks to others after a racial incident to help one manage one's reaction; Confrontation, which involves direct interaction with the parties involved in the racial incident; Empowered Action, where one uses community or legal action to address racism; Spirituality, where one uses prayer and meditation to ease the stress of racism; Racial Consciousness, which involves taking action against racism; and Constrained Resistance, which includes active and passive forms of protest and activity to redress racism. In a separate study by Forsyth and Carter (2012), in which they put the racism-related coping strategies with Black racial identity status attitudes and explored related mental health symptoms, they found four distinct cluster groups: (a) Encounter bargaining, (b) Pre-encounter constrained resistance, (c) Immersion cultural hypervigilance, and (d) Internalization-empowered confrontation. The results of statistical analyses indicated that there were significant differences between the groups in psychological symptoms but no differences in well-being. Overall, the analyses revealed that the combination of racial identity status attitudes and coping strategies uncovered important information about how participants used coping styles in the context of the racial identity statuses to deal with racial discrimination. For instance, the Internalization-empowered confrontation cluster group had lower levels of psychological symptoms when compared to the Encounter bargaining and Immersion cultural hypervigilance cluster groups. Based on this information, Johnson and Carter used four of the racism-related coping scales in their study: Confrontation, Empowered Action, Spirituality, and Constrained Resistance.

Johnson and Carter (2020) tested via empirical analyses whether a set of Black cultural values and practices were interrelated and whether, together, these practices and beliefs would indicate Black cultural strengths. If so, would the cultural strengths be positively related to psychological well-being, life satisfaction, quality of life, and other pro-social states? Their study used *structural equation* modeling to explore how particular measured and latent variables were related. The unobserved or latent (not directly measured) variables are listed below, with the measured scales or instruments that were used to assess the variable in question. So, for instance, mature racial identity was not directly measured but was indicated by the scales from the respective instruments. In the tested model, there were five constructs (e.g., positive racial socialization or effective racism-related coping). The list shows the constructs and the scales given to participants in the study to determine whether, as a group of constructs, the notion of Back cultural strengths could be indicated and empirically established.

- *Mature racial identity*, indicated by three scales:

  a BRIAS Internalization status attitudes scale
  b MIBI scale of Centrality
  c MIBI scale of Private Regard

- *Positive racial socialization*, captured by two racial socialization scales:
  - a Preparation for bias
  - b Cultural socialization
- *Effective racism-related coping*, predicted by four racism-related coping scales:
  - a Constrained resistance
  - b Empowered action
  - c Spirituality
  - d Confrontation
- *Communalism*, indicated by the two scales;
  - a Communalism scale
  - b African American collectivism scale
- *Cultural spirituality*, indicated by
  - a Daily spiritual experiences
  - b African American spirituality scale

Together, on the left side of the model were indicators, in the form of measured instrument scores, and the respective latent variables of *Mature racial identity, Positive racial socialization, Effective racism-related coping,* and *Communalism and Cultural spirituality* that predicted Black cultural strength. On the right side of the structural model was the latent variable psychosocial health that was related to the cultural variables on the left and was indicated or predicted by two measured variables or scores from the Mental Health Inventory that assesses psychological well-being as well as scores from a life satisfaction instrument.

The Johnson and Carter (2020) study found empirical evidence for Black cultural strengths and psychosocial health. Communalism was most strongly related to Black cultural strength, followed by mature racial identity, cultural spirituality, positive racial socialization, and, finally, effective racism-related coping.

The study indicates that one's level of connectedness with other Blacks is an essential part of Black cultural strength in that lacking a communalistic orientation limits one's ability to develop a mature racial identity, recognize and then learn to effectively cope with racism, and absorb racial socialization messages.

It appears that these Black cultural values, beliefs, and practices work to the benefit of members of the Black community and help people to stay mentally healthy. The presence of Black cultural strength indicates that Black people did not lose their minds, their will, or their resolve in the face racial oppression. Consider a Black employee in a predominantly white workspace who may be encouraged to assimilate to white work culture and be accepted by their co-workers. However, the Black employee is either unsuccessful at assimilating, isolated, or rejected by his peers. However, given the presence of high racial regard, a history of pro-Black racial socialization, and high communalism, this same individual may reach out to other Black workers for support, in or outside the workplace, and learn ways of coping with isolation in the workplace, and not internalize personal blame for a poor fit with white employees in the organization.

Alternatively, the absence of one or more of these cultural beliefs, practices, or values may contribute to increased psychological distress. In using the previous example, the Black employee who could not assimilate to his predominantly white work culture comes to think that he is the problem and as a result harbors negative feelings about himself and about being Black, which could potentially be harmful to his mental state.

Johnson and Carter's (2020) study documents important cultural values that should be promoted and reinforced with Black clients in therapy. Clients should be helped to adopt, be aware of, and practice these Black cultural values and beliefs to bolster them and to enhance their mental health and psychological well-being. Clinicians and laypeople should be taught about these cultural practices, beliefs, and values and how they impact the psychological functioning and overall life satisfaction of Black people. Mental health professionals must learn to work with Black clients from a Black cultural strength approach. Johnson and Carter (2020) put it this way:

> In addition, the findings point to cultural values that should be promoted and reinforced for Black American clients in therapy. Clients may be facing pressures to conform to White cultural values in a variety of settings (e.g., academic). Clinicians should consider ways in which the student may regain their sense of communalism, even within an institution, which does not reflect their own cultural values (e.g., joining the Black student union).
>
> Clinicians may serve the role of additional racial socializers, and suggest racism-related coping strategies that have been empirically proven to be effective. For instance, a clinician may find that a client relies heavily on cognitive racism-related coping. The clinician may suggest that the client "get out of their head" and confront the parties involved. Furthermore, a clinician can rely on their knowledge of the client's spirituality to suggest they also utilize spiritual coping strategies as well (e.g., praying). Even if the individual does not regularly engage in formalized religious practices, clinicians should be aware that they may endorse high levels of spiritual coping.
>
> *(p. 83)*

It is imperative that policy makers and program developers design and implement systems and methods that promotes the use of Black cultural strengths to advance their psychosocial well-being. And now the story moves to a new chapter - all has not been told as of yet. But I hope as did my ancestors for a brighter future.

References

Alegria, M., Fortuna, L. R., Lin, J. Y., Norris, F. H., Gao, S., Takeuchi, D. T., Jackson, J. S., Shrout, P. E., & Valentine, A. (2013). Prevalence, risk, and correlates of posttraumatic stress disorder across ethnic and racial minority groups in the United States. *Medical Care*, 51(12), 1114–1123.

American Psychiatric Association (APA). (2021, January 18). APA's apology to Black, Indigenous, and people of color for its support of structural racism in psychiatry. American Psychiatric Association. https://www.psychiatry.org/news-room/apa-apology-for-its-support-of-structural-racism.

American Psychiatric Association (APA). (2013). Diagnostic and statistical manual of mental disorders. (5th ed.), Text revision. American Psychiatric Association.

American Psychological Association (APA). (2015). Ethical principles of psychologists and code of conduct. https://www.apa.org/ethics/code.

American Psychological Association (APA). (2017). Multicultural guidelines: An ecological approach to context, identity, and intersectionality. http://www.apa.org/about/policy/multicultural-guidelines.pdf.

American Psychological Association (APA). (2019). Task force on race and ethnicity guidelines in psychology. APA guidelines on race and ethnicity in psychology. https://www.apa.org/about/policy/guidelines-race-ethnicity.pdf.

American Psychological Association (APA). (2021a). Resolution on harnessing psychology to combat racism: Adopting a uniform definition and understanding. https://www.apa.org/about/policy/resolution-combat-racism.pdf.

American Psychological Association (APA). (2021b). Equity, diversity and inclusion framework. https://www.apa.org/about/apa/equity-diversity-inclusion.

American Psychological Association (APA). (2021c, October 29). Apology to people of color for APA's role in promoting, perpetuating, and failing to challenge racism, racial discrimination, and human hierarchy in U.S. https://www.apa.org/about/policy/racism-apology.

Becares, L., Nazroo, J., & Jackson, J. (2014). Ethnic density and depressive symptoms among African Americans: Threshold and differential effects across social and demographic subgroups. *American Journal of Public Health*, 104(12), 2334–2341.

Belgrave, F. Z., & Allison, K. W. (2019). *African American psychology: From Africa to America*. Sage.

Bennett, L. (1988). *Before the Mayflower: A history of Black America*. Johnson Publishing.

Blackstock, U. (2024). *Legacy: A Black physician reckons with racism in medicine*. Viking.

Boyd-Franklin, N. (1989). *Black families in therapy: A multisystem approach*. Guilford.

Boyd-Franklin, N. (2006). *Black families in therapy: Understanding the African American experience*. Guilford.

Boykin, A. W., Jagers, R. J., Ellison, C. M., & Albury, A. (1997). Communalism: conceptualization and measurement of an Afrocultural social orientation. *Journal of Black Studies*, 27(3), 409–418.

Brown, C. L., Love, K. M., Tyler, K. M., Garriot, P. O., Thomas, D., & Roan-Belle, C. (2013). Parental attachment, family communalism, and racial identity among African American college students. *Journal of Multicultural Counseling and Development*, 41(2), 108–122.

Carter, R. T. (1995). *The influence of race and racial identity in psychotherapy*. Wiley.

Carter, R. T. (Ed.). (2005). *Handbook of racial-cultural psychology and counseling*, Vol. 2, *Training and practice*. Wiley.
Carter, R. T., & Helms, J. E. (1987). The relationship of Black value-orientations to racial identity attitudes. *Measurement and Evaluation in Counseling and Development*, 19, 185–195.
Carter, R. T., & Pieterse, A. (2020). *Measuring the effects of racism: Guidelines for the assessment and treatment of race-based traumatic stress injury*. Columbia University Press.
Cross, W. E., Jr., & Vandiver, B. J. (2001). Nigrescence theory and measurement: Introducing the Cross Racial Identity Scale (CRIS). In J. G. Ponterotto, J. M. Casas, L. A. Suzuki, & C. M. Alexander (Eds.). *Handbook of multicultural counseling* (pp. 371–393). Sage.
Cummings Center for the History of Psychology. (2021). Examining psychology's contributions to the belief in racial hierarchy and perpetuation of inequality for People of Color in the United States. Cummings Museum and Center for the History of Psychology. Akron, Ohio.
Erving, C., Thomas, C., & Frazier, C. (2019). Is the Black-white mental health paradox consistent across gender and psychiatric disorders? *American Journal of Epidemiology*, 188(2), 314–322.
Faber, S., Khanna Roy, A., Michaels, T., & Williams, M. (2023). The weaponization of medicine: Early psychosis in the Black community and the need for racially informed mental healthcare. *Frontiers in Psychiatry*, 14, 1098292. doi:10.3389/fpsyt.2023.1098292.
Forsyth, J., & Carter, R. T. (2012). The influence of racial identity status attitudes and racism-related coping on mental health among Black Americans. *Cultural Diversity and Ethnic Minority Psychology*, 18(2), 128–140.
Forsyth, J., & Carter, R. T. (2014). The development and preliminary validation of the racism-related coping scale. *Psychological Trauma: Theory, Policy, Research, and Practice*, 6(6), 632–643.
Franklin, H. J., & Moss, A. A. (2000). *From slavery to freedom: A history of African Americans* (8th ed.). McGraw-Hill.
Gates, L. H., Jr. (2021). *The Black church: This is our story, this is our song*. Penguin.
Gibbs, T., Okuda, M., Oquendo, M., Lawson, W., Wang, S., Thomas, Y., & Blanco, C. (2013). Mental health of African Americans and Caribbean blacks in the United States: Results from the National Epidemiological Survey on alcohol and related conditions. *American Journal of Public Health*, 103, 330–338.
Gray-Little, B., & Hafdahl, A. (2000). Factors influencing racial comparisons of self-esteem: A quantitative review. *Psychological Bulletin*, 126(1), 26–54.
Grier, W. H., & Cobbs, P. M. (1992). *Black rage*. Basic Books.
Griffith, E. E. H., Jones, B. E., & Stewart, A. J. (2019). *Black mental health: Patients, providers and systems*. American Psychiatric Association.
Harrington, M. (1963). *The other America: Poverty in the United States*. Penguin.
Helms, J. E. (1990). *Black and white racial identity: Theory, research and practice*. Greenwood.
Hill, R. B. (1972). *The strengths of black families*. Emerson Hall.
Himle, J., Baser, R., Taylor, R., Campbell, R., & Jackson, J. (2009). Anxiety disorders among African Americans, Blacks of Caribbean descent, and non-Hispanic whites in the United States. *Journal of Anxiety Disorders*, 23, 578–590.
Horton, J. O., & Horton, L. E. (2005). *Slavery and the making of America*. Oxford University Press.

Hughes, M., Kielcolt, K. J., & Keith, V. (2022). Racial identity and the racial paradox in mental health. In M. Elliot (Ed.). *Research handbook on society and mental health* (pp. 115–135). Edward Elgar Publishing.
Hylton, A. (2024). *Madness: Race and insanity in a Jim Crow asylum.* Legacy.
Jensen, A. R. (1968). Social class, race, and genetics: Implications for education. *American Educational Research Journal*, 5(1), 1–42.
Johnson, V., & Carter, R. T. (2020). Black cultural strengths and psychological well-being: An empirical analysis with Black American adults. *Journal of Black Psychology*, 46(1), 55–89.
Jones, J. M. (2003). TRIOS: A psychological theory of the African legacy in American culture. *Journal of Social Issues*, 39(1), 217–242.
Kardiner, A., & Ovesey, L. (1951). *The mark of oppression: Explorations in the personality of the American Negro.* Norton.
Keyes, C. L. M. (2009). The Black-white paradox in health: Flourishing in the face of social inequality and discrimination. *Journal of personality*, 77(6), 1677–1705.
Liu, W. M., & Pope-Davis, D. B. (2005). The working alliance, therapy ruptures, and impasses and counseling competence: Implications for counselor training and education. In R. T. Carter (Ed.). *Handbook of racial-cultural psychology and counseling*, Vol. 2, *Training and practice* (pp. 148–167). Wiley.
Louie, P., Upeneiks, L., Erving, C., & Tobin, C. (2022). Do racial differences in coping resources explain the Black-white paradox in mental health? A test of multiple mechanisms. *Journal of Health and Social Behavior*, 63(1), 55–70.
McLaughlin, K. A., Alvarez, K., Fillbrunn, M., Green, J. G., Jackson, J. S., Kessler, R. C., Sadikova, E., Sampson, N. A., Vilsaint, C. L., Williams, D. R., & Alegría, M. (2019). Racial/ethnic variation in trauma-related psychopathology in the United States: A population-based study. *Psychological Medicine*, 49(13), 2215–2226. doi:10.1017/S0033291718003082.
Price, J. H., & Khubchandani, J. (2019). The changing characteristics of African-American adolescent suicides, 2001–2017. *Journal of Community Health*, 44, 756–763.
Price, J. H., & Khubchandani, J. (2022). Childhood suicide trends in the United States, 2010–2019. *Journal of Community Health*, 47(2), 232–236. doi:10.1007/s10900-021-01040-w.
Roberts, A. L., Gilman, S. E., Breslau, J., Breslau, N., & Koenen, K. C. (2011). Race/ethnic differences in exposure to traumatic events, development of post-traumatic stress disorder, and treatment-seeking for post-traumatic stress disorder in the United States. *Psychological Medicine*, 41(1), 71–83. doi:10.1017/S0033291710000401.
Sellers, R. M., Smith, M. A., Shelton, J. N., Rowley, S. A., & Chavous, T. M. (1998). Multidimensional model of racial identity: A reconceptualization of African American racial identity. *Personality and Social Psychology Review*, 2(1), 18–39.
Stewart, E. C., & Bennett, M. J. (2011). *American cultural patterns: A cross-cultural perspective* (2nd ed.). Nicholas Brealey Publishing.
Sue, D. W., Sue, D., Neville, H., & Smith, L. (Eds.). (2019). *Counseling the culturally diverse: Theory and practice* (8th ed.). Wiley.
Thompson, V. L. S., Bazile, A., & Akbar M. (2004). African Americans' perceptions of psychotherapy and psychotherapists. *Professional Psychology: Research and Practice*, 35(1), 19–26. doi:10.1037/0735-7028.35.1.19.
Twenge, J. M., & Crocker, J. (2002). Race and self-esteem: Meta-analyses comparing whites, blacks, Hispanics, Asians, and American Indians and comment on Gray-Little and Hafdahl (2000). *Psychological Bulletin*, 128(3), 371–408; Discussion, 409–420.

Upenciks, L., Louie, P., & Hill, T. D. (2023). Welcome to the dark side: The role of religious/spiritual struggles in the Black-white mental health paradox. *Society and Mental Health*, 13(2), 151–168.

Underwood, L. G., & Teresi, J. A. (2002). The daily spiritual experience scale: Development, theoretical description, reliability, exploratory factor analysis, and preliminary construct validity using health-related data. *Annals of Behavioral Medicine*, 24(1), 22–33. doi:10.1207/S15324796ABM2401_04.

U.S. Department of Health and Human Services. (2001). Mental health: Culture, race, and ethnicity—A supplement to mental health: A report of the Surgeon General. U.S. Department of Health and Human Services, Substance Abuse and Mental Health Services Administration, Center for Mental Health Services.

Vontress, C. E., & Epp, L. R. (1997). Historical hostility in the African American client: Implications for counseling. *Journal of Multicultural Counseling and Development*, 25(3), 170–184. doi:10.1002/j.2161-1912.1997.tb00327.x.

Webber, T. L. (1978). *Deep like the rivers: Education in the slave quarter community, 1831–1865.* Norton.

Williams, D. R., & Mohammed, S. A. (2013). Racism and health I: Pathways and scientific evidence. *American Behavioral Scientist*, 57(8), 1152–1173. doi:10.1177/0002764213487340.

INDEX

For Product Safety Concerns and Information please contact our EU
representative GPSR@taylorandfrancis.com
Taylor & Francis Verlag GmbH, Kaufingerstraße 24, 80331 München, Germany

www.ingramcontent.com/pod-product-compliance
Ingram Content Group UK Ltd.
Pitfield, Milton Keynes, MK11 3LW, UK
UKHW020154200926
475702UK00016B/2703
* 9 7 8 0 3 6 7 6 2 9 4 7 2 *